GOVERNING NEW YORK STATE

Governing New York State

Fifth Edition

Edited by
Robert F. Pecorella
and
Jeffrey M. Stonecash

STATE UNIVERSITY OF NEW YORK PRESS

Published by
State University of New York Press, Albany

© 2006 State University of New York

For information, address State University of New York Press,
194 Washington Avenue, Suite 305, Albany, NY 12210-2384

Production by Marilyn P. Semerad
Marketing by Fran Keneston

Library of Congress Cataloging in Publication Data

Governing New York State / edited by Robert F. Pecorella and Jeffrey M. Stonecash.—5th ed.
    p. cm.
  Includes bibliographical references and index.
  ISBN 0-7914-6691-4 (alk. paper) — ISBN 0-7914-6692-2 (pbk. : alk. paper)
  1. New York (State)—Politics and government—1951– 2. New York (State)—Economic
policy. 3. New York (State)—Social policy. I. Pecorella, Robert F., 1948– II. Stonecash,
Jeffrey M.
JK3416.N48 2006
320.9747—dc22

                                                              2005008572

  13-digit ISBN: 978-0-7914-6691-9 (hardcover : alk. paper)
  13-digit ISBN: 978-0-7914-6692-6 (pbk. : alk. paper)

                    10 9 8 7 6 5 4 3 2 1

Contents

Part III. Public Policy

Illustrations

Figures

Tables

PART I

Political Conflicts and Their Representation

Introduction to Part I

The Sources of Conflict

JEFFREY M. STONECASH

Democracies exist because people have different values and needs. The political process represents these differing wants to politicians who must struggle with trying to reach publicly accepted policy decisions. The greater the conflict within a society, the more difficult it is to reach accommodations. New York state represents a state where the diversity is considerable and the conflicts are acute. Part 1 of this book focuses on the conflicts within the state that politicians struggle with in trying to reach decisions. There are significant conflicts that revolve around region, class, and race. These conflicts make it difficult to reach decisions within the state.

One of the enduring sources of conflict within the state revolves around New York City and its population. Robert Pecorella reviews how New York City differs from the rest of the state in terms of its ethnic and racial composition and its economy, and how those differences lead to conflicts within the political process. New York City has a higher percentage of renters and minorities. It has more people who rely on mass transit. It has many low-income individuals, who have many needs for government social programs. These differences create a sense that New York City is different. The rest of the state, of course, has substantial numbers of low-income individuals, but the political perception has emerged that New York City has very different needs, and that it spends more on social programs than the rest of the state.

This creates a continual concern with whether New York City is getting more or less than it deserves.

Here are also significant disputes that stem from intergovernmental programs. As Don Boyd indicates, the state receives large sums of money from the federal government and provides extensive fiscal aid to local governments. The state adopts programs such as Medicaid that create state obligations and require state revenues. When the state adopts programs, it often results in the state imposing accompanying obligations on local governments. While the state defines what it will do regarding Medicaid and welfare, counties must pay part of Medicaid costs, and counties administer welfare programs. Many at the local level are not happy with the burdens imposed by the state in these policy areas, and want the state to either cut mandates or provide more revenue. The same conflicts over mandates and state aid occur with local education.

There are also consistent differences among demographic groups, and these become bases for differences between the parties. The nonwhite population has grown in the state, and nonwhites tend, on average, to be more liberal than whites. Nonwhites are generally more concerned with social programs and jobs. Urban populations differ from suburban and rural populations. Urban areas, for example, have less affluent tax bases and need more state aid for schools than suburban communities do. The affluent have less need for government assistance to go to college than those with lesser incomes. In New York nonwhites, urban groups, and the less affluent tend to align with the Democratic Party, while whites, suburban and rural groups, and the affluent are more likely to align with the Republican Party. These differences between the parties in their electoral bases become the basis for ongoing policy disputes within the state, and are reviewed by Amy Widestrom and my staff. There are also significant third parties in New York, and Robert Spitzer examines their role.

The political arena also draws the attention of many interest groups that want to make sure that their interests are considered and protected. While there are broad conflicts revolving around geographical areas, race, class, and intergovernmental programs, in New York politics there is also a steady stream of lobbyists who present arguments for specific groups. Rogan Kersh presents an overview of the diversity of groups seeking attention. He argues that lobbying activities have grown in recent years. This activity is part of the endless process of attempting to persuade state officials that specific concerns need to be addressed. While the conflicts of region, class, and race may receive more media coverage, the presentations of lobbyists are enduring and crucial in the political process.

Finally, there is the important issue of how much the electorate is informed about the issues and conflicts within the state political process. Journalists must regularly decide how much information to convey to the public about policy conflicts, what events should have priority, and how news about policy conflicts should be presented. Elizabeth Benjamin, a *Times-Union* reporter, presents an overview of the relationship between the press and elected officials.

CHAPTER 1

The Two New Yorks
in the Twenty-first Century

The City and the State

ROBERT F. PECORELLA

In the wake of the September 11, 2001, terrorist attacks, there was broad
support and even open affection expressed for New York City from around
the rest of the state and nation. Given the horrific nature of the attacks and
the heroic responses of the city's uniformed services, it is not surprising that
positive feelings about the city were so widespread. Given the history of
social tension and political conflict in the city-state relationship, however, it
is also not surprising that the intensity of the positive feelings was temporary.
The social, economic, and political divisions between New York City and
much of the rest of the state remain as fundamental as ever and although
they may now play out with slightly less open hostility, play out they will.
Indeed, such diversity of interests always promotes political conflict in democratic societies.

People from New York City and people from other areas of the state
often view each other with emotions ranging from bemusement to hostility.
Although tensions between residents of cities and surrounding areas are not
unusual, the extent of the mutual animosity in New York State is notable. As
creations of modernity, cities challenge traditional culture by incubating liberal social and political attitudes and, as the nation's most modern and international city, New York represents the greatest challenge to traditional values.

7

The differences between people in New York City and those in the rest of the state are both long-standing and easily summarized: City residents have been and are less Protestant, more ethnically diverse, more likely to be foreign-born, and far more likely to be Democrats than people in the rest of the state. David Ellis writes, "Rural folk and city dwellers in many countries and over many centuries have viewed each other with fear and suspicion. . . . [T]he sharp differences—racial, religious, cultural, political—between New York City and upstate have aggravated the normal rural-urban cleavages."[1]

The rural/urban dichotomy, however, is not based solely in culture and demography; it is also a function of each area's different relationships with government. Given the social interdependence that defines their existence, cities need more activist governments than do rural areas. The urban econ-omy, for example, requires public transportation systems. While nearly 53 percent of New York City residents use mass transit to get to work, fewer than 7 percent of residents in other parts of the state do. Urban density makes government regulation of multifamily housing construction and maintenance a critical issue. While nearly two-thirds of New York City households live in rental units, many of which are government price stabi-lized, fewer than 27 percent of households outside the city reside in rental units. Moreover, the nature and extent of urban social problems require roughly two-thirds of all state spending on welfare and health care programs. (For an analysis of health care issues, see chapter 14). These diverse needs generate rural-urban conflicts over the size and scope of government gener-ally as well as conflicts over the degree of autonomy that city government should have.

For much of New York State's history these political conflicts were con-sidered within a context that defined New York City as downstate and every-thing else as upstate.[2] Although this dichotomy still has substantial cultural and psychological import, it excludes important aspects of more recent state politics. The suburbs around New York City, geographically downstate but in many ways philosophically upstate, have emerged as a potent political force and the larger upstate cities now share many of the urban concerns once associated exclusively with downstate politics.

With these caveats in mind, this chapter takes a threefold approach to examining the relationship of New York City to the rest of the state in the first part of the twenty-first century. First, it examines the legal context for the political interactions between state and local governments in New York. Second, it explores the socioeconomic bases underlying the political interac-tions between representatives of New York City and those of the rest of the state in Albany. And third, it analyzes New York City's relative influence within the arenas where the political interactions occur.

THE LEGAL RELATIONSHIP:
STATE CONSTRAINTS ON CITY AUTONOMY

With 42 percent of the state's population, a proportion that increased for the first time in decades during the 1990s, New York City has a critical role in the state's social, economic, and political life. Indeed, elected and appointed state and city officials interact constantly on a host of intergovernmental issues including school aid formulas, Medicaid costs, and tax policy. Such interactions, whether between the governor and mayor, representatives of state and city service agencies, or city lobbyists and state legislators, are constrained by legal rules as well as by political variables.

The primary legal principle guiding state-city relationships in the United States is quite direct: cities are public corporations created by state law with authority derived solely from the state.[3] (For a complete analysis of state-local relations in New York, see chapter 2). As they have in other states, local governments in New York have sought relief from the legal straightjacket of state control in the principle of home rule, that is, the practice of providing localities with some degree of governing autonomy. After years of effort, advocates of local autonomy saw home rule enacted in New York. An amendment to the state constitution, incorporated in 1923, and the City Home Rule Law, enacted a year later, codified home rule in New York by defining local government authority over local "property, affairs and government."[4] However, when the principles of state preeminence and home rule conflict, as they often do, state courts have ruled consistently that a "state-concern" doctrine preempts home rule in New York.[5]

Despite the formal adoption of home rule, therefore, the state government continues to exercise considerable influence on local policymaking. Such influence takes the form of general rules applicable to all local governments in the state as well specific mandates applying only to New York City. Although state restrictions of and mandates upon local governments are universal in New York, the specific nature and extent of state involvement vary depending on the type of local government as well as local fiscal circumstances. There are four basic types of state constitutional and statutory restrictions that impact on New York City's autonomy, including limits on the city's revenue-raising authority; limits on the city's debt-issuing authority; state

mandates requiring city action; and provisions for state administrative supervision of city operations.

Article XVI of the state constitution limits local governments to state-
specified taxing authority that, once granted, is subject to continual state
review. As a result, for New York City officials to institute a tax or change the
rates of any revenue other than the property tax, they must first receive
approval from the state legislature. In 2003, with the city facing its most
severe fiscal problems since the mid 1970s, Mayor Michael Bloomberg,
having failed in his efforts to secure state reinstatement of the commuter tax
on suburbanites who worked in the city, had to obtain state legislative
approval for increases in the city's income and sales taxes on its own residents. Even the city's property tax, the only constitutionally defined local
revenue, is limited to an annual total of 2.5 percent of the "average full valuation of taxable real estate" in the city.[6]

The rigid state control of local revenue-raising capacity is coupled with
strict constitutional limitations on local authority to contract debt and provide for its long-term capital needs. In New York City, total debt is limited
to 10 percent of a five-year rolling average of the full valuation of annual taxable real estate.[7] One consequence of having debt limits calculated as a percentage of the value of real property is that when property values decrease, as
they did from the mid-1980s to the mid-1990s in New York, the debt limit
is reached more quickly and the City is forced to search for alternative methods to finance its capital programs. Increases in property values since the
mid-1990s have lessened the pressure somewhat on city debt. By 2004,
although New York City's debt level was significantly higher than that of any
other major American city, it was well within constitutional limits.

State mandates, the other side of the fiscal restrictions coin, require
local governments, that is, counties and New York City, to undertake some
action; partially funded or unfunded mandates require them to assume some
or all of the costs for the action. Studies have shown that New York State
imposes a comparatively large number of mandates that collectively have a
substantial fiscal impact.[8] State legislative mandates, for example, force New
York City to expend billions of dollars annually on its share of Medicaid
costs, public-employee pension programs, and construction costs.

Although the norm to one degree or another throughout New York,
state administrative involvement in local governance is particularly notable
in New York City. City agencies operate under administrative regulations
that mandate state preclearance for and review of agency actions. Public

authorities, created by the state legislature and governed by boards appointed largely by state officials, have administrative control of important services. The governor's appointees, for example, control a majority of the seats on the Metropolitan Transportation Authority, which runs the city's transit system. Moreover, state fiscal monitors, created as a consequence of the 1975 fiscal crisis, still emerge periodically as influential participants in city politics.[9] In 2003, the Local Governments Assistance Corporation, yet another state fiscal monitor, held up a budget agreement passed by the state legislature over the governor's veto requiring the state to assume a portion of New York City's long-term debt payments. State regulations also control how city administrators implement the Safety Net Assistance Program, which by 2004 had already enrolled thousands of families who had reached their five-year federal deadline for welfare benefits.

On balance, therefore, court interpretations of the state constitution, continuing and recent statutory restrictions, and the increased use of public authorities provide the government in Albany with substantial influence over New York City. As a result, city officials must come to the state capital with hats in hand, seeking the resources and waivers from controls they need to govern effectively.

THE SOCIAL AND ECONOMIC ROOTS OF POLITICAL CONFLICT

Legal primacy aside, New York State and City interact within a web of political relationships. Politics concerns choices about who gets what share of scarce resources and one group's share is often perceived as another's loss. Political relationships, therefore, involve the conflicts emerging from the socioeconomic differences among groups of people that to a large extent determine the nature of their interaction with government. Given its diversity, New York provides a solid empirical base to study the political conflicts emerging from group differences.

Demographics and Political Conflict

In 2004, New York City remains more heterogeneous than any other area of the state or nation (see table 1.1). Despite the constancy of the fact of

TABLE 1.1.
New York State: A socioeconomic profile by region
(percentages)

	United States	New York State	New York City	NYC suburbs[a]	Upstate cities[b]	Rural counties[c]
African American	12.3	15.9	26.6	9.8	34.1	3.1
Latino	12.5	15.1	27.0	11.4	8.4	2.6
Asian	3.6	5.5	9.8	3.8	2.3	1.1
Foreign born	11.1	20.4	35.9	16.6	6.4	3.7
Non-English[d]	8.1	13.0	23.7	8.5	5.4	2.0
Median income[e]	0.9	1.0	0.9	1.6	0.6	0.8
Below poverty	9.2	11.5	20.8	6.5	24.6	12.9
On public assistance	7.8	10.4	15.0	5.1	18.4	
No high school diploma	19.6	20.9	27.7	14.5	24.7	19.6

[a] *NYC suburbs:* Nassau, Putnam, Rockland, Suffolk, and Westchester counties (includes city of Yonkers).

[b] *Upstate cities:* Albany, Buffalo, Rochester, and Syracuse.

[c] *Rural counties:* 22 NYS counties not within Standard Metropolitan Areas (SMAs).

[d] Self-description on the 2000 census form; the category is non-English language background.

[e] As percentage of NYS median household income ($43,393).

demographic differences between the City and the rest of the state, however, the nature of these differences has changed over the years. During the first half of the twentieth century, religious and ethnic divisions carried regional political implications. New York City was home to large numbers of Catholic immigrants from southern and eastern Europe who supported the Democratic Party as well as Jewish immigrants active in liberal reform movements, while upstate was populated largely with the Republican descendants of northern European Protestants. This division, reflected in local political conflicts over Prohibition, legislative reapportionment, and aid to parochial schools, came to have national implications as the city's ethnic voters helped form the national urban electoral base for the Democrats' "New Deal coalition" while upstate remained firmly Republican.

By the 1960s, much of the ethnic tension had been superseded by racial distinctions between an increasingly African American and Latino New York City and the European-American rural areas and suburbs. In the 1950s and 1960s, millions of white residents, encouraged by federal subsidies, left the cities of the Northeast and Midwest to settle in suburbs. One of the largest such migrations was the eastern and northern exodus from

New York City. Initially settling in Nassau and Westchester Counties, the suburban migrants would eventually expand into Suffolk County on the east end of Long Island, and Putnam and Rockland Counties to the north.[10] Indeed, by the beginning of the twenty-first century, Catholic ethnics were dispersed widely around the state, particularly in the suburbs, where, although they are often hostile to urban interests, they are less conservative than original suburban populations.

While large numbers of white families were leaving New York City for the suburbs, the mechanization of Southern agriculture, the racist policies of Southern states, and the expectation of employment in the cities were producing a northern migration of African Americans. Following train lines north, blacks transformed themselves from a rural to an urban population and in so doing transformed national and state politics. As a Twentieth Century Fund report noted, "Between 1950 and 1974, as a result of the net out-migration of whites and in-migration of blacks and Hispanics, New York's [City] black and Hispanic population rose from about 13 percent to 42 percent."[11] The 2000 census indicated that "people of color" make up a majority of New York City's population, a fact first evident in the 1990 census report.

From a macro perspective, the New York City's racial make up is quite distinct from that of the rest of the state. A more focused analysis, however, yields more nuance. Although largely white, the suburbs include areas like Mt. Vernon and Yonkers in Westchester County as well as communities in Nassau and Suffolk Counties with significant minority populations. In recent years, African-Americans have been relocating to inner-ring suburbs, although racial discrimination makes that process more difficult than it was for their European American counterparts.

Upstate cities also include large minority populations. In the last three decades of the twentieth century, for example, the African American populations in Buffalo and Rochester increased substantially. By 2000, African Americans accounted for nearly 38 percent of Buffalo's population and nearly 39 percent of Rochester's population. Because the negative impacts of racism are not geographically bounded, these upstate cities experience many of the same social and economic problems manifest in race relations downstate. Therefore, the general demographic picture affirming that New York City remains the most racially heterogeneous area of the state, while correct overall, may be masking important social nuances with potential cross-regional political implications.

The New York City experience with foreign born residents is sui generis in the state and in the nation. In 2003, the city's population included representatives of more than two hundred ethnic groups. For all of its history, the city has been the port of entry for immigrants from around the globe. At the turn of the twentieth century, roughly 33 percent of New York City's population was foreign born; at the turn of the twenty-first century, over 35 percent of the City's population is foreign born. The majority of the most recent arrivals are from Latin America; there are also substantial numbers from Eastern Europe and Asia.

New York City's role as port of entry continues to have political implications. The Mayor's Office of Immigrant Affairs and Language Services maintains close relationships with nearly three hundred community groups involved in providing services to immigrants from around the world. Both Mayors Giuliani and Bloomberg have identified themselves with the "immigration supportive" wing of the Republican Party.

Economics and Political Conflict

Economic status is a primary influence on group relationships with government: "Politics generally comes down, over the long run, to a conflict between those who have and those who have less. In state politics the crucial issues tend to turn around taxation and expenditure."[12] In considering New York City's political relationships with the state then, it is useful to examine the economic resources the city brings to the state and the economic demands it makes on state government.

New York City's economy in the early twenty-first century is characterized by a fundamental contradiction that began to appear three decades earlier. At the same time that the city acts as the financial center of an increasingly global economy, it is also the regional center for very difficult social and economic problems. And, in a related paradox, while the city's financial sector provides state government with large amounts of revenues, the extent of its social problems demands equally large amounts of state expenditures.

At the top of New York's economy is a world-class city that "accounts for half of all securities traded on a global basis, leading London and Tokyo by a wide margin."[13] In 2004, New York City was home to well over 3,000 international firms representing more than one hundred countries and employing nearly 250,000 people.[14] With slightly more than 42 percent of the state's population, the city accounted for 44 percent of the state's personal income and more than 50 percent of total state jobs in finance, insurance, and real estate.[15] The importance of the city's financial institutions to the state's overall fiscal health has been clearly evident in recent years. The national downturn that began in 2000 was driven by problems in the financial sector and, as a result, had a particularly negative impact on business in New York City and consequently on New York State's economy.

Conversely, the city has a greater concentration of social and economic problems than rural areas and other cities in the state and far greater difficulty than the suburbs (see table 1.1). As a consequence of the concentration of social and economic problems, over 60 percent of all the state's households on public assistance and 72 percent of all Medicaid personal-care cases reside in New York City and two-thirds of all state funds allocated for these two programs are spent in the city.[16] Maintaining state spending on social welfare programs, therefore, will be of primary interest to a population with such needs, just as reducing such spending is of interest to people further removed economically and geographically from the problems.

Such contradictions are not new. New York City's economy has always included large numbers of people at polar ends of the economic continuum, as the wealth produced by the city's business sector existed side-by-side with the poverty of newly arrived immigrants. In years past, the economic chasm was bridged by a growing middle class employed largely in the city's once substantial manufacturing sector. Since the 1970s, however, part of the middle-class bridge has left the city, as have many of the manufacturing jobs that supported them. By the 1990s, the income gap between rich and poor in New York State was greater than in any other state and a large part of it results from the bifurcation in New York City's economy.[17] Moreover, the gap between low-income people and other city residents has become increasingly rigid as poor families, locked into poor neighborhoods with substandard schools, see their economic plight perpetuated from one generation to the next. With the highest unemployment figures in the state and with over 30 percent of its school-age population not finishing high school, the city may be seeing several more generations locked into economic stagnation.

New York City's socioeconomic dichotomy, a result of national and international economic transformations and segregated housing and job markets, produces intense political reactions among the victims, which, in turn, generates increased resistance from beneficiaries of the status quo. The resulting deep political divisions hold the potential for maximum political tension and minimum political accommodation among the diverse groups and the public officials representing them.

In summary, New York City remains generally distinct from the rest of the state in terms of the overall diversity of its population and the extent of its socioeconomic problems. In the past, these characteristics encouraged the city's representatives in Albany to be the state's primary spokespeople for liberal social and economic programs. In the early 2000s, we should expect that city representatives, particularly those who represent communities with severe social and economic problems, will continue to take the lead in fighting the political battle against retrenchment of the welfare state. It is useful to note, however, that the social problems that plague New York City are also present in upstate cities and in some parts of rural communities. In many of these areas, the counterbalance of growth at the top of the economy is not present as it is in New York City. As the century ends, it may be only the psychological depth of the upstate/downstate chasm that keeps cross-regional coalitions from redefining state politics.

THE ARENAS OF POLITICAL CONFLICT

The political conflicts generated by the diverse interests outlined above are most directly evident in three arenas: the two houses of the state legislature, gubernatorial election contests, and the ongoing interactions between the mayor of New York City and state government officials. Within each of these three venues the city's political forces seek to secure a statewide urban agenda by counterbalancing the influence of the state's other regions.

New York City and Legislature Politics

Since 1975, control of the state legislature has been divided, with the Democrats firmly in charge of the assembly and the Republicans holding a majority in the senate. (For an analysis of the regional basis of legislative politics in New York, see chapter 8). In fact, no other state has had as long a history of divided party control of its legislature.[18] Under a highly partisan system, majority-party conferences charge their legislative leaders with developing unified policy positions and representing them in negotiations with

TABLE 1.2
The New York State Legislature: An ideological profile*
(average conservatism rating)

Assembly			Senate		
Democrats		*Republicans*	*Democrats*		*Republicans*
14.4	Overall	53.1	23.9	Overall	39.3
13.9	NYC	n/a	23.9	NYC	36.9
15.2	Outside NYC	53.1	n/a	Outside NYC	40.3

Source: The Conservative Party of New York State, *Ratings of the 2003 Legislature.*
*The higher the rating, the more conservative the voting record.

the other house and the governor. To assist the leaders in their task, the conferences grant them the authority to select the chairs and majority members of committees, to fill lower leadership positions, and to allocate staff among members. The majority-party conference, therefore, empowers its leaders to make the policy decisions for each house.[19]

The majority conferences in the two houses reflect the regional nature of party politics in the state. While the Republican majority in the senate includes mostly suburban and rural members, there is a decided "downstate cast" to the Democratic conference in the assembly. Since gaining control of the assembly in 1974, more than 60 percent of the Democratic conferences each session and all five assembly speakers have been from New York City.

Given the city's influence, it is not surprising that for three decades, the assembly has emphasized a liberal or progressive approach to government that includes support for increased social spending and protection of civil liberties. At the beginning of the twenty-first century, Democrats in the assembly continued to be significantly more liberal than Republicans and New York City Democrats remain the most liberal of the regional groupings (see table 1.2). The liberal approach is evident in the assembly's strong support for rent regulations, increased state aid for city schools, and the extension of civil liberties protections to those with alternative lifestyles.

The Democratic conference, however, is not ideologically monolithic. Party conferences in the legislature reflect the diversity of party interests in the electorate and issue positions that may appear rock solid on the floor are usually the result of negotiations among conference factions. As table 1.2 also indicates, upstate Democrats are less liberal then their New York City counterparts. The point is that no matter how liberal the Democratic leadership is or wishes to be, it simply cannot ignore the interests of these upstate members if the party is to hold its majority in the assembly.

The diversity within the Democratic conference is not solely regional. Although the New York City delegation in 2004 includes a majority of liberals, it also contains a small group of moderates who represent white working-class areas of New York City and who emphasize more conservative social agendas. These more moderate city Democrats often reflect the views of single-family homeowners from the "outer boroughs" who have at times distinct policy differences with what they sometimes view as "Manhattan liberals."

In May of 2000, ideological, managerial, and personal conflicts within the Democratic majority conference turned into open rebellion when the then majority leader, Michael Bragman, sought to unseat the speaker of the assembly, Sheldon Silver. By most accounts, Silver's coupling of personal political skills with the institutional powers available to him as the speaker enabled him to regain control of the conference, put a stop to the rebellion, and maintain his power. In the wake of the upheaval, two assembly members who had supported the insurgency were stripped of their committee chairs and Bragman was replaced as majority leader and later left the assembly.

Although the 2000 revolt was a dramatic exception to the rule, it did highlight the point that assembly leadership must always be attentive to the diversity of interests represented in the majority conference. Nevertheless, as presently constituted, the assembly majority will continue to take policy positions reflective of its New York City base. The consistent liberal direction of these positions, which are often unpopular in upstate districts as well as in some city neighborhoods, reflects both the political culture and the nature of constituency concerns in New York City.

In contrast, the majority conference in the senate is composed largely of upstate rural conservatives and suburban moderates, a situation enhanced significantly by the 2002 redistricting. Of the 38–24 majority that Senate Republicans held in 2004, twenty seats were from upstate, twelve were from downstate suburban districts (including nine from Long Island), and only six were from New York City. In the wake of the 2002 redistricting, therefore, for the first time in recent memory, a floor majority of Republican votes can be maintained without any support from New York City representatives.

During the 1990s, Senate Republicans generally held a seven- or eight-vote majority that included five seats from New York City. As a result, city Republicans were influential within the conference because their electoral viability was critical for maintaining Republican control of the senate. Indeed, on issues of particular importance to their constituents, city Republicans could threaten to act as a swing vote and deprive the leadership of a floor majority. In 1997, for example, Senate Majority Leader Joseph Bruno, under increasingly vocal pressure from New York City Republicans in his conference, abandoned his effort to end rent regulations.

Such dramatic and public showdowns occur only rarely because potential swing voters in a party are as willing as others to negotiate within conference and settle for a compromise that keeps in place the benefits of strong leadership. Moreover, as was evident in the wake of the 2000 leadership rebellion in the assembly, in extreme cases, legislative leaders can impose severe sanctions on rebellious members. Such open conflicts, therefore, are likely to occur only on issues of conscience or when the fear of external sanctions, like the reaction of angry and organized constituents, outweighs concerns over leadership authority.

New York City and Statewide Elections

The unwritten rule for winning statewide elections in New York is simple: Republican candidates must maximize their winning margins in upstate New York, secure the suburban vote, and hold down their losing margins in New York City. Democratic candidates, on the other hand, need to carry the city by a wide margin, run close in the suburbs, and hold down their losing margins upstate. (For a complete analysis of election politics in New York, see chapter 3). Since the end of World War II, successful gubernatorial candidates from both parties have built campaigns around this strategy. Republican governors, like Thomas Dewey and Nelson Rockefeller, attended to New York City interests and were rewarded with sufficient urban support to win seven statewide contests (see table 1.3). Rockefeller, in particular, developed good working relationships with union leaders and prominent Democrats in the city that served him well in his four gubernatorial campaigns. Democrats Averell Harriman, Hugh Carey, and Mario Cuomo based their combined six victories at least in part on the overwhelming support of New York City voters.

Historically then, New York City's vote bloc has been an important statewide political resource. The growth of the suburbs and the proportionately smaller turnout of the city's increasing number of low-income voters,

TABLE 1.3.
Percent of vote by region for successful
Republican gubernatorial candidates

	NYC	Suburbs	Upstate cities[a]	Rural counties	NYC % of state vote
Republican vote:					
2002 (Pataki)	38	59	42	58	30
1998 (Pataki)	30	61	53	69	31
1994 (Pataki)	27	53	49	65	30
1970 (Rockefeller)	47	58	47	59	41
1966 (Rockefeller)	39	53	40	52	41
1962 (Rockefeller)	44	64	49	65	42
1958 (Rockefeller)	43	65	56	68	41
1950 (Dewey)	44	68	54	69	49
1946 (Dewey)	46	76	60	73	51
1942 (Dewey)	37	68	59	71	48

[a]Data for upstate cities reflects county vote.

however, have decreased the salience of the city vote over the years. As recently as 1950, New York City voters accounted for nearly one-half of the votes cast in statewide elections; in the 2002 election, that total dropped to barely 30 percent while the suburban vote rose from 12 percent to nearly one-quarter of the total. In an era where the allocation of state resources is increasingly seen as a zero-sum game, the fact that the city is losing statewide electoral influence relative to the suburbs has important political implications.

In 1994 and again in 1998 George Pataki won election with a smaller percentage of the New York City vote than any other successful gubernatorial candidate in the twentieth century. He did this in 1994 by winning a substantial majority of a notably large upstate turnout; in 1998, Pataki maintained his upstate support and increased his share of the suburban vote. It is well worth noting that whereas previous Republican governors had averaged roughly 40 percent of the New York City vote, Pataki captured just over one-quarter of the city's electorate in 1994 and less than one-third in 1998.

In 2002, however, with his support upstate declining and the challenge of the Independence Party candidate, Thomas Golisano, in that region increasing, Pataki employed a more historically traditional Republican gubernatorial campaign strategy. Refusing to acknowledge the impending budget deficits facing the state, Pataki focused on downstate Democratic constituencies. By coupling his moderate image on social and environmental issues with active support for pay increases for teachers and health care workers, Pataki assembled a coalition of downstate interests that earned him nearly 40 percent of the New York City vote and reelection to a third term.

The Mayor in Albany

Much of New York City's influence in the period between statewide elections is played out in the ongoing relationships between the mayor and state officials. The governor and mayor have conflicting institutional responsibilities. It is the mayor's job to secure the city's interests in Albany; it is the governor's job to consider those interests within the context of the entire state: "As the two leading elected officials in a populous and nationally influential state, the governor and mayor cannot avoid friction or even overt collision; their cooperation is always tense."[20]

Mayors push the city's agenda in a variety of ways. They lobby in Albany for or against legislation impacting the city's interests, particularly when budget issues are in play. Mayors use their political base at home to influence state legislators from city districts and their media access to make the city's policy positions more broadly known around the state. In the 1960s, Mayor John Lindsay attempted to create a coalition of the "big six" city mayors in the state as an urban lobbying force in Albany. And mayors have had a continuing institutional presence in the state capital in the form of New York City's Legislative Affairs Office. This office monitors policy proposals to ascertain their impact on the city and lobbies for the mayor's legislative initiatives in Albany and against initiatives perceived as harmful to city interests.

The interactions between the mayor and state officials are inherently political. While the governor holds the legal upper hand in the relationship, a persuasive mayor can influence the governor's political fortunes with city voters. In that regard, however, political party appears to play a limited role in the relationship between the two executives. Indeed, several of the better working relationships have been between governors and mayors of different parties while some of the more intensely negative ones have involved executives from the same party. Democratic governor Herbert Lehman and Republican mayor Fiorello LaGuardia had a notably positive working relationship, as did Republican governor Nelson Rockefeller and Democratic mayor Robert Wagner. On the other hand, Rockefeller and John Lindsay, a Republican mayor for his first term, were open political enemies and the interactions between Democratic governors Hugh Carey and Mario Cuomo with Democratic mayors Abraham Beame and Ed Koch were often quite tense.

Personality issues notwithstanding, there may be more systemic explanations for this counterintuitive dynamic. Party labels often mean something very different to executives than they do at the legislative level. As mentioned above, the historic need for Republican governors to hold down their margin of loss in New York City has encouraged them to broaden their political base and address city interests, a process which can only prove helpful to Democratic mayors and distressing to Republican Party loyalists. Moreover, sharing partisan affiliations may actually further strain inherent institutional tensions by generating intraparty leadership competition between the state's chief executive and the mayor from the world's media capital.

Democratic mayors, like David Dinkins and Ed Koch, were able to rely on generally strong support for their initiatives from the assembly majority. As Republican mayors, however, Rudy Giuliani and Michael Bloomberg have more complicated relationships with state officials. Giuliani's relationship with Pataki was tempered initially by the mayor's endorsement of Governor Cuomo's reelection in 1994. After some initial tension, he and Governor Pataki built a reasonably amicable public relationship over the years cemented by their joint handling of the aftermath of the September 11 attacks.

The emergence of Giuliani's successor, Michael Bloomberg, is unique in modern New York City history. He is the first Republican to succeed another Republican as mayor; he is the first Republican to win the mayoralty without significant third-party support; and he has built his political base around his immense personal wealth. Yet, many of Bloomberg's problems in Albany are similar to those encountered by traditional fusion mayors: "Fusion mayors encounter upstate Republican legislators who doubt the mayor's party loyalty and New York City Democratic legislators who regard him as a city hall interloper."[21]

Mayor Bloomberg has dealt with this tension by trying to walk a political tightrope between the assembly Democrats on the one hand and the Republicans in the senate and the governor's office on the other. Although Democrats in the assembly are focused on helping their constituents in New York City, they are not especially interested in doing this in ways that benefit a Republican mayor. Such hesitancy on their part was reenforced by

Bloomberg's reticence to criticize Governor Pataki's budget policies (perhaps nonpolicies) either during or in the aftermath of the 2002 campaign. As a consequence, since taking office, Mayor Bloomberg's relationships with the assembly Democrats have been strained. On the other hand, with the state facing large budget deficits, the most Pataki and the senate majority were prepared to do for Bloomberg's budget problems was to permit the mayor to raise taxes on city residents.

CONCLUSION

Historically, the relationship between New York City and the state has been one of both constancy and change. The city remains the most heterogeneous area in the state, although the nature of the heterogeneity has changed; the city continues to generate substantial wealth for the state although it makes expensive demands on state social-service resources; and it continues to be a center of Democratic Party and Liberal politics in the state despite more than a decade of Republican mayors. Moreover, the once all-encompassing upstate/downstate has been complicated by suburban growth and the appearance of downstate economic and social problems in upstate cities.

In Albany, the elected representatives of these diverse forces contest for their constituents' share of state resources. In the early years of the twenty-first century, a slower national economy, an even more pronounced decline in the state's economy, and a conservative national government continue to threaten the social programs so critical to many city residents. The election and subsequent reelections of a Republican governor, coupled with increasing Republican strength in the senate, which by 2003 had a working floor majority of suburban and rural members, makes the assembly the last bastion of New York City interests in Albany. Despite an urban floor majority in the assembly, regional and intracity divisions within the Democratic Party's majority continue to make consensus building in that body a formidable task. There is every reason to expect a continuation of the kind of geographically based partisan politics characterized by the current tripartite breakdown of political power.

There is, however, an alternative scenario based on reformulated political coalitions. The spread of economic and social problems to the suburban inner rings and the ubiquity of these problems in upstate cities may eventually lead to the development of a cross-regional political coalition favoring devoting more money to social programs. Such a coalition would find much of its conservative opposition not in another region of the state, but from wealthier areas of the same cities and suburbs that provide the new coalition with support. Under such a scenario, cross-regional partisan battles would supersede the geographical partisanship so apparent today.

NOTES

1. David Ellis, *New York: State and City* (Ithaca, NY: Cornell University Press), p. 198.

2. For a more complete discussion of this historical regional dichotomy, see Robert F. Pecorella, "Upstate Downstate Relationships," in *The Encyclopedia of New York State* (Syracuse, NY: Syracuse University Press, 2005), pp. 1619–1622.

3. The common legal term for state preeminence is "Dillon's rule."

4. See Article IX of the New York State Constitution, and *New York Laws of 1924*, chapter 363.

5. For a discussion, see Richard Briffault, "Intergovernmental Relations," in *The New York State Constitution: A Briefing Book,* ed. Gerald Benjamin (New York: The Temporary State Commission on Constitutional Revision, 1994), pp. 119–38.

6. New York State Constitution, article 8, section 10.

7. New York State Constitution, article 8, Section 4.

8. See Citizens Budget Commission, *Fixing New York State's Fiscal Practices*, November 2003.

9. For an analysis of the potential influences of fiscal monitors, see Robert F. Pecorella, *Community Politics in a Postreform City* (Armonk, NY: M. E. Sharpe, 1994), chapter 5. For a report on the activities of the fiscal monitors during the 2003 budget season, see James C. McKinley Jr., *New York Times,* August 1, 2003, p. B4.

10. By the beginning of the twenty-first century, the New York metropolitan region included three states and thirty-one counties. See Gerald Benjamin and Richard P. Nathan, *Regionalism and Realism* (Washington, D.C.: Brookings Institution Press, 2001), pp. 3–4.

11. Twentieth Century Fund, *New York World City* (Cambridge, MA: Oelgeschlager, Gunn & Hain, 1980), p. 62.

12. V. O. Key, *Southern Politics* (New York: Knopf, 1949), p. 307; quoted in Jeffrey Stonecash, *American State and Local Politics* (Ft. Worth: Harcourt and Brace, 1995), p. 7.

13. Robert D. Yaro and Tony Hiss, *A Region at Risk* (Washington, D.C.: Regional Plan Association, Island Press, 1996), pp. 26–31.

14. New York City Commission for the United Nations. *International Business in New York City, 2003 Directory* (New York: Zicklin School of Business, Baruch College, 2003).

15. 2000 census data.

16. Citizens's Budget Commission, *New York City and New York State Finances: Fiscal Year 1997–98* (Pocket Edition), table 7; New York City Comptroller's Office News Report, May 27, 1997; *Statistical Abstract of the United States*, 1995 (Washington, D.C.: Department of Commerce, 1995), Table K-24.

17. Richard Perez-Pena, *New York Times*, Dec. 17, 1997, p. 1. For a report on income inequality in the early 2000s, see Janny Scott, *New York Times*, March 5, 2003, p. B1.

18. See Richard Benjamin's analysis in *Fixing New York State's Fiscal Practices*, Citizens Budget Committee Background Report (Citizen's Budget Commission, November 2003, New York), pp. 24–26.

19. For an excellent analysis of in-house legislative politics in New York, see Edward Schneier and John Brian Murtaugh, *New York Politics: A Tale of Two States* (Armonk, NY: M. E. Sharpe, 2001), chap. 6.

20. Wallace Sayre, "The Mayor," in *Agenda for a City*, ed. Lyle Fitch and Annmarie Hauck Walsh (New York: Sage, 1970), p. 586.

21. Ibid., p. 587.

CHAPTER 2

Political Conflict and Intergovernmental Fiscal Relations

DONALD J. BOYD

New York state and its local governments decide upon spending and tax policies in a complicated political, legal, and fiscal environment. This environment can pit one state against another and one part of New York against another, but it also can create surprising incentives to work together.

FEDERAL-STATE FISCAL CONNECTIONS AND TENSIONS

The federal government influences state and local governments—and especially states—in many different ways. It provides grants in aid that can be large relative to state and local budgets. It designs grant programs in ways that encourage some kinds of activity while discouraging others. The federal government imposes mandates on state and local governments, with or without money, telling them how they must implement programs. It also influences state and local governments in far more subtle ways as a result of the tax rates it chooses and the deductions it allows.

The Federal Government and New York Spending Policy

The most obvious way the federal government affects state and local government finances is through grants in aid, and indeed these are large. In fiscal year 2003, the federal government distributed $387 billion in grants to state and local governments, accounting for 24 percent of all federal domestic spending and 26 percent of all state and local spending (when spent by recipient governments).[1]

New York's state and local governments received an estimated $41 billion of these grants.[2] Most of these grants are paid to the state government, not local governments. In fiscal year 2000 (the latest year for which appropriate data are available), 90 percent of federal grants to state and local governments in New York were paid to the state government, while only 10 percent were paid to local governments.[3] As a result federal grants accounted for 31 percent of the state government's general revenue, but only 3 percent of local governments' general revenue. In some cases the state government distributes aid it receives from the federal government to local governments, creating tensions among the state, localities, and federal government. For example, in 2003 U.S. Senator Charles Schumer attempted to cajole the state government into sharing half of a one-time infusion of federal fiscal relief with New York's local governments.[4] A U.S. senator's influence is greater in Washington than in Albany, and the effort was unsuccessful.

Federal grants are dominated by Medicaid, a health program for the poor and medically needy.[5] (See the analysis of health policy in chapter 14). It is mandated by the federal government, with some flexibility granted to states to choose services and populations they will cover. In most states Medicaid is financed jointly by federal and state governments, but in New York, counties and New York City also finance a large share. Figure 2.1 shows that Medicaid dwarfs other federal grant programs. It is nearly eight times as large as the number two program, Temporary Assistance to Needy Families (TANF, the nation's main welfare program), and in fact is larger than the 40 next largest programs combined (including TANF).[6]

Medicaid is a major source of tension between the federal government and the New York State government. First, it is a huge program, with total federal-state spending expected to exceed $300 billion in fiscal year 2005.[7] Second, it is growing rapidly, with the state share of spending growing faster than 10 percent annually in recent years, at a time when revenue has been growing very little. Third, Medicaid costs are very difficult to control—the federal government imposes some minimum care standards on states, the health care system generally lacks incentives that help control costs, many of the constituencies that benefit from Medicaid, particularly health care providers, are very powerful politically, and federal cost sharing makes it less

FIGURE 2.1.

Medicaid dwarfs other federal grant programs:
Five largest federal grants to state and local governments
in New York, fiscal year 2002

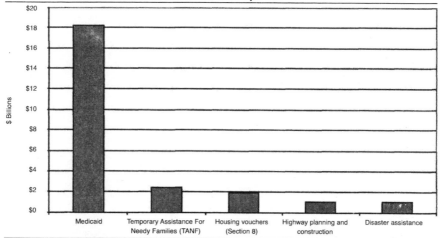

Source: U.S. Bureau of the Census, Consolidated Federal Funds Report for Fiscal Year 2002

attractive to cut the program.[8] Fourth, because Medicaid is an uncapped entitlement over which states have some policy control, the federal government bears considerable fiscal risk—the more creative states are at spending money in ways that qualify for federal cost sharing, the greater the risk to the federal treasury. New York is widely "respected" in Medicaid policy circles for its success at maximizing its draw on the federal treasury.

The federal share of Medicaid varies by state under a formula that provides a higher federal match for low-income states.[9] In ordinary years, the federal share can be as high as 83 percent for a very low-income state and as low as 50 percent for a high-income state.[10] This effectively changes the "price" a state pays to provide health care for its poor and medically needy: a state with an 80 percent match rate pays only twenty cents to purchase a dollar of health care while a state with a 50 percent match rate pays fifty cents to purchase a dollar of care, or two and one-half times as much as the low-income state. The intent of this price change is to encourage low-income states to spend more on health care for the needy than they otherwise might.

New York's per-capita income has long been well above the national average, leaving New York with the lowest possible federal match rate of 50 percent. Many New York analysts have argued that the formula is unfair to New York because it only takes into account the state's capacity to pay without taking into account its need—New York historically has had a higher-than-average poverty rate, a rough proxy for need.

The second-largest grant program in New York is TANF, the nation's primary welfare program. When the federal government enacted TANF in 1996, replacing the former Aid to Families with Dependent Children (AFDC), it made major changes to the fiscal incentives states face for welfare programs. AFDC was an open-ended entitlement program for individuals and for state governments—the federal government would pay its share for as many individuals as a state allowed to participate under its eligibility rules, with no cap on the federal cost.

The federal share was the same for AFDC as it was for Medicaid—50 percent of actual expenditures in the case of New York. As a result, New York's criticism of the federal match rate for not taking need into account applied to the AFDC match rate as well. Those criticisms have since gone away—the new program instead gives states a fixed block grant and great flexibility to determine which services to provide, such as child care, job training, counseling, and other services that may help recipients become more self-sufficient. AFDC, by contrast, was primarily a cash assistance program. The change to a block grant changed the price of welfare—as new individuals become eligible for TANF, the state will pay the full cost of their services, with no cost sharing, while under the old program the federal government shared half of the incremental cost.

One possible source of intergovernmental tension relates to how the block grant was set. AFDC grants were based on actual state spending. New York was a very high-spending state, and so its federal grant, even with a 50 percent federal share (lower than the average share) was far above average. The initial TANF grants were based primarily on the old AFDC grants. As a result, New York's block grant is about 80 percent higher per person in poverty than the average state's grant. Other states might be expected to argue that New York (and other relatively high-income, high-benefit states) should not receive more welfare aid per poor person than poorer states such as Mississippi and West Virginia. While this issue may arise in future TANF reauthorization debates, it does not yet appear to be a serious consideration.

Federal regulation of programs can be particularly irksome for states when the federal government provides little financial support. For example, the No Child Left Behind act (NCLB) imposes profound requirements on states for the single largest thing they do—elementary and secondary education—if they wish to accept federal aid. NCLB requires certified teachers in every classroom, annual standardized testing of students, demonstration of adequate yearly progress in student performance, and other rules that regardless of their educational merits can be expensive to implement. The federal government contributes very little financially to elementary and secondary education—providing less than 6 percent of school district revenue in New York[11]—leading many states to chafe under these requirements. More than one education official has referred derisively to NCLB as "no cost left behind."[12]

One perennially contentious issue is the question of whether any given state is getting its fair share of federal grants. New York has 6.7 percent of the nation's population but in 2002 New York state and local governments received more than 10 percent of federal grants.[13] Per-capita grants in New York were $763 higher than the U.S. average, with $560 of this due to New York's Medicaid grant, which was 80 percent above the national average. (Despite New York's low federal match rate, its Medicaid grant is high because it spends much more on Medicaid than any other state.) Former U.S. Senator from New York Daniel Patrick Moynihan argued that looking just at grants misses the story—that New Yorkers pay far more in taxes to the federal government than residents of the typical state because of their high incomes, and they receive far less benefit from nongrant federal spending than the typical state. He also argues, as many others have, that New York is disadvantaged by a low federal share of Medicaid that does not take into account New York's above-average need.[14]

When it comes to the distribution of funds across states, even data on how federal funds are distributed can be a political hot potato. For many years the president's proposed budget included a section known as *Budget Information for States* (BIS) which provided a state-by-state breakdown, by program, of aid anticipated in the budget—politically sensitive information. In the fiscal year 2004 budget, which proposed to cut grants to state and local governments, the president did not include the BIS state-by-state details by program, eliminating more than four hundred pages of tables. According to the *Washington Post*, the Office of Management and Budget said it was eliminating the report to reduce the cost and paper involved in producing another volume.[15] In a January 2004 statement labeled "The Bush Wall of Secrecy," U.S. senator from Connecticut Joseph Lieberman, who was campaigning for president, said, "Rivaling the Nixon administration, George W. Bush has pursued an arrogant policy of denying the American people access to important information about their government" and included the elimination of the BIS in a list of examples of how, he argued, the Bush Administration was making government more secretive.[16]

The Federal Government and New York Tax Policy

By contrast to the enormous role the federal government plays in state expenditure decisions, it plays a far smaller role in influencing tax policy decisions—there are very few federal limits on what states can tax and how. The most important current issue results from the commerce clause of the U.S. constitution, which reserves to Congress the power "to regulate commerce . . . among the several states." The Supreme Court has interpreted this as prohibiting states from burdening interstate commerce absent specific approval from Congress. This is the crux of the Internet sales tax issue: under current interpretations, because the complex web of different state and local sales taxes around the nation could create a burden on interstate commerce, a state cannot force an out-of-state business to collect sales and use taxes due on Internet or mail-order transactions unless the business has a sufficient physical presence in the state, known as "nexus."

As a result, in-state sellers are required to collect sales tax but out-of-state sellers (those without physical presence) are not. A New York student seeking to order the prior edition of *Governing New York State* can open two browser windows, one at *www.barnesandnoble.com*, a bookseller with a New York presence, and one at *www.amazon.com*, which has no physical presence in New York. In early 2004, both sites priced the book at $26.95 with free shipping, but Barnes & Noble added tax of about $1.96 (depending on the purchaser's local sales tax rate) while Amazon collected no tax. Seeing this difference most people might choose to purchase at Amazon. While tax is legally due by the purchaser, the Amazon buyer (and most other New Yorkers) understandably might not send a separate check to the New York State Tax Department for $1.96.

This arrangement obviously disadvantages the retailer with a New York presence, and also causes the state to forgo sales tax revenue. But the state cannot resolve this problem on its own—its tax policy is held hostage by the federal government and other states. Congress could choose to loosen nexus rules so that large firms with a substantial economic presence but no physical presence (such as Amazon) are required to collect sales tax. Most observers believe Congress is unlikely to do this unless states simplify their sales taxes and make them more uniform across states. A multistate effort known as the Streamlined Sales Tax Project (*www.StreamlinedSalesTax.org*) is underway to accomplish exactly this, and the New York legislature recently passed legislation requiring New York to join the effort.[17] Many states hope that if they simplify and conform sales taxes sufficiently, Congress will allow states to require collection of sales and use tax on Internet and mail-order transactions. Whether states will simplify their sales taxes sufficiently and whether Congress will choose to respond the way these states wish remains to be seen.

A second way in which the federal government influences state tax policy is through deductibility of state and local taxes. Under current law, when people compute their federal income taxes they can deduct payments for income, property, and certain other taxes, but not sales taxes. With federal tax rates that can reach 35 percent, this effectively reduces the cost of deductible state and local taxes by as much as 35 percent, depending on the circumstances of an individual taxpayer. This benefit is largest for high-income taxpayers (who pay the highest federal tax rates) in states with high income and property taxes. New York has a disproportionately large number of high-income individuals, and very high income and property taxes.

In 1985 President Ronald Reagan proposed a comprehensive reform of the federal income tax that would do away with many deductions, including deductions for income, property, and sales taxes (which were then deductible). New York governor Mario Cuomo treated this as an attack on New York's taxpayers and governments and led the charge to retain deductibility of state and local taxes. In the end, the federal government retained the deduction for income and property taxes but did away with the deduction for sales taxes, a compromise that benefits middle- and upper-income New York taxpayers dramatically relative to the original proposal. This episode is a good example of how New York state and local governments usually speak with one voice in Washington—with the state doing most of the speaking—despite the many within-New York tensions discussed in the next section.

A mild form of the tax deductibility debate is likely to reemerge in the next few years. A provision of federal law known as the "Alternative Minimum Tax" being phased in between now and 2010 will reduce the benefit of state and local tax deductibility for as many as thirty-three million households nationwide.[18] This effect is widely acknowledged to be unintended, but it is expensive to undo. If the AMT provisions phase in fully, New Yorkers, especially those in New York City, will face significant increases in their federal income tax. According to one analysis, New York City taxpayers already are paying more than $440 million in additional federal taxes due to the AMT and this will increase substantially as the AMT provisions are phased in.[19]

Finally, states gain many administrative and compliance efficiencies as a result of the federal tax system. States with income taxes generally conform to most federal definitions of income, allowing taxpayers, auditors, and others to apply already-settled federal laws and regulations, and to use books and records they use for federal purposes. For example, when taxpayers prepare their income tax returns, most items of income and deduction will be the same for state and federal purposes, or will require only minimal adjustment, saving taxpayers enormous work and frustration. When the federal government adjusts a taxpayer's income on audit, that change generally will flow through to state income taxes with relatively little state effort or expense.

These efficiencies can be so large that states conclude they must conform to federal policy even if they would prefer different policies. For example, when President George W. Bush proposed eliminating income taxes on dividend income, states were concerned that if the federally imposed systems for reporting and taxing dividends were eliminated, states would no longer be able, as a practical matter, to tax dividends. Similarly, many states conform to federal estate tax rules, and with impending elimination of that tax states generally have concluded it would not be administratively or politically practical to impose their own estate taxes in absence of a federal tax.

STATE-LOCAL FISCAL CONNECTIONS AND TENSIONS

Local Governments in New York

The U.S. Constitution does not mention local governments—they are "creatures of the state legislature" with only those powers expressly granted. This is known as Dillon's Rule, after Iowa judge John F. Dillon, who in 1868 enunciated this interpretation. States can grant home-rule power and freedom to local governments in state constitutions and statutes, and they do so to varying degrees. New York sometimes is considered a strong home-rule state, giving local governments more power than the typical state.[20]

This may be true in nonfiscal matters, but the fiscal relationship between New York and its localities is more like a controlling and complicated parent-child relationship. The parent decides how the child can (and cannot) earn income and controls the credit card. The parent provides an allowance to support favored activities and sometimes dictates what the child must spend income on. In what must be infuriating meddling, sometimes neighbors and distant relatives play a major role in deciding what the child can and cannot do. But if the child gets into deep financial trouble the parent usually will bail the child out—after allowing a period of worry. In the end, though, children grow up and break free—but local governments do not.

One distinguishing feature of state-local finance in New York is that local governments bear a greater share of state-local responsibility than in other states. For example, local governments in New York raise 52 percent of state-local taxes compared with only 39 percent in the United States as a whole. They also bear a greater share of combined state-local spending (64 percent) than in the United States as a whole (57 percent). (See table 2.1.) This reflects choices that local taxpayers make plus policies that the state government has adopted.

New York has more than three thousand enormously varied local governments, as table 2.2 shows. One local government stands out among all others: New York City, the largest city in the nation by far. (See the discussion of New York City in chapter 1). It has 42 percent of the state's population, and is far more urban than the rest of the state (its population density is more than six times that of other cities in New York and more than thirteen times that of the average village).

Outside of New York City, the state has a complicated web of overlying and overlapping governments. The fifty-seven counties cover the entire non-New York City geography and do not overlap each other. Just over half of the state's counties have cities, which do not overlap each other or towns

TABLE 2.1.
Local government share of state-local responsibilities in 2000

	New York	United States
Local share of state-local taxes	52.0%	38.3%
Local share of state-local direct spending	64.8%	57.1%

Source: U.S. Bureau of the Census, State Government Tax Collections, http://www.census.gov/govs/www/statetax.html.

TABLE 2.2.

Population characteristics of local governments in New York State

	Number of governments	Population in 2000 (millions)	Population density (per square mile)
New York City	1	8.01	26,404
Other local governments	3,167	10.97	234
Counties	57	10.97	234
Cities	61	2.27	3,957
Towns	932	8.69	188
Villages	554	1.87	1,988
School districts	705	10.97	234
Fire districts	858	n/a	n/a
Statewide total	3,168	18.98	402

Source: Office of the State Comptroller, *Comptroller's Special Report on Local Government Finances for New York State* (Albany: Office of the Comptroller, April 2003).

and do not cross county borders. Most counties have many towns, which do not overlap each other and rarely cross county borders. Many towns include all or part of one or more villages, which generally are urbanized areas within towns created to provide enhanced services. Villages do not cross county borders and do not overlap cities. The final major form of local government is school districts, which go this way and that, crossing town borders, village borders, and even county borders, but do not overlap each other. The five largest cities in the state have "dependent" school districts that are part of the city government. (The state also has independent fire districts but they are of minor fiscal importance.) It is very common for citizens in upstate New York to pay taxes to four separate governments: general purpose county, town, and village governments, and a separate school district.[21]

By contrast, New York City is a comprehensive government, with no other local governments within its borders. (It does have five boroughs— Manhattan, Bronx, Brooklyn, Queens, and Staten Island—sometimes called counties, each of which has a borough president. However, the boroughs are not separate governments. The borough president appoints members of community boards and plays an advisory role in the City budget, land-use planning, and other matters.)[22] New York City performs functions that separate counties, towns, villages, and school districts perform in upstate New York.

It is difficult to generalize about each kind of general-purpose government in New York because they are extraordinarily diverse. For example,

Nassau County, with a population of 1.3 million people, spent more than $2.8 billion in 2001 while Hamilton County, with only 5,400 people, spent only $11 million.[23] Other kinds of government are similarly diverse. Still we can make some rough generalizations. Counties once were considered an administrative arm of the state but now are more independent, although vestiges of this history remain.[24] Counties and New York City tend to be the major local government providers of economic assistance to their residents, including health care, foster care, job training, cash assistance, and other forms of aid, on average spending a third of their budgets on these purposes. Cities outside New York City, by contrast, spend more than a third of their budgets on police, fire, and other forms of public protection. Villages spend nearly a third of their budgets on sewer, water, electricity, and other utility-like services, and also spend a large amount on public protection. By contrast, the largest item in the typical town budget is for transportation services such as maintaining roads and highways.[25]

Table 2.3 shows the relative size of local government budgets in 2001, the latest year for which comparable data are available. Local governments collected nearly $100 billion in revenue—about one-quarter more than the state's $81 billion of revenue.[26] Here New York City stands out even more

TABLE 2.3.
Local governments revenue in New York State

		Fiscal year 2001	
	Number of governments	Total revenue ($ millions)	Average revenue ($ millions)
Local government total	3,168	$ 99,789	$ 31
New York City	1	52,370	52,370
Other local governments	3,167	47,420	15
Counties	57	15,038	264
Cities	61	3,036	50
Towns	932	4,547	5
Villages	554	1,715	3
School districts	705	22,680	32
Fire districts	858	404	0

Sources: Office of the State Comptroller, Comptroller's Special Report on Local Government Finances for New York State (Albany: Office of the Comptroller, April 2003); Rockefeller Institute, NYS Statistical Yearbook 2003 (Albany: Rockefeller Institute, 2003): Table F-2.

Note: State government total receipts in FY 2001 were $81 billion.

than in the earlier figure, accounting for 52 percent of local government revenue, compared with 42 percent of population. The average upstate government had about $15 million in revenue, compared with New York City's $52 billion.

Although New York City has 42 percent of the state's population and 52 percent of all local government revenue, and can at times wield substantial power in the state legislature, at other times it must go to Albany hat in hand. New York City legislators dominate the state assembly, where 61 percent of the majority-party Democratic legislators are from the city, but in the state senate only 8 percent of the majority-party Republican legislators are from the city (see table 2.4). In addition, Republicans dominate the senate in Long Island and upstate; Democrats are overwhelmingly dominant in New York City but are a minority in the rest of the state. (See the analysis of regional conflict in the legislature in chapter 8). As a result legislation desired by New York City residents or the City government is not assured easy passage, and the City sometimes has to pay a high price to achieve its objectives. In other cases elected officials outside the city can impose their will on New York City against its will, as we will cover later in our discussion of the New York City commuter income tax.

TABLE 2.4.
Regional differences in legislative party membership,
New York State Legislature, 2004

	Senate	Assembly
Composition of the house		
Majority party	*Republican*	*Democrat*
Majority percent	59.7%	68.0%
Geographical composition of majority party		
New York City	8.1%	60.8%
Long Island	24.3%	8.8%
Rest of state	67.6%	30.4%
Sum of regions, majority party	100.0%	100.0%
Share of a region's legislators who are from a majority party		
New York City	21.4%	95.4%
Long Island	100%	42.9%
Rest of state	64.1%	48.4%
Share from majority party, statewide	59.7%	68.0%

Sources: New York State Board of Elections and legislative member directories.

The New York State Government and Local Spending Policy

The governor's budget office, the press, and others often note that about two-thirds of New York state's budget is devoted to aid to local governments. As the budget is presented this is technically correct, but this is because in its budget documents New York calls the state share of Medicaid spending "aid to local governments." However, New York is the only state that requires local governments to pay a significant share of the cost of Medicaid (25 percent for costs other than long-term care, and 10 percent of long-term care, as noted earlier). A state that pays for 100 percent of the cost of Medicaid—the usual situation—would not treat its spending on Medicaid as if it were aid to local governments.

Table 2.5 shows total revenue of different classes of local government, along with state aid as it is recorded in the books of those local governments (where the state share of Medicaid is not treated as aid from the state government, except for a small amount of explicit aid). What is called state aid here is far smaller than we would see if Medicaid were included. By far the

TABLE 2.5.
State aid to local governments in New York State

	Fiscal year 2001		
	Total local government revenue ($ millions)	State aid ($ millions)	State aid share of revenue (%)
Local government total	$ 99,789	$ 23,224	23%
New York City	52,370	9,604	18%
Other local governments	47,420	13,619	29%
Counties	15,038	2,454	16%
Cities	3,036	543	18%
Towns	4,547	416	9%
Villages	1,715	94	5%
School districts	22,680	10,112	45%
Fire districts	404	–	0

Sources: Office of the State Comptroller, *Comptroller's Special Report on Local Government Finances for New York State* (Albany: Office of the Comptroller, April 2003); Rockefeller Institute, *NYS Statistical Yearbook 2003* (Albany: Rockefeller Institute, 2003): Table F-2; State "STAR" payments reclassified as state aid by Rockefeller Institute.

Note: State government total receipts in FY 2001 were $81 billion.

TABLE 2.6.

State aid to general-purpose local governments outside New York City,
fiscal year 2001

	Aid from the state government ($ millions)					
	General purpose	Social services	Health	Highway and transp.	Other	Total
Counties	$ 10	$ 1,066	$ 559	$ 174	$ 645	$ 2,454
Cities	335	0	1	43	163	543
Towns	240	0	3	88	85	416
Villages	40	–	1	23	31	94
Total	$ 625	$ 1,066	$ 564	$ 329	$ 924	$ 3,508

Source: Office of the State Comptroller, *Comptroller's Special Report on Local Government Finances for New York State* (Albany: Office of the Comptroller, April 2003).

largest component of state aid is school aid—$10 billion outside of New York City, and more than $4 billion of the $9.6 billion in aid to New York City is school aid. Thus it accounts for more than 60 percent of total state aid. As is apparent from table 2.5, state aid relative to overall revenue is most important for school districts, cities, New York City, and counties. State aid is relatively less important for towns and villages.

Table 2.6 shows the distribution of aid to general-purpose local governments outside New York City. In dollar terms, social services and health aid to counties is most important—much of this is for programs such as foster care, child care, family assistance, and administrative costs of social service programs. For cities and towns, general-purpose aid is by far the most important.

As table 2.5 shows, state aid to school districts is the most significant grant program to local governments in New York. A recent decision in New York's highest court, the court of appeals, will make it even more so. That decision, known as the *Campaign for Fiscal Equity* (CFE) *v State of New York*, places responsibility for New York City children's opportunity to obtain a sound basic education squarely on the state, in each and every school in the city. It suggests that the state is responsible for increasing education spending in lagging New York City schools but does not require the state to come up with the money—the state could, conceivably, require New York City to tax itself to pay for additional spending, although undoubtedly an approach like that would be back in court quickly. (See the analysis of state education aid in chapter 12).

By its terms the CFE decision only applies to New York City. The legal reasoning would pertain elsewhere (that is, the state is responsible for ensuring adequate opportunity to learn) if the facts in other districts are sufficiently dire and if those other districts wend their way through the courts. It may be years before any school districts outside New York City obtain similarly favorable court orders requiring the state to improve educational opportunity. But as a practical matter, any acceptable political resolution to the CFE decision will require action by the state legislature, and it is highly unlikely that upstate legislators will vote for a large increase in school aid for New York City without additional aid increases in the rest of the state. Thus, the ultimate resolution to the CFE issue is likely to be statewide and very expensive.

Although the state share of Medicaid is not state aid, Medicaid still is one of the two most important state-local fiscal issues in New York—in its role as a mandate. Counties in New York have been complaining vociferously about the large and rising cost of Medicaid, the fact that they have almost no control over the cost, and the fact that unlike the state, they do not have the ability to rely on significant tax bases other than property and sales taxes to finance this growth. The New York State Association of Counties is leading an effort to build support for a state takeover of Medicaid costs, and the senate majority leader and governor have both come out in favor of modest proposals to be begin phasing in a state takeover.[27] Approximately two-thirds of local government Medicaid spending is in New York City,[28] and so New York City will benefit disproportionately from a state Medicaid takeover (and would argue that it is disproportionately disadvantaged now), and so the distributional politics of a takeover debate will be quite interesting.

The state government affects local government spending in many other ways, some of which are extremely hard to measure. Two of significance are: (1) a policy known as the "Wicks Law," which generally prevents local governments from hiring general contractors on a capital project, requiring governments to act as their own general contractors instead, and (2) the state's system of regulating teacher labor markets. In the first case, there are no studies showing how much the Wicks Law costs, but local government officials say they believe it can add approximately 15–30 percent to the average construction cost, and that if it were a good approach to managing projects we would see it done that way in the private sector.[29]

In the latter case, the New York State Education Department establishes minimum qualifications for teachers, requiring that they complete approved programs of teacher preparation, pass certain certification exams, and earn a master's degree (even if teaching preschool). These rules have the effect of restricting the supply of teachers and invariably driving up salaries of teachers. By and large these rules are not based on research showing that these requirements actually lead to teachers who are more effective in teaching students.

The New York State Government and Local Tax Policy

Local governments in New York have very limited ability to set their own tax policy. As a rule they can assess property for tax purposes on their own and set their own property tax rates, but most other policies either are strictly constrained or require explicit approval by the legislature. Counties can only impose sales taxes within limits established by the state, and cities, villages, and towns generally do not have this option. During times when the economy is weak and local government revenue is suffering, individual counties often seek authorization from the legislature to increase their sales taxes, and each such action requires approval by a majority of the full legislature.

New York City as always is different. The state legislature has authorized a full complement of taxes for New York City, giving it a tax structure more like that of a large urbanized state than other local governments in New York. The city has a large personal income tax with a progressive rate structure, a corporate income tax, a bank tax, and many other individual taxes. But even New York City can only do what the state legislature allows.

In 1999 the state legislature demonstrated how powerless New York City can be over its tax policy, and how it can be held hostage to legislators outside the city. New York City imposes an income tax on its residents, plus for many years had a non-resident earnings tax imposed at a very low rate (0.45 percent of wages at most) on commuters. A Rockland County senate seat was up for a special election that fall and in an apparent one-upmanship bid in each house to garner votes for their party (senate Republicans hoping for a Republican to win the senate seat, and assembly Democrats hoping for a Democrat to win the senate seat), the legislature voted to repeal the commuter tax for New York State residents who commute to New York City (such as those in Rockland County, Nassau, and Westchester) while keeping the tax in place for out-of-staters in New Jersey, Connecticut, and elsewhere.

Some analysts at the time argued that the selective repeal obviously was unconstitutional—violating the rights of New Jersey and Connecticut commuters to equal protection of the laws, and burdening interstate commerce. The law, however, included a "severability" clause that told the courts precisely what to do if the selective repeal was found unconstitutional: the entire tax was to be repealed, rather than declaring the entire law invalid, which would have restored the tax on in-state commuters. A cynic might think the legislature knew the law was unconstitutional at the time it was enacted. Sure enough, the new law wound up in court, the court struck it down, and the entire New York City commuter tax was repealed at an annual cost to the city of more than $350 million—all because, at least in the minds of the press and several other observers, the legislature and governor were seeking to please Rockland County residents.[30]

WHAT DOES THE FUTURE HOLD?

The three biggest federal-state fiscal issues in coming years are likely to be (1) continued pressure at the federal level to constrain the costs of Medicaid, in an environment in which the federal budget is likely to be in deficit as far as the eye can see (an environment in which it is not reasonable for states to expect increases in intergovernmental aid, and in which cuts are likely), (2) state efforts to resolve the difficulty of collecting sales tax on Internet and mail-order transactions, and (3) death by a thousand cuts in grants to state and local governments, as federal officials try to reign in the federal deficit, which is now projected to grow at astonishing rates.

The two largest state-local fiscal issues are likely to be (1) continued pressure to control costs of Medicaid and to shift costs from counties to the state, and (2) the state's effort to respond to the CFE decision in a way that will satisfy the courts. State responses to both of these issues will have dramatically different effects on different regions of the state and among different kinds of local governments, creating tensions among regions and governments.

NOTES

1. Budget of the United States Government, Fiscal Year 2005, *Budget Information for States*, (Washington, DC: Government Printing Office, 2005), table 8.3).

2. State-by-state data on grants for federal fiscal year 2003 are not yet available. However, in FY 2002 New York received 10.7 percent of federal grants, according to U.S. Bureau of the Census, *Federal Aid to States for Fiscal Year 2002* (Washington, DC: U.S. Government Printing Office, May 2003). Applying this percentage to the 2003 total yields the $41 billion estimate.

3. U.S. Bureau of the Census, State and Local Government Finances for 2000, www.census.gov, files 00slss1.xls and 00slss2.xls.

4. *Schumer Presses State on Sharing New Aid with NY's Local Govts,* press release, June 10, 2003, available at www.senate.gov/~Schumer/ SchumerWebsite/pressroom/press_releases.

5. Medicaid often is thought of as serving the traditional poor and working poor, and this is true in terms of numbers of people served: about two-thirds of Medicaid enrollees are low-income children and nonelderly, nondisabled adults. However, the disabled and elderly are far more expensive to serve, particularly when provided long-term care in nursing homes and other settings, and they account for more than 70 percent of Medicaid payments. See *A Profile of Medicaid: Chartbook 2000* (Washington, DC: Health Care Financing Administration, U.S. Department of Health and Human Services, 2000.)

6. U.S. Bureau of the Census, *Consolidated Federal Funds Report for Fiscal Year 2002* (Washington, DC: U.S. Government Printing Office, May 2003).

7. Congressional Budget Office, *The Budget and Economic Outlook: Fiscal Years 2005 to 2014,* (Washington, DC: CBO, January 2004).

8. Donald J. Boyd, "Health Care within the Larger State Budget," in *Federalism & Health Policy,* ed. J. Holahan, A. Weil, and J. Weiner, (Washington, DC: Urban Institute Press, 2003).

9. This match rate is known by policy wonks as the FMAP (pronounced "F-MAP"), or Federal Medical Assistance Participation rate. Aspiring health-finance policy analysts and administrators should be prepared to say this naturally in job interviews.

10. See Catalog of Federal Domestic Assistance, http://www.cfda.gov, program 93.778, Medical Assistance Program.

11. Elise St. John, "Revenues and Expenditures for Public Elementary and Secondary Education: School Year 2000–01," *Education Statistics Quarterly* 5, no. 2 (2003): table 2.

12. Overheard by the author at a meeting of education officials.

13. U.S. Bureau of the Census, *Federal Aid to States for Fiscal Year 2002* (Washington, DC: U.S. Government Printing Office, May 2003). Population data are from U.S. Bureau of the Census, 2000 Decennial Census.

14. See Senator Moynihan's introductions to *The Federal Budget and the States*, various years, a series of reports initiated by Senator Moynihan and produced by the Taubman Center for State and Local Government, John F. Kennedy School of Government, Harvard University.

15. DanaMilbank, "Seek and Ye Shall Not Find," *Washington Post*, March 11, 2003, p. A21.

16. As reported by the Federation of American Scientists' Project on Government Secrecy, http://www.fas.org/sgp/news/2004/01/lieb-wall 010904.html.

17. S. 2850 (2003).

18. See Leonard E. Burman, et al., *AMT Relief in the FY2005 Budget: A Bandaid for a Hemorrhage* (Washington, DC: The Urban Institute, February 4, 2004).

19. Karen Schlain, *New York City and the Federal AMT: The Future is Now*, presentation to the Federation of Tax Administrators Conference on Revenue Estimating and Tax Research, September 2003, Office of Tax Policy, New York City Department of Finance, available at http://www.tax-admin.org/fta/meet/03revest_pres/schlain.pdf.

20. See Joseph F. Zimmerman, "State-Local Relations," in *The Government and Politics of New York State* (New York: New York University Press, 1981), for a discussion of the growth of home-rule power in New York.

21. In addition, tax bills may give the impression that taxpayers pay taxes to several additional entities—special assessment districts within towns or counties—but these districts typically are part of town or county government and are simply a mechanism for apportioning taxes to areas that benefit from them. Some analysts refer erroneously to these districts as governments, thereby raising the total number of governments to about ten thousand. These districts do not have independent governing boards or power to tax, and are not separate governments.

22. Local government relationships can be complicated, and there are other quasi-governments within New York City's borders. For example the Metropolitan Transportation Authority is a state-created, quasi-independent entity that provides and finances mass transportation services in New York City and seven suburban counties. Still, the New York City government is

probably the second-most comprehensive large government in the nation, after the District of Columbia, which performs the functions of a state in addition to those of a county, city, and school district.

23. Nassau is the highest-spending county in the state, but its next-door neighbor, Suffolk, has a slightly higher population, at 1.4 million. Hamilton is the smallest county in terms of population and expenditures. Office of the State Comptroller, *Special Municipal Report 2001*, file 2001county.xls.

24. See *Local Government Handbook*, 5th ed., (Albany, N.Y.: New York State Department of State), January 2000, for historical development of local government in New York.

25. See Office of the State Comptroller, *Comptroller's Special Report on Local Government Finances for New York State* (Albany, N.Y.: Office of the State Comptroller, April 2003): file 2001summary.xls.

26. Local government in New York also is larger than state government if we measure by own-source revenue rather than total revenue. Here we need to use data from the Census Bureau to obtain the most appropriate comparison. In the latest available year of data, 2000, own-source state government revenue was $52.2 billion and own-source local government revenue was $62.4 billion, or about 20 percent larger than state revenue. See http://www.census.gov/govs/estimate/00sl33ny.html.

27. See *Message to NYS Legislature: Medicaid Relief Means Tax Relief!* at www.nysac.org, and similar efforts on the web pages of individual counties.

28. New York State Department of Health, *Monthly Medicaid Managed Care Enrollment Report* (Albany, N.Y.: Department of Health, 2005), file cy02.xls.

29. Interview on February 19, 2004, with Edward Farrell and Peter Baines, executive director and deputy director, respectively, of the New York Conference of Mayors. Also, see the *Wicks Tax Exemption Toolkit*, available from the New York State School Boards Association (www.nyssba.org) and the New York State Association of School Business Officials (www.nysasbo.org).

30. See Alan Rothstein, "The New York State Legislature: How Albany Controls the City," *Gotham Gazette*, January 01, 2001, http://www.gotham gazette.com/article//20010129/201/149; Michael Jacobs, "Eliminating the Commuter Tax: Fiscal Impacts," New York City Independent Budget Office,

1999; and Professor John Yinger, Maxwell School of Citizenship and Public Affairs, Syracuse University, class notes for ECN 635/PPA 735, State and Local Government Finance, Case: A Commuter Tax for New York City?, http://faculty.maxwell.syr.edu/jyinger/ppa735/Com-Tax%203%20Case.htm.

CHAPTER 3

Political Parties and Elections

JEFFREY M. STONECASH AND AMY WIDESTROM

Political parties are central to New York politics. Their electoral bases differ significantly, and they "organize" political debates by taking differing positions on policy issues. The policy positions taken by the legislative parties shape policy negotiations. At the same time, however, parties must cope with a changing partisan environment. The percentage of the public registering to vote as party members—Democrat, Republican, or some third party—is less now than was the case in the 1950s. Split-ticket voting is greater than it was in the 1950s. In many legislative districts independents are the pivotal group that candidates must attract to win an election.

These two situations—the enduring dominance of parties while partisan attachments are not as strong as they once were—might seem contradictory. They are not, however. The crucial matter is that partisan attachments and voting are regionally concentrated. These regional divisions provide strong electoral bases for each party. There are areas where loyalties are divided, and these become political battlegrounds, but most areas have clear partisan inclinations. These differing electoral bases lead to parties taking differing policy positions and a continuing role for parties in the process.

This chapter reviews the electoral bases of the parties, the decline in attachment to the parties, and the response of party organizations to these changes over the years. The role of the parties in structuring the political debates within the state will then be examined.

THIRD PARTIES

The focus here is on the two major parties, though state law also allows for additional parties. Any party whose gubernatorial candidate receives at least fifty thousand votes is certified as a legitimate party until the next election. In New York the current third parties are the Conservative, Independence, Right-to-Life, Green, Libertarian, Marijuana Reform, and Working Families parties. The Liberal Party did not receive the minimum number in 2002, but individuals are still enrolled in that party. (For a full discussion of third parties see chapter 4.) The Conservative Party began in 1963 as a reaction to domination of the Republican Party by the relatively liberal governor Nelson Rockefeller. The Right-to-Life Party began in 1978 as an effort to make abortion issues an explicit part of campaigns. None of the "third" parties enroll large numbers of individuals. As of April 2005 the total number of registrants was 11,733,051, with 5,548,871 enrolled as Democrats, and 3,172,706 as Republicans. The third-party enrollments were Independence, 328,752; Conservative, 156,186; Liberal, 73,554; Right-to-Life, 42,504; Green, 37,874; Working Families, 28, 922; and Libertarian, 567. There were also 2,340,575 who chose no party, and are listed as nonenrolled in a party. In New York they are also characterized as independents.

Third parties have influence primarily through their strategies of endorsing major-party candidates. A candidate can be endorsed by more than one party. On the ballot each party has a row to list its candidates, and candidates can appear on more than one party line. Voters can vote for a candidate under any line. Candidates seek to run on third-party lines because they believe it allows voters to register a more specific political message (voting on the Conservative line) in addition to voting for a candidate. Candidates also do not want opponents to receive the endorsements. The Working Families Party usually endorses Democrats, while the Conservative and Right-to- Life parties endorse Republicans.[1] The power to endorse is of some consequence because candidates believe an endorsement and the additional line can provide more votes. While some candidates worry about endorsements a great deal, evidence from the last forty years indicates that votes on third-party lines provide the margin of victory in only about 3 percent of legislative races.[2] In gubernatorial and mayoral races, there are occasions where votes on third-party lines play a significant role, however. In 1982 Mario Cuomo won the governor's race with the votes on the Liberal line. The Liberal party also played a major role in helping Republican Rudy Giuliani defeat incumbent Democrat David Dinkins for mayor of New York City in 1993. Republican George Pataki's votes (328,605) on the Conservative Party line in 1994 provided his margin of victory to beat Mario Cuomo. Third parties can be pivotal in some races, but the major parties continue to dominate the state.

PARTY ELECTORAL BASES: REGIONALISM, CLASS, AND RACE

The important matter for politics is whether the parties represent different groups and serve as advocates of different policies. Political parties in New York draw upon very different constituencies. Results from polls conducted by CBS / New York Times, indicate that individuals who identify themselves as liberals tend to identify with the Democratic party, while conservatives tend to identify with the Republican party.[3] Differences by income are not as pronounced, but there are still differences. Low-income individuals in urban areas are more likely to identify with the Democratic Party, while high-income individuals are more likely to identify with the Republican Party.[4] This aggregate portrait of party bases is helpful, but it is relevant primarily for statewide candidates. For the legislative parties the important matter is how regions and districts differ by party disposition, income, and race and how party success varies with these traits.

Region has been significant for some time. Republicans do well upstate and in suburban areas around New York City. Democrats do well in New York City and a few upstate urban areas. There has been a long-standing division between upstate and downstate areas. Much of this division has been driven by a sense among upstate residents that New York City is different (see chapter 1). The influx of immigrants, seen as "different," into the city in the late 1800s played a significant role in this. The Democratic machine (Tammany Hall) built a strong base among ethnics, which further convinced Republicans upstate that New York City politicians and Democrats were not to be trusted.[5] This regional dominance was not complete, but it was sufficient for areas of the state to have clear political identities.[6] Republicans enjoyed an enormous edge in upstate areas in party enrollment and the ability to win legislative races. The regional dominance of the parties can be seen in the geographical bases of the legislative parties across time. Figure 3.1 presents the proportion of assembly seats held by Democrats for New York City and the rest of the state since 1900. Democrats have

FIGURE 3.1.

Democratic proportion of assembly seats, by area, 1900–2002

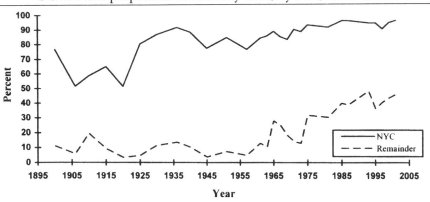

dominated New York City for a long time, while Republicans have dominated upstate. These regional differences in support for parties have, with
few exceptions, also prevailed in gubernatorial elections.[7]

Because of these different party bases, for much of the last century,
many policy proposals were seen as benefiting either New York City or the
rest of the state. Issue differences might have split along urban versus suburban-rural lines, with Buffalo and Rochester aligning with New York City,
but, instead, the division between New York City and the remainder of the
state dominated politics.

In turn, many people in each area who might normally have been in a
different party stayed in the dominant party of their region because of hostility to the other region. Many blue-collar workers upstate, for example,
might normally have been Democrats, but were Republicans because their
primary concern was opposition to New York City.[8] Many wealthy residents
of New York City were Democrats because they felt that Republicans were
unsympathetic to New York City needs.

As Figure 3.1 indicates, the sharp division in support by region for the
parties has declined somewhat since the early 1970s, largely because Democrats made some inroads into areas outside New York City. The 1974 election
was particularly important for increasing Democratic success outside New
York City. In 1975 the Democrats became the majority party in the assembly. Assembly Democrats took 21 seats that were held by Republicans and
lost 2 to the Republicans for a net gain of 19. Most of these Democratic seat

changes (14 of 21) were upstate. That election gave the party a significant base upstate. In 1974 Democrats held 10 of the 64 upstate seats (16 percent). After the 1974 elections the Democrats held 24 of 64 seats (38 percent). In subsequent years the Democrats won even more seats upstate and expanded their legislative base. In 1982, 1992, and 2002 Democrats used their control over drawing district lines to create more districts favorable to Democrats, which increased the number of seats they held.[9] By 2003 they held 39 of 85 (45 percent) of the seats outside New York City. The assembly Democratic Party is now more of a statewide urban party than a New York City party. While change has occurred, the parties still differ greatly in how they fare by region of the state. Table 3.1 presents success for the majority parties in each house, by area of the state, for the 2002 elections. Republicans, who control the senate, win a much higher percentage of the seats in upstate rural and suburban areas. Democrats, who control the assembly, win a high percentage of the seats in New York City and urban areas.

The parties also differ in their class bases. Democrats do better in less affluent districts, while Republicans do much better in more affluent districts.[10] Lower-income individuals are more likely to live in communities that need more state aid for schools. They are more likely to need help with job training and assistance to go to college. They are less likely to have health insurance (see chapter 14).[11] Affluent individuals are less likely to need this government assistance and many are less likely to be sympathetic to those needing this assistance.

There are also significant differences by race in attitudes toward government. Blacks and Latinos, on average, have lower incomes than whites. Minorities are more likely to believe that discrimination is still a significant problem in housing, jobs, and civil rights. They are more likely to support government activity and spending to deal with problems of race relations, increasing job opportunities, and integration. Blacks are more likely to

Table 3.1.

Geographic bases of parties: percent of seats won by area, 2002

Regions	Assembly			Senate		
	N	% Dem	% Rep	N	% Dem	% Rep
Upstate rural	31	32.3	67.7	11	0	100.0
NYC suburbs	33	48.5	51.5	14	14.3	85.7
Upstate urban	21	61.9	38.1	11	27.3	72.7
NYC	65	96.9	3.1	26	80.8	19.2

TABLE 3.2.

Race bases of parties among nonwhite voters:
percentage of seats won by district race, 2002

	Assembly			Senate		
Percentage nonwhite	N	% Dem	% Rep	N	% Dem	% Rep
0–9	35	25.7	74.3	13	0	100
10–19	28	46.4	53.6	13	23.1	76.9
20–29	16	81.3	18.8	9	33.3	66.7
30 plus	71	94.4	5.6	27	74.1	25.9

support state tax increases for schools. They are more likely to see state and federal government action as beneficial to them, rather than local action.[12] In general, minorities are more supportive of state government action, and they are much more likely to see the Democratic Party as more responsive to their concerns than the Republican Party.

Table 3.2 indicates for the 2002 elections how party success varies by the racial composition of state legislative districts.[13] The majority parties in each house in New York clearly have electoral bases that differ by region, race, and income. Senate Republicans do very well in districts with a low percentage of nonwhites, while assembly Democrats do very well in districts where the percentage nonwhite is relatively high.

PARTY BASES AND POSITION TAKING

The electoral bases of the parties affect their policy concerns. Democrats have held the assembly since 1974, while Republicans have held the senate, with only minor disruptions, for most of the century. The parties, with differing electoral bases, use their control of the separate houses to advocate different policy positions and negotiate legislation favorable to their constituencies.[14] Republicans continually advocate policies that they believe will encourage more economic competition and new businesses within the state. They propose lower taxes because they argue that high taxes make it harder to retain business and professional workers.[15] They advocate fewer regulations on business and less government bureaucratic intervention in business practices. They advocate reductions in Medicaid and other social programs. Republicans consistently argue that too much is spent on welfare and Medicaid, and that there should be limits on the benefits clients receive.

Democrats, on the other hand, are much more likely to speak of compassion for the needs of working- and lower-class interests. They seek to restrain increases in tuition at the state universities. They consistently support social services and making the tax structure more progressive.[16] They seek to maintain welfare benefits, while restraining the reimbursement paid to providers. They support building more public housing, and seek to preserve public housing built in the past.

These party differences are reflected in the ratings that interest groups give the parties. Interest groups select bills important to them and score legislators according to whether they vote "right." The higher a score, the more the legislator has voted in accordance with the interest group. Averages by party provide an indication of each party's compatibility with different interest-group concerns.

The 1994 ratings indicate party differences. In the senate, Republicans averaged 57 in their Conservative Party ratings, while Democrats averaged 22. For the Environmental Planning Lobby, Republicans averaged 58, while Democrats were at 78. In the assembly, Republicans averaged 74 for the Conservative Party, while Democrats averaged 10. For the EPL, Republicans averaged 72, while Democrats averaged 88. Past ratings indicate the same differences between parties.[17] While some argue the parties do not differ,[18] interest-group ratings indicate there are clear differences.

The parties in New York serve as vehicles for presenting different ideas about the role of government and its relationship to society. Republicans are worried about the decline or stagnation of the state's economy, and think individualism and economic activity can be encouraged by cutting state programs and reducing tax and regulation burdens. Democrats have argued for maintaining more of a state role to help people who they see as vulnerable and in need of assistance.

MODERATING PARTY DIFFERENCES

While New York's parties are generally regarded as cohesive and different, there are tensions within each party which lead to some moderation of the general stances just described. Many assembly Democrats, and particularly those from Queens and upstate, are more moderate and conservative than liberal. This creates continual tensions within the party, which must be worked out in party conferences. Within the senate, upstate Republicans tend to be more conservative than those from the New York City metropolitan area. The nine Republicans on Long Island are continually seeking more school aid to hold down local property taxes. This requires maintaining state taxes to maintain revenue flows, which leads to a continuing tension within the party over whether to cut taxes or keep revenues.

Each majority party has fundamental tensions. As table 3.1 indicates, each party does very well in its traditional areas, *but each, in order to retain power, also needs the seats it has in areas less receptive to its core approach to government.*[19] In the assembly, the Democrats hold almost all the seats in New York City. The key to their majority in the assembly, however, lies in the 39 Democratic seats held outside New York City. These areas outside New York City are often not as liberal as the areas within New York City and do not support New York City needs. The need to maintain suburban members, for example, led in 1999 to the assembly speaker supporting repeal of the commuter tax, or an income tax on suburban residents to support the Metropolitan Transit Authority. The senate said it would repeal it, and the Assembly did not want to look as if it was unsympathetic to suburban needs.[20] In the senate, the areas of Republican dominance are the upstate rural areas and Long Island. They hold 23 out of 25 seats in these areas. But Republicans could not hold the senate without the seats they hold in New York City and upstate urban areas. They hold five seats in New York City and three seats in upstate urban areas. Much as with the Democrats, the Republicans control their house by being able to win seats in areas that are not inclined to elect Republicans. For both parties, some moderation of policy stances is forced on the center of the party because of the members from areas outside the party's strength.

There have also been tensions between the legislative and gubernatorial wings of each party. The Republican Party's primary base of support is outside New York City, but for the last fifty years Republican gubernatorial candidates have needed to win substantial votes in relatively liberal New York City because the city constitutes over 40 percent of the electorate. Governors such as Dewey and Rockefeller were able to get elected and reelected only by adopting relatively liberal Republican stances, which created clashes with their more conservative legislative party.[21] The Republican Party was sometimes less conservative than it might have wanted to be because of the moderate to liberal leanings of the governor.

Democratic gubernatorial candidates also have tensions with wings of their party. The Democratic Party's strongest base of support is in New York City, but Democratic candidates have usually had to be sensitive to the need to gather votes outside the city. As New York City's population has declined, Democratic candidates have become even more concerned about this. Lee Miringoff argued that the key to Mario Cuomo's vote success during the 1980s was his popularity in the suburbs around New York City.[22] Table 3.3 indicates how much Cuomo's success depended on areas outside New York City for 1990. The table presents the proportion of the vote Cuomo received in each area, along with the percent of his total vote which came from the area. The first indicates his popularity within an area, and the second indicates how much he relied on votes from each area. In 1990 Cuomo faced Republican and Conservative Party candidates, winning by 53 percent of the vote. Cuomo was able to achieve 50 percent of the vote in the New York City suburbs and upstate urban counties and derived about two-thirds of his total vote from areas outside New York City. In 1994, his support in the New York City suburbs and upstate urban areas declined, and his reliance on New York City increased. His inability to do well outside New York City lead to his loss.

The elections of George Pataki have provided mixed results as to the importance of New York City to Republicans (see chapter 7). New York City was over 50 percent of the state population for many years, but that percent has now declined to just over 40. The lesser turnout in 1994 by New York City voters (just under 50 percent) compared to upstate voters (about 70 percent) reduced the importance of New York City in the gubernatorial election. This made it possible for Republican George Pataki to win, even though he won only 28 percent of the vote in New York City (see table 3.3). This vote proportion in New York City was the lowest percentage won by a winning Republican candidate in over sixty years and suggested that the governor would not have to cater to New York City in the budget process.[23] This possibility of Republican political estrangement from New York City was despite the presence of Rudy Giuliani, the Republican mayor of New York City, elected in 1993 and 1997. In the 1994 election Giuliani endorsed Cuomo, further separating Pataki from New York City and leaving him in a situation where he was not indebted to Giuliani. As table 3.3 indicates, Pataki received only 17 percent of the total of his votes from New York City, so he was less dependent on that area for votes.

While New York City may have declined as a percentage of the state's electorate, the 2002 election indicates it still presents difficulties for

TABLE 3.3.
Gubernatorial electoral bases, 1990–2002

Area of state	1990 % Dem. Vote		1994 % Rep. Vote		1998 % Rep. Vote		2002 % Rep. Vote	
	Within	From	Within	From	Within	From	Within	From
NYC	73	35	28	17	34	18	39	24
NYC Suburbs	50	25	55	31	57	32	60	32
Upstate urban	48	20	51	21	55	19	43	16
Upstate rural	43	21	65	32	80	31	56	28

Sources: Legislative Manual, various years; New York State Board of Elections official results, 1994–2002.
Note: The first column for each year indicates the proportion of the vote each governor won within each area. The second column indicates the percent of his entire vote that came from that area. New York City suburban counties are Dutchess, Nassau, Orange, Rockland, Suffolk, and Westchester. Upstate urban counties are Albany, Broome, Erie, Monroe, and Onondaga.

Republican gubernatorial candidates. George Pataki, running amidst a recession, won reelection with only 45.5 percent of the vote. He won 60 percent of the vote in the New York City suburbs, and 56 percent in the upstate rural counties, but he received only 43 percent in the upstate urban counties. He received 34 percent of the vote in New York City, which constituted 24 percent of his vote total. New York City became an important source of votes for a Republican governor, just as it was in the 1950s and 1960s.

These tensions within parties are not confined to just the majority parties. The minority parties in each house also have internal conflicts, but those conflicts are less significant because the minority party does not control policy decisions, so party members have more freedom to vote as they wish.

POLITICAL CHANGE: PARTY VOTING
AND ELECTORAL COMPETITION

The situations of New York political parties are in some ways very stable. The bases of the parties are relatively clear and stable, and divided control of the legislature has persisted for some time. But, amidst this continuity, considerable change is occurring in the situation the parties face in the electorate. Three related changes in electoral behavior have emerged in recent decades. The proportion of independents has increased, split-ticket voting has increased since the 1950s, and party competition in legislative elections has declined in the 1980s and 1990s.

The Rise of Independents

As figure 3.2 indicates, two significant changes have occurred in party enrollment since 1950.

First, independents are increasing as a percentage of registrants. By 2003, independents had risen to 20 percent. Independents create problems for parties and their candidates. Voters without party attachments are more volatile than partisans in their vote choices. They rely on other criteria such as familiarity with the candidate, personalities, reactions to current events, and positions on specific issues, rather than some enduring partisan attachment, to make their vote choices. The reliance on factors other than partisanship makes voting patterns inconsistent from election to election and results in voters splitting their vote among candidates from different parties.

The impact of these independents in New York politics will also grow in the future. Enrollment in parties is strongly associated with age. Older individuals are more likely to be enrolled in a party, while younger individuals are much more likely to choose the independent category.[24] As the voting population gets older, those without partisan attachments will constitute a

FIGURE 3.2.
Party enrollment trends in New York, 1950–2003

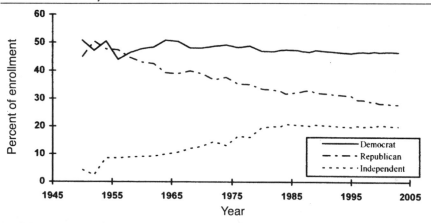

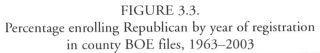

FIGURE 3.3.
Percentage enrolling Republican by year of registration
in county BOE files, 1963–2003

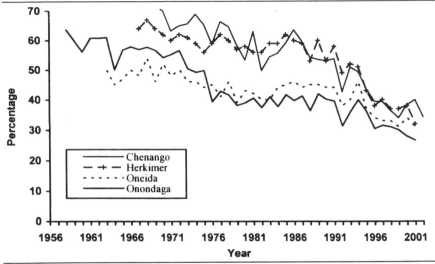

larger part of the electorate. Unless younger people develop stronger attachments to parties as they age, candidates will face an electorate less and less likely to vote regularly for one party.

Second, while Democrats have remained about 50 percent of all registrants, enrollment in the Republican Party has steadily declined since the 1950s.[25] Perhaps most significantly, the problem is steadily getting worse for the party. County Board of Election (BOE) files record the year that individuals register. It is possible to sort these files by the year an individual last registered, and then determine the percentage who enroll as Republicans by the year of registration. The pattern for upstate counties is one of a continual slide in Republican enrollment. If this continues, and older registrants, who are more Republican, leave the state or die, Republican enrollment will be much lower in the future (see figure 3.3).

The Rise of Split-Ticket Voting

There has also been a rise in split-ticket voting in state legislative elections. Split-ticket voting is defined here as the difference in the vote for assembly

FIGURE 3.4.
Percentage difference Assembly and Senate Democratic
vote, 1910–2003

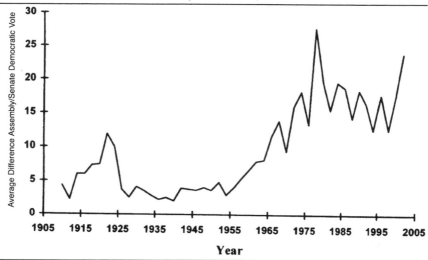

Democratic candidates and senate Democratic candidates within the same county.[26] Figure 3.4 presents the average of differences in assembly and senate vote proportions by county. The trend is clearly toward more ticket splitting. As politicians are aware, the party vote for an assembly candidate within a county often diverges considerably from the senate vote. If straight-party voting is declining, then candidates can focus more on creating personal images. It may also lead to less inclination of legislators to work with and be associated with the party. If the electorate is not engaging in as much party voting, it may be politically expedient for legislators to be cautious about their association with the party and its image. This behavior makes it more difficult to create cohesive party positions within the legislature.

The Decline of Electoral Competition

Many observers of politics argue that it is crucial to have competition between political parties within legislative districts so voters have a real choice. Electoral competition has changed dramatically in New York. Since 1900 the average margin of victory (percentage points by which the winner leads the loser) in legislative elections has steadily increased from a little over twenty to the current level of over fifty percentage points.[27] Few districts have close elections. As the proportion of independents has risen, and as split-ticket voting has increased, incumbents have been able to win with larger and larger margins. This decline in party competition within districts has occurred at the same time that the parties have continued to differ in the legislature. This seeming contradiction will be discussed later.

As competition has declined, there is considerable concern that the decline is a product of the level of spending on campaigns by incumbents. Figure 3.5 presents the average expenditure by incumbents and challengers from 1984–2002 in assembly and senate elections. The figures, unadjusted for inflation,[28] indicate there has been a steady rise in spending by incumbents. In the assembly in 1984 incumbents on average spent $22,625. By 2002 the average had increased to $108,625. In the senate, the average expenditure increased from $35,054 in 1984 to $328,228 in 2002.

While incumbent spending relative to challenger spending has increased, the impact of spending on election outcomes is not so clear.[29] In regions such as upstate rural counties and New York City, one party has such an overwhelming advantage in party enrollment that there are no close elections in these areas. This lack of closeness would be the case even if incum-

FIGURE 3.5.

Incumbent and challenger average campaign expenditure, by year, 1984–2002, New York State Assembly and Senate

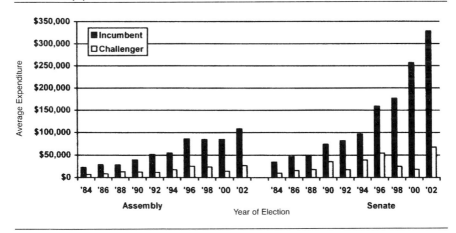

FIGURE 3.6.
Percentage enrolling Republican by year of registration
in county BOE files, 1963–2003

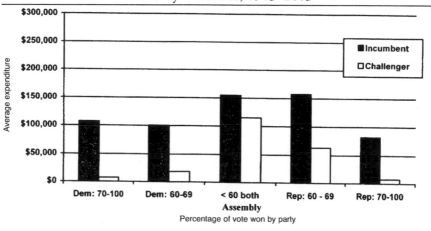

bents in those areas did not spend more than challengers. The greater fundraising by incumbents in recent years has probably served to increase the margins, but not to fundamentally change the differences in party support by area. In other areas of the state, such as the suburbs around New York City and some of the upstate urban areas, party enrollment is more evenly divided and elections are closer. The closer elections are, the more money is spent on elections in an effort to win these marginal seats.[30] When elections are close, the amount of money spent by incumbents and challengers is closer. Figure 3.6 presents spending in 1996 races for the assembly and senate by how close the election was. There is, to be sure, a dynamic between closeness and fundraising. Competitive elections prompt candidates to raise more money, and spending more money can make a race closer. What causes what is often not clear, but it is clear that the most money is spent in the close races.

What is not clear about elections is how much money may have created a decline in the competitiveness of elections. In fact, we do not know what has caused this change. Fundraising advantages of incumbents are one possibility. It is also very possible that the decline in closeness is a product of more legislators devoting more time to their position. As will be discussed in chapter eight, there has been a significant increase in the proportion of legislators who are only legislators and do not hold a private sector job. Legislators now have district offices, and more staff resources to work with constituents. With legislators devoting more time to their position, and having more resources to present themselves to constituents, the increase in electoral margins may be more a product of what is done while in office than what is spent during campaigns.[31]

EVOLVING PARTY ORGANIZATIONS

The organizations used by politicians to pursue political goals have experienced considerable changes over recent decades. While governors continue to create their own campaign committees and use the state party committee as a means to mobilize supporters and to raise funds, the organizations relied upon by legislators have changed. Local county organizations have declined as the primary party organizations used by state politicians. The legislative parties have created legislative campaign committees, and legislative candidates now have their own campaign organizations.

These changes emerged gradually. At one time, most political party activity was organized by county organizations. We have no detailed studies of how significant their roles were, but numerous accounts of the county party organizations indicate they had a significant role in shaping nominations, mobilizing volunteers, and raising money for candidates from the local arca.[32] Governors could at one time negotiate state legislative agreements with county leaders and count on the county leader being able to "deliver" a county delegation.[33] County leaders no longer have those powers over legislators. County organizations have fewer patronage positions to distribute and have more difficulty attracting volunteers.[34] With the rise of independents, candidates now create organizations separate from county party organizations so they can make their own personal presentations to the electorate. With the rise of television and direct mail campaigns, candidates raise their own funds and plan their own campaigns. All these changes have reduced the role of county organizations. They still play a role in interviewing candidates, gathering petition signatures, raising some funds, and various other activities, but candidates now can be and generally must be more independent and entrepreneurial in conducting their campaigns.

The legislative parties, responding to the decline of county organizations and desiring to affect the success of legislative candidates, formed legislative campaign committees. During the 1970s the parties in the legislature became concerned about having the resources to conduct their own campaigns so they could preserve their incumbents and add new ones. These organizations have grown to considerable significance. Each party in each house has developed its own organization. The committees are directed by the leadership of each party in each house. They raise substantial funds within each election cycle (from $4 to $6 million for the majority party in each house in the late 1980s). They conduct their own polling and they plan their own campaign strategies. Their primary focus is on marginal races, or races where they face the greatest risk of losing a seat, or have the greatest potential of gaining a seat.[35] The greatest resources go to the closest elections, and the organizations have sufficient discipline to deny resources to those who do not need them.[36] In 2000, for example, the assembly Democrats directly spent as much as $82,000 on candidates in close elections, while Republicans in the assembly spent as much as $135,000. These are funds spent by the campaign committees independently of what candidates spend. In the senate the Republicans spent as much as $560,000 on close elections, while Democrats spent as much as $98,000. Close races draw the overwhelming bulk of party money, as the parties seek to win marginal seats, or seats where an incumbent has chosen to retire.[37]

These legislative campaign committees (LCCs) have become a significant part of the state party organization scheme. Legislative candidates receive virtually no funds from state committees, and almost no direct financial support from gubernatorial candidates. LCCs have emerged to provide that assistance. The organizations raise their own funds, engage in recruiting candidates for office, and even help candidates who run for local offices. Although the point should not be stretched too far, the legislative campaign committees have become somewhat of the permanent party organization. They worry about recruiting candidates, raising funds, and the long-term position of the party.

These organizations have not completely replaced local organizations. Indeed, some research suggests that local organizations have revived somewhat from the decline that occurred during the 1960s and 1970s.[38] On many campaigns the local and state organizations work together. On other races and concerns there is some friction between the two.[39] While their status and significance is not entirely clear, it is clear that party organizations are changing in the state, and that healthy party organizations exist, but in more diverse forms.

The emergence of these organizations does not mean that legislators are less constituent oriented. Organizations in the capital may design strategy, write and print brochures, conduct polls, and mail literature, but all these activities are designed around the nature of the constituency in specific districts. Legislators receive assistance in passing legislation which is pertinent to their district. The focus continues to be on the local district, but the resources to respond to that constituency and to design a campaign for that constituency are more likely to come from Albany.

The effects of this transformation in party organizations are not entirely clear, but it surely has contributed to maintaining party cohesion within each house of the legislature. The legislative parties have their own resources and organization. Legislators may have relied on these resources in the past, or anticipate needing them in the future. Since this reliance is greatest among marginal legislators, it may create some loyalty among those most likely to otherwise be mavericks within the party. But this presumption of an impact on loyalty among these legislators must be tempered by a recognition that the party also is dependent on the survival of these marginal legislators, and is more likely to understand that they need considerable autonomy from party discipline to survive.

These electoral trends and new party organizations have also increased the independence of the legislative parties from the governor. Legislators know their elections are not tied to gubernatorial results, and they have campaign resources independent of the governor.

CONCLUSION

Parties are significant in New York. They play a major role in organizing the electorate, but their political environment is changing. The electorate votes less on the basis of party. This discrepancy between partisan conflict in the legislature and the decline of party affiliation in the electorate may appear to be puzzling. If the electorate is less concerned with parties, then why do such strong party competition and conflict persist in the legislature? Why do legislators line up in opposition while the electorate is less concerned about such divisions?

The answer lies in the spatial clustering of the population. Areas of the state differ in their populations and dominant concerns. Those areas in turn elect legislators typical of the area. Rural areas tend to be Republican and relatively conservative and they invariably elect someone typical of their area. Urban areas tend to be Democratic and relatively liberal, and they also elect legislators typical of the area.

When legislators assemble in Albany, members within each party find themselves in rough agreement with each other on many major issues, and they find themselves in opposition to legislators from other areas. Organized partisan competition persists in Albany even while partisan attachments are declining in the electorate.

NOTES

1. Robert J. Spitzer, "Third Parties in New York," in *Governing New York State*, 3rd edition, ed. Jeffrey M. Stonecash, John K. White, and Peter W. Colby, (Albany: State University of New York Press, 1994), p. 107.

2. Chao-Chi Shan, "The Decline of Electoral Competition in New York State Senate Elections, 1950–88" (Ph.D. dissertation, Department of Political Science, Syracuse University, 1991), p. 45.

3. The data were compiled by Gerald Wright, Indiane University, and Robert Brown, University of Mississippi. We greatly appreciate their willingness to allow us to use their data. Low Income was defined in the *New York Times* polls as less than $12,500. High income was defined as above $50,000. Robert D. Brown, "Party Cleavages and Welfare Effort in the American States," *American Political Science Review* 89 (March 1995): 23–33.

4. Other analyses report similar finds. See John K. White, "New York's Selective Majority," in *Party Realignment and State Politics*, ed. Maureen Moakley (Columbus: Ohio State University, 1992), p. 217; and, Jeffrey M. Stonecash, "Political Parties and Partisan Conflict," in Stonecash, White, and Colby, p. 89.

5. David Ellis, "Upstate vs. Downstate," in *New York: State and City* (Ithaca, NY: Cornell University Press, 1979).

6. Stuart Rice, *Quantitative Methods in Politics* (New York: Knopf, 1928.)

7. Jeffrey M. Stonecash, "'Split' Constituencies and the Impact of Party Control," *Social Science History* 16, no. 3 (Fall 1992): 455—477.

8. Ralph Straetz and Frank Munger, *New York Politics* (New York: New York University, 1960).

9. Jeffrey M. Stonecash, "New York," in *Redistricting in the 1980s*, ed. Leroy Hardy, Alan Heslop, and George S. Blair (Claremont: Rose Institute of State and Local Government, 1993), p. 185–190.

10. Mark D. Brewer and Jeffrey M. Stonecash, "Parties and Elections," in *Governing New York State*, ed. Jeffrey M. Stonecash, 4th ed. (Albany: State University of New York Press, 2001), 48. The same pattern prevails nationally—see Jeffrey M. Stonecash, *Class and Party in American Politics* (Boulder: Westview Press, 2000).

11. For overviews of differences in policy concerns by class, see John J. Harrigan, *Empty Dreams, Empty Pockets: Class and Bias in American Politics* (New York: Macmillan, 1993); and Lawrence Mishel, Jared Bernstein, and John Schmitt, *The State of Working America, 1996–97* (Armonk, NY: M. E. Sharpe, 1997).

12. For a review of race differences with specific regard to New York, see Ester R. Fuchs and J. Phillip Thompson, "Racial Politics in New York State," in Stonecash, White, and Colby, *Governing New York State*, pp. 23–48.

13. To compare New York's situation with other states, see Jeffrey M. Stonecash, "Political Cleavage in State Legislative Houses," *Legislative Studies Quarterly* 24, no. 2 (May 1999): 281–302.

14. For an analysis of differences in the 1960s and 1970s, see Alan G. Hevesi, *Legislative Politics in New York* (New York: Praeger, 1975).

15. The Public Policy Institute, *The Comeback State* (Albany: The Business Council, 1994).

16. Diana Dwyre et al., "Disorganized Politics and The Have-Nots: Politics and Taxes in New York and California," *Polity* 27, no. 1 (Fall 1994): 25–47.

17. Jeffrey M. Stonecash, "Political Parties and Partisan Conflict," in Stonecash et al., *Governing New York State*, 3rd ed., p. 90.

18. Ken Auletta, "Profiles: Governor Mario Cuomo—Part II," *The New Yorker*, April 16, 1984.

19. See also Gerald Benjamin, "The Political Relationship," in *The Two New Yorks*, ed. Gerald Benjamin and Charles Brecher (New York: Russell Sage Foundation, 1989).

20. Richard Perez-Pena, "Dual Interests Leave Speaker in the Middle," *New York Times*, May 19, 1999, p. B1.

21. Judith Stein, "The Birth of Liberal Republicanism in New York State, 1932–1938," (Ph.D. dissertation, Yale University, 1968); Jeffrey M.

Stonecash, "Political Cleavage in Gubernatorial and Legislative Elections: Party Competition in New York, 1970–82," *Western Political Quarterly* 42, no. 1 (March 1989): 69-81; Jeffrey M. Stonecash, "'Split' Constituencies"; and, John K. White, "New York's Selective Majority," in *Party Realignment in the States*, ed. Maureen Moakley (Columbus, OH: Ohio State University Press, 1992), pp. 210–24.

22. Lee M. Miringoff and Barbara L. Varvalho, *The Cuomo Factor* (Poughkeepsie, NY: Marist Institute for Public Opinion, 1986).

23. James Traub, "Dollface." *The New Yorker*, January 15, 1996, p. 34.

24. A 1985 statewide survey conducted at the Maxwell School of Citizenship and Public Affairs, Syracuse University, showed this same pattern across the state. In that survey people were asked to indicate with which party they identified. A 1986 survey also provides evidence of this. A survey conducted during that year by the *Syracuse Herald-Journal* in the upstate counties of Madison and Onondaga during the 1986 election found that registering as an independent is much higher among younger individuals. In my own polling in various counties in the state I also found that to be the case.

25. Jeffrey M. Stonecash, "An Eroding Base: The GOP's Upstate Foundation Is Showing Some Cracks," *Empire State Report*, May 1986, 53–58.

26. The ideal way to assess the existence of this would be to have individual-level data across years which indicate the proportion of voters who choose opposing party candidates. Such data do not exist. It is possible to achieve an analysis somewhat equivalent by using counties as the unit of analysis. Legislative results have been reported in the *Legislative Manual of New York* since 1900. The results are presented by legislative district and then by county within districts. It is possible to construct a county-by-county analysis of partisan voting for assembly and senate races. This approach is limited in that some counties represent only a part of a district while others represent combinations of several or numerous districts (particularly in New York City and other large urban areas). Nonetheless, this is the only feasible way to undertake a historical analysis of party and split-ticket voting over any period of time. Using these data, it is possible to calculate for each county the extent to which the partisan vote for each house is the same. That is determined by subtracting the partisan vote for one house from the partisan vote for the other house. If the two are the same, the difference will be zero. If the difference is zero across all counties, then it indicates that the

electorate is voting essentially a straight-party ticket. (The aggregate data may conceal some ticket splitting, but this approach provides a reasonably good estimate of ticket-splitting.) If the difference between assembly and senate votes is high in a county, this suggests a great deal of ticket splitting. If the difference is high across all counties, this suggests that ticket splitting is a widespread practice in state legislative elections.

Those calculations were made for assembly and senate races from 1900 to 2002 for each county. The differences were expressed in terms of absolute scores (a difference of -12.5 percent becomes a difference of 12.5, and +12.5 becomes 12.5) to allow a calculation of average differences across the state. Once the difference was determined for each county, the average of the scores across all counties was calculated. The results give an indication of the divergence of assembly and senate results over the years.

27. Chao-Chi Shan and Jeffrey M. Stonecash, "Legislative Resources and Electoral Margins: The New York State Senate, 1950–1990," *Legislative Studies Quarterly* 19, no. 1 (February 1994): 79–93.

28. The figures are presented in nominal dollars, or the current dollars of each year, so the magnitudes will be comparable to other published figures on campaign spending that readers may encounter. It would be difficult to compare adjusted figures. If the figures were adjusted, the apparent rise in spending by incumbents would be considerably less.

29. Jeffrey M. Stonecash, "Chickens and Eggs, Money and Votes: What's the Question and Does it Matter?" (paper presented at the Conference on Campaign Finance sponsored by the Committee for the Study of the American Electorate, Washington, D.C., July 29–30, 1994).

30. Jeffrey M. Stonecash, "Money, Elections, and Public Policy in New York Politics," in *We Get What We Pay For . . . Or Do We: The Impact of Elections on Governing*, ed. Paul Scheele (Wesport, CT: Greenwood Press, 2000).

31. For a critical presentation of this argument, see Morris Fiorina, *Congress: Keystone of the Washington Establishment*, 2nd ed., (New Haven: Yale University Press, 1989).

32. Roy V. Peel, *The Political Clubs of New York City* (New York: G. P. Putnam's, 1935); Norman M. Adler and Blanche Davis Blank, *Political Clubs in New York* (New York: Praeger, 1975); and Jerome Krase, *Ethnicity and Machine Politics* (Lanham, MD: University Press of America, 1991).

33. Robert H. Connery and Gerald Benjamin. *Rockefeller of New York: Executive Power in the Statehouse* (Ithaca, NY: Cornell University Press, 1979); and Alan Hevesi, *Legislative Politics in New York* (New York: Praeger, 1975).

34. David R. Mayhew, *Placing Parties in American Politics* (Princeton, NJ: Princeton University Press, 1986).

35. Jeffrey M. Stonecash, "Working at the Margins: Campaign Finance and Party Strategy in New York Assembly Elections," *Legislative Studies Quarterly* 13, no. 4 (November 1988): 477–93; Jeffrey M. Stonecash, " Campaign Finance in New York Senate Elections," *Legislative Studies Quarterly* 15, no. 2 (May 1990): 247–62; and Jeffrey M. Stonecash, "Where's the Party: Changing State Party Organizations," *American Politics Quarterly* 20, no. 3 (July 1992): 326–44.

36. Jeffrey M. Stonecash and Sara E. Keith, "Maintaining a Political Party: Providing and Withdrawing Campaign Funds," *Party Politics* 2, no. 3, (July 1996): 313–328.

37. As an example of how money can affect results in close races, see Jeffrey M. Stonecash et al., "Maintaining A Republican Senate in New York: Apportionment, Incumbency, and Campaign Spending," *Comparative State Politics* 19, no. 4 (August 1998): 19–29.

38. Cornelius P. Cotter et al., *Party Organizations in American Politics* (New York: Praeger, 1984), pp. 51–56.

39. Daniel M. Shea, "The Myth of Party Adaptation: Linkages Between Legislative Campaign Committees and Party," (a paper presented at the 1991 New York State Political Science Association Meetings, New York City).

CHAPTER 4

Third Parties in New York

ROBERT J. SPITZER

I believe that the people of the state of New York are finding that the
minor parties are the tail that wags the dog, and are seeking to
impose their candidates on the major parties.
—Edward I. Koch, Mayor of New York City, 1982

The closest and most bitterly fought moment in the 2002 New York State
gubernatorial election was, surprisingly, not election day itself, November 5. By then, the outcome was clear. Incumbent Republican governor
George Pataki easily outdistanced his opponents: in a crowded field of candidates, Pataki won just under 50 percent of the vote, followed by Democratic challenger Carl McCall, with 34 percent, and billionaire businessman
Tom Golisano who, running on the Independence Party line, received 15
percent of the vote.

No, the climax of the election occurred two months earlier in the hotly
contested primary contest to choose the Independence Party's gubernatorial
nominee. That contest pitted Golisano against Pataki, who was trying to
force Golisano off the ballot, thereby eliminating Golisano (who had already
spent nearly $30 million in a campaign marked by sharp criticism of Pataki)
from the race. The Pataki campaign's desire to win the Independence primary was so great that it hired workers to enroll new pro-Pataki Independence Party members. In the summer before the primary, they enrolled
about eighteen thousand new voters. In a move that garnered unwelcome
attention, the campaign hired bikini-clad women to gather new enrollee

signatures.[1] When the dust had settled in the September 10 primary, Golisano had squeaked by the governor, winning the Independence nod by fewer than a thousand votes.[2] Had Pataki won the primary, this would have eliminated Golisano from the state ballot entirely, and while Pataki was in no danger of losing to the billionaire regardless of the outcome of the primary, Golisano's elimination would have also eliminated a major source of campaign irritation for the governor.

Anyone acquainted with American politics knows that America is a two-party system (see chapter 3). Despite periodic regional and national third-party thrusts,[3] party politics has been dominated by the Democrats and Republicans since the Civil War. Yet as the 2002 gubernatorial race again demonstrates, third parties in New York State can play a decisive role in election politics, underscoring the truth of former Mayor Koch's "tail that wags the dog" comment. Why and how do minor parties play such an important role in New York?

The answer begins with the acknowledgment that the structure of federalism in the United States has engendered not merely one national party system, but fifty-one party systems: one at the national level, and one for each of the 50 states. The U.S. Constitution left to each state the responsibility of formulating and regulating its own electoral structure. Thus, many states have evolved unusual if not unique party practices, and New York's system is certainly one of the more esoteric. But aside from illustrating how federalism causes electoral permutations, the case of New York also demonstrates the decisive importance of electoral and legal structures in shaping party politics, and the key role minor parties can play, especially when the two major parties compete actively, as they do in New York.

HISTORY

New York has witnessed the emergence of no fewer than sixteen minor parties during the twentieth century.[4] Of these, four maintained an automatic slot for all elections on the state ballot from 1994 to 2002. These four, in order of formation, are the Liberal Party, the Conservative Party, the Right to Life Party, and the Independence Party. A fifth, the Freedom Party, existed from 1994 to 1998. Two new parties, the Green Party and the Working Families party, were established after the 1998 elections. Yet three of these failed to garner the necessary fifty thousand votes in the 2002 gubernatorial race, and thus disappeared from the New York ballot—the Liberals, Right to Life, and Greens.

The oldest of these, the Liberal Party, was an offshoot of the American Labor Party (ALP). The ALP was formed in 1936 by a group of socialists and trade unionists seeking a way to support President Franklin Roosevelt and other liberal-leftist candidates without working through the corrupt state Democratic Party, then dominated by Tammany Hall.[5] The success of the Labor Party in bargaining with the major parties was such that it attracted more radical elements, and in 1943 many of the original founders, including labor leader Alex Rose, broke away and formed the Liberal Party. The ALP faded from existence in 1954, but the power of the Liberal Party grew. Dominated by Rose until his death in 1976, the Liberal Party generally sided with liberal Democratic candidates, although it has occasionally supported moderate Republicans. Over the years, it has sought to promote such causes as full employment, consumer rights, rent control, progressive taxation, equal rights, and expanded social welfare programs.[6] The party's primary power base traditionally rested with urban Jewish voters. In the 1980s and 1990s, however, it sought to expand its base by trying to win black and Hispanic support. Yet these efforts failed to produce results; instead, the Liberal Party was increasingly seen as a patronage-driven machine orchestrated by its leader, Raymond Harding, whose two sons were given high-ranking jobs in New York City Republican mayor Rudolph Giuliani's administration, as the party had endorsed Giuliani in his successful bid for office. Anger directed against Harding and his party culminated in 2002, when Democratic gubernatorial nominee McCall refused to seek or accept the Liberal Party's endorsement, which instead went to the other Democrat seeking the Democratic nomination, Andrew Cuomo. Cuomo pulled out of the race shortly before the Democratic primary, and refused to campaign. On election day, Cuomo garnered only 16,399 votes on the Liberal line, with the result that the Liberal Party disappeared from the ballot. Few mourned its passing; one analyst observed that "there was a strong sense among Liberals that it was time for them to go."[7]

The Conservative Party was also founded as a result of dissatisfaction with a major party. After his election as governor in 1958, Nelson Rockefeller dominated New York's Republican Party until 1974, when he resigned to become vice president. But Rockefeller's brand of liberal Republicanism was distasteful to many traditional conservative Republicans, especially in the business and professional class, and a group of them combined in 1961 to offer a conservative alternative to Rockefeller Republicanism. They also hoped to pressure the Republicans to move to the right.[8] The Conservatives have generally identified with conservative Republicans, especially after Rockefeller's departure, although they too periodically support conservative Democrats. In the 1980s, the conservative perspective received a boost with the election of Ronald Reagan as president. This national ideological swing helped the party maintain its position as New York's main conservative voice. In recent years, however, the party has lost some of its sway in the state, as state political leaders, including Governor Pataki (elected with Conservative endorsement) and the Republican-controlled state senate, enacted such liberal positions as tax increases, gay rights legislation, and a ban on smoking in restaurants in 2002 and 2003. State Conservative Party Chairman Michael Long noted with dismay that these and other recent actions were "a clear indication the elected officials in this state have moved to the left."[9]

Unlike the Conservative and Liberal Parties, which were founded by political and business elites, The Right to Life Party (RTLP) began inauspiciously among a book discussion group in the home of a Merrick, Long Island, housewife. The party's grassroots beginning was prompted by attempts in the State Legislature to liberalize the state's abortion law. Those attempts succeeded in 1970, and the concerns of these formerly apolitical individuals with anti-abortion sentiments accelerated when the Supreme Court ruled in 1973 (*Roe v. Wade*) that women had a right to a safe legal abortion.[10] Unlike New York's other minor parties, the RTLP was predicated on a single issue—that of opposition to abortion. The salience of this issue for some New York voters was evidenced when, in 1978, the RTLP succeeded in establishing its own line on the New York ballot after a brief attempt to work within the major parties (notably, party founder Ellen McCormack sought the Democratic Party nomination for president in 1976). Aside from fielding candidates in state races, the RTLP has also run minor party candidates for president. Yet this party's fortunes gradually declined in the 1990s. In 1984, the RTLP endorsed twenty-one winning state assembly candidates and four winning state senate candidates; by 2002, only seven assembly and no state senate winners opted for their endorsement. And in the 2002 gubernatorial race, RTLP candidate Gerard Cronin received only 42,000 votes, spelling the party's loss of formal recognition.[11]

Two new state parties were founded in 1994. During that year's gubernatorial election, millionaire businessman Thomas Golisano ran for governor on what was initially called the Independence Fusion Party. Emulating the campaign approach at the presidential level of Ross Perot, Golisano spent his own money on an extensive media advertising campaign, and gained over 217,000 votes in the general election—enough for his party, renamed the Independence Party after the election, to win the fourth spot on New York ballots (below the Democrats, Republicans, and Conservatives). Based in Rochester, the Independence Party has endorsed many candidates, including Republicans and Democrats as well as independents, for local and state office. In 1995 alone, it endorsed about one thousand candidates. In 1996, Ross Perot used this line for his presidential bid. In 1998, Tom Golisano again ran for governor, this time garnering 364,000 votes, making him the third leading vote getter for governor. In 2002, Golisano received 423,000 votes, which also kept for his party the third ballot position, behind the Republicans and Democrats. According to the party's state chair, its primary goal is to link up with other, similar third parties in other states (including the Perot movement) in order to create a coherent national third party. Its issue concerns include ballot initiative and referendum options, the reduction of government spending and taxing, stemming the influence of political action committees, and other government reform proposals.[12]

The other party emerging from the 1994 elections was the Freedom Party. While other state minor parties have found alliance with a major party, the Freedom Party went beyond this in that it was expressly created by state Republican party leaders to boost the candidacy of gubernatorial candidate George Pataki. It was initially called the Tax Cut Now party, and Pataki received 54,000 votes on this line, qualifying it as an established party. The Freedom Party was run out of Albany by state party leaders, and was available only to Republican candidates.[13] As a direct creature of the state Republican Party, it represented the clearest expression yet of the value attached to multiple endorsements. In the 1998 election, this party fielded no candidate for governor, so it ceased to exist.

In the 1998 elections, two more new parties emerged. Unlike the state's other minor parties, efforts to form a state Green Party were preceded by an already-established national and international Green Party. While known primarily for its devotion to stronger environmental and consumer protection, as reflected in its nomination of consumer activist Ralph Nader for president in 1996 and 2000, the Greens advocate a series of liberal positions, including increasing the minimum wage, universal health care, opposition to the death penalty, repeal of the tough Rockefeller drug laws, and cracking down on corporate misdeeds. Despite limited resources, the state Greens received considerable attention in the 1998 election by nominating actor and political activist Al Lewis (known as "Grandpa Munster" for playing that role in the 1960s television show *The Munsters*) for governor. He received 52,533 votes in the election. Four years later, however, despite the energetic campaigning of college professor and activist Stanley Aronowitz, gubernatorial votes fell short, with Aronowitz receiving only 40,000 votes, so it, too, lost official ballot recognition, although the party continued to function actively in the state.

The other party to emerge from the 1998 election was the Working Families Party. Propelled by labor unions and others who felt that neither the state Democratic nor Liberal Parties were sufficiently responsive to the needs and concerns of workers and their families, this state party, also preceded by a national effort to form a union-centered party, nominated Democratic gubernatorial candidate Peter Vallone. He received 51,325 on this line. In 2002, the party retained its line by endorsing Democratic gubernatorial nominee McCall, who also earned more than the requisite 50,000 votes on this line.

Despite the disappearance of three parties in 2002, minor party recognition attempts persisted in that year, as the Marijuana Reform Party gubernatorial candidate received 22,000 votes, and the Libertarian Party candidate 9,000 votes. The fact that minor parties continue to try to gain the minimum vote total and the method by which successful minor parties have established themselves and extended their influence over the state's electoral landscape reveal both the potency of electoral structures and the ability of minor parties to encroach on major party turf.

NEW YORK'S ELECTORAL STRUCTURE

To understand how electoral structures encourage parties in New York, one must begin with the initial establishment of a party. According to state election law, and as noted in the previous discussion, a political party may establish an automatic ballot line for all New York elections by fielding a candidate for governor who receives at least 50,000 votes on that party line in the general election.[14] If this threshold is reached, the party is guaranteed a ballot position in all New York elections for the next four years (until the next gubernatorial election). If no automatic ballot slot exists for a party or candidate, an individual seeking statewide office must obtain at least 20,000 petition signatures (signature requirements are less for nonstatewide offices). Any registered voter may sign an independent candidate's petition, regardless of the voter's party affiliation, unless the voter has already signed a competing candidate's petition.

In comparison with ballot access requirements in other states, New York's is one of the more demanding. Despite this fact, however, determined and organized third parties can endure in New York where they cannot in other states by virtue of another characteristic of state law—the *cross-endorsement* rule. This key provision of New York election law says simply that parties may nominate candidates already endorsed by other parties. The votes a candidate receives on all lines are then added together in the final count to determine the winner. This practice dates back to the post–Civil War era, when political opponents of New York City's powerful Tammany Hall political machine would join together in what were called "fusion" movements. Fusion candidacies incorporated multiple endorsements, and were common in the United States in the nineteenth century, but they declined by the start of the twentieth century when most states banned multiple-party endorsements.[15] Nine other states permit candidates to be endorsed by more than one party.[16] But the ability to cross-endorse does not alone explain New York's vigorous third-party activity, as New York's multiparty history is also a vital factor. Moreover, third-party attempts in other states face additional obstacles. In Connecticut, for example, state law sets a 20 percent gubernatorial vote threshold as a requirement for party recognition.

Cross-endorsement is a regular feature in New York elections. Not surprisingly, the Conservative Party usually sides with the Republicans, and the Liberal and Working Families Parties with the Democrats. From 1974 to 1998, for example, every Democratic candidate for governor has also been endorsed by the Liberal Party, and every Republican gubernatorial candidate has won the endorsement of the Conservative Party, except for the 1990 Republican gubernatorial nominee, Pierre Rinfret, who will be discussed later.

Table 4.1 summarizes the endorsement patterns of New York's then-four minor parties for the 212 state legislative races in 2002 (150 assembly seats and 62 state senate seats). In the senate 47 of 62 Conservative Party endorsements went to Republican candidates, while only 2 endorsements went to Democratic candidates. In the assembly 79 of 149 Conservative Party endorsements went to Republicans. In contrast, the Liberal and Working Families Parties gave most of their endorsements to Democrats. The

TABLE 4.1.
Minor-party endorsements of major-party candidates for
New York State legislative races, 2002*

Minor-party endorsements	Major-party candidates			
	Democratic	Republican	Other	None
State senate (62 seats)				
Working Families	21	5	3	33
Liberal	11	4	5	42
Independence	5	38	2	17
Green	3	0	7	52
Right to Life	0	1	13	48
Conservative	2	47	5	8
State Assembly (150 seats)				
Working Families	83	11	6	49
Liberal	37	3	6	103
Independence	40	48	15	46
Green	6	1	26	116
Right to Life	1	19	24	105
Conservative	40	79	25	34

*Based on count of state legislative seats in each house: 150 in the state assembly, and 62 in the state senate. In some districts, the minor party did not endorse anyone, so those are classified as "None." Tabulations include major-party candidates receiving more than one minor-party endorsement. Percents are rounded to nearest whole percent. If the minor party endorsed a candidate who was not a Republican or Democrat, the endorsement is listed under "Other."

Independence Party endorsed more Republicans in both houses. The RTLP, on the other hand, mostly endorsed non-major-party candidates.

The cross-endorsement system has a number of consequences for the New York party system, the sum total of which causes New York to resemble, in certain respects, European multiparty systems. First, this provision removes a major impediment to voters casting votes for minor parties—that is, the "wasted vote" syndrome. Voters frequently have preferences for third-party candidates, but refrain from voting for them because of the feeling that they are throwing away their votes on candidates or parties that cannot win. But according to the cross-endorsement rule, votes cast for a candidate anywhere on the ballot are added to the candidate's total.

Second, one can easily calculate how many votes a party contributes to a candidate by observing the vote count on each line. Many quickly point out that a candidate would probably receive about the same total number of votes whether appearing on one line or several, but candidates perceive that every line helps, especially in this politically competitive state. In addition, some voters do feel more comfortable supporting a candidate with an alternate party label. In 1994, for example, Republican gubernatorial nominee George Pataki sought out the Conservative Party nomination, only clinching the nod when party leaders agreed to give Conservative gubernatorial candidate Herbert London the Republican party nomination for state comptroller. In addition, Republicans created the Freedom Party line (originally called the Tax Cut Now Party), so that Pataki's name appeared on the ballot three times. These efforts were considered necessary if Pataki was to have any chance of unseating popular three-term Democratic governor Mario Cuomo. Pataki picked up 328,000 votes on the Conservative line, and 54,000 votes on the Freedom line. In all, he defeated Cuomo by 173,798 votes. As one state Republican Party leader noted, the added lines offered "a perception that [the extra lines] give non-Republican voters an alternative."[17]

Evidence of the importance candidates attach to multiple party endorsements can be seen in the frequency of cross-endorsements. In 1996, for example, of New York's 31 representatives in the house, 26 were elected with more than one party endorsement, and the winners averaged just over two endorsements per house member. Of New York's 61 state senators, 52 were elected with more than one endorsement, and they averaged about 2.5 endorsements per senator. Of New York's 150 state assembly races, 120 won election with more than one endorsement, and they averaged over 2.3 endorsements. Despite the belief that these endorsements are crucial, a study of all New York State Senate races from 1950 to 1988 demonstrated that third-party endorsements provided a winning edge for candidates in only about 3 percent of the races.[18]

Third, minor parties may go beyond merely offering an additional line by offering the only line for a candidate denied a major-party line. While not a common occurrence, there have been instances of candidates denied a major line who have gone on to win election on a minor-party line. In 1969, then incumbent Republican New York mayor John Lindsay was defeated in the Republican primary by John Marchi. But Lindsay was nevertheless reelected by running on the Liberal Party line, defeating Marchi and conservative Democrat Mario Procaccino. It was later said that as a reward for Liberal Party support, no Liberal Party activist seeking a municipal job went without work. In 1970, the Conservative Party succeeded in electing one of its own, James Buckley, to the U.S. Senate in a three-way race against the

Democratic nominee, Richard Ottinger, and the liberal anti-Nixon Republican incumbent, Charles Goodell.

Fourth, minor parties can run their own candidates, or endorse others, to punish major-party candidates by depriving them of votes. In 1966, the Liberal Party ran the popular Franklin D. Roosevelt Jr. for governor, instead of endorsing the Democratic candidate, Frank O'Connor. Incumbent Republican Nelson Rockefeller was viewed as being vulnerable to defeat that year, and the over one-half million votes garnered by Roosevelt deprived O'Connor of the election (O'Connor lost by 392,000 votes). Alex Rose, then the leader of the Liberal Party, commented later that the move to nominate someone other than the Democratic nominee was sparked at least partly by a desire for retribution against Democratic leaders who were so sure of victory with or without Liberal support that they brushed aside attempts by Rose to have influence in the process of nominating the Democratic candidate.[19] Indeed, influence over major-party nomination decisions is often a key objective of minor-party leaders.

Fifth, minor parties can nominate candidates before the major parties to try to influence the choices of the major parties. Recent New York politics is replete with examples. In 1982, the Liberal Party moved early to nominate Lieutenant Governor Mario Cuomo for governor. This early endorsement, coming before the Democratic primary, gave a critical boost to Cuomo's campaign against the front-running candidate, Ed Koch. It also meant that Cuomo would appear on the general election ballot even if he lost the Democratic primary to Koch. If that happened, Democratic-Liberal votes would be split as in 1966, allowing Republican Lewis Lehrman to be elected. Thanks in part to the Liberal endorsement, Cuomo upset Koch in the Democratic primary and went on to be elected governor. In 1980, an unknown town supervisor from Hempstead, Long Island, Alfonse D'Amato, received a critical early boost in his campaign for the U.S. Senate by receiving the nomination of the Conservative Party. He then went on to defeat incumbent Jacob Javits in the Republican primary and win election in November.

Major-party anxiety over this "tail that wags the dog" syndrome in the 1980s encouraged leaders of both major parties to propose that the cross-endorsement provision be wiped from the books.[20] In 1997, the *New York Times* scornfully referred to the Liberal Party as a "moribund shell."[21] Despite this uneasiness with third-party influence, the major parties have lived with insurgent parties and factions for many decades, in part because these insurgent party movements served to vent public displeasure arising from disclosures of corrupt and autocratic major-party practices in the first half of the twentieth century. Those minor parties that survived, such as the Liberals, soon made their peace with the major parties. If major-party bosses had succeeded in suppressing dissident reformist parties, enhanced public outrage might have cost the bosses control of their own party machines. This possibility caused party leaders to at least tolerate the existence of these dissident elements.

These five factors outline a significant degree of electoral potency for New York's minor parties, and it is evident that the major parties are often uncomfortable with the extent of minor-party influence. Successful moves to change the system have been blocked in recent years, however, by a state legislature populated with representatives who have benefited from the system.

MINOR-PARTY LEVERAGE

New York's third parties are interested in maximizing their influence, but their primary goal is not supplanting one of the major parties, since New York's system allows them to acquire rewards and influence without actually winning elections on their own. First, minor parties can trade their lines and their support for patronage, usually in the form of jobs, as the Liberals received after Lindsay's reelection. Liberals reaped similar patronage rewards after the party's endorsement of Republican New York City mayoral candidate Rudolph Giuliani, who won a close race in 1993 over Democrat incumbent David Dinkins. Republicans found themselves in competition for patronage positions with Liberal Party members throughout the city. Aside from the high-level city jobs won by Liberal party leader Raymond Harding's two sons, Harding's law firm lobbying business boomed.[22]

Second, minor parties may exchange their ballot lines for ideological and policy support. The RTLP in particular was motivated by the desire to impel state lawmakers to curtail liberalized abortion practices. As party leaders have made clear, they have been less interested in running their own candidates, and much more interested in endorsing major party candidates who could be persuaded to advance the right-to-life position in government in exchange for the RTLP line. The party's stated goal was to end abortions, not elect candidates.[23]

The Conservative Party has also pressed ideological concerns. In 1993, for example, the state head of the Conservative Party threatened Republicans in the state legislature with the withdrawal of Conservative endorsement support if they voted for a civil rights bill aimed at protecting gays and lesbians. Support for the bill would have been "close to a fatal issue" as far as party leader Michael Long was concerned.[24] The measure was defeated that year.

THE CONTINUED POTENCY OF MINOR PARTIES

Gubernatorial and mayoral elections continued to demonstrate the attractiveness of New York's electoral system to minor parties (see accompanying state ballot in figure 4.1).

The 1990 governor race elevated the minor-party role to an even greater degree, nearly precipitating a crisis for the Republican party. The near-certain reelection of Mario Cuomo deterred prominent state Republicans from challenging him. After numerous unsuccessful appeals to over twenty potential candidates, the party settled on an unknown but affluent economist, Pierre Rinfret. The Rinfret endorsement enraged the state's conservatives, who objected to his support for abortion rights and lack of conservative credentials. The Conservative Party turned instead to New York University dean Herbert London; the Right to Life party endorsed a Staten Island consultant and Republican, Louis Wein.

Rinfret proved to be an inept candidate who seemed uninformed about and uninterested in state issues. London, on the other hand, campaigned hard, and preelection polls showed the two running neck-and-neck for second place. A third-place showing for Rinfret would have been disastrous for the Republicans, as it would have reduced the party to the status of a third party, making the Conservatives the state's other major party. The Republicans would lose control over appointed patronage positions in every county in the state, and suffer a nearly incalculable loss of prestige. In the election, party loyalty prevailed, but just barely: Rinfret received 22 percent of the vote to London's 21 percent. Cuomo swept the election with 53 percent of the vote; but had Cuomo faced a single strong opponent, the race would have appeared far closer. Four years later, unknown state senator George Pataki scored his upset victory over Mario Cuomo with the help of three party endosements (Cuomo had two endorsements, the Democratic and Liberal lines). Indeed, Cuomo actually received more votes on the Democratic line than Pataki did on the Republican.

Figure 4.1.
A sample NYS ballot: 2004 elections

Sheet No: 1 59 Election Districts County of Onondaga 25th Congressional District 49th Senatorial District 119th Assembly District City of:Syracuse Ward 5 E.Dis: 8 Ward 8 E.Dis: 1 Ward 9 E.Dis: 5 Ward 10 E.Dis: 3-5 Ward 12 E.Dis: 1-4 Ward 13 E.Dis: 1-6 Ward 14 E.Dis: 1-3, 8 Ward 15 E.Dis: 1, 2, 4 Ward 17 E.Dis: 1-17 Ward 18 E.Dis: 1, 2 Ward 19 E.Dis: 1, 2, 4, 5 Town of:DeWitt E.Dis: 1-27	PROPOSITIONS ARE LOCATED ON THE REVERSE SIDE OF THIS BALLOT	MARKING INSTRUCTIONS: Correct Mark: ●	•Mark in blue or black pen or pencil. •To vote for a candidate whose name is printed on this ballot, completely fill in one oval above the name of the candidate. •To vote for a person whose name is not imprinted on this ballot, write the name and fill in the oval in the blank space which appears at the bottom of the column under the title of the office. •**To vote on a proposal located on the reverse side of this ballot**, completely fill in the "Yes" or "No" oval contained in the box setting forth such proposal. •Any other mark or writing, or any erasure made on this ballot outside the voting ovals or blank spaces provided for write-in may void this entire ballot.

OFFICE	1 PRESIDENTIAL ELECTORS FOR PRESIDENT AND VICE PRESIDENT (Vote ONCE)	2 UNITED STATES SENATOR (Vote for ONE)	3 STATE SUPREME COURT JUSTICE 5th Judicial District (Vote for any TWO different candidates even if in same column)	4	5 REPRESENTATIVE IN CONGRESS 25th District (Vote for ONE)	6 STATE SENATOR 49th District (Vote for ONE)	7 MEMBER OF ASSEMBLY 119th District (Vote for ONE)	8 FAMILY COURT JUDGE (Vote for ONE)	9 COUNTY CLERK (Vote for ONE)	10	11
A REPUBLICAN	1A Republican ELECTORS FOR **George W. Bush** FOR PRESIDENT **Dick Cheney** FOR VICE PRESIDENT	2A Republican Howard **Mills**	3A Republican Donald A. **Greenwood**	4A Republican James P. **Murphy**	5A Republican James T. **Walsh**	6A Republican Nancy Larraine **Hoffmann**	7A Republican Charles M. **Iavarone**	8A Republican Bryan R. **Hedges**	9A Republican M. Ann **Ciarpelli**		
★B DEMOCRATIC	1B Democratic ELECTORS FOR **John F. Kerry** FOR PRESIDENT **John Edwards** FOR VICE PRESIDENT	2B Democratic Charles E. **Schumer**	3B Democratic Alan J. **Pierce**	4B Democratic Richard J. **Brickwedde**		6B Democratic David J. **Valesky**	7B Democratic Joan K. **Christensen**	8B Democratic Vanessa E. **Bogan**	9B Democratic Marthe **Ngwashi**		
C INDEPENDENCE	1C Independence ELECTORS FOR **Ralph Nader** FOR PRESIDENT **Peter Miguel Camejo** FOR VICE PRESIDENT	2C Independence Charles E. **Schumer**	3C Independence Donald A. **Greenwood**	4C Independence James P. **Murphy**	5C Independence James T. **Walsh**	6C Independence Thomas V. **Dadey, Jr.**		8C Independence Bryan R. **Hedges**	9C Independence M. Ann **Ciarpelli**		
D CONSERVATIVE	1D Conservative ELECTORS FOR **George W. Bush** FOR PRESIDENT **Dick Cheney** FOR VICE PRESIDENT	2D Conservative Marilyn F. **O'Grady**	3D Conservative Donald A. **Greenwood**	4D Conservative James P. **Murphy**	5D Conservative James T. **Walsh**	6D Conservative Thomas V. **Dadey, Jr.**		8D Conservative Bryan R. **Hedges**	9D Conservative M. Ann **Ciarpelli**		
WF E WORKING FAMILIES	1E WF Working Families ELECTORS FOR **John F. Kerry** FOR PRESIDENT **John Edwards** FOR VICE PRESIDENT	2E WF Working Families Charles E. **Schumer**				6E WF Working Families David J. **Valesky**	7E WF Working Families Joan K. **Christensen**	8E WF Working Families Vanessa E. **Bogan**			
F PEACE AND JUSTICE F BUILDERS	1F Peace and Justice ELECTORS FOR **Ralph Nader** FOR PRESIDENT **Peter Miguel Camejo** FOR VICE PRESIDENT	2F Builders Abraham **Hirschfeld**			5F Peace and Justice Howie **Hawkins**						
SWP G SOCIALIST WORKERS	1G SWP Socialist Workers ELECTORS FOR **Roger Calero** FOR PRESIDENT **Arrin Hawkins** FOR VICE PRESIDENT	2G SWP Socialist Workers Martin **Koppel**									
H LIBERTARIAN	1H Libertarian ELECTORS FOR **Michael Badnarik** FOR PRESIDENT **Richard V. Campagna** FOR VICE PRESIDENT	2H Libertarian Donald **Silberger**									
I GREEN		2I Green David E. **McReynolds**									
WRITE-IN	WRITE-IN	WRITE-IN	WRITE-IN	WRITE-IN	WRITE-IN	WRITE-IN	WRITE-IN	WRITE-IN	WRITE-IN		

The 1989 New York City mayoral contest illustrated how minor-party fortunes could revive. After its successful endorsement of Mario Cuomo in 1982, the Liberal Party succumbed to a fierce intraparty power struggle during a time when liberalism seemed out of favor. Teetering on the edge of extinction, the Liberals came back by patching up their differences and emerging as an important force in the mayoral race. Early in 1989, Liberal Party leader Raymond Harding openly courted Republican U.S. attorney Rudolph Giuliani, who had expressed interest in running for mayor.

The incumbent, Ed Koch, had been no friend to liberal causes, and Harding believed that none of the other Democratic challengers, including borough president David Dinkins and city comptroller Harrison Goldin, could mount a strong enough challenge to defeat Koch. The link between Giuliani and the Liberals raised some eyebrows, as Giuliani's liberal credentials were less than impeccable. Although a Liberal supporter of Democrat George McGovern in 1972, Giuliani had switched parties and was appointed to his position as federal prosecutor by President Reagan. In addition, Giuliani opposed abortion and supported the death penalty. Despite the ideological compromise, the subsequent Liberal endorsement immediately made the Liberals major players in what promised to be a close election in a crowded field. Giuliani later won the Republican nomination, making him an even more formidable challenger. And in a concession to his newfound Liberal supporters, Giuliani backtracked on some of his conservative positions, including a disavowal of his opposition to abortion. To the surprise of many, Koch was defeated in the Democratic primary by Dinkins, who went on to win the election by a 3 percent vote margin over Giuliani.

Liberal Party leader Harding had gambled on Giuliani and lost. Nevertheless, the early endorsement signaled Democratic leaders that the Liberals could not be ignored or taken for granted, and that they continued to exercise influence. Even Governor Cuomo's threat to shun the Liberal designation in his next race for governor if they endorsed Giuliani did not deter them. Echoing the words of party founder Alex Rose, Harding said that his party's purpose was to "keep Democrats liberal and Republicans honest."[25]

Four years later, the Liberal Party enraged Democrats and African Americans by again endorsing Giuliani, against Mayor Dinkins (the city's first-ever black mayor). This time, however, Giuliani won a narrow victory. As the *New York Times* noted, the race turned on "slivers of Liberal vote."[26] In the process, the Liberals had renewed their party, won substantial patronage, and moved a Republican closer to the Liberal camp. In 1997, the Liberals again endorsed Giuliani, who handily won reelection, ignoring other mayoral candidates with stronger liberal credentials than the mayor.

CONCLUSION: PARTY REVIVAL OR
THE FRENCH FOURTH REPUBLIC?

As these examples reveal, predictions of the demise of New York's minor parties are at the least premature, and at the most inaccurate. By surviving the turbulent 1980s, New York's minor parties demonstrated their staying power, as well as their political flexibility. The 1990s saw a resurgence of third-party activity, although the start of the new century saw the eclipse of several minor parties. Nevertheless, the entrenched rules and political culture of New York State continue to cultivate and encourage third-party efforts.

Minor- and major-party leaders cooperate when it is in their interest to do so. But ideological differences, personal disputes, and attempts to enhance power often turn cooperation into conflict. In examples like John Lindsay's 1969 reelection, or the 1990 gubernatorial race, the minor parties were the tail that wagged the dog.[27] But more often in state politics, the dog wags the tail, as in the case of the Republican-controlled Freedom Party. Indeed, it would be a mistake to attribute too much influence to the minor parties. That holds true in particular for the Right to Life Party, which found itself in a position where major-party candidates sympathetic to their point of view frequently turn down invitations to accept the RTLP endorsement because of its reputation for inflexible extremism, which in turn surely hastened the party's demise.[28] The RTLP also illustrates most vividly the importance of electoral structures in shaping electoral behavior. Without question, New York's cross-endorsement and party-recognition rules explain the otherwise anomalous fact that one of the most strongly pro-choice states in the union was also the home of the nation's only antiabortion political party.

Finally, what does this near-multiparty system offer for the voters of New York? As previously mentioned, many major-party leaders, newspapers, and others have come to vilify the current system,[29] fearing, in the extreme, political paralysis characterized by institutionalized factionalism brought about by too many parties—as occurred for example during the French Fourth Republic after World War II.[30] These fears have been heightened by the spread of single-issue politics since the 1970s, of which the RTLP is an obvious example, and the generalized "decline of parties."[31] On the other hand, the New York system may offer, apart from the virtues or vices of particular parties, a feasible avenue to reinvigorate party politics[32] by providing voters with a greater variety of party and, therefore, policy options. A vote for a candidate on the Green Party line, for example, is clearly an issue vote. Moreover, the presence of more parties can only help diversify an electoral landscape considered by most voters to be uninteresting at best. Few could deny that the multiparty system sparks greater interest in the electoral process.

E. E. Schattschneider observed many years ago that competition was the hallmark of a vigorous party system, and that democracy was unthinkable without vigorous parties.[33] The current national electoral malaise leans clearly toward the side of decay and disinterest. The New York example offers a good reason to believe that party competitiveness, considered a hallmark of effective and responsive party politics, is enhanced by the presence of minor parties.[34] Those who complain about the woeful state of political parties in America might be well advised to give the New York system a closer look.

NOTES

1. Kerry Burke, "New (Pataki) Voters Wanted," *New York Daily News*, July 3, 2002, 32; Seanna Adcox, "Golisano: Pataki Used Bikinis to Sign Up Voters," *Cortland Standard*, August 29, 2002, p. 12.

2. Randal C. Archibold, "Candidates Are Bracing for an Ad Blitz," *New York Times*, September 12, 2002, p. A22.

3. See, for example, Daniel Mazmanian, *Third Parties in Presidential Elections* (Washington, D.C.: Brookings, 1974); Frank Smallwood, *The Other Candidates* (Hanover, NH: University Press of New England, 1983); D. Stephen Rockwood, et al., *American Third Parties Since the Civil War* (NY: Garland, 1985); Steven J. Rosenstone, Roy L. Behr, and Edward H. Lazarus, *Third Parties in America* (Princeton, NJ: Princeton University Press, 1996).

4. New York minor parties, and their years of official ballot status: Prohibition (1892–1922); Socialist Labor (1896–1904); Socialist (1900–1938); Independent League (1906–1916); Progressive (1912–1916); American (1914–1916); Farmer Labor (1920–1922); Law Preservation (1930–1934); American Labor (1936–1954); Liberal (1946–2002); Conservative (1962–); Right to Life (1978–2002); Independence (1994–); Freedom Party (1994–1998); Working Families (1998–); and Green (1998–2002).

5. Robert Karen, "The Politics of Pressure," *The Nation*, September 20, 1975, pp. 236–37.

6. For more on the history of the Liberal Party, see Warren Moscow, *Politics in the Empire State* (New York: Knopf, 1948).

7. Erik Kriss, "Some Minor Parties Lost Automatic Ballot Status," *Syracuse Post-Standard*, November 7, 2002, p. A14.

8. Robert A. Schoenberger, "Conservatism, Personality and Political Extremism," *American Political Science Review*, September 1968, p. 869.

9. Marc Humbert, "Conservative Party Leader Longs for the Old Days," *Cortland Standard*, October 14, 2003, p. 6.

10. Robert J. Spitzer, "A Political Party Is Born: Single-Issue Advocacy and the New York State Election Law," *National Civic Review*, July/August, 1984, pp. 323–24.

11. Richard Perez-Pena, "Where the Politics of Abortion Stand Now," *New York Times*, November 20, 2002, p. B6.

12. "New York Party to Work for Perot," *Syracuse Post-Standard*, September 27, 1995, p. A8; Erik Kriss, "State GOP Controls Third Party," *Syracuse Herald American*, September 17, 1995, p. G7; Maureen Nolan, "State's Party Policy Complicates Elections," *Syracuse Post-Standard*, November 6, 1995, [. C3.

13. Kriss, "State GOP Controls Third Party"; Maureen Nolan, "State's Party Policy Complicates Elections," *Syracuse Post-Standard*, November 6, 1995, p. C3.

14. Ballot position is determined by gubernatorial vote. The party whose gubernatorial candidate receives the largest vote appears first on all New York ballots, followed by the other parties, according to their gubernatorial vote. If a party does not field a gubernatorial candidate, it forfeits the line.

15. Howard Scarrow, "Fusion Party in New York City," in *Political Parties and Elections in the United States*, 2 vols. (New York: Garland, 1991), p. 417. The first known instance of fusion was a New York gubernatorial election in 1854; at the presidential level, the first instance of fusion was in 1856, when the Whigs and Know-Nothings both endorsed Millard Fillmore for president. Howard Scarrow, "Duverger's Law, Fusion, and the Decline of American 'Third' Parties," *Western Political Quarterly* 39 (December 1986): 634–47.

16. The other states are Arkansas, Connecticut, Delaware, Idaho, Mississippi, South Carolina, South Dakota, Utah, and Vermont. Linda

Greenhouse, "Law Barring Multiparty Ballot Listing of a Single Candidate is Challenged," *New York Times*, May 29, 1996, p. A14.

17. Ian Fisher, "Minor Parties File Petitions for Pataki and Rosenbaum," *New York Times*, August 24, 1994, p. B4.

18. Chao-Chi Shan, "The Decline of Electoral Competition in New York State Senate Elections, 1950-1988" (Ph.D. dissertation, Syracuse University, 1991), p. 45.

19. Karen, "The Politics of Pressure," p. 236.

20. A Democratic party resolution considered briefly by state party leaders denounced cross-endorsements in saying, "The process has led to many cases where the people able to dispense such cross-endorsements obtain influence out of all proportion to the people they represent." See Maurice Carroll, "State Democrats Attack Cross-Endorsement Policy," *New York Times*, January 29, 1982, p. B2. See also Milton Hoffman, "Major Parties Might Lose Top Ballot Positions," *Ithaca Journal*, August 26, 1982, p. 10. The Republicans considered a similar resolution. See Frank Lynn, "Conservatives and a Political Gamble in New York," *New York Times*, January 26, 1982, p. B7; Maurice Carroll, "Minor Party Once Again Has a Major Effect on Politics," *New York Times*, March 14, 1982, p. E7.

21. "A Party for Hire," *New York Times*, February 24, 1997, p. A14.

22. Alison Mitchell, "Liberals and Republicans Scrambling for Giuliani Jobs," *New York Times*, December 20, 1993, p. B1; Kevin Sack, "A Liberal's Patronage Dividend," *New York Times*, February 15, 1994, p. B3; "A Party for Hire."

23. Robert J. Spitzer, *The Right to Life Movement and Third Party Politics* (Westport, CT: Greenwood Press, 1987), chapter 2.

24. David Bauder, "Supporters of Gay Rights Criticize Fear of Conservatives," *Cortland Standard*, June 3, 1993, p. 11.

25. Sam Roberts, "Tiny Liberal Party Set to Wag Some Big Dogs," *New York Times*, March 13, 1989, p. B1.

26. Todd S. Purdum, "Mayoral Race May Turn on Slivers of Liberal Vote," *New York Times*, August 12, 1993, p. 1.

27. In Cayuga County in upstate New York, local Republicans say that "the lack of a Conservative endorsement . . . is the kiss of death to a campaign." This is true even though the local Conservative Party is considered poorly organized and has a small enrollment. Charley Hannagan, "Small Conservative Party Still Powerful in Cayuga County," *Syracuse Post Standard*, June 6, 1989, p. B2.

28. Jacqueline Arnold, "Party Lines Tug Executive Candidate," *Syracuse Post-Standard*, June 16, 1995, p. C3; Irving Long, "Weighing Effects of Cross Endorsements," *Newsday*, April 17, 1997, p. A35.

29. Howard Scarrow, *Parties, Elections, and Representation in the State of New York* (New York: New York University Press, 1983), chapter 2.

30. One symptom of the continued concern about the minor parties was seen in 1986, when the liberal *New York Times* called in an editorial for the dissolution of the Liberal Party, citing its factional disputes and apparently declining influence.

31. William Crotty, *American Parties in Decline* (Boston: Little, Brown, 1984).

32. For more on this argument, see Spitzer, *The Right to Life Movement and Third Party Politics*, chapter 4. See also Mazmanian, *Third Parties in Presidential Elections*, chapter 5; Theodore J. Lowi, "The Party Crasher," *New York Times Magazine*, August 23, 1992, p. 28. Lisa J. Disch argues for the reintroduction of the fusion/cross-endorsement rule as a way to reinvigorate party politics. See *The Tyranny of the Two-Party System* (New York: Columbia University Press, 2002).

33. E. E. Schattschneider, *Party Government* (New York: Holt, Rinehart and Winston, 1942), p. 208.

34. Spitzer, *The Right to Life Movement and Third Party Politics*, chapter 4.

CHAPTER 5

Interest-Group Lobbying in New York State

ROGAN T. KERSH

At least since the term "lobbying" was coined in Albany in the early nineteenth century, New York State has been a showcase for interest-group
activity of every type. Labor, high-tech, environmental, industrial, consumer-
rights, education, financial, agricultural, religious—these and many other sectors of the U.S. polity (aptly termed an "interest group society" a few years
ago)[1] have worked to establish or maintain a powerful presence in the state.
In recent years, the extent of lobbying activity has reached new heights in
New York, measured both in total group expenditures, sheer number of lobbyists, and eye-opening events such as an infamous "$500,000 phone call," of
which more below. This continued expansion of an already-saturated interest-
group sector has helped fuel calls for toughening New York's lobbying laws,
pressure that scarcely abated in the wake of a 1999 reform act. As interest
groups settle more firmly into the role of an informal but undeniably powerful fourth branch of government in Albany and across the nation, their place
in New York governance deserves extended examination.

This chapter first provides a short summary of the growing prominence
of interest groups in contemporary U.S. state politics, with particular reference to New York. The next section then looks broadly at the details of lobbyists' work and influence on state policymaking. A review of New York's
fierce battles over lobbying reform since the mid-1990s follows in the third
section, which also features selected highlights of interest-group activity in
New York over the past few years. The chapter concludes by reviewing the
drawbacks—and legitimate benefits—of lobbyists' increasing centrality in
state and national policymaking.

AN "INTEREST-GROUP SOCIETY" INDEED

Interest group activity, in both Washington and state capitals, continues at rates that, by any measure, grow greater each year. Total expenditures on federal lobbying in 2003 approached $2 billion, up more than 10 percent from the previous year. Contributions to federal campaigns by interest groups, measured in constant dollars, reached new highs in 2000 and again in 2002; despite a new "soft money" ban, those records almost certainly will be shattered in the 2004 national elections. And state and local lobbying is growing at an even greater pace. During 2003, lobbyists in forty-one states (nine states do not have formal reporting requirements) spent nearly $900 million to influence their lawmakers—notably, that $900 million figure excludes campaign contributions. New York featured the nation's third-highest state spending total: lobbyists spent just under $120 million to affect Albany policymaking in 2003, a 30 percent increase over the previous year. (Just under 3,600 lobbyists registered with the state in 2003, another new high; forty-four different interests each spent over $250,000 to influence state lawmakers.) In New York City, an estimated $22.6 million was spent on lobbying activities in 2002, more than doubling the figure for five years earlier.[2]

What do lobbyists—and the clients they represent—receive for all this largesse and professional activity? Despite an enormous amount of research and speculation, no one really knows. Many interest-group scholars, as well as journalists and Americans more generally, are firmly convinced that campaign contributions, for example, primarily represent "bribes" (essentially, money in exchange for votes or other favors) or at the very least a reliable means of access to policymakers. Yet, at the federal level, one exhaustive study of lobbying concluded recently that "votes are not purchased and contributions do not facilitate opportunities for direct contact with legislators."[3] That political-action committee (PAC) donations are intended to sway election outcomes seems intuitively obvious, but their efficacy in this regard appears limited at best. Another group of researchers concluded recently that "individual PAC contributions have little to no value at the margin to incumbents in either House or Senate elections."[4] Still, PAC spending continues to soar, totalling $316 million to federal candidates and party committees in the 2000 election cycle—a 30 percent increase over 1996; 2004 figures had topped $200 million by early August, well on the way to another new high.[5] If not to secure favors or guarantees of access, what could all this money be for?

One possibility: lobbying, including campaign contributions and other types of interest-group spending, provides a form of insurance in a deeply uncertain political world. Just as homeowners don't pay fire-insurance premiums with the expectation that their house will burn down, many lobbyists and their clients make contributions not because they have concrete expectations of influence or even access, but because they fear not doing so—in large part because their competition, that is, opposing lobbyists, are making donations.

Efforts to empirically account for the purposes of interest-group lobbying will assuredly continue. But in the short term, researchers' difficulty in identifying the payoff of political contributions and other types of lobbyist spending reaffirms one scholar's lament from more than a decade ago: "Despite years of research . . . the extent to which money actually buys political influence on a regular basis remains a mystery."[6]

State interest group activities are even less well understood, given the patchwork of lobbying disclosure requirements across the fifty states (not to mention hundreds of metropolitan localities, all attracting growing knots of lobbyists as well) and the relative paucity of research in this area. It seems plausible, given the fewer number of actors and relatively compact scale of decision making, that face-to-face interactions yield more reliably fruitful policy results for prominent state lobbyists than seems to be the case in Washington. A study by three lobbying researchers bluntly concluded that "campaign contributions and gifts buy access to legislators in New York State." Yet political uncertainty, which drives much lobbying at the federal level, has also been increasing in many state governments. As one expert notes, "In state legislatures, as in Congress, it is no longer possible to make one's case with a powerful few. Instead, the lobbyist has to contact a wider group of members and touch more bases. . . . [Even] in the New York legislature, where power still is concentrated in top leadership, it is not as concentrated as it used to be."[7]

This increasingly dispersed power within state governments, combined with devolution of governing responsibilities from the federal to state level and the growing complexity of issues faced by state officials, has resulted in more elaborate state lobbying efforts. The past decade has seen rapid growth in the number of lobbyists registered in Albany, like other state capitals, as well an increase in the types and sophistication of lobbying techniques. Among the U.S. states, New York has long attracted considerable attention as a haven for intensive interest-group activity. Usually this attention is followed by proposals for significant reform; recent years are no exception.

NEW YORK LOBBYING: OVERVIEW

Of the handful of nineteenth-century lobbyists still considered legendary, the two most notorious—Thurlow Weed and Samuel Ward—both got their start as influence seekers in Albany and New York City. And with good reason: into the twentieth century, New York was both the largest U.S. state and a frequent source of political innovations.[8] While California has supplanted the Empire State in both respects, New York remains a haven for lobbying activity. And dramatic scandals involving interest-group influence are also part of the New York tradition still in evidence today.

Past glories (and embarrassments) aside, how does interest-group influence in New York compare to that of other states? Lobbyists in New York politics are seen by researchers not as "dominating" policymaking, as is the case in a few states like Florida and Nevada, but rather as "complementary" to state legislators and bureaucrats. New York lobbyists work closely with decision makers, but are constrained in their influence by institutional actors like political parties and executive-branch officials, as well as by competition with other lobbying groups.[9] Groups' extensive jostling for influence reflects both a relative balance among public and private, corporate and labor/public-interest, and other coalitions of opposing lobbying sectors, as well as the growing number of lobbyists active in the state. A record 3,598 New York firms and individuals registered as lobbyists in 2003, almost certainly a small percentage of the actual number of organized groups actively seeking to influence policymakers' decisions.

Such influence seeking, as noted earlier, comes at an ever-higher price. Corporate clients and members of public-interest groups earmark tens of millions of dollars to support their efforts to secure favorable outcomes in Albany. For a recent snapshot of those most concerned about New York legislative activity, see table 5.1, which lists the highest-spending groups during 2003. Unions, teachers, health care organizations, trial lawyers: all faced major state legislative battles affecting their concerns, and spent large sums—over $11 million in one case—on their lobbying efforts.

What does all this money buy—or, in other words, what do the thousands of registered lobbyists do? Much of the public's awareness of lobbying is in the context of scandals, certainly in no short supply in New York or any other political realm. But the reality of lobbying differs vastly from the familiar caricature of corrupt bargains between special interests and lawmakers, struck in shadowy corners of the capital. Some recent headline-making

TABLE 5.1.
Top 10 Clients: 2003 lobbying expenses

1. Service Employees International Union & Greater NY Health Assn. Healthcare Education Project	$ 11,067,696
2. United Teachers (NY State)	$ 2,292,528
3. Seneca Nation of Indians	$ 1,993,207
4. Public Employees Federation	$ 1,560,792
5. Civil Service Employees Association (CSEA) & CSEA PAC	$ 1,489,038
6. Healthcare Association of NY State	$ 1,244,083
7. Medical Society of the State of NY	$ 1,231,880
8. United Federation of Teachers	$ 1,009,748
9. Trial Lawyers Association	$ 1,009,116
10. Greater NY Hospital Association	$ 972,052

Source: New York State Temporary Commission on Lobbying, *2003 Annual Report.*

stories of lobbyist malfeasance or overreach are profiled below, in the next section's account of lobbying reform. But to judge New York's interest-group activity on the basis of these is no more accurate than would be an analysis of doctors or engineers that focuses primarily on accounts of medical malpractice or collapsing buildings.

To some degree, a New York lobbyist's work depends on the type of group the lobbyist represents. Researchers usually divide the interest-group world into three basic varieties: *single-firm* lobbyists, who represent one corporation or public-interest group, such as IBM or the Sierra Club; *trade-association* or *issue-based* representatives, who work on behalf of a particular industry or policy topic (dairy farmers, oil companies) or concentrate on a single policy topic (solar energy, health care); and *contract* lobbyists, who represent a variety of clients and are usually among the more seasoned and best-known political operatives in Albany. The nature of a lobbyist's responsibilities flows in part from their location in this triad: a lobbyist for a particular firm or trade association, for example, will focus attention on a handful of issues each year. When a bill or agency decision relevant to their interests is under consideration, their activity reaches a climax: buttonholing legislators and their staff or executive officials, testifying or arranging client testimony before legislative committees, or orchestrating a "Legislative Lobby Day" in Albany to bring their group's concerns straight to lawmakers. In a typical example of the latter, New York's Business Council organized an annual "Small Business Day and Manufacturing Lobbying Day" on March 25, 2003, during consideration of a bill to reduce health-care costs for business. Members attended morning panel discussions on health-care and tort law reform, then fanned out to assembly and state senate offices in the afternoon. Rare is the week in Albany (and, increasingly, New York and other major cities) that one or more such events is not scheduled. As one political scientist notes, "Even though such grassroots visits consume a great deal of the time available during session days, legislators welcomed them. Visits by group members present an opportunity to gather important information about the impact of existing or contemplated policies on specific constituencies."[10]

A contract lobbyist, in contrast, typically works on a wide variety of different policy matters. Lobbyists for the New York City-based firm Bolton St. John, for example, in the first three quarters of 2004 represented some seventy different clients, including the County Nursing Facilities of New York, Verizon Wireless, the Gay Men's Health Crisis, Nassau Off-Track Betting, the Committee for Taxi Safety, and Monroe County. The contrast between single-firm representatives' in-depth knowledge of a particular subject and the generalist's approach required of contract lobbyists can be striking. But all in all, more similarities than differences mark the regular work of a lobbyist in Albany or a major state metropolis.

Though much of their activity is out of the public eye, given that "[interest] group politics in the states is now similar to group politics in Washington," it is possible to draw on detailed knowledge of federal lobbyists' practices for a better understanding of interest-group work in New York State.[11] The bulk of lobbying targets the legislature in Albany, the most accessible of the three branches, but both the executive and judiciary are important to lobbyists as well. Much of lobbyists' work, in Albany or New York City as in Washington or other state capitals, is mundane: researching policy options, monitoring legislative and executive activity such as hearings and committee debates, reporting to clients, providing information to lawmakers or (more often) their staff members, attending fund-raisers and other campaign events, meeting with reporters, planning grass-roots strategies with group members or other supporters, and so forth. Far less often do lobbyists engage in the nitty-gritty of active advocacy, which might include testifying at public hearings, pressing a point directly with government officials, drafting legislation or administrative regulations, or brokering high-stakes meetings between clients and policymakers. These activities do take place, but they are the exception (if, for many lobbyists, a personal professional highlight) rather than the ordinary.

Lobbyists' principal influence on governance lies in monitoring and exchanging information. Like federal interest-group representatives, many New York lobbyists now employ research staff to develop in-depth studies of policy issues, designed to help make a client's case in the capitol. Decision makers, pressed for time and research support themselves, are often able to make use of these reports in preparing legislation or policy recommendations. In turn, the typical lobbyist spends hours each day trolling for legislative or administrative tidbits, talking to staffers, policymakers, and—most often—other group representatives. A fundamental rule of the twenty-first-century lobbying game: anticipating legislative or executive activity, even if most lobbyists have little power to affect outcomes, can be immensely helpful to clients or group members.

In sum, rather than persuading a legislator to vote their way, or weighing in decisively on vital legislative matters, virtually all New York lobbyists spend the vast majority of their time on routine efforts to keep abreast of political developments and to report those to their clients. This is important work, essential to helping lubricate the elaborate machinery of policymaking. But the professional activity of most lobbyists seems considerably removed from the familiar description of sinister influences wielding a stranglehold over the legislative process in Albany, New York City, or elsewhere around the state. In one representative example, the *New York Times* editorialized early in 2003: "How deeply New York State's decision makers remain in the thrall of special interests. . . . Virtually nothing happens in Albany in which the desires of lobbyists aren't taken into account."[12] Such rhetoric has fuelled ongoing efforts to expand regulation of interest-group activity in New York.

REGULATING NEW YORK'S INTERESTS:
THE LOBBYING ACT AND BEYOND

As in many U.S. states, efforts to regulate lobbying in New York began during the early-twentieth-century burst of American reform known as the Progressive Era. A governor-appointed commission, headed by the respected state senator William W. Armstrong, was convened in 1905 to investigate interest groups' influence on state legislation. The Armstrong Committee's recommendation that lobbyists be required to register with the secretary of state was enacted the same year, a novel regulatory step—and one not replicated at the federal level until after World War II. Like most other initial efforts at lobbying restrictions, however, this requirement was essentially toothless. State secretaries had scant authority to punish those failing to register, nor could they initiate investigations of corruption by lobbyists.

Although sporadic and occasionally high-profile reform efforts were mounted thereafter, it was more than seventy years before a stronger lobbying law was passed. This came in 1977, during another (post-Watergate) reform era; the Regulation of Lobbying Act toughened registration and reporting requirements and created an independent bipartisan state commission on lobbying regulation. Though intended to be short-lived, the Temporary Commission on Regulation of Lobbying has endured and, indeed, seen its powers strengthened. A boost in the commission's authority occurred in 1999, when a new lobbying act empowered the six-member commission to mount investigations and audits, enforce penalties, recommend further legislative changes in lobbying regulation, and expand its presence as a clearinghouse for information on lobbying in Albany and major New York metropolitan areas.

Unlike its 1905 and 1977 predecessors, the 1999 Lobbying Act was the result of in-state pressures, rather than part of a national antigovernment corruption effort. A spate of negative stories about interest-group influence in municipal and local New York governments was one source of calls for change. As a result, the 1999 act requires lobbying groups to register when lobbying on local issues. In 2002, the year that provision went into effect, 255 lobbyists did so, and informal reports suggest that the number has grown steadily in the two years since. The act also reflected widespread public concern—fuelled by media reports—that legislators were unduly swayed by gifts; the response was a ban on all gifts over seventy-five dollars in value. The gift ban was subsequently criticized as vague and ambiguous: it is unclear, for example, whether the seventy-five-dollar ceiling refers to individual gifts or the maximum value of all gifts a lobbyist can make to a policymaker in a single year.

Despite this expansion of the lobbying law, the drumbeat of reform calls has continued virtually unabated. Some critics of New York lobbying deplore regulation that does not focus on the legitimacy or nature of group influence, but merely seeks to ensure transparency via disclosure. Such concerns owe partly to the steady rise in volume of lobbying activity, again as

FIGURE 5.1.
Lobbying expenditures, New York State (in constant dollars)
1978–2003 (in millions)

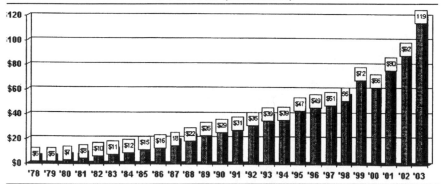

Source: New York State Temporary Commission on Lobbying, *2003 Annual Report.*

measured in lobbying expenditures (research, salaries, transportation, and the like). Figure 5.1 demonstrates this graphically: even adjusted for inflation, state lobbyist spending has increased tenfold over the past two decades.

But recent reform efforts go beyond concerns about the "demosclerotic" effects of too many lobbyists clogging the lifeblood of New York governance. Compared to other states, New York's disclosure laws are essentially the weakest lobbying regulations in the country. In one recent comparative ranking of state lobbying restrictions, New York ranked next to last—ahead of only New Hampshire, which features a very feeble state legislature and comparatively limited lobbying activity. Most other states require some combination of the following: strict restrictions on (or, in several states, prohibition of) lobbyist campaign contributions, tough rules governing lobbyist gifts to lawmakers, investigation and audit powers, punitive measures for lobbyists who fail to register or violate campaign-finance restrictions, and full disclosure of lobbying activities.[13] New York's lobbying laws are relatively weak on all these fronts. Most controversial at present are the first (campaign finance) and last (lobbying disclosure); an overview of each area follows.

Campaign Finance

To critics, New York's regulation of campaign financing is "quite lax."[14] Contribution limits are more generous than in most other states: counting both primary and general elections, individuals, PACs, labor unions, and corporations are permitted to donate up to $6,800 per assembly candidate, $13,900 to a senate candidate, and $50,100 to a candidate for governor. Overall limits also apply: corporations may give only $5,000 per year to all New York state candidates, while individuals and PACs can give up to $150,000.

Whatever one makes of the size of these dollar limits, loopholes exist in the New York campaign-contribution system. For example, the ostensibly tough $5,000 aggregate ceiling on corporate giving is skirted by the fact that most corporations make donations through their PACs. Moreover, contributions up to $84,400 each year can be made to state party committees, which are then permitted to redistribute funds to candidates for state office, with no limit.[15] Thus an enterprising donor could donate the maximum $13,900 to a senate Democratic candidate (for example), split between a $5,400 primary-election and $8,500 general-election donation. The donor could then contribute an additional $84,400 in 2003 to the New York Democratic Party, and the same amount in 2004, funds which the party could then pass on to the donor's desired senate candidate. Finally, so-called "soft money" is also still legal in New York, though banned in 2002 at the national level; political parties can receive unlimited contributions for activities designated as "party building," such as voter registration drives and televised ads, as long as they do not ask viewers to vote for a particular candidate.

Campaign finance is a thorny perennial in the American political landscape; the point here is not to address normatively the vexing issue of money in elections. Rather, compared to many other states, New York ranks toward the bottom in terms of restrictions on contributions. More than half the U.S. states either prohibit lobbyist contributions altogether or ban fundraising during a legislative session. And, as one study notes, over the past few years "the trend among the states [is] toward greater restrictions on gift giving and campaign contributions."[16]

Full Disclosure

As the 2003 legislative session concluded in midsummer, virtually every major media outlet in the state lamented Albany's failure to address what the *New York Times* called "the desperate need for lobbying reform."[17] (Similar laments were sounded during the 2004 session, which ended too late to be included in this draft.)[18] The heart of the *Times* editors' and many other critics' concern is a loophole in the existing law's reporting requirements. Those mandate that lobbyists must report all efforts to influence legislators, but only executive-branch lobbying related to rules, regulations, or rates is subject to registration requirements. Interest-group lobbying concerning state contracts, procurement, or other agency decisions, or lobbying of judges or state authorities are not covered by the disclosure laws.

State authorities, such as the Metropolitan Transportation Authority (MTA) or the Long Island Power Authority, are little understood public private hybrid organizations, established by the governor and in some cases wielding considerable power. Media and other public attention to lobbying of state authorities was inspired by a series of scandals, affecting such agencies as the Long Island Power Authority (which, among other questionable acts, paid its acting financial officer $582,000 for fourteen months' work, some four times the going salary) and the Empire State Development Corporation, formed to distribute federal funds to New York businesses in the wake of the September 11 terrorist attacks. Attracting most public attention were two notorious cases involving lobbying of state authorities, details of which follow.

• **The $500,000 Telephone Call.** During a May 2003 Assembly hearing, developer Tamir Sapir testified that he was able to secure a $230 million loan to continue construction on the MTA's new headquarters thanks to the timely intervention of U.S. senator-turned-lobbyist Alfonse D'Amato. "God bless Mr. D'Amato, because if not for him my business would be broke," Sapir told the Assembly Committee on Corporations, Authorities and Commissions. Under questioning from the committee's chair, assemblyman Richard Brodsky (D-Westchester), Sapir indicated that his firm had paid D'Amato's lobbying firm $500,000 for a phone call to the MTA chairman promoting Sapir's construction work. In late October 2003, an official inquiry into the matter was launched by the MTA's investigative arm, inspired in part by media reports that MTA officials had expressed "misgivings" before the loan was approved "about Sapir's ability to finish the job on time and on budget."[19]

• **The $30,000 Canal Caper.** Late in 2002, a notice appeared in the "Contract Reporter," a state-issued newsletter with very limited circulation, advertising the sale of shoreline development rights along a stretch of the Erie

Canal. Only a single developer responded, Richard Hutchens of Buffalo, and his bid of $30,000 was accepted—a price that the *New York Times* later described as "highway robbery." Public attention was initially aroused by a series of articles in the Syracuse *Post-Standard,* which noted that dozens of potential developers had expressed interest in canal-front property, but none had the option to bid on this forty-five-mile stretch. It also emerged that Hutchens was planning 10 luxury housing developments on the property, the first of which was valued at $95 million. State Comptroller Alan Hevesi eventually stepped in the following October and cancelled the contract. Concluded the *Times* editors, "[Governor] Pataki and the Legislature have to open the doors to this cozy little club to let the public know who's lobbying for contracts, what's being sold for peanuts, and how this secret government operates."[20]

These and similarly disturbing revelations about interest groups and state authorities were echoed in other venues, keeping lobbying reform in the headlines. The 2002 battle over New York's redistricting, especially intense after the state lost two U.S. congressional seats after the 2000 census, saw at least two members of Congress hire lobbyists to press the case in Albany for leaving their districts largely intact. And late in 2003, the Commission on Lobbying itself was embroiled in a controversy involving hip-hop artist and producer Russell Simmons, who sponsored a rally on June 4, 2003, condemning New York's Rockefeller drug laws. Members of the commission requested from Simmons extensive materials concerning the rally that was scheduled during legislative consideration of proposals to reform the drug laws. Eventually Simmons filed a First Amendment lawsuit against the commission, joined by the American Civil Liberties Union (ACLU) because, as ACLU officials explained, "The [commission's] approach may lead to groups having to account to the government . . . about all kinds of activities that never before have been considered lobbying—like marches and demonstrations."[21]

Both chambers of the state legislature passed bills during the 2003 session to further strengthen New York's lobby laws, but for procedural reasons no changes were enacted. Although, to reiterate a point made earlier, lobbyists spend most of their time on relatively dull matters of information seeking and policy analysis, the well-publicized examples of illegal or questionable interest-group behavior will continue to dominate public discussion until reform is achieved. With the most lenient regulations in the nation, New York would seem to have plenty of room for improvement.

WHAT GOOD ARE LOBBYISTS IN GOVERNING NEW YORK?

Given the preceding discussion of lobbying reform, one might well conclude (as many political observers do) that New York is in thrall to special interests in a way that endangers responsible governance. It is also arguable, however, that lobbyists provide genuine benefits to state politics and policymaking, and even help enhance democratic features of New York's political system. A review of four principal contributions made by interest groups follows.

1. *Representation.* While many lament the continuing increase in lobbyists' presence in Albany, this "advocacy explosion" may also be seen as potentially furthering the democratization of New York politics. A greater range of interest groups seeking influence can translate into better representation of the wide variety of interests in the state. From the Uniformed Firefighters Association and the Neighborhood Retail Alliance (representing bodegas, greengrocers, and independent supermarkets) to the Coalition for the Homeless and the New York Nannies' Association, every imaginable group, concern, or collection of like-minded individuals occasionally seeks to influence New York's government, and many seek professional lobbying help in their efforts. (The Uniformed Firefighters Association, for example, in 2003 retained New York City's largest lobbying firm, Davidoff & Malito, for assistance with contract talks and other issues.)

Not all interests are equally represented, of course. Resources, organization, and political context all greatly affect a group's ability to turn policymakers' attention into concrete legislative or agency results. But the expansion of lobbying groups and access to legislators over time at least suggests the possibility of gaining a hearing with a public official, the first step to more meaningful political representation.

2. *Information transmission.* Also arguably advancing democratic politics in New York is improved communication between the state's governing officials and citizens, communication that is frequently enhanced (or even originated) by interest-group representatives. An ongoing revolution in communications technology has expanded the strategies and tactics available to interest groups attempting to make members' views known to officials, and vice versa. The result, as any Albany policymaker or state official will attest, is a vast increase in the policy information available to them. Thus, at least in principle, assembly members and state senators hear more informed points of view before making public decisions. And lobbyists are often those supplying the information, as noted above.

Sometimes this information provision can represent an abuse of the process, as interest groups skew studies to reflect their own points of view. This is rarer than might be imagined, however—most lawmakers and staffers draw on a range of groups for background information on any given policy issue. Ultimately, if lawmakers do indeed seek a range of inputs on a policy issue or agency decision, the variety of information and possible new perspectives represented by interest-group analyses can enhance the quality of New York's lawmaking, as well as the deliberative process. Is this a utopian folly? Not necessarily, as a variety of recent examples suggests. To take one, New York City in 2002 sought enhanced enforcement powers for the city's Department of Consumer Affairs (DCA), requiring state legislation. When the enforcement bill stalled in Albany, Consumer Affairs commissioner Gretchen Dykstra, who had consulted a host of consumer-rights lobbyists as well as representatives of small business, met privately with the lead lobbyist for retailers, Richard Lipsky. As one press account noted, "Small businesses, including food stores and used-car dealers, fear [the bill] would give DCA too much power." After Dykstra met with Lipsky and members of his Neighborhood Retail Alliance, an accommodation was struck and the legislation passed.[22]

3. *Mobilization.* Interest groups engage in a variety of efforts to mobilize public awareness of policy issues. These range from issue advocacy (television and other media advertisements on a policy topic) to old-fashioned door-to-door voter-registration drives. Such mobilization activity was once the province of political parties, but interest groups have largely filled the void since the 1970s. Mobilization efforts, as party leaders were long aware, are essential to boosting voter turnout and citizen involvement in the political process—goals of any representative democratic polity.

4. *System stability.* As lobbyists monitor practically every action taken by state and city officials, usually with competing groups actively promoting their view on most sides of all issues, one result may be to promote deliberate, even slow state policymaking. Bold policy changes become rarer, given a legislative process that features countless checks and balances and hundreds of lobbyists seeking to manipulate these to block or alter bills not to their liking. New York's policy outcomes thus are typically incremental in nature. To be sure, a slowed legislative process may strike many readers as counterproductive, rather than beneficial. But one by-product can be government stability. A system that changes relatively little, or over long periods of time, enables reasonably reliable predictions about regulatory costs

and the like. In something of a paradox, one of the chief results of the vast amount of interest-group lobbying activity in New York may be greater stability in the state's policymaking.

Given this roster of potential benefits, how to maximize these while minimizing the costs of interest-group activity? Government itself plays an especially vital role, even in an age of popular suspicion of government. Jeffrey Berry makes four points in this regard, here adapted to the New York example.[23] First, New York's governor and legislature must ensure that interest-group spending does not overly influence the political process. Second, the political process must be made as open and transparent as possible—exclusionary or favoritist policies, although sometimes the coin of the realm in Albany, should be avoided. Third, it could be useful to strengthen New York's political parties. Parties are able to aggregate citizen preferences in broad ways, helping to ensure that a particular group or coalition of interests doesn't dominate policymaking to an unfair extent. And finally, government officials must seek to ensure that disadvantaged sectors of New York's polity, many of which are inadequately represented by interest-group lobbyists, receive a fair hearing. This helps maximize representation, as discussed above.

In sum, interest-group lobbying has become an integral part of governing New York State. Though that fact is routinely deplored by political candidates, media watchdogs, and ordinary citizens, lobbyists are increasingly less often—indeed, usually are not—sources of obstruction, policy obfuscation, and even graft. Instead their contributions and public standing has begun to resemble that of more traditional professions like engineering or medicine.[24] Whether this translates into improved democratic governance in New York, perhaps along the dimensions explored above, is still an open question.

NOTES

1. Jeffrey M. Berry, *The Interest Group Society,* 3rd ed. (New York: Longman, 1997).

2. Figures from www.opensecrets.org; www.politicalmoneyline.org (both last accessed August 12, 2004); Stewart C. Wagner, *New York Temporary State Commission on Lobbying: 2003 Annual Report* (New York: Temporary State Commission, 2003) (New York State figures); Wendy Blake,

"Lobbying Spending Sets Record," *Crain's New York Business*, August 26, 2003 (New York City figures).

3. Marie Hojnacki and David C. Kimball, "PAC Contributions and Lobbying Contacts in Congressional Committees," *Political Research Quarterly* 54 (2001), p. 177.

4. Jeffrey Milyo, David Primo, and Timothy Groseclose, "Corporate PAC Campaign Contributions in Perspective," *Business and Politics* 2 (2000), p. 83. Thomas Mann summarizes a "broad consensus that campaign spending affects (but does not determine) election outcomes," though "scholars continue to wrestle with and disagree over the specifics of that relationship." Thomas E. Mann, "Linking Knowledge and Action: Political Science and Campaign Finance Reform," *Perspectives on Politics* 1, no. 1 (2003): 75.

5. Larry Makinson, *The Big Picture: The Money Behind the 2000 Elections* (Washington, D.C.: Center for Responsive Politics, 2001), p. 3, 2004 figures are from the Federal Election Commission (author's compilation).

6. Jack Snyder, 1992. "Long-Term Investing in Politicians, or Give Early, Give Often." *Journal of Law and Economics* 35:1.

7. Alana S. Jeydel, Blair Horner, and Russ Haven, "Lax Lobbying Laws? An Analysis of the Fifty States," *Comparative State Politics* 20, no. 2 (1999): 43; Alan Rosenthal, *The Third House: Lobbyists and Lobbying in the States,* 2nd ed. (Washington, D.C.: CQ Press, 2001), p. 88. See also Edward Schneier and John Brian Murtaugh, *New York Politics: A Tale of Two States* (Armonk, NY: M. E. Sharpe, 2001).

8. Among hundreds of illustrative examples, consider New York's role as inspiring creation of the National Endowment for the Arts in 1965. See Robert H. Salisbury and Lauretta Conklin, "Instrumental Versus Expressive Group Politics: The National Endowment for the Arts," in *Interest Group Politics*, ed. Allan J. Cigler and Burdett A. Loomis (5th ed., Washington, D.C.: CQ Press., 1998), pp. 288–90.

9. Clive S. Thomas and Ronald J. Hrebenar, "Interest Group Power in the Fifty States: Trends Since the Late 1970s," *Comparative State Politics* 20, no. 4 (1999): 12–13.

10. David Louis Cingranelli, "The Influence of Interest Groups," in *Governing New York State,* ed. Jeffrey M. Stonecash (Albany: State University of New York Press, 2001), p. 81.

11. Anthony J. Nownes and Patricia Freeman, "Interest Group Activity in the States," *Journal of Politics* 60, no. 1 (1998): 109. The following description is drawn largely from my ongoing observations of lobbyists at the

federal level; an overview of this project is in Rogan Kersh, "Corporate Lob-byists as Political Actors: A View from the Field," in Cigler and Loomis, *Interest Group Politics.*

12. "New York's Secret Lobbying," *New York Times,* January 14, 2003 (unsigned op-ed).

13. Jeydel, Horner, and Haven, "Lax Lobbying Laws?," pp. 40–43.

14. Ibid., p. 39.

15. New York State Board of Elections, 2003–04 Contribution Limits.

16. Jeydel, Horner, and Haven, "Lax Lobbying Laws?," p. 43.

17. "A Broken Legislature," *New York Times,* June 25, 2003 (unsigned op-ed).

18. See, e.g., Michael Trupo, "Session Ends with Finger Pointing, No Budget," *New York Legislative Gazette,* June 28, 2004.

19. See Joshua Robin, "D'Amato $500,000 MTA Call Probed," *Newsday,* October 30, 2003; Michael Gormley, "Inquiry Targets D'Amato Call to Head of MTA," *Albany Times-Union,* October 31, 2003.

20. "The $30,000 Canal Caper," *New York Times,* October 13, 2003 (unsigned editorial); Erika Rosenberg, "State's Hevesi Bans Canal Contract," *Rochester Democrat & Chronicle,* October 21, 2003.

21. Christopher Dunn and Donna Lieberman, "Lobby Laws Should-n't Intimidate," *New York Daily News,* November 14, 2003.

22. Philip Lentz, "Progress on Consumer Affairs Enforcement," *Crain's New York Business,* July 12, 2002.

23. Berry, *The Interest Group Society,* pp. 238–40.

24. On the ongoing "professionalization" of lobbying, see Rogan Kersh and Mark Schlesinger, "Interest-Group Lobbyists as Professionals," paper presented at the Midwest Political Science Association annual meetings, April 2004.

CHAPTER 6

Reporters and Politicians in Albany

Access, Reciprocity, and News Management

ELIZABETH BENJAMIN

EDITOR'S INTRODUCTION

News about state politics comes to most citizens from the media. Newspapers are perhaps the most important sources of state news. Television tends to cover national or local news, leaving to print journalists the task of providing the bulk of state coverage. The important questions are: How much do newspapers cover state politics? What aspects of politics do they decide to cover? How are political issues presented?

Two conclusions emerge from research on the print media. First, state politics generally does not receive as much coverage as national and local concerns. Second, there are ongoing tensions between journalists and politicians about what to cover and how to cover issues. Politicians continually complain that they do not get the right kind of coverage and that issues do not get enough attention, while journalists are always wary of being used to provide free publicity for a politician's views or career aspirations.

Although there are numerous commentaries on the performance of the press, the perspectives of the journalists themselves get little attention. In this chapter, Elizabeth Benjamin, a political reporter for the *Albany Times Union*, provides an up close and personal perspective on the job of covering state politics. Her chapter highlights a number of important points, including different gubernatorial strategies designed to manage the news; the importance of a reporter's terminology in framing stories; and the daily grind and competitive energies involved in covering state politics. Concerning the tensions between journalists and politicians, Benjamin concludes that "when things get too manipulative and negative, the result is a vicious cycle and then everyone loses."

ᕦᕤ

J ay Gallagher came to Albany in August 1984 to head Gannett News Service's capitol bureau. The story of the moment was Governor Mario Cuomo's impending keynote address at the National Democratic Convention in San Francisco. Gallagher called the governor's press secretary, Tim Russert, and asked if Cuomo would be willing to offer a preview of his speech. Within a few days, arrangements had been made, and Gallagher had a front-page story for Gannett's member newspapers.

Fast forward almost two decades to the fall of 2003—eight years after a little-known but ambitious Republican state senator, George Pataki, surprised political observers by ousting Cuomo, by then a Democratic icon who had once been considered a possible presidential candidate. Gallagher was now on leave from his bureau chief post to do a yearlong special project on New York's economy that he planned eventually to publish as a book. He called Pataki's press office and asked for an interview with the governor.

Although he had covered Pataki's rise to the state assembly, his controversial win in a primary against his former mentor, the sitting Republican senator Mary Goodhue, and the triumphal 1994 gubernatorial campaign, Gallagher—a fixture in the state capitol press corps—had never been granted a personal audience with Pataki after he became governor. In general, since taking office in January 1995 the Pataki administration had steadily diminished reporters' access to the governor, and provided virtually no one-on-ones. But in this instance, Gallagher was hopeful his request would be granted. He was working on a book on the economy, one of Pataki's signature issues. The governor frequently spoke of how the state's business climate had improved dramatically as a result of the tax cuts he had approved during his time in office.

For two weeks, Gallagher said, his call to Pataki's press office went unanswered. Repeated follow-up calls also received no response. Gallagher became resigned to the fact that he wouldn't be sitting down with the governor—over the years his bureau had simply stopped asking for interviews with Pataki, since they were never approved. But the editors and publishers at the Gannett newspapers in New York were furious. They proposed writing a joint letter to the governor's office, demanding that Pataki see Gallagher.

As a courtesy, Gallagher said, he called Pataki's Communications Director, Lisa Dewald Stoll, and informed her of what the Gannett officials planned. Stoll urged him to tell them not to go forward, and assured him something would be worked out. Not long afterward, Gallagher got a forty-five-minute interview with Pataki on the second floor of the state capitol. Also present were Pataki's chief of staff, John Cahill, his budget director, Carole Stone, his top health and education aides, and several members of his press office.

Ironically, after all the effort that went into trying to avoid the interview, Pataki "did fine," Gallagher said. "He's a smart guy, and he laid out a very good defense of what he was doing. I thought it was a very productive interview, and it added a lot to my story."[1]

Jay Gallagher's experience is indicative of the Pataki administration's overall strategy for dealing with the press. The governor has truly treated information as power. In addition to control of access to himself and his agency heads, Pataki has in general sought to release information about state government on his own terms and in his own time, information that in previous administrations was once readily available.

While press access to the governor has decreased since Pataki took office, access to the two top legislative leaders—state senate majority leader Joseph Bruno (R-Brunswick) and state assembly speaker Sheldon Silver (D-Manhattan)—has improved in recent years, veteran capitol reporters said. Both men hold regular press conferences in the capitol and are easily reachable by phone through their press offices.

The other 210 rank-and-file legislative members are also very accessible. Indeed, they are anxious for coverage, but few are privy to many inside details of high-level negotiations on key issues between their leaders and the governor. In fact, it's not uncommon for legislators to call reporters or stop them in the halls of the capitol in an effort to find out what's going on.

Lobbyists are another potential source. Some represent the state's major interests on a range of issues. Others are more narrowly focused. On occasion, lobbyists are on the inside and privy to negotiations going on behind closed doors. Of course, as with almost everyone at the capitol, they have an agenda and are often trying to get reporters to write about their clients or their issues in an effort to ratchet up public pressure on elected officials to act in their favor.

Similarly, capitol reporters are routinely inundated with requests for coverage from nonprofit groups, good-government activists, and others. There are far more potential stories than there is time to write them or space in which to publish them. Thus simply by deciding which stories to cover, reporters help set the agenda at the capitol. Such is the power of the press.

Reporters also have the ability to influence opinions through the words and phrasing they choose to employ in their stories. To say someone was "not available for comment" sends a very different message than "refused to return calls for comment." Typically, a reporter may employ the latter when it is felt that an official is stonewalling—not calling back because the official doesn't want to be in a story.

The way an official responds to a story can dictate how—and where—it is played in the paper. In 2004 I wrote about U.S. representative John Sweeney (R-Clifton Park), whose biggest campaign expense was for a well-known former capital region strip club owner who had tangled with local officials numerous times over his businesses. The man, Harwood McCart, was listed on Sweeney's Federal Election Commission filings as a "transportation and security consultant." He was also on the congressman's federal payroll as a "staff assistant." Sweeney refused repeated requests for an interview to explain why he needed McCart's services, which were unusual, according to other congressional staffers in Washington. Largely because of Sweeney's refusal to sit down and talk, the story had many unanswered questions and rose to a higher level of importance than it might have otherwise. Under the glare of front-page publicity in the *Times Union*, McCart resigned from Sweeney's payroll.

THE GOVERNOR, THE PRESS CORPS, AND NEWS MANAGEMENT

There is an intricate and ongoing dance between state officials and the reporters who cover them. Politicians and their aides need us to get information out to the public and build support for their programs or campaigns. We need them for stories to meet our deadlines, satisfy our editors and, of course, serve our readers. Both sides understand this mutual dependence.

Like any relationship, the connection between politicians and reporters goes through some periods of relative calm and others of great upheaval. Sometimes the press gets frozen out. Other times, reporters are courted.

Whether from the executive chamber, the legislature, or a lobbyist's office, when someone calls a political or statehouse reporter with a tip, that reporter is always trying to calculate the angles. What does this person want to achieve? What is their agenda? Is this story important enough to write, even though it might benefit the tipster? Sometimes reporters get played. They get used. That's part of the game that is political reporting. The more time reporters spend on the beat, the better they get at sniffing out stories and the motivations of sources, and get used less.

There are roughly forty-four active members in the Legislative Correspondents Association (LCA)—the reporters who cover state government full time in Albany. Most work for the state's biggest daily newspapers and news wire services, but weekly papers, television and radio stations, and websites are also represented.

The majority of the LCA reporters are jammed together in close proximity to each other in an office on the third floor of the capitol—a factor that just serves to enhance competition to break good stories. But there is also great camaraderie, most evident in the annual LCA dinner. Here again the reciprocal relationship between the news gatherers and the newsmakers is evidenced as reporters satirize the state's top leaders—and then weather the not-too-gentle responses delivered by representatives from both the Republican and Democratic Parties.

The first sure sign that members of the LCA were in for a big change when George Pataki took office was his decision to lock down the capitol's second floor, where he and his executive-chamber staff are housed. Where reporters once entered freely to chat with Governor Cuomo's top aides, they were now prevented entry by an armed state police trooper.

Throughout his years in office, Governor Pataki has spent very little time in Albany. He kept his family and main residence in Garrison, in Putnam County. Moreover, when he is in Albany, the governor holds very few press conferences. He prefers instead to travel the state and grant interviews to local reporters who don't follow the day-to-day news in Albany and are therefore less likely to ask tough questions about the nuances of his proposals or policy decisions.

At the rare capitol press conferences he does hold, Pataki is unlikely to answer questions directly. Instead, he often responds by touting his record.

Another technique is to promise to "take a look" at whatever controversial subject on which reporters are seeking his opinion on any given day, thereby dodging a potentially problematic response.

The Pataki administration seems bent on controlling the press through disenfranchisement. The less you say, some politicians seem to believe, the less they'll be able to say about what you said. They have even sought to control access to the historic record. The governor ceased publication of his public papers, a practice that had been in place for more than a century before he came to office.

In a story than ran on September 28, 2003, in the *Times Union*, Michael Gormley of the Associated Press captured a quintessential example of Pataki's avoidance strategy at a news conference the governor had held in Albany two months earlier: "Pataki was asked if he would return campaign contributions from principals in the New York Racing Association, whose management was under investigation for ignoring employees' illegal activities. The governor's answer: 'I'm very proud of the role that the state Racing and Wagering Board is playing with the attorney general to make sure that NYRA along with all the different—whether public or private—entities meet the highest possible standards. And I have instructed the Racing and Wagering Board to make sure they continue to work with the attorney general. I'm confident they will, and I'm confident that racing in New York, which is tremendous, is just going to get better.' He never mentioned NYRA's campaign contributions."[2]

One weapon reporters have when access is being managed is to make the lack of access itself a story. At the height of Pataki's bid for a third term in 2002, James C. McKinley Jr. of the *New York Times* noted, "Mr. Pataki's stealthy style goes beyond an election year strategy, and beyond handling the press. Throughout his two terms, he has limited his public exposure to planned events, usually away from Albany. Aside from his annual message to the State Legislature, his policy speeches are rare."[3]

Pataki's reticence has led veteran capitol reporters to wax nostalgic about the Cuomo era. In those days it wasn't unusual for the governor to wake up members of the media with early-morning phone calls during which he hotly debated their stories of the day.

"More than once he called me," recalled Dave Hepp, co-producer of the public television show *Inside Albany* who has covered New York state government for close to three decades. "One time, I went to cover a real free-for-all of a forum when (Cuomo) was embroiled in trying to shut down the

Shoreham (L.I.) Nuclear Plant. He met with people and let them vent. The next morning, I got a call at 7:30. It was Cuomo, spinning the event and what our coverage might be. He called before it even aired."[4]

Reporters who complain to Pataki's press office about his lack of response to questions are typically told that the problem is not the governor, but their expectations of how he should act. Or, as Pataki's Dewald Stoll told Gormley, "The governor is always thoughtful and clear in his responses to questions from the press. Just because there may be times that the press doesn't like the answer, it doesn't mean he didn't give one."[5]

Some good government activists and reporters note that the situation has worsened since the September 11, 2001, attacks on Manhattan, which provided the administration with ample cover for refusing to discuss certain topics or release information in the name of maintaining the public's security. That strategy is not unusual. The Bush administration, too, has been criticized by reporters for reducing access to the president and curtailing the flow of information from the White House. Like Pataki, Republican president Bush rarely holds press conferences, preferring instead to appear at highly orchestrated events that translate best on television.

AIDES AND RELATIONSHIPS

Reporters deal far more with aides than they do with political principals. Zenia Mucha, the governor's first communications director, is credited with crafting Pataki's "say nothing" media strategy and setting a combative tone with reporters. Mucha, former press secretary to U.S. senator Alfonse D'Amato (R-NY), came into Pataki's employ during his 1994 campaign. (D'Amato, assisted by former New York State GOP chairman Bill Powers, had largely engineered Pataki's gubernatorial nomination and rise to power).

In his September 28 story, Gormley recounts a meeting held by Mucha with the state's public information officers soon after Pataki took office in the ornate Blue Room of the capitol, once the chambers of the court of appeals, the state's highest court. According to a former Pataki-administration employee who spoke to Gormley on the condition of anonymity, Mucha ordered new rules for handling public information—namely that everything would be approved by the governor's second-floor press office before being related to reporters or the public: "'It was made clear. You were very much working for downtown,' said the former public information officer, referring to Pataki's Capitol Chambers. 'Everything that was released after that was much more tightly controlled.' Implied at the meeting, the source said, was this message: The press is the enemy out to get Pataki, so act accordingly. Mucha later said the meeting was designed to get the public information officers to understand the central messages of the new governor and to speak with a united voice on public policy."[6]

It was not unusual for a reporter to receive an angry and confrontational phone call from Mucha or one of her staff if they were displeased by a story—either already published or in the works. Mucha left the Pataki administration in February 2001 to take a top job with the ABC television network. But her number two, Michael McKeon, enthusiastically took up her mantle. McKeon adopted Mucha's aggressive style, frequently berating reporters when he didn't approve of their stories or, in the perceptions of some reporters, seeking to bully them out of printing articles he deemed inappropriate or unseemly.

The tone in Pataki's press office softened somewhat with the arrival in early 2003 of Dewald Stoll, who is married to the governor's 2002 campaign manager and political adviser, Adam Stoll. Dewald Stoll, who was Pataki's deputy campaign manager in 2002 and D'Amato's deputy campaign manager in 1998, is not a screamer and has elevated press officers who are less aggressive in their style. But the feeling that the press corps and the press officers are on opposite sides of a never-ending battle remains.

Reporters often know the people they cover quite well after spending several years watching them and chronicling their every word. With the 99 percent reelection rate in the state legislature, capitol reporters are virtually guaranteed to run into the same elected officials and political operatives again and again. Things can get nasty. If a reporter writes a story an official doesn't like, the reporter might be "punished" by being cut off for a period of time. That means phone calls are not returned, tips are not shared, and important stories are leaked to the competition. This can last for weeks, or even years.

Often, sources play on the fact that reporters know them personally. They might lobby to keep a story out of the paper or at least to have it altered significantly. But unflattering and embarrassing stories do get printed. And then reporters continue to work the beat. Congressman Sweeney's spokesman, Demetrios Karoutsos, called me repeatedly in an effort to get the Harwood McCart story killed. He called my boss as well. Friends of the congressman also called me in an effort to talk me out of running the story. Sweeney never called me personally, but it isn't unusual for the subject of a contentious story to call and ask for it not to run.

The best a reporter can do is to be fair and give equal time to as many sides as a story might have. Pure objectivity is impossible. Simply by selecting which stories we cover and what words we use, we are bringing our opinions into our work.

COMPETITION AND CAMARADERIE

Statehouse reporters spend a lot of time together. This is particularly true during campaign season, when they are on the road for days at a time. A tense closeness develops among them: they are good friends, but they are also competing against each other for stories. Typically, the relationships between New York City reporters (particularly those who work for the *New York Post* and the *Daily News*, which compete head-to-head) are more fraught with tension than those between downstate and upstate reporters, whose agendas are very different.

Within the competitive environment, there are certain realities that cannot be changed. The bigger papers take precedence in the minds of elected officials—with the exception of local papers that are courted by the legislators whose constituents are readers. In particular, the *New York Times* is routinely leaked stories by members of the governor's staff on down, and *Times* reporters are often given access not offered to other reporters. We grouse about it, but there is nothing that can be done. The *Times*, with its large circulation and considerable reputation, simply reaches more readers and influences more important people than do the other publications.

TV reporters have become more important as the number of people who get their news from television has increased over the years. At press conferences or campaign events, press officers are often most concerned with setting up shots and meeting the needs of TV reporters, knowing they can follow up with print reporters later.

One example of the rising power of the TV reporter can be drawn from Governor Pataki's trip to Iraq in the winter of 2004. The governor could bring one reporter. He chose Dave Evans of Channel 7, the ABC news affiliate in New York City. Reporters don't like politicians playing favorites—this makes it look like they have less access than their peers and also allows someone else to get exclusive stories. Members of the capitol press corps were angry not only because the trip was kept secret until Pataki was safely on the ground, but also because Evans worked for a channel affiliated with the company where former Pataki staffer Zenia Mucha held considerable sway. It is well known that Mucha's advice is still regularly sought by the governor and his aides. But the Pataki administration has repeatedly insisted that the Mucha connection had nothing to do with Evans's inclusion in the trip.

THE DAILY GRIND

Most of the time, covering the capitol is not glamorous. Negotiations on the budget and nonbudget bills alike take place between legislative and administrative staffers behind closed doors. The governor and the legislative leaders get together in the governor's offices on the capitol's second floor to hash out their budget deals—the infamous "three men in a room" meetings. While they meet, reporters sit on the stairs outside the governor's third-floor offices, waiting for the three men to come out and provide a briefing. Specifics are rarely available, and nothing is ever provided on paper. That is for aides and staffers to hash out later.

Though state lawmakers may not be allowed inside the room where the three men negotiate, hip-hop mogul Russell Simmons spent close to seven hours closeted with the governor and legislative leaders trying to reach an agreement on Rockefeller Drug Law reform in the final days of the 2003 legislative session. State assemblyman Jeffrion Aubry (D-Queens), who authored the bill that Simmons, Pataki, Bruno, and Silver were wrangling over, was stuck waiting on the stairs with the press corps to learn whether a deal had been reached. Although things looked promising when the meeting broke after one o'clock that morning, the agreement fell apart shortly thereafter.

The stone stairs on which reporters sit—sometimes for hours—are not comfortable. And the scrum of reporters pushing against the glass doors leading into Pataki's inner sanctum in an effort to get close to him or one of the two legislative leaders during their postmeeting press conferences can get downright dangerous. At the height of budget negotiations in 2003, a reporter deep in the "gaggle" almost fainted, leading her colleagues to mount a campaign for the Pataki administration to allow members of the media to wait in one of the spacious rooms on the second floor while the three men negotiated. This request was never met, although folding chairs appeared outside the governor's office when budget negotiations began in earnest in 2004.

WHAT YOU LEARN IN SCHOOL
VERSUS WHAT YOU REALLY DO

Young reporters coming out of journalism programs are not adequately pre-pared to handle the realities of state politics. I am an alumna of Columbia's Graduate School of Journalism. The primary text for our basic reporting class was Melvin Mencher's *News Reporting and Writing*. Mencher had the following to say about dealing with politicians and candidates for public office: "The political reporter has a sense of what the public considers impor-tant, and this becomes the substance of questions directed to the candidates. Their answers can provide voters with more information than can the source-originated handbook, speech or television commercial."[7]

Nowhere does Mencher offer any advice on what a reporter should do when a candidate—or elected official—refuses to answer a question, even when it is repeated over and over. I wonder what Mencher would have said about the following exchange between a reporter and Pataki about the state's warehousing of mentally ill patients in nursing homes and their mistreat-ment there. The questioning came during the governor's 2002 campaign for a third term, and was detailed in the *The New York Times*.

"At the announcement of the United Federation of Teachers' endorsement of Pataki, a reporter tried to follow up after the gov-ernor had ignored her question on who made the decision to place mentally ill patients in nursing homes and whether he had been lobbied by a campaign contributor to do so. "We are looking for ways where the mentally ill who need structured residences can have those structured residences, and we're going to continue to look to see how we can accomplish that," the governor said. The reporter pressed, "But how was that decision made to release them to nursing homes?" "That was made by the health professionals," the governor said. Mr. McKeon, the spokesman, jumped in. "O.K. Thank you." "Thank you," the governor said, waving and turning to leave. "Did you know about it yourself?" the reporter asked. "Thank you," Mr. Pataki said. "Did you know about it yourself?" the reporter asked again. "When did you learn about them?" another reporter asked. "It was made by the health profes-sionals," the governor said. "When did you learn though?" the second reporter asked again. "Do you still have confidence in those health professionals?" a third reporter asked. At the doorway, the governor turned, hesitated, nodded and left the room."[8]

The philosopher Bertrand Russell once said, "Our great democracies still tend to think that a stupid man is more likely to be honest than a clever man, and our politicians take advantage of this prejudice by pretending to be even more stupid than nature made them."[9]

Mencher counsels fledgling journalists to ward against cynicism, saying it "disables the reporter in the task of helping the public to articulate its demands of its officials. The cynic believes that the process is futile or the actors in it are hopelessly corrupt or so inefficient nothing can work."[10] By the same token, Mencher also warns against acting as a "stenographer to officialdom," saying that it is "equally useless since by failing to use his or her knowledge and experience, essential issues may not become part of the agenda for public debate."[11]

But it is difficult not to be cynical when Pataki and other state-level officials have effectively relegated reporters to providing readers and viewers not real answers to questions about important issues, but simple sound bites. It is equally difficult to call an administration spokesperson in order to provide balance in a story when one can be reasonably certain the answer will be formulaic and most likely closely resemble any number of responses that are interchangeably employed no matter what the question may be.

In fact, the problem has generalized to become more the rule than the exception throughout state government. "The trend has been for political people, politicians, to go over the press's heads with a set message," Dave Hepp told me. "It used to be that it would just happen during the campaign. But now it happens regularly. I think our expectations have lowered dramatically. You call the press office, and the response of the day is read from a script. You can even predict what they're going to say. You should ask the questions anyway, but, speaking for myself, you pretty much know what you're going to get."[12]

The lack of real substantive information coming out of state government acts as a kind of Catch-22—the less information there is, the less editors are interested in running stories about state government and the fewer resources they are willing to dedicate to it. As a result, readers end up knowing less and less about what their elected officials are up to.

When things get too manipulated and negative, the result is a vicious cycle. And then everyone loses: Politicians are even more negatively portrayed. Members of the media reinforce the stereotype of the vulturelike reporter, interested only in "gotcha" stories and scandals. Voters can't make informed decisions when there is no real information available. The public, already disconnected, becomes even more skeptical about government. We need leaders who give real answers. If politicians refuse to provide these, we reporters start trying to dig them up ourselves. Nothing is more dangerous to a politician than a reporter with time on his or her hands. Politicians tend to think less is more when it comes to information provided to the media. But by opening the floodgates, they might be pleasantly surprised to find the number of in-depth, meaningful stories increasing while shallow quick hits diminish.

NOTES

1. Telephone interview with Gannett News Service reporter Jay Gallagher, January 30, 2004.

2. Michael Gormley, Associated Press, "Open Meeting Backers See Politics in SUNY Secrecy," *Albany Times Union*, September 28, 2003. Capital Region Section, p. D7.

3. James C. McKinley Jr., "By Saying Very Little, Pataki Sticks to Script," the *New York Times*, Section A, p. 1, October 17, 2002.

4. Telephone interview, November 13, 2003.

5. Gormley, "Open Meeting Backers."

6. Ibid.

7. Melvin Mencher, *News Reporting and Writing*, 7th Edition (Madison, WI: Brown & Benchmark Publishers, 1997), 550.

8. McKinley, "By Saying Very Little."

9. Bertrand Russell, *New Hopes for a Changing World* (London: G. Allen & Unwin, 1951), p. 164.

10. Mencher, *News Reporting and Writing*, p. 551.

11. Ibid, p. 552.

12. Telephone interview, November 13, 2003.

PART II

Political Institutions and Decision Making

Introduction to Part II

State Government Institutions

GERALD BENJAMIN

New York State's government, like that of the nation and other states, is one of separate institutions sharing governmental powers. The system provides for executive, legislative, and judicial institutions that are distinct and politically independent of each other, while using each, in some measure, to check the power of the others in their primary spheres of action.

This approach contrasts with the distribution of power in parliamentary democracies and most American local governments. There the executive is chosen by or from a directly elected legislature, and is responsible to it. There is no legal or national constitutional barrier to the adoption of parliamentary institutions in an America state, but no state has ever adopted a parliamentary system. The persistent adherence of state governments to the separation-of-powers model over several centuries is a powerful testimonial to the centrality in the American political culture of the idea, expressed by James Madison in *Federalist* #51, that "to control the abuses of government . . . ambition must be made to counteract ambition. The interest of the man must be connected with the constitutional rights of the place."[1]

Separate Institutions. The legislative power in New York is located in the senate and assembly (Article III of the state constitution), and the executive power in the governor (Article IV). The state constitution, though it deals in great detail with the court system, nowhere specifically vests the judicial power in it. A change in language accomplishing this was offered in the draft constitution of 1967 (rejected in toto at the polls). Separation is further achieved, and the powers of the branches of government defined, by the assignment to each of specific functions.

Separation of the branches is assured by the constitutional prohibition against a sitting state legislator accepting a civil appointment to a state or city office created during his or her term or for which the emoluments were increased as he or she served, and by the requirement, with narrow exceptions, that a legislator resign his or her seat upon acceptance of an elected or appointed post in national, state, or city government (Article III, Section 7). The provision in New York's constitutionally defined budget process that the governor transmit the legislative and judicial budgets along with the executive budget "without revisions" is additional acknowledgment of the separate status of the three major branches of state government (Article VII, Section 1). Judges too are constitutionally barred from other public office, and from political party office, while serving on the bench (Article VI, Section 20. 1b and 3).

The constitutional distinctions between the executive and legislative branches are consequential. In 1987, for example, the court of appeals found that sweeping state health department regulations barring smoking in public places went beyond the powers delegated in law to the department. They were judged unconstitutional as the exercise of legislative power by the executive branch on separation-of-powers grounds.

Sharing Powers. Separation, however, in not absolute. The clearest example is the power of the executive to veto legislation. The senate, for its part, must confirm most important gubernatorial appointments. The assembly has the power of impeachment, with trial before a court that includes members of the senate. The court of appeals is the final arbiter of the constitutionality of state legislation. These are all, of course, purposefully crafted and familiar techniques to limit government that are, as noted, endemic to American systems.

A number of other New York constitutional provisions do not conform to the separation-of-powers principle. The gap between the executive and legislative branches is partially bridged by the lieutenant governor, who is elected with the governor but presides over the state senate and has a casting vote (Article IV, Section 6). The governor submits appropriation bills to the legislature as part of the budget process; on all other matters the submission of the legislation is a prerogative of elected members (Article VII, Section 3). As noted below, the legislature appoints the head of the education department, the Board of Regents, though appointing department heads is generally regarded as an executive function (Article V, Section 4). The majority leader of the senate and the speaker of the assembly, though legislative branch leaders, are in the line of executive succession, if both the governorship and lieutenant governorship simultaneously become vacant (Article IV, Section 6).

The Electorate: Additional Checks on Government. As a further check on the governor and legislature, the electorate in New York selects the comptroller and attorney general by direct statewide election. This method of filling these offices, instituted in 1846, is designed to assure independence for each official in the execution of their duties.

Additionally, the electors of the state, voting within cities, towns, counties, and judicial districts, select most judges. This remains a highly debated process, and has been the source of frequent proposals for constitutional change. Until 1977 judges on New York's highest court, the court of appeals, were also elected. In that year a constitutional amendment was adopted that provided that court of appeals judges be appointed by the governor from a group recommended by a panel appointed by the governor, the chief judge, and the legislature leaders.

The statewide electorate must be asked once every twenty years if they wish a constitutional convention to be held. Additionally, the electorate must ratify constitutional amendments before they are effected, and approve any pledge of full faith and credit of the state. Unlike constitutions in twenty-one other states, however, New York's does not give citizens the powers of initiative, the right to petition to put policy questions or constitutional amendments on the ballots, or referendum, or the right to a popular vote on these questions. A variety of constitutional amendments adding initiative and referendum to the New York Constitution have been proposed in recent years, but none has been approved.

Qualifications and Election of State Officers. State legislators, the governor, and lieutenant governor must be American citizens and five-year residents of New York State. Legislators have an additional district residence requirement: all are required to swear or affirm support of the United States Constitution and the New York Constitution. Salaries of offices named in the constitution may not be increased or reduced during a term of office.

The governor and lieutenant governor must be thirty years old. They are elected in tandem, statewide, in even-number nonpresidential years at the general election for a four-year term by a plurality-winner system. There is no age requirement for senators and assembly members. They are also chosen at the general election, though the date of their election may be altered by the legislature.

The members of both legislative houses are selected within single-member districts for two-year terms, also on a plurality-winner basis. Legislative districts are reapportioned decennially by the legislature itself in accord with national constitutional and statutory standards and detailed state constitutional provisions. However, many of these state constitutional provisions have been found by federal courts to be in conflict with national standards and therefore void. The 1967 draft constitution (not adopted) provided for a legislative districting commission. There are no term limitations for any office, though constitutional amendments creating them have recently been proposed.

The Legislature. The New York State legislature is bicameral, as are those of all states except Nebraska. The legislature assembles annually on the first Wednesday after the first Monday in January. The number of assembly members is fixed at 150 while the number of senators, at least 50 and currently 62, is variable.

The power of the legislature is plenary, except insofar as it is limited in the constitution. The most important of the legislature's powers is the power of the purse—the authority to both raise and spend funds. It is separately treated in great detail in two articles of the constitution, and further constrained and defined in the legislative article (Articles VII and XVI and Article III). Additionally, the legislature is explicitly given the power to regulate "practice and procedure" in the courts, and to remove court of appeals and supreme court judges for cause by concurrent resolution upon two-thirds vote of both houses (Article VI, Sections 23 and 30).

The legislature is also empowered to provide for filling vacancies in the offices of comptroller and attorney general (Article V, Section 1). The recent use of election by the legislative houses meeting jointly to fill a vacancy in the comptroller's office led to proposals for an amendment of the constitution to alter this procedure, and demonstrated how breaking political events may bring attention to otherwise obscure constitutional provisions.

For bills to become laws they must be passed by a majority of the members elected to each house, following the form of the enacting clause prescribed in the constitution. The legislature may override a gubernatorial veto by a two-thirds vote of those elected to each house. Proposed constitutional amendments that pass the legislature are not subject to gubernatorial veto, nor are its actions on executive budget bills.

Bills may originate in either house and be freely amended in either house, with a majority required for a quorum to do business, except that many fiscal actions require a quorum of three-fifths. Each house adopts its own rules, is the judge of the qualifications of its own members, and selects its own leaders. By a constitutional change adopted in 1975, two-thirds of the elected members of each house may petition to call the legislature into special session for the specified purposes. Neither house may adjourn for more than two days without the consent of the other.

Both the senate and assembly must keep and publish a journal and meet in open session, though secrecy is permitted if deemed by the legislature to be in the interest of the "public welfare." To assure free debate on controversial matters, members may not be "questioned in any other place" for remarks made in the legislature.

The senate must give its advice regarding and consent to the appointments by the governor of heads of departments and members of boards and commissions, but has no role in their removal (Article V, Section 5). Upon recommendation of the governor, the senate can remove judges of the court of claims, the county court, the surrogate's court, and the New York City courts by two-thirds vote (Article VI, Section 23). Additionally, its members sit as a part of the court in trial of impeachment, if charges are brought by a majority of elected assembly members against the governor, lieutenant governor, or a state judge.

The legislature is restricted in numerous procedural and substantive ways by the state constitution. Process requirements, often stimulated by past abuses in New York and elsewhere, seek to assure that there is an opportunity for members to familiarize themselves with proposed legislation prior to voting. Thus, bills may not be amended following their final reading nor made applicable by reference. Private bills must be limited to one subject, identified in the title. Similarly, tax laws must clearly identify the nature and object of taxation. Absent a special message of necessity from the governor, bills must be printed and sit on members' desks in final form for three calendar days before passage. Two-thirds of each house must support any appropriation of public money or property for private or local purposes. In budgeting, other appropriations may not be considered until after those offered by the governor are taken up, and then must be made by separate bills, for a single purpose (Article VII, Sections 5 and 6).

Substantially, the legislature is barred from passing private or local bills on fourteen different subjects, for example changing of names of persons, incorporating villages, or granting a person, corporation, or association "any exclusive privilege, immunity or franchise whatever" (Article III, Section 17). The gift or loan of state money or credit for private purposes is prohibited (Article VII, Section 8). A number of key articles or provisions of the constitution—for example those establishing the "merit and fitness" principal for civil service employment (Article V, Section 6); restricting borrowing authority (Article VII, Section 11); granting powers of home rule to local government (Article IX); establishing a general process of incorporation (Article X); and keeping the forest preserve "forever wild" (Article XIV) are major limits on the legislature's sphere of action.

The substantive limits were adopted for a number of reasons. Constraints on special legislation at once removed opportunities for patronage and corruption and focused the legislature on general matters, making it more efficient. Guarantees of home rule would, it was thought, both advance local democracy and, again, enhance legislative efficiency. (In fact home rule, or the power of local governments to act independently of state authority, has been greatly weakened by court interpretation.) And the inclusion of broad policy commitments in the constitution put these beyond the sphere of ordinary politics, making them more enduring.

The constitution also contains numerous policy directives that the legislature act to give constitutional provisions force and effect, while in other areas it indicates that the legislature may act if it wishes to do so. Thus, for example, the legislature *must* provide for "the maintenance and support of a system of free common schools" (Article XI), but *may* provide low-rent housing and nursing home accommodations (Article XVIII). Requirements that the legislature act in an area are in some degree limiting on its discretion, though they are not, of course, defining of the action it takes.

The governor must "take care that the laws be faithfully executed." The governor reports to the legislature annually on the condition of the state, and makes policy recommendations to it that comprise a legislative agenda (Article IV, Section 3). The governor may expedite legislation or allow special legislation applicable to local governments other than New York City, with a message of special necessity (Article II, Section 14; Article IX, Section 2). After the legislature has acted, the governor is presented with legislation for approval or veto. On appropriation bills not originally submitted by the governor, the governor may exercise an item veto, striking one or more items without invalidating the entire bill. The definition of an "item" has been the subject of litigation.

If the legislature is in session, a veto must be exercised within ten days of receipt of a measure, and may be overridden by a two-thirds vote of the members elected to each house. During the session there in no pocket veto; if the governor fails to sign a bill within ten days it still becomes law. If the legislature had adjourned, the veto period is thirty days and a bill may not become law without the governor's signature (Article IV, Section 7). Since the mid-1970s the legislature has adopted the practice of recessing rather than adjourning, which keeps the legislature in session, and this practice has mitigated the effect of this provision.

The governor's key priorities are often encompassed in the executive budget, produced through a process defined in detail in a separate constitutional provision (Article VII). It requires that annually, by February 1 in gubernatorial election years or by the second Tuesday following the first day of annual meeting of the legislature, the governor submit the executive budget to the legislature, including a "complete plan of expenditures," revenue estimates, the basis of these, and recommendations for additional revenues, if needed. The budget must be accompanied by appropriation bills and proposed implementing legislation. The form of the budget, and the inclusiveness of the appropriation bills, have been subjects of disputes between the branches settled in the court of appeals.

The governor is the commander in chief of the state's military and naval forces. The governor may call the entire legislature, or senate alone, into special session and set the agenda for that session, though the legislature is not required to act upon the matters brought to it. The governor may grant reprieves, commutations, or pardons for all offenses except treason and those subject to impeachment, and may suspend execution of a sentence for treason until the legislature has had time to consider and act upon it. With certain exceptions specified in the constitution and noted below, the governor appoints department heads and, subject to processes prescribed in law, may remove these officials. Following constitutionally prescribed procedures, the governor may also remove elected sheriffs, county clerks, or district attorneys for cause (Article XIII, Sections 13 a and b).

Regarding the judiciary the governor has considerable appointing authority. The governor appoints judges to the court of appeals and the court of claims, appoints judges to fill vacancies in the supreme court, appoints four members of the Commission on Judicial Conduct, and designates justices of the appellate divisions of supreme court (Article 6, Sections, 4c, 9,

21, 22). Additionally, the governor may appoint an extraordinary term of the supreme court, designate the presiding justice at such a term, and replace that justice as the governor sees fit (Article VI, Section 27). The governor may recommend to the senate removal of judges of the court of claims, the county court, the family court, the surrogate's court, and the New York City courts (Article VI, Section 23).

The lieutenant governor, as noted, presides over the senate and has a casting vote. The lieutenant governor *becomes* governor and serves out the term if the governor dies, resigns, or is removed; or *acts* as governor if the governor is impeached, is absent from the state, or is unable to discharge his or her duties, until the temporary condition is meliorated (Article IV, Section 5).

The comptroller is the head of the Department of Audit and Control. The comptroller is charged in the constitution with the preaudit of all vouchers, the audit of the state's accounts, and the audit of the accrual and collection of revenues. The comptroller also prescribes state accounting methods. Absent an audit by the comptroller, state monies may not be paid out. As provided for by the legislature, the comptroller also supervises the accounts of the state's local governments and oversees some limited aspects of real estate taxation. In aggregate these powers are sources of considerable influence over the management of the governmental system.

The constitution specifies that the comptroller may not be assigned additional administrative duties by the legislature, presumably to keep the audit function distinct from daily state government operations (Article V, Section 1). The comptroller is also charged with the management of sinking funds for the retirement of certain local debts, and may be required by the legislature to certify local debt that may be incurred outside of ordinary limits (Article 8, Sections 2a, 4, 5, and 7).

Interestingly, the constitution is silent on the comptroller's very considerable powers in the management of the state retirement system and role in the incurring of state debt. These are entirely based in statute.

The attorney general is the head of the Department of Law. The constitution is almost entirely silent on the powers of this office. When a constitutional amendment is proposed, the attorney general must within twenty days report to the legislature on its affect on other portions on the constitution.

The court system is created in detail in the constitution and includes at the state level: the court of appeals, the appellate divisions, the supreme court, the court of claims, the county court, the surrogate's court, and the family court. Court of appeals and supreme court judges serve for fourteen years. Surrogates, county court judges, and family court judges have ten-year terms, and the term of court of claims judges is nine years. Whether judges are elected or appointed, long terms are regarded as a necessary condition for judicial independence. All judges on these courts have a mandatory retirement age of seventy. Court of appeals and supreme court judges may be certified to continue to perform the duties of a supreme court justice for an additional six years, in two-year increments.

The highest court, the court of appeals, has a chief judge and six associate judges. Its quorum is five, with four in agreement required for a decision. Upon request by the court of appeals, the governor may temporarily appoint up to four supreme court judges to serve on this court and assist with its work, their services to cease upon certification by the court that the need for help has passed. Among the duties of court of appeals judges is to sit on courts of impeachment, together with members of the state senate.

Local courts with constitutional status include a separately defined New York City court system and district, town, city, and village courts outside New York City. In New York City civil court judges are elected to ten-year terms, while criminal judges there are appointed by the mayor to terms of the same length. District court judges outside New York City serve six-year terms in districts within counties created by the legislature upon local request and after acceptance at local referendum. City and village courts may be discontinued by the legislature upon its own decision, but discontinuance of town courts must be approved by referendum in the affected jurisdiction. In towns, justices of the peace are elected for four years.

The four judicial departments, for appellate division purposes, and eleven judicial districts, for supreme court purposes, are also constitutionally defined. For all courts, jurisdiction is specified in the constitution. Processes for appeal, and possible actions on appeal, are also specified.

Administrative supervision of the court system is given to a chief judge of the court of appeals who, with the advice and consent of an administrative board of courts comprised of the chief judge and the presiding judges of the appellate division of each department, appoints a chief administrator of the courts. Judges may be assigned outside of their immediate jurisdiction under the constitution, and may perform duties of more than one court outside the city of New York if required to do so by legislation. The constitution creates an eleven-person Commission on Judicial Conduct, with multiple appointing authorities, to hear complaints concerning judges, initiate investigations, and make independent determinations of their fitness. Upon review of the commission's findings, the court of appeals may sanction judges in a range of ways, including removal.

The detailed specification of the state and local court systems in the constitution contrasts substantially with the broader provision concerning the judiciary in the national constitution and that of some other states. There are continuing efforts, described below, to simplify these provisions, further unifying the courts and reorganizing them by constitutional amendment. Another regular object of amendment, also described below, concerns the creation of a Fifth Judicial Department.

Departments and agencies: The constitution limits departments to twenty in number. This limitation, designed to constrain the size of government, is in practice overcome by the location of many units, not called "departments," in an omnibus "Executive Department." Unlike in many other states, the governor has limited power to reorganize the executive branch. It is the legislature that is constitutionally empowered to reduce the number of departments; create temporary commissions or executive offices of the governor; and enhance, diminish, or alter the powers and functions of departments, officers, boards commissions, and executive offices. Enhanced authority in this area has been sought by the governor through constitutional amendment (Article V, Sections 2 and 3).

As noted above, with the exception of departments headed by elected officials and the Department of Education, headed by legislatively appointed regents who in turn select a commissioner to serve as the chief administrative officer, department heads are appointed by the governor with the advice and consent of the senate. The senate, however, does not share the removal power (Article V, Section 4). The governor's authority over departments is further solidified by the constitutional requirement that department heads provide the governor with required budgetary information, as part of the executive budget process (Article VII, Section 1).

No department rule or regulation, except those entirely for internal management, may be effective until filed with the Department of State.

Public authorities emerged in New York during the post–World War I period, but were first constitutionally regulated by the amendments adopted in 1938. Authorities are autonomous entities delivering services largely outside the departmental structure of state government, and are therefore not subject to many of the rules and regulations that govern the operations of ordinary state departments and agencies. Under the constitution, authorities must be created by special act of the legislature. They are authorized to contract debt and to collect fees to pay for the facilities they build and operate (Article X, Section 5).

The state is not liable for the obligations of public authorities, nor can it be made liable for these by legislative act, though the legislature may act to acquire the property of these corporations and assume the indebtedness on this property (Article X, Section 5). The accounts of public authorities are subject to review by the comptroller. Specific exceptions allow state guarantees for authority debt to construct thruways, purchase railroad cars, finance certain economic development activities, and finance housing and nursing home accommodations for low-income persons (Article VII, Section 8.3; Article X, Sections 6–8; Article XVIII, Section 2).

Techniques developed by the state over time to bypass the prohibition of state guarantees of authority debt, including "moral-obligation" borrowing and lease-purchase arrangements, have made this an area of continuing political and constitutional controversy. State courts have permitted these practices. Numerous constitutional amendments have been proposed as a result, some to strengthen limits on authority borrowing and the use of de facto state guarantees and others to remove existing limits as ineffectual, leaving regulation to the financial market.

CHAPTER 7

New York's Governorship

"What Happens Now?"

GERALD BENJAMIN AND ELIZABETH BENJAMIN

In 1994 there were 1.43 million more voters enrolled as Democrats than as Republicans in New York State (see chapter 3). George Pataki was a little-known state senator. Mario Cuomo was the three-term incumbent Democratic governor of New York, often mentioned for the presidency, and a national party icon.

Pataki was nominated, ran and won the governorship. By 1998 New York's Democrats outnumbered Republicans by 1.86 million. Now an incumbent, Pataki won again. By 2002, the Democratic enrollment margin had grown to 2.12 million. Pataki won still again.

From Pataki's first election to his third, the number of New Yorkers eligible to vote grew substantially. The state's registered voters totaled 11.25 million in 2002, 27.5 percent more than in 1994 (8.82 million). Yet for each of the years that he ran, the number of actual voters in the state declined, from 5.3 million in 1994, to 4.99 million in 1998, to 4.69 million in 2002. Even with shrinking participation, the GOP never provided a majority for Pataki in a statewide race. Head-to-head in 1994, the Democrats in New York outpolled the Republicans for governor. Pataki gained his first statewide victory with votes provided by the Conservative Party's cross-endorsement. Still, he was only a plurality winner in 1994 (47.7%), as he was again in 2002 (48.2%). As a one-term incumbent, Pataki gained a majority in 1998 (51.5%) only when the votes on the Republican and Conservative lines were combined.

Writing in the *New York Times Magazine* in June of 2003, Jennifer Senior likened George Pataki's stellar political performance in a solid Democratic state to "living in a tremulous state of equipoise, as if perched on the top of a bowling ball."[1] Clearly, Pataki was very good at getting elected under adverse circumstances. On the run up to his first gubernatorial win, he beat one incumbent Democrat to become mayor of Peekskill, another to enter the state assembly, and (in a primary) an incumbent state senator to enter that body.

But repeatedly winning office does not by itself assure a governor's place in history. That place is established by what is accomplished while in office. For George Pataki, like for all governors before him, the question is the same as for Robert Redford (as Bill McKay) in the famous movie about American politics, *The Candidate*: "What happens now?"

In an essay published in 1982 about the "ten outstanding governors of the twentieth century," George Weeks, former chief of staff to Governor William G. Milliken of Michigan, commented, "Based alone on the caliber of its governors, [New York] could have accounted for half the top ten if there had not been some attempt to recognize different times and circumstances." Indeed, even after adjusting his analysis to avoid overemphasizing New York, Weeks included three of the state's governors—Smith, Dewey, and Rockefeller—on his final list of the ten greatest.[2]

One measure of success may be the ability to contest for even higher office. Historically, New York's governorship has been a springboard for presidential aspirants. Eight New York governors became the presidential nominees of their party between the Civil War and 1948. Of these eight, three won the presidency: Grover Cleveland, Theodore Roosevelt, and Franklin Delano Roosevelt. The five remaining governors—Horatio Seymour, Horace Greeley, Samuel J. Tilden, Charles Evans Hughes, and Thomas E. Dewey—failed in their presidential bids. Since the Dewey candidacy of 1948, however, no New York governor has appeared on a national ticket.

On the Democratic side, the New York governor is still a factor in national politics. Hugh Carey was mentioned for vice president and Mario Cuomo's declarations of noncandidacy took on the air of a quadrennial ritual. But in the national GOP Nelson Rockefeller's eclipse marked

> the end of New York Republicanism as a national force. In 1960 the newly elected New York governor threatened to take the pres-

idential nomination by storm. The price Rockefeller extracted for removing himself from contention was the famous "compact of Fifth Avenue" concerning the substance Republican platform, negotiated with his rival, Vice President Richard Nixon. In 1964 Rockefeller was the center of a jeering confrontation at the national convention, as the party turned decisively rightward and nominated Barry Goldwater for president. In 1976 Gerald Ford, under conservative pressure, removed Vice President Rockefeller (appointed, not elected, to the post) from his ticket. Despite George Pataki's ambitions, no New York Republican has been a serious contender for the national ticket since.[3]

To those with a more than casual interest in government and politics, New York's governors are better measured by their performance in the office than by their presidential ambitions. This includes providing both governmental and political leadership in such areas as responding to social and educational needs, building the state's economy, protecting its environment, achieving efficiency in governmental operations, and advocating effectively for resources from the national government. If for no other reason, the level of distinction achieved by many of the office's incumbents in these areas makes the New York governorship worthy of study. What is it about this office that has attracted people widely acknowledged for their quality, and what about New York's political system has allowed them to rise?

In order to find answers to these questions, we need to understand a number of complex factors: the presence in New York of social diversity and political economy that demands and supports strong leadership, a constitutional design that provides the framework for such leadership, and a history of the use of executive power, which creates the expectation that the governor will be the center of energy in the state political system.

THE FRAMEWORK

Commenting before New York's 1967 Constitutional Convention Committee on the Executive Branch, Governor Nelson Rockefeller observed, "Great men are not drawn to small offices." Rockefeller noted further that the governor's powers "comprise a substantial grant of authority. And because our governors possess this authority, we have enjoyed leadership that has established New York as a pioneering, innovating, and eminently successful state."[4]

Rockefeller's somewhat self-serving hyperbole notwithstanding, it is indeed true that over its history New York has been less chary of a strong executive than most states. During the Revolutionary era, a one-year term, limited succession, and legislative selection of the governor were the norm. New York's constitution, drafted later and in a more conservative political milieu than prevalent in the other original states, provided for a three-year term, unlimited succession, and popular election. At a time when the veto power was anathema, identified as it was with royal authority, New York nevertheless allowed its governor first to share such a veto with a Council of Revision and then, in 1821, made it his alone. In that same year, the authority to make state appointments was taken from a Council of Appointment and given to the governor, subject to state senate approval.

Despite its early inclination to empower the executive, New York in the first half of the nineteenth century was subject to the same tides of Jacksonian democracy that swept the rest of the nation. In 1821, the governor's term was shortened to two years, and in 1846, the number of statewide elected officials was increased to thirteen, with an impact on the power of the chief executive that one authority has called "devastating."[5] During the rest of the century, incremental advances of gubernatorial power—the addition of the item veto and a slight reduction in the number of statewide elected boards, for example—still failed to leave New York's governor in control of the administrative establishment.

Progressive reform reached its zenith in New York at the Constitutional Convention of 1915. At that convention, Elihu Root and others sought to reempower the governorship by consolidating administrative agencies (there were 169, including 108 boards and commissions), by adopting a "short ballot" system to minimize the number of statewide elected officials, and by giving budgeting authority to the executive. Ironically, the state constitution that emerged from this convention (a model for other states) was rejected by New Yorkers when offered to them in a comprehensive package. It remained for Governor Al Smith, a Democrat and product of Tammany Hall, to push through piecemeal the progressive reforms implementing the short ballot (1925) and the executive budget (1927).

With the adoption of a four-year term (1938), the formal powers of the modern New York governorship were in place. Comparative analysis of tenure, appointive, veto, and budget powers shows it to be one of the strongest in the nation.[6] Taking advantage of the absence of term limitation, modern New York governors have regularly served multiple terms. As a result of severe budget battles between the legislature and governor during the Pataki years, the New York courts confirmed the governor's dominance in budgeting.[7] Only in the authority to independently reorganize state government is New York's governor significantly less strong than the governors of many other states. Here, despite efforts at constitutional revision in 1967 and 1968, the Legislature has remained, at least in form, predominant.[8]

Interestingly, this did not prevent Governor Pataki from using reorganization to put his stamp on state government. The functions of the old Department of Social Services were dispersed among the Departments of Health and Labor, and newly created Offices of Children and Family Services and Temporary and Disability Assistance within a newly constituted Department of Family Assistance, signaling a major policy redirection in response to sweeping national welfare reform. Economic development activities in both state agencies and public authorities were concentrated in the hands of a single individual, Charles Gargano—a prodigious fundraiser for Pataki. At the same time that this centralization of authority took place, construction-oriented public authorities were consolidated into the Dormitory Authority, reducing costs and, incidentally, demonstrating the degree to which their independence from gubernatorial control was a political fiction. Pataki's early efforts to reshape public authorities were boosted by Mario Cuomo's practice of allowing trustees with expired terms to remain as interim appointments, making them vulnerable to swift replacement by his successor. Later, in Pataki's third term, the accountability of these of authorities, their number, and the size and scope of their activities again became a major issue in state government.

Though the New York governorship cannot be understood without a review of its formal powers and duties, it also cannot be known only by reading the state constitution and statutes. Constitutionally required to "communicate by message to the legislature at every session the condition of the state, and recommend such matters to it as he shall judge expedient,"[9] the governor is expected by the people and principal political actors of the state, even those elected statewide, to provide leadership. Regardless of the actual locus of authority, the governor is praised if things go well and blamed if they go wrong.

Regular independent public opinion polling measures the degree to which the state's chief executive is meeting others' expectations that he lead. Strong poll numbers are themselves a source of power, suggesting to legislators and others the peril of resisting the governor's political priorities. George

Pataki's ability to generate strong approval ratings provides one clue to his success as a Republican in a Democratic state. These were persistently low during his first months in office. Pataki's early budget cuts were painful to many constituencies, his leadership was untested, and his style was unfamiliar. But as his first reelection approached, the state economy improved, revenues flowed, the wraps were taken off spending, and Pataki's popularity rose. At 47 percent only sixteen months before, the governor's approval in the respected Marist College poll exceeded 60 percent in February of 1998. The governor's poll ratings peaked at 81 percent approval just after the September 11, 2001, terrorist attacks on Manhattan and Washington. A year later, that number returned to earlier but quite respectable levels (62 percent in September 2002). Even the embarrassment of the legislature's override of his budget vetoes in May 2003 didn't have much of an effect on Pataki's popularity. True, his approval rating dropped to 43 percent—the lowest since he took office in 1995—but 62 percent of the 1,059 individuals questioned by the Quinnipiac University Polling Institute said they considered Pataki a "strong leader" and 65 percent found him likable. This led Quinnipiac pollster Maurice "Mickey" Carroll to call Pataki "the Teflon governor." "He's negative on all the issues, yet people still think he's a good leader," Carroll said.[10]

The expectation that the governor lead is most evident during crises. In 1975, the New York State Urban Development Corporation (UDC) defaulted on its bonds, and New York City and state tottered on the brink of fiscal chaos. Though only in office a few months, Governor Hugh Carey responded. His ability to organize public and private resources to avoid the fiscal collapse of the state, its public authorities, and its local governments won him wide praise; it proved to be his finest hour.

The power-enhancing qualities of crisis are well known to governors, and at times lead them to cultivate a crisis atmosphere. Governors Harriman, Rockefeller, Carey, and Cuomo each emphasized in their first budget message the severe, even unique, fiscal crisis they claimed to have found upon assuming office. Similarly, George Pataki's first budget message, in 1995, referred to New York's "5 billion dollar crisis, a budget gap larger than the total annual budgets of 31 other states." The rhetoric bolstered Pataki's justifications for spending cuts to reduce the deficit. Unlike his predecessors, however, he asked not for tax increases but for tax cuts to boost economic growth and therefore revenues.

Though Mayor Rudy Giuliani took the lead in responding to the September 11 attacks in New York City, Governor Pataki was omnipresent at his side, and joined in providing on-the-scene leadership and follow-up to seek federal assistance (though there were later disputes about how it would be shared between the state and city). Pataki knew, as he wrote in his autobiography of an earlier tragedy, the crash of TWA Flight 800 off the coast of Long Island, "that one of the most important functions a governor can fulfill is to extend a caring hand to people in despair."[11] Later, during the 2002 primary campaign, Andrew Cuomo questioned the governor's performance in crisis. "Pataki stood behind the leader," Cuomo said. "He held the leader's coat. He was a great assistant to the leader. But he was not a leader." The public, appreciative of Pataki's approach, especially in light of his earlier disputes with Giuliani, rallied to support the governor; Andrew Cuomo's gubernatorial candidacy never recovered.[12]

Crisis presents leaders not only with opportunity but also with peril. Nelson Rockefeller's handling of the 1971 Attica prison uprising, in which forty-three people died, subjected him to the most severe criticism of his tenure. The resolution of a prison uprising at Ossining during Governor Cuomo's first month in office in 1983 without death or any major concessions by the state, especially with Attica still vivid in the memories of key New York state decision makers, illustrates another point about gubernatorial power. Success for a governor, however obtained, breeds later success by creating a political environment in which others expect the governor to not only lead, but to prevail.

Expectations may, however, be unrealistic, especially when they result from extraordinary circumstances. During his second term, after the success of his dramatic efforts to stave off fiscal disaster in his first, Governor Carey was quoted as responding to his critics, "What am I supposed to do, save New York City twice?"[13]

William Ronan, secretary to the governor during the Rockefeller years, remarked, "New York is a big, dynamic, high-powered state, and it wants a big, dynamic, high-powered man for its governor."[14] Indeed, formal gubernatorial powers do tend to be enhanced in those American states, such as New York, that are large in size and have heterogeneous populations and great social and economic diversity. It is as if a center of substantial political power is needed to offset, balance, and broker the diversity of interests and concerns within these states.[15]

It is not insignificant, too, for gubernatorial power in New York that the state's principal city is a national and international media center. In all states, as in the nation, the chief executive—a single person, representative of and known to a broad constituency—tends to be the focal point of media attention, and therefore is advantaged over others in the political arena.[16] The situation in New York is complicated by the fact that the state is home to the nation's largest and greatest city, a world financial capital and the fourth largest government in the United States. New York City's mayor is a world-class political figure and, therefore, a natural rival to the governor for media attention. But both share an advantage over other state and local leaders because New York politics is the "local story" for media enterprises of national and international importance.

During the 1994 gubernatorial campaign, New York City mayor Rudolph Giuliani, a Republican, endorsed Governor Cuomo over Pataki. After Pataki took office, he and Giuliani cohosted the national NBC television show *Saturday Night Live* in a skit intended to show that the political hatchet had indeed been buried. Many local political figures engage in feuds, both personal and professional. Rare, however, is the local dispute that finds its way into the national popular culture.

Pataki's relationship with New York City's current mayor, Democrat-turned-Republican Michael Bloomberg, has been outwardly more amiable than the one he shared with Giuliani (and it should be noted, Giuliani and Pataki have publicly claimed to be the best of friends since weathering September 11 together). Bloomberg, a billionaire businessman, used his personal wealth not only to win his own office, but also to fatten the coffers of the Republican Party in New York and assist GOP candidates, including Pataki. A less pugnacious presence than Giuliani, Bloomberg has usually avoided knock-down, drag-out public fights with Pataki—even when that hurt him and New York City, as when the governor nixed reinstating the commuter tax, or raised subway fares even though he pledged not to during the 2002 campaign. One exception, however, was an open dispute between the two chief executives about the city and state sharing of post-9/11 aid.[17]

New York's importance in the nation and the world attracts to it an array of enormously talented people, providing for the governor a source of informal assistance and advice that is unsurpassed in range and depth. Given the success previous governors have had in attracting the paid and unpaid services of such advisors as Henry Kissinger and Felix Rohatyn, a criticism made of the Pataki administration in its early years was that it failed to take advantage of such resources. Later the governor attracted such nationally prominent New Yorkers as Frank Zarb and Ira Millstein to head important commissions, the first on financing elementary and secondary education, the second on public authority reform.

Gubernatorial power is also subtly served by the ambitions of staffers who wish to hitch their wagons to a political star, riding to a desk at the White House. When the demands of service chafe too greatly, senior aides move to the private sector, leveraging their experience into top positions with investment banks, national law firms, national media networks, and multinational corporations. There, they grow affluent and are still available to the governor for advice and counsel. The Pataki administration's first counsel to the governor was Pataki's close friend and long-time political associate, Michael Finnegan. Finnegan, agent and architect of many Pataki environmental policy successes, left the administration after three years to become a managing director at J. P Morgan Securities on Wall Street. Later Zenia Mucha, Pataki's former communications director, became a spokeswoman for the Disney Corporation, while remaining on tap for the administration.

The governor also serves as "chief of state," a ceremonial role that puts the governor in touch with the many worlds of New York, providing contacts across the lines that usually separate these worlds. The governor's presence adds status and luster to events. Far more invitations are offered than can be accepted. Each opportunity chosen to cut a ribbon, give a speech, or greet a visiting notable creates an opportunity to do a favor, provide recognition, and develop a wellspring of later support.

Incumbent governors have traditionally held sway within their party at the state level and have used that influence in varying ways. Like Hugh Carey, Mario Cuomo came to office without the support of the Democratic Party organization. During his twelve years in office, Cuomo exercised party leadership largely to advance his own interests and ambitions, often at the expense of other Democratic officeholders and aspirants, and certainly not for the benefit of his party as an organization.

George Pataki's election, however, owed much to a striking resurgence of the Republican Party as a statewide institution in New York. Captive under Rockefeller and moribund during much of the Cuomo administration, New York's Republican Party was reincarnated following the electoral debacle of 1990, in which its gubernatorial candidate, Pierre Rinfret, came within a handful of votes of placing third. Party leadership was provided by U.S. senator Alfonse D'Amato and his close associate, then-state GOP chairman William Powers. D'Amato entered into a power vacuum to fill a purely partisan role unknown for a U.S. senator in New York since the time early in the twentieth century when holders of this office were still elected by state legislatures. With Powers, D'Amato ramrodded George Pataki's 1994 gubernatorial nomination through the state convention and assured that there would be no primary challenge.

Clearly, during the early years of the Pataki administration, the state Republican Party organization remained a political force independent of the governor to a degree rare in the history of modern New York politics. In 2001, Pataki finally took organizational control. Powers departed from his position as state chairman, and was replaced by the governor's close friend, Alexander "Sandy" Treadwell, the former Essex County GOP chairman and a staunch Pataki supporter—both financially and ideologically. But, as noted, little was accomplished over the Pataki years before or after the governor's assertion of party control to build the New York State GOP voter base at the grassroots.

THE INSTITUTIONAL GOVERNORSHIP

The governor is assisted in the exercise of his powers, both formal and informal, by a substantial staff. In recent years, New York's executive-chamber offices have been budgeted at over $12 million per year, and more than two hundred people, about a third of them professional, have been employed in the chief executive's service. In addition, a number of "control agencies" in the executive office, the most important of which is the Division of the Budget, are used for key policymaking and implementation tasks. Staffed primarily by career professionals, the budget division, one of the most powerful agencies of its kind, is responsible for both the development of the governor's financial plan and its implementation throughout the year.

In modern New York government, the three top aides to the governor have traditionally been the counsel, the secretary, and the budget director. Recent years have seen the director of State Operations and Policy Management and the governor's communications director join these three aides as key members of the governor's staff. The importance of other staff members fluctuates in response to specific concerns, and none have had the staying power of the five key positions.

Any discussion of the roles of top staff on New York government is necessarily artificial. It tends to obscure the degree to which the responsibilities of the governor's key aides overlap and thus understate the extent to which, as Governor Dewey liked to observe, theirs is a team effort.[18] It is fair to say that the counsel to the governor and the governor's assistants serve as architects of the legislative program and as advisors on state legal matters. The budget director oversees preparation and administration of the budget and fiscal plan. The secretary to the governor is the governor's chief of staff, prime negotiator with the legislature, and liaison to local governments; and the director of Operations and Policy Management is charged with policy development and day-to-day coordination of state bureaucracy.

Upon taking office, most governors have expressed concern about concentrating too much power in the hands of one staff member. Over time, however, one aide has always seemed to emerge as a pivotal figure. Indeed, William Ronan, secretary to Governor Rockefeller, and Robert Morgado, secretary to Governor Carey, wielded such power in state government that they were widely thought of as surrogate governors. In retrospect, Ronan described his role thus: "The Secretary acts on behalf of the Governor and, in his name, deals with the department and agencies of state government in liaison, also with the legislature in many matters, and with various individuals and public groups who have business with the chief executive of the state."[19]

And of working with his secretary, Governor Rockefeller commented: "I know him. I trust his judgment. I know his background. We have worked together. I get the feel of the thing and I can make that decision very fast if he feels that he should ask me about it. Or he will inform me of decisions he has made. I just don't have time to hear these people. If a department feels very strongly that they have been shortchanged on a decision and it was wrong they will come to me and I will listen to them. But he is a fair-minded man and they have confidence in him."[20]

Opponents criticized Governor George Pataki for failing to give sufficient direction to state government on key issues. Long-time Democratic assemblyman William L. Parment, for example, noted that he "talked about [education finance reform] . . . in his State of the State speeches, but his budgets have never attempted to correct the inequities in school financing."[21] In contrast, supporters praised Pataki's open, consensus-driven management style. Lisa Dewald Stoll, Pataki's press secretary, said "the governor's style, in the end, is to call upon the better nature of people to rise to the challenge, to say 'Let's get together, let's build a consensus.'"[22] Pataki, who over his three terms had his share of confrontations—especially with Democratic assembly speaker Sheldon Silver—nevertheless described himself as "always prefer[ring] cooperation to confrontation."[23]

A consensus-oriented style, however, does not preclude certain staff members from attaining the status of primus inter pares. In the early Pataki years Brad Race, ex-chief of staff, and Zenia Mucha, former director of communications, were regarded as particularly enjoying the governor's confidence. Pataki met Race while working on Nelson Rockefeller's 1970 reelection campaign. Mucha, former press secretary to D'Amato, joined Pataki's campaign in that role and remained with him after the election. The two played differing, but equally important, roles in the early days of the administration. Race was viewed as the governor's top policymaker, while Mucha was Pataki's very public, very zealous imagemeister. Later in the administration's second term John Cahill, an old Pataki friend and former Department of Environmental Conservation commissioner, was appointed to succeed Race as secretary to the governor and became the key staffer in the executive chamber.[24]

Because Governor Pataki took office after his party had been out of control of the executive branch for a generation, much of his top staff was recruited from among long-time personal associates—Republican legislative staffers, especially from the assembly minority, state party activists, and interestingly, political leaders and professionals in local government. Early accounts suggested the presence of intrastaff tensions between more moderate, pragmatic personal loyalists and government professionals and more ideologically conservative party activists and others recruited from outside state government. Governor Pataki was captured by neither camp, though his public policy priorities clearly became more centrist as the time for reelection approached.

As interest in a policy area is aroused, a governor may get intensely involved with it, only to move on to another area after establishing a tone or direction. National surveys of state commissioners have systematically shown that the New York governorship is one of the nation's strongest in directing administration. Those few departments that are not headed by gubernatorial appointees still feel the governor's influence via the executive budget process. For example, members of the Board of Regents are elected by a joint session of the state assembly and senate, in which legislative Democrats hold a sizable majority. The regents, in turn, select the commissioner of education. Presumably insulated from executive influence by this process, the commissioner must still submit his department's spending request for review and approval by the governor's Division of the Budget before its inclusion in the annual Executive Budget.

As on the national level, cabinet meetings in New York are rarely the locus of policymaking. Commissioners enjoy relative autonomy within each administration's policy parameters, looking to the governor and staff for support or direction as appropriate. Some commissioners gain responsibilities beyond their titles as a consequence of their performance, their personal relationship with the governor, or the importance of the function they head. Such was the case with Bob King, appointed director of the governor's Office of Regulatory Reform upon its creation by Governor Pataki in 1995. King, formerly a Pataki colleague in the state assembly and Monroe County executive, spearheaded the deregulation effort central to Pataki's goal of making New York's government more business friendly.[25] In February, 1998, Pataki moved King to oversee another area of special concern, appointing him budget director upon Patricia Woodworth's resignation. King was also mentioned as a possible 1998 running mate for Pataki, to replace Lieutenant Governor Betsy McCaughey-Ross. Instead Pataki tapped King—a lawyer, not an academic—to head the state university system, extending the governor's influence through their personal relationship over the vast SUNY system.

Lieutenant governors have little formal power and must enjoy the confidence of the governor to be effective. Specially recruited from outside electoral politics to balance the Republican statewide ticket in 1994, McCaughey-Ross's relationship with the governor was troubled from the start. She bolted from the Republican Party in 1997 and positioned herself as a potential challenger to Pataki. McCaughey-Ross was replaced with former Rensselaer County district attorney Mary Donohue, whose most defining distinction in office has been her willingness to provide unstinting support for Pataki and his proposals. Because Donohue had the added benefit of coming out of the Rensselaer County Republican machine, controlled by Senate Majority Leader Bruno, her selection as his No. 2 helped the governor cement his relationship with Bruno.

However extensive the governor's administrative powers, they are vulnerable to significant restraint by court action. In 1975, the Willowbrook Consent Decree was signed by Governor Carey after scandalous conditions at a state mental hospital led to federal litigation. Negotiated between the state and civil liberties and mental health groups and carried out under judicial supervision, the decree established detailed criteria and a timetable to improve the delivery of a state service that once was entirely within the governor's control.[26] More recent court actions have mandated changes in state police hiring practices and prison conditions. In another limitation on executive discretion, the state's highest court, the court of appeals, ruled that local assistance funds (virtually 60 percent of the state budget) could not be impounded by the governor once appropriated by the legislature.[27] Also, in an area that has been little remarked upon, rules on the standing of a taxpayer to sue state officials on constitutional grounds were eased considerably by the courts and the legislature in the mid-1970s, opening a wide range of official gubernatorial actions to challenge in the courts.[28] One such suit, brought in 1990 against the use of state funds to publicize the proposed Twenty-First Century Environmental Quality Bond Act (which ultimately failed at the polls), resulted in the issuance, by a state judge, of a gag order temporarily preventing the governor and other state officials from offering any public comment on the issue.[29]

Dependence on federal funds and the policy requirements attached to their appropriation, often characterized with considerable hostility as "mandates," has historically constrained the governor's autonomy in the administrative sphere (see chapter 2). However, recent changes in federal law, most notably the 1996 Personal Responsibility and Work Opportunity Reconciliation Act (welfare reform), have increased the state's latitude in administering and establishing social services programs. The extent to which New York will avail itself of that opportunity is attenuated by both the power of the state assembly's Democratic majority and a unique state constitutional provision giving New York's poor an affirmative right to assistance from the state.[30] Mindful of these constraints, Governor Pataki, as noted above, has sought programmatic and managerial change through departmental reorganization.

Though the ground rules have changed, the federal government continues to play an enormous fiscal role in New York. New York's governor, acting individually and in concert with his colleagues in the northeast and the National Governors Association, must be a lobbyist for the state in Washington. Through an office in the nation's capital, the governor seeks to organize New York's congressional delegation on a bipartisan basis in support of maximizing the resources made available for the state. With a majority of governors in the Northeast and the nation Republican, and the Congress held by Republicans, a new dynamic formed in the mid-1990s. With Republican governors across the nation, Governor Pataki continued to seek more state discretion in how federal dollars are spent.

RELATIONS WITH THE LEGISLATURE

Nowhere are the demands upon the governor for leadership as prominently on display as in the annual legislative process. Each year the governor systematically canvasses the state bureaucracy and his advisors, both within and outside government, and then sets the policy agenda in the state of the state and budget messages. Department chiefs and interest groups alike struggle to have their priorities included in these messages, to marshal behind them the clout of the chief executive. Often, the governor's messages are leaked piecemeal to the press over a week's time, to maximize their political impact.

As the counsel's office puts programs in bill form, lines up key committee chairmen and other leaders in both houses (and parties) for sponsorship and support, and tracks the progress of "program bills," the governor may reinforce his priorities with special messages. In addition, there is the authority of the governor to veto bills or items of appropriation (within ten days if the legislature is in session or thirty days if it has adjourned), subject to override by two-thirds of the membership of both houses, and to call the legislature into special sessions for a specific purpose, if the governor feels the need to do so.

There are three key dimensions to the governor's relationship with the legislature: the institutional, the partisan, and the personal. Institutional tensions arising from the division of executive and legislative authority are the necessary and desired result of the system of separation of powers. Partisanship distributes power within political institutions, providing a framework for their organization and ensuring a debate over alternative goals for state government. Personality is an inevitable element in any organization where strong, independent people must cooperate to get things done.

Traditionally, New York has had a highly disciplined legislature, organized along partisan lines (see chapter 8). In fact, both Charles Breitel, when he was counsel to Governor Dewey, and William Ronan likened executive-legislative relationships in the state during the 1940s, 1950s, and early 1960s to those in a parliamentary system.[31] During those less complex times, the governor bargained with the speaker of the assembly and the majority leader of the senate, and when a deal was struck the leaders delivered the necessary legislative majorities. Things went most smoothly when the governor's party controlled both houses, but with some modifications, the system still operated when the legislature was of a different partisan stripe than the governor, or even when control was divided. In control of all the resources of the executive and on the job full-time, the governor dominated the part-time amateur legislature.

Things began to change in the mid-1960s, however, as service in the legislature became a full-time occupation.[32] Reapportionment increased the legislature's representation of urban and suburban areas, and weakened party organizations diminished the ability of the governor to discipline those legislators through home-county party chairs. During the same period, the legislature significantly increased its professional staff, giving the institution, and its members, sources of information and expertise to rival those of the governor.

The task of gubernatorial leadership was further complicated by the elections of 1974, when the Democratic Party gained control of the state assembly, while the state senate remained under Republican leadership. This partisan division of legislative power has persisted since then, creating enormous incentives for each house to develop independent analytic and fiscal capacity. Where once the executive possessed sole leadership of the policy-development apparatus, the governor now holds but one corner in a triad of power.

During the Carey administration, institutional tensions between the governor and the legislature grew as legislators continued to assert themselves. The state constitution was amended to allow special sessions without gubernatorial initiative, and the leaders took to recessing rather than adjourning their bodies, so that they could be called back at any time. In the context of recurring fiscal austerity, in part dictated by economic circumstances and in part the result of conscious policy choices, state politicians became less distributive and more redistributive. With less to go around, executive-legislative confrontation became more and more common.

Institutional differences were exacerbated too by bad chemistry between Governor Carey and legislative leaders—Warren Anderson in the senate and Stanley Steingut and Stanley Fink in the assembly—and by Carey's ill-disguised dislike for the legislature, which he once publicly characterized as a zoo. The results were constantly missed budget deadlines, precedent-setting aenate rejection of gubernatorial appointees for major posts, a lawsuit that, for the first time, gave the legislature a role in distributing federal funds in New York, and renewed use by the governor of the long-dormant item veto as he fought to retain fiscal control.[33]

Succeeding Carey in 1983, Mario Cuomo initially pursued a conciliatory course with the legislature. The turning point, however, came in 1987 as headlines carried news of a scandal over the use of public resources to support political campaign activities. Fresh from his landslide reelection in 1986, Cuomo gained passage of an ethics-in-government law over stiff legislative opposition. In achieving this victory, Cuomo portrayed himself as a people's tribune, battling a faceless, and obstructionist legislature. Legislators took exception to this characterization, and Cuomo's legislative effectiveness diminished greatly during his third term, as measured by both opinion polls and legislative approval for his initiatives. Gubernatorial relations with the legislature may have reached a historic nadir during the 1992 state of the state address when Anthony Seminerio, an assembly member of the governor's own party from Cuomo's home borough of Queens, interrupted and heckled Cuomo during the speech.

Like Cuomo in 1983, Pataki in 1995 sought at first to calm the legislative waters. George Pataki was New York's first elected governor since Franklin D. Roosevelt to have served in the state legislature, and the first since Alfred E. Smith to be elected directly from the legislature. Indeed, Pataki referred to his legislative roots in the opening paragraphs of his first state of the state message, telling the assembled legislators that "because, for me, friends always stay friends—the door to this governor's office is always open to each of you."

Despite these claims, Pataki was willing to play a role in changing leadership in the senate. A coup on Thanksgiving Day, 1994, engineered by a group of senators allied with Pataki deposed Marino as Republican Senate majority leader and installed senator Joseph Bruno in his place. During Pataki's term in the Senate, both he and his political patrons chafed at Marino's low-key legislative style and his accomodationist relationship with Governor Cuomo. Marino's greatest heresy, however, may have been his late and lukewarm endorsement of Pataki's candidacy for governor.[34]

Having had to "play defense" for twenty years in response to initiatives from Democratic governors, the Republican-led senate embraced the opportunity to support a governor of their own party. As majority leader, Senator Bruno is a skilled, telegenic partisan. He has also, however, been willing to confront the governor with those assets to protect the institutional stakes of his house where there were clear philosophical differences between his majority and the governor. A notable example, from 1997, was Bruno's lengthy and public effort to eliminate rent-control laws benefiting mostly New York City tenants. (Most of the Republican majority in the senate is from upstate and suburban districts, where rent control does not apply.) The controversy delayed the extension's enactment until long after the law's expiration date and caused Governor Pataki extreme political discomfort. Speaker Silver's artful exploitation of the issue led to such substantial concessions from the governor that his credentials as a conservative were questioned on the editorial pages of the *Wall Street Journal*. With the Democratic Party voter advantage in New York, Republican George Pataki simply could not afford to alienate millions of middle-class voters living in rent-controlled apartments in the city and still hope to win reelection.

With Pataki the governor, the state assembly—Democratic since 1974—came to be the locus of the "loyal opposition" in New York state government that the Republican senate had been under Carey and Cuomo. Though all New York's statewide offices except governor and lieutenant governor were held by Democrats at the beginning of the twenty-first century, it was assembly speaker Sheldon Silver, elected from the Manhattan district once represented by Al Smith, who most frequently locked horns with the governor and acted as the party's standard bearer. Silver won the Speaker's post in 1994. His Democratic majority, formerly almost entirely from New York City, has more recently been comprised of members from all regions of the state with a wide range of views on issues. From time to time, identification with Silver's program of opposition to a popular Republican governor places the more conservative members at political risk.

Early in Pataki's tenure, the state Republican party mounted televised political attacks in some upstate districts, emphasizing links between local Democratic legislators and "liberal" New York City and illustrating a centuries-long theme in New York politics—the upstate/downstate split. These attacks failed and, in fact, may have strengthened the speaker. Political tensions within the assembly Democratic conference led in 2000 to an unsuccessful coup attempt by Majority Leader Michael Bragman, a Syracuse-area lawmaker.[35] Overcoming this challenge further strengthened Silver. Though plagued in 2003 and 2004 by a string of embarrassing scandals, including his former top counsel pleading guilty to sexual assault of an assembly staffer, Silver remained the state's foremost Democratic leader and the governor's principle adversary in state government.

As was the case in the Carey years, during the early twenty-first century interpersonal enmity exacerbated the structurally driven institutional and partisan tensions that inevitably arise between the governor and the Assembly speaker in state government. Governor Pataki and Speaker Silver just did not like each other, and their dislike often surfaced in public. For example, remarking on Pataki's proposed response to court-ordered enhanced school aid for New York City in June of 2004, Silver said of the governor, "There is no presumption that he ever tells you the truth." In response, Pataki likened Silver to "the guy who killed his parents claiming he was an orphan." The governor then continued, "We have to consider the fact that there is a realistic possibility that the speaker is not really interested in reaching an agreement."[36]

Over the last half-century, New York governors have regularly vetoed between a fifth and a quarter of the bills passed by the legislature, a far larger percentage than in most states.[37] This practice, and the fact that no veto had been overridden since 1870, made the mere threat of a veto a powerful tool in negotiations, and led to regular legislative cooperation in the recall of measures from the governor's desk for changes to avoid the veto. A court of appeals decision in 1993 found this practice unconstitutional, reducing gubernatorial flexibility and adding to the likelihood that there would be greater resort to formal constitutional powers.[38]

The politics of the veto can be complex. Sometimes, as Governor Rockefeller once explained, legislators "went along" with bills to please individual members as a "courtesy" on purely local matters, only because they were confident that there would be a gubernatorial veto. "I'll be the guy who vetoes the bill," Rockefeller said. "This is all part of the act."[39]

Despite the fact that Governor Carey used his veto far less than his predecessors, during his tenure the gubernatorial negative was overridden for the first time in a century in 1976. With this psychological barrier smashed, such actions became relatively common during the Carey years.[40] Governor Cuomo was regularly able to sustain his vetoes. Despite differences with Mayor Giuliani, Governor Pataki has consistently used his veto to protect New York City's fiscal interests and governmental authority. In 1996, however, the legislature overrode Governor Pataki's veto of a bill that allowed arbitration of police salaries by a state agency.

Death-penalty vetoes and nearly successful override attempts were annual events during the administrations of Governors Carey and Cuomo. Ironically, Cuomo's success in this regard may have played a role in his loss to George Pataki, who honored a campaign pledge by pushing through and signing a death-penalty bill early in his first year in office.

The string of late state budgets, which Pataki, as a gubernatorial candidate in 1994, vowed to halt, continued under the Pataki administration, with every budget during his tenure enacted after the April 1 deadline.

In 1995 George Pataki became New York's first governor in fifty-two years to propose an executive budget that reduced general-fund spending from the previous year. While New York's fiscal condition had been the centerpiece of Pataki's campaign, neither he nor the public learned until after the election that New York's budget deficit had reached $5 billion. Many observers felt that this news would force the newly elected governor to renege on his pledges to simultaneously reduce taxes and spending. The new governor, however, surprised many—some of his allies among them—not only by proposing a budget that would do all that he had promised but also for the tenacious manner in which he sought its enactment. Pataki threatened draconian consequences if the legislature failed to adopt a budget by the April 1 outset of the state fiscal year; he was embarrassed when compelling timely action proved beyond his power. But when push came to shove, Pataki sacrificed process for substance, as had other governors before him. And after waging what was then the second-longest budget battle in state history, Pataki won on each essential point. As finally adopted, the budget reduced state taxes and general-fund spending and eliminated ten thousand positions from the state payroll.

Pataki's biggest budget battle with the Legislature came in 2003. In anticipation of his 2002 reelection campaign, the governor spent freely to gain the support of organized labor, including the powerful health care workers and teachers' unions—traditionally Democratic voters—drawing upon nonrecurring revenues to do so. Preelection spending was a major element that led conservative writers to denounce Pataki's departure from his earlier austere fiscal agenda.[41] Throughout the 2002 campaign Pataki played down the state's mounting fiscal woes, exacerbated by the nationwide economic downturn and compounded by the costs of responding to the September 11 attacks and jobs lost in that horrific incident. Experts spoke of the mounting multi-billion-dollar deficit—Pataki's fellow Republican, Senate

Majority Leader Joe Bruno estimated it at $10 billion. Yet the governor continued to insist that the state was fiscally sound.

The message changed after the election. Pataki soon acknowledged a deficit of historic proportions—more than $11.5 billion. His $90.8 billion budget proposal included increased security spending but cuts of more than $1 billion for both public education and health care, areas that had been advantaged the year before. School districts predicted record-high property tax increases and hospitals warned of a reduction in services—or worse, closed facilities. Led by Assembly Speaker Silver and Senate Majority Leader Bruno, lawmakers reacted by adding $2 billion in spending to Pataki's plan, funded largely by temporary personal income tax increases. Warning it would be a "fiscal train wreck" for the state, Pataki used 119 separate vetoes to scuttle the legislative budget. Less than sixteen hours later, the legislature overrode every single one.

WHAT HAPPENS NOW?

The governor of New York is powerful, but not all-powerful. He can succeed in pursuit of his vision for the state and its people only by marshaling the full array of authority and resources that are temporarily at his disposal. And even then success is not assured. Bringing a focus on tax and spending cuts, economic development, social policy reform, and toughness on crime, George Pataki was able to launch New York on a new path during his first term. But as the need to get reelected asserted itself, his conservative ideological agenda gave way to pragmatic political considerations.

There were some consistent themes in the Pataki governorship. One was a devotion to environmental values, deeply rooted in the governor's childhood in the Hudson Valley as part of a Hungarian-immigrant farming family. Another was an effort to improve the business climate, though success in encouraging economic development was highly variable across the state. But over time, conservatism on social policy gave way to support for gay rights and gun control. Budgets, persistently late, remained structurally imbalanced. Spending, at first restrained, came to grow at a rate faster than under Mario Cuomo, Pataki's "liberal" Democratic predecessor. State taxes were cut, but costs displaced downward kept local taxes among the highest in the nation.

Massive borrowing for building projects pleased construction unions, but kept New York among the states that had most mortgaged their futures.

Perhaps the greatest contradiction was Pataki's condemnation of political careerism while building a career in successive elective offices. In 1998 Pataki wrote in his autobiography, "I believe term limits are vital to the long-range health of this nation, at every level of government. We should get in, have our say, and get out. . . . We should vote our conscience, as elected officials, and enact legislation because we think it's the right thing to do, not because it's what we think we need to do to get reelected." And he added, "To people for whom politics is all there is, a term limit poses a real threat. . . . But to someone for whom politics is simply part of a balanced life, a point of pause in a varied career, term limits are only natural."[42] In the year these word were published Pataki ran for reelection. Four year later he ran again. He did whatever was necessary to win. And he won.

During the past third of a century, New York's governors frequently operated in a corrosive environment of partisan division and institutional dysfunction in the legislature and persistent resource scarcity. Distributive politics prevailed in good times. The late 1990s are a case in point. Things were so good that Governor Pataki could cut state taxes and still grow spending at a rate faster than inflation. But more often demands upon state government far in excess of available resources assured that politics would be redistributive, with governors having to cope with vocal, well-organized interest groups competing for larger slices of a shrinking pie.

Historian Donald Roper has written that New York's most successful governors in this century were guided by a philosophy of "positive liberalism," a belief that the state could be an affirmative force in meeting the needs of its people.[43] Mario Cuomo sought to govern in accord with this core value. In contrast, in the 1970s (well before the Reagan presidency), after a frightening fiscal crisis and in response to the cumulative effect of decisions taken in the Rockefeller years, state government came to be regarded not as an engine for progress but as a source of mischief. It was seen, in short, as a danger against which New Yorkers had to be protected.[44] George Pataki sought to govern in accord with this core value.

We began by noting the exceptional quality of the people who have served as New York's governors. In three terms as governor of New York, the great powers of the governorship notwithstanding, neither Democrat Mario Cuomo nor Republican George Pataki—both extraordinarily able, both extraordinarily politically effective—could fundamentally redirect state government. The legislature is noncompetitive, entrenched, and dysfunctional. Interest groups are well financed and served by an elite corps of influential lobbyists. The electorate is disaffected and nonparticipating. In this context, the question for New York in the twenty-first century is whether even the very best person as governor can lead effectively, or whether—to restore real executive leadership—we must have serious structural change in state government.

NOTES

Robert Lawton was coauthor of earlier versions of this essay.

1. Jennifer Senior, "Going for Broke," *New York Times Magazine,* June 15, 2003, p. 40.

2. George Weeks, "A Statehouse Hall of Fame," *State Government* 55, no. 3: 69, 1982.

3. Gerald Benjamin "The Republican Party's Diminished Strength in New York," *Gotham Gazette,* June 7, 2004. http://gothamgazette.com.

4. Nelson Rockefeller, *Public Papers of the Governor* (Albany: Office of the Governor, 1967), p. 209.

5. Thomas Schick, *The New York State Constitutional Convention of 1915 and the Modern State Government* (New York: National Municipal League, 1978), p. 8.

6. Joseph A. Schlesinger, "The Politics of the Executive," in *Politics in the American States,* ed. Herbert Jacob and Kenneth Vines, 2nd ed. (Boston: Little, Brown, 1971), p. 232.

7. In *Silver v. Pataki* 96 NY2d 532 (2001. *Pataki v. Assembly* 2004 NYSlipOp 02980), decided April 22, 2004. In this later case the court ruled that state legislators had unconstitutionally rewritten some appropriations bills sent to them by Pataki in connection with the 2001-2002 fiscal year and improperly sent the governor back bills in inappropriate forms. The forty-six "baseline" budget bills adopted by the legislature in August 2001 were an attempt by lawmakers to force the governor to the negotiating table. (The budget process was later completely derailed by the September 11 attacks). The move did not work from a political standpoint—Pataki did not yield—

and neither was it legal because, according to the court, under the state constitution lawmakers are not authorized to change language in spending bills received from the governor. They may only strike out or reduce specific appropriations or add new ones. The constitutional action, the court said, would have been for lawmakers to refuse to pass the Pataki appropriation bills and forced him to the bargaining table to work out new bills agreeable to all sides. The Democrat-dominated state assembly pledged to appeal the decision to the court of appeals.

8. Thad Beyle, "The Governor's Power of Organization," in *State Government,* 1982, pp. 79-87.

9. New York State Constitution, Article IV, Section 3.

10. Elizabeth Benjamin, "Pataki Still Seen As Strong Leader," *Albany Times Union,* June 26, 2003, p. B2.

11. George Pataki with Daniel Paisner, *Pataki: An Autobiography* (New York: Viking Press, 1998), p. 210.

12. Ron Dreher, "Where the Son Doesn't Follow," *National Review On Line.* September 4, 2002, http://www.nationalreview.com/dreher/.

13. *New Yorker,* February 22, 1982, p. 105.

14. Robert Connery and Gerald Benjamin, *Rockefeller of New York: Executive Power in the Statehouse* (Ithaca: Cornell University Press, 1979), p. 418.

15. See Schlesinger, *Politics of the Executive,* p. 233.

16. Larry Sabato, *Goodbye to Goodtime Charley,* rev. ed. (Washington, D.C.: CQ Press, 1982), p. 8.

17. Jennifer Steinhauer and Raymond Hernandez, "City and State at Odds on Aid to Fight Terror," *New York Times,* April 3, 2003, p. 1.

18. Richard Norton Smith, *Thomas E. Dewey and His Times* (New York: Simon and Schuster, 1982), chap. 11.

19. Connery and Benjamin, p. 117.

20. James E. Underwood and William Daniels, *Governor Rockefeller in New York: The Apex of Pragmatic Liberalism in the United States* (Westport, CT: Greenwood Press, 1982), p. 110.

21. Al Baker. "As a Leader, Pataki Makes No Decision Before Its Time," *New York Times,* April 6, 2004, p. B1.

22. Ibid.

23. Ibid.

24. Elizabeth Benjamin, "Pataki Aide Brings Own Style to Key Job," *Albany Times Union,* March 18, 2002, p. A1.

25. "The Governor's Chief Bureaucracy Buster," Interview with Robert L. King, *Rockefeller Institute Bulletin* (1998), pp. 104–109.

26. Barbara Grumet, "Willowbrook Reforms: A Pandora's Box?" *Empire State Report,* December 1975, pp. 469–63.

27. *County of Oneida v. Berle,* 49 N.Y 2nd 515 (1980).

28. *Boryszewski v. Bridges,* 37 N.Y 2nd 361 *(1975).*

29. *New York Times,* October 4, 1990, p. B9.

30. New York Constitution, Article XVII.

31. Connery and Benjamin, p. 91; and Gerald Benjamin and T. Norman Hurd, eds., *Rockefeller in Retrospect: The Governor's New York Legacy* (Albany: Nelson A. Rockefeller Institute of Government, 1984).

32. For a detailed analysis, with particular reference to decision making regarding budgeting, see Gerald Benjamin, "Reform in New York: The Budget, the Legislature and the Governance Process," paper given at the Citizens Budget Commission Conference on "Fixing New York State's Fiscal Practices," November 13–14, 2003, New York City.

33. Janice Prindle, "Assessing the Legislature's Saratoga Session," *Empire State Report,* September 1976, pp. 296–302; *Anderson v. Regan,* 53 N.Y. 2nd 367 (1982); and Joseph F. Zimmerman, "Rebirth of the Item Veto in New York State," *State Government,* 54 (1981): 51–52.

34. Pataki with Paisner, pp. 202–209.

35. See Edward Schneir and John Brian Murtaugh, *New York Politics: A Tale of Two States* (Armonk, NY: M. E. Sharpe, 2001), pp. 192–194.

36. Marc Santora, "Democrats Seek Bigger Aid Rise to City Schools," *New York Times,* June 3, 2004, p. B8.

37. On the veto, see generally Frank Prescott and Joseph F. Zimmerman, *The Politics of the Veto of Legislation in New York,* 2 vols. (Baltimore: University Press of America, 1980).

38. *King v. Cuomo,* 81 N.Y. 2nd 247 (1993).

39. *New York Times,* December 3, 1972, p. 41.

40. Humphrey Tyler, "The Legislature, Profile in Rancor," *Empire State Report* (May 1976): 31ff.

41. George Marlin. "New York's Republican Stumble: How Governor Pataki Fed, Rather Than Fought, Government Bloat," *American Enterprise* (October-November, 2003): 44ff. See also Noam Schneider, "Liberal Arts: the Political Reeducation of George Pataki," *New Republic,* June 17, 2002, p. 20ff.

42. Pataki with Paisner, p. 118.

43. "The Governorship in History," in *Governing the Empire State,* ed. Robert Connery and Gerald Benjamin (New York: Academy of Political Science, 1974), p. 16. Underwood and Daniels, *Governor Rockefeller in New York,* strike a similar theme using the term "pragmatic liberalism."

44. See for example, Peter D. McClelland and Alan L. Magdovitz, *Crisis in the Making* (New York: Cambridge University Press, 1981).

CHAPTER 8

The Legislature, Parties, and Resolving Conflict

JEFFREY M. STONECASH AND AMY WIDESTROM

The legislature is the primary political institution for representing the
diversity of public concerns within the state, and within New York there
is considerable diversity to represent. Legislative districts vary from an average income of $17,000 to over $125,000. Their local property tax bases vary
accordingly, creating large differences in the ability to provide tax revenue for
local schools. The percentage nonwhite within districts varies from 1 percent
to over 99 percent. Some districts are completely rural and others are densely
urban. These differences create conflicts among legislators about what policies should be pursued, what taxes should be imposed, and how benefits
should be distributed. The continual challenge facing the legislature is how
to reconcile the conflicting policy needs emerging from these districts and
reach some policy agreements.

For the last thirty years the struggle for policy agreements has been
shaped by parties and the divided partisan control of the legislature. Since
1974 the Democrats have held the majority in the assembly, and Republicans have held the majority in the senate. The majority parties in each house
have very different constituency bases, which leads to very different policy
preferences between the two parties. Democrats in the assembly do much
better in districts that are urban, lower income, and dominated by nonwhites. Republicans in the senate do better in districts that are suburban and
rural, higher income, and largely white.

While the majority parties differ significantly in their primary constituencies, there are tensions within each party. Each majority party may

have, on average, a typical constituency, but, as noted in chapter 3, *each party needs to retain the seats it has in areas less receptive to its core approach to government.*[1] Assembly Democrats hold almost all the seats in New York City. The party has a strong Black, Puerto Rican, and Hispanic Caucus with forty-one members.[2] Members from the caucus seek more resources for New York City and for minorities. New York City members in general lobby for the party to be liberal and address urban problems. The key to retaining the majority in the assembly, however, lies in the Democratic seats held outside New York City. Following the 2002 elections Democrats had 102 seats and 39 of them were from outside New York City. These members from outside New York City are generally not as liberal as the members from areas within New York City. These members argue that they cannot run for reelection as a part of a party that is consistently seen as liberal and supporting higher taxes and more redistribution to urban and minority populations. As the Democratic Party approaches bargaining with the senate and the governor, the party must reconcile the needs of these diverse and contending perspectives before it can bargain with the senate or the governor.

In the senate, the areas of Republican dominance are the upstate rural areas and Long Island. They hold almost all of the seats in these areas. But Republicans could not hold the senate without the seats they hold in New York City and upstate urban areas. Following the 2002 elections they held 5 seats in New York City and 31 seats outside New York City. The New York City Republicans are generally more liberal (particularly on civil liberties issues) than their upstate colleagues, and they advocate for more consideration for New York City's problems. Much as with the Democrats, the Republicans control their house by winning seats in areas that are not predisposed to elect Republicans. The Republican Party, as we shall see later with the rent control issue in 1997, cannot ask the New York City members to vote against New York City. The senate must reconcile the needs of these diverse constituencies before it can bargain with the assembly and the governor. For both parties, the process of reconciling differences within the party is crucial and continuous as the decision process evolves.

THE ENDURING IMPORTANCE OF LEADERSHIP

Bringing legislators together to reach policy agreements is not an easy task. The New York legislature has resolved this problem for sometime by relying on strong leadership.[3] The leadership of each house allocates resources among members, presides over the party conferences, plays a major if not dominant role in setting party strategy, and represents the party in most policy negotiations. This leadership is not, however, unrestrained. It is ultimately based in the wishes of the members. The leadership has considerable power, but it does not control members. It is granted this power because the members generally support a significant leadership role in shaping behavior within the legislature.

The practice of granting the leadership such authority exists for several reasons. The formal rules of both houses grant the leadership considerable discretion in allocating resources and positions. Leadership positions and committee chairs do not have to be appointed on the basis of seniority, and these positions are designated at the discretion of the leadership. Each member is guaranteed a minimal staff budget of approximately fifty thousand dollars, a very small amount of money for hiring staff. Much larger staff budgets are awarded at the discretion of the leadership.

These rules exist because the majority of the members find that strong leadership generally suits their needs. David Rhode provides a succinct summary of what creates strong leadership:

- The key to understanding legislative leadership lies in the membership, not in the leaders.
- If a party has sufficient consensus on issues, it may create strong leaders to act as its agents in pursuing the party's legislative agenda.
- The members sacrifice a *limited* amount of their independence to the leaders, because the commonality of preferences ensures that most members would only rarely be pressured to take an action they do not prefer.
- Instead of party leadership being the cause of high party cohesion, cohesive parties are the main precondition for strong leadership.
- Strong leaders are still possible in an era of individualistic members, but the collective membership becomes "the Boss."[4]

In the New York Legislature, understanding the dominance of parties and leaders within parties begins with recognizing the different constituencies within the parties. They recognize that they must find a way to reconcile their conflicting interests. They want leadership which works toward a consensus, while using their interests as the basis for that consensus. To most members, strong leadership is a self-inflicted "necessary evil" to achieve agreement. As long as the leadership is responsive to member needs, the members are likely to continue to support a strong leadership system.

THE EMERGENCE OF PROFESSIONAL LEGISLATORS

While strong leadership has a long tradition in the New York Legislature, that tradition faces continuing challenges. The legislature has changed, and those changes have created even greater needs for leadership, but they have also made the task of providing leadership more difficult. Perhaps the most significant change has been the emergence of full-time legislators who seek to be reelected, stay in office for numerous terms, and devote themselves full-time to the position. These legislators are more independent and less inclined to neglect their constituency just to comply with the need of a leader for their vote. It is harder to form a consensus among these new legislators.

Across the country there has been a gradual increase in the desire of legislators to remain in legislatures.[5] In New York,[6] as shown in figure 8.1, from the latter part of the 1800s through the 1930s, there was a gradual and steady increase in the percentage of legislators seeking reelection—rising from about 40 percent to 90 percent during that period. It has stayed at around that level since then. For reasons we do not understand, the legislature became a very attractive place to return to by the 1930s. This occurred even though the real value of legislative salaries was gradually eroding due to inflation.

The success of incumbents in winning reelection, shown in figure 8.1, has been relatively stable in New York since 1900. The percentage of incumbents (among those seeking reelection) winning reelection has generally been above 90 percent over the last century. The major change has been the steady increase in the percentage seeking reelection. The consequence of increased pursuit of office and a steady rate of success in retaining it has been a rise in the average number of years legislators remain in the legislature. More and more of these legislators have turned it into a career and devote themselves full-time to the position.[7] Figure 8.2 indicates, for the first year of each new legislative session, the average number of years those legislators have been in office. The average has increased steadily since 1900.

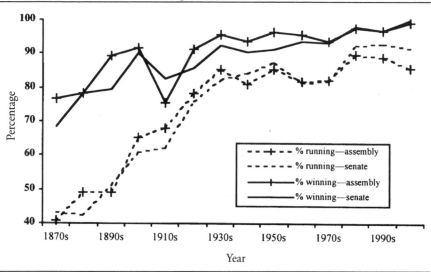

FIGURE 8.1.
Percentage of assembly members and senators seeking
and winning reelection, 1870–2000

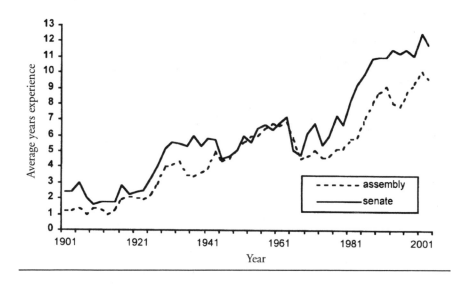

FIGURE 8.2.
Average years in office at start of each new session, 1901–2003

The emergence of professional legislators has had two significant consequences. The legislature is now comprised of politicians who are very concerned about having an impact and who want to have an effect on public policy. They have a strong interest in having the legislature be an equal partner with the governor in making decisions.

These same reasons, however, make it more difficult to get legislators to form a policy consensus.[8] Almost all of them want to be reelected, they are concerned with forming policy that is good for their districts, and they are less inclined to comply with leaders just to reach an agreement. They are more likely to hold out for budget and policy agreements which serve the needs of their constituents. These motives create a legislature that seeks to have an impact, but one in which the process of reaching agreements is not easy. In this situation—internally diverse parties, with members who are less docile and more interested in the decisions made—the role of leadership in forging a consensus becomes crucial. The members may not want strong leadership, but they continue to find it very valuable.

LEADERSHIP: RESPONDING TO MEMBER NEEDS

The task of the leadership is to pull together the diverse members within their parties, and then negotiate with the other house and the governor. The task requires some delicacy and relentless hard work. If leaders are to succeed, they must listen to members and respond to their needs, but push them to compromise when necessary. Leaders fulfill this role through several practices. First, leaders explicitly derive their ongoing policy positions from the members by consistently relying on party conferences to hear what the members are willing to accept as policy positions. Party conferences are closed-door sessions held off the chamber floor on a regular basis for legislators only. In those sessions, members are free to make arguments about policy directions. It is within these conferences that the limits of what the members can accept are determined. The leadership is then generally free within those limits to negotiate with the other house and the governor over policy. This reliance on member opinions is crucial for leadership legitimacy. While the news media continually underplay this interaction between members and the leadership, it is essential to maintaining the system.

With the process of member needs ongoing, specific negotiations can then be delegated to the leaders. This delegation is valuable for the members.

Legislators want to have some impact on policy and they want to get reelected. Conference and informal discussions with the leadership give members opportunities to try to influence policy. Turning negotiations about specifics over to the leadership frees the members to spend more time focusing on and dealing with district concerns that will enhance their reelection chances. With this arrangement, legislators do not need to be in the state capital on a full-time basis because the leadership assumes responsibility for negotiations and the management of day-to-day legislative business. This allows the practice regularly witnessed every session, in which members devote as little time as possible to remaining in Albany.

Members also find the strong leadership system valuable because it organizes the concerns of legislators and constrains legislators from becoming fragmented as each seeks to pursue individual concerns. As Jim Tallon, the former majority leader of the assembly, put it, the party recognizes it must ultimately govern and make decisions. A strong leadership system allows members to argue about what policies to pursue, but it imposes discipline without which decisions might not get made. Many members look with dismay upon practices in Congress, where decision making is decentralized and members must spend all their time in Washington negotiating fine points of the law.

A strong leadership system also persists because leaders use their power to distribute resources to each member according to need. More senior members, who understand the legislative process better, and who may want to play a greater role in shaping policy, are allocated more leadership and committee chair positions. They also pass more bills.[9] This allows senior members to have more influence on legislation, and it allows them to build records of passing and claiming credit for legislation. Regardless of whether members wish to actually change social conditions or just claim credit for legislation, this satisfies more senior members.

Newer members often have other concerns. Some are very ambitious and concerned with establishing a record of legislative accomplishments. These members receive help from the leadership in terms of staff assistance with bills.[10] Others are more concerned with their next election. They may have faced a close election in their initial run for office and they want to build up their name recognition in the district. Their concern is likely to focus on receiving assistance in campaigns and obtaining aid from the legislative party campaign committees.[11] To be able to allocate campaign resources to these new and marginal members, the party leadership has to have enough discipline to deny resources to members who do not face close races.[12]

The party leadership continually faces the task of responding to the varying needs of the members. It must convince younger members and members with small electoral margins that the party will respond to their needs and try to enhance their reelection chances. It must also convince newer members that their policy views will be heard and their concerns accommodated. At the same time the leadership must satisfy more senior members who have waited their turn and now want to have a greater role in the process. Thus far, leaders appear to have done this well.

The inclination of members to continue with a strong leadership system is increased because of the importance of majority control. The majority party controls the bulk of legislative resources. It determines which bills pass, and it is able to raise more money than the minority within its house because of that power. These advantages provide a powerful incentive to remain in the majority. Majority members are inclined to work together as a party to retain this majority power. The members are willing to make the leader the individual responsible for marshaling and distributing party resources to keep the party in power and maintain their control over legislative resources.

There are, to be sure, some members who are less satisfied with strong leadership. At times the number dissatisfied can increase sufficiently to lead to a change in leadership or a challenge to leadership. In 1989 the president of the senate, from an upstate district, was displaced by a member from Long Island because of dissatisfaction among the Long Island members over the amount of school aid negotiated for that area with the governor. In 2001 an assembly member challenged the existing speaker, arguing that he was not listening to the members enough. The speaker, using all of his resources to reward and punish dissenting members, was able to beat back the challenge. The lesson to leaders is that it is crucial to listen to members and maintain their support.

While most members see virtues in strong leadership, there are political trends that may push legislators to be wary of being too amenable to leadership influence. Ticket splitting by voters has increased, negative ads can have a quick and devastating effect, and legislators always want to stress their image of independence. They know that it is important to fight for the needs of their district when decisions are made. All this makes them less amenable to leadership domination.

Faced with the political needs of individual legislators, the leadership must act with some skill. Leaders must listen and respond while pushing for consensus and party cohesion. In recent decades, exerting influence over legislators has been harder because of their independence. As recent leaders have argued in public interviews, it is now necessary to work very hard to listen to make sure district needs are accommodated while seeking to form a consensus.

In 1998 the leaders of both houses responded to media criticism of the dominance of leaders in negotiating budgets and the grumbling of some members and created conference committees joining members from both houses to negotiate parts of the budget. The leadership of the two houses first agreed on a total budget amount and then had committees focusing on specific policy areas negotiate budget agreements within their area, within the confines of the overall budget agreement.[13] This was a way to get more members involved.

This experiment, however, did not fundamentally change the role of leadership and has not been used much since then. It was clear that even with this new approach, leaders played a significant role in setting the broader parameters of the committee negotiations. In addition, in 1998 it may have been easier to use this approach, since there were no major policy issues to resolve and the state was running an enormous surplus, making it easier to reach agreement. Finally, and perhaps most important, as discussed above, the system of strong leadership, as it works now, provides many benefits to members. The members are unlikely to be willing to abandon the system.[14]

The continuation of strong leadership may also be helped along by the fact that most legislators in New York do not have close elections. In 2002, for example, the average margin of victory—the difference between winners and losers—was 58 percentage points in the assembly and 65 percentage points in the senate. Only 10 percent of all winners won with less than 60 percent of the vote. Few legislators face close elections, and that may give them more room to grant discretion in policy negotiations. There are also a limited number of new legislators entering the system every two years. This may make it easier to socialize new members into accepting this practice. For all these reasons, strong leadership persists.

The durability of this approach is indicated by the abrupt but smooth transition in the assembly in 1991 from Mel Miller to Saul Weprin, and then to Sheldon Silver in 1994 when Weprin became incapacitated by illness. The question was who would become speaker, not whether there would be some sort of change in the system. When Joe Bruno replaced Ralph Marino as president of the senate in a leadership battle, the strong leadership pattern persisted.

"THREE MEN IN A ROOM"

The press and the public generally do not see such a reciprocal relationship between leaders and members. The general conclusion is that members are dependent on dominating leaders. From this perspective, the primary concern of members is to retain their seats, have a safe legislative district drawn for them, avoid controversy, be appointed to positions that carry an extra stipend in pay, and be able to claim they brought home benefits ("pork") to specific groups. Leaders can help members avoid having to make controversial votes by keeping conflictual issues off the floor. Leaders can also acquire considerable influence over members by selectively providing campaign funds, controlling appointments as chair of a committee, or doling out budgetary funds for local projects. Members who do not comply with the leadership can have all these benefits withdrawn, which can intimidate members. In this view, influence runs only one way, from leaders over members.

The suggestion of this portrayal of relationships is that members are largely bullied, compliant, and perhaps even docile. Most troubling is the vague suggestion that members either restrain their advocacy for their district or are pressured to vote against district needs, to vote as the leadership wishes. As a result, policy debates are more reflective of the desires of stubborn leaders than of the collective concerns of members. To critics of the process, representation is distorted and democracy is not well served.

Despite the pervasiveness of this view in the press,[15] these portrayals hinge on a dubious presumption about the nature of assembly members. The most important issue in this portrayal is representation, and the assumption that members are pressured to vote against district interests to serve the needs of leaders. Such behavior would encourage members to risk giving challengers material to use against them in a campaign. It presumes that members would risk appearing out of touch with their district and gamble their position to please a leader. It presumes a leader would risk losing a member for personal reasons (which are never really articulated). *It presumes that members would systematically risk a position to keep it.* Every member knows that the opposing party is continually looking for such votes and has campaign workers and money ready to help a challenger who could use such information. Very few will risk setting off such a response by the opposing party. In reality, members are continually preoccupied with understanding and representing their district, and while there may be a few members who are relatively compliant to the leadership, there is no evidence that many fall into this category. Critics seem to adopt the approach that leadership, regardless of who holds positions, is prone to be abusive and is not desired by the members. Rather than assess how leader-member interactions work and vary by issue, critics and journalists generally simply assume they are detrimental to representation and dispense this view uncritically to the public.

THE RISE OF PROFESSIONAL STAFF

The emergence of legislators desiring to have an impact has also lead to a significant increase in the capacity of the legislature to play a role in policy debates. There has been a tremendous increase in legislative staff during the last several decades. During the Nelson Rockefeller era (1959–1973) the legislature was widely perceived as subordinate to the governor and incapable of making policy initiatives in most areas. It was generally in a position of responding to gubernatorial initiatives.[16] This dependence was recognized by both legislative parties and both parties supported a significant increase in legislative resources in response to that situation. Support for these changes also came from various groups outside the legislature, such as the New York Bar Association and academics.[17]

To increase the capability of the legislature, there has been a significant increase in the number of staff, the amount of office space, and the use of computers to handle information. These changes were intended to give the legislature the ability to conduct its own research and analyses and formulate its own policy positions.[18] During the early 1970s the legislature also created district offices so legislators could independently receive and respond to constituent concerns.

The legislature now also meets longer. During the 1950s it met approximately one hundred days a year. Sessions usually ended sometime in March or April. During the 1960s the number of session days began to increase. By the end of the 1970s the legislature was regularly in session until July 1. Eventually it decided to not adjourn at all so it could reconvene at its own discretion. Otherwise the legislators could meet only when the governor called them into session. This reduces the ability of the governor to act without the involvement of the legislature.

To do all these things, the legislature has allocated itself more money. There has been a significant increase in the overall budget since the 1950s. The most significant increases occurred from 1960 through 1990. The increase has gone almost entirely into general legislative resources—staff, equipment, telephones, and so on—and not into the salaries of legislators. Figure 8.3 indicates the growth of the legislative budget, expressed in real dollars—adjusted for inflation—since the early 1900s. The total budget is presented, along with the portion going to legislator salaries. The difference between the two provides a crude indicator of the growth of staff resources, including office space and equipment. The significant growth in general staff resources began in the 1960s.

The legislature now has the staff to conduct its own analyses and to form its own proposals. There are now staff members who have been through numerous budget negotiations and who are able to quickly determine the governor's position. They have "institutional memory" and are not ignorant of past debates and decisions. There are staff who conduct long range studies on policy development and oversight. Staff of the Assembly

FIGURE 8.3.
New York legislative budget, in real dollars, 1900–2002

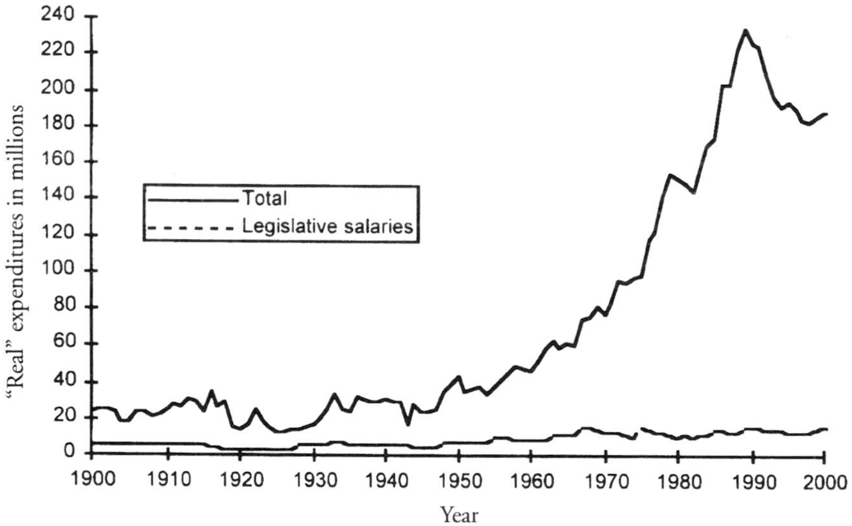

Ways and Means Committee and the Senate Finance Committee either conduct or contract for economic forecasts for the state to help guide them in conducting analyses of anticipated revenues. Legislative staff members still rely on executive branch agencies for information, but the era when the legislature had to rely on executive branch personnel for interpreting that information is over. All these changes have made the legislature a more active and independent participant in the decision process. The legislature as an institution is less passive and reactive than twenty years ago.

This assertion of influence has not gone unchallenged by the governor. During the early 1990s Governor Pataki asserted his right to veto selected language in bills passed by the legislature, resulting in a lawsuit by the legislature over the constitutionality of that assertion. Subsequently the governor vetoed specific budgetary appropriations that were additions to his budget, arguing that the legislature had to accept his budget or not, but could not add to it. That generated another lawsuit. These lawsuits are pending. In 1999 when the legislature wanted an increase in salary, having gone without one since 1989, the governor agreed to the change only if the legislature agreed to a provision that would withhold their pay until the budget passed, while his pay would not be withheld.

This developing institutional tension may explain how passage of the 2003 budget was resolved. After years of not passing a state budget by the April 1 deadline, the legislature and governor entered the 2003 budget cycle under pressure to achieve agreement on time. Yet as the date approached it became clear that for the nineteenth year in a row this would not be possible.[19] Unique to this cycle, however, was the "unusual agreement" between Senate Majority Leader Joe Bruno, a Republican, and Assembly Speaker Sheldon Silver, a Democrat.[20] When Pataki vetoed the legislature's budget, this agreement allowed the legislature to override Pataki's veto in just four hours and pass the 2003 state budget independent of the governor's approval. This display of legislative independence would not have been possible without the institutional growth that had been occurring over the past several decades.

THE LEGISLATURE IN THE DECISION PROCESS

All these changes have affected the speed with which issues are resolved in Albany. The legislature has evolved from playing a minor role to a major role:

"In the early 1950s when Thomas E. Dewey was governor, the legislative leaders were called to the governor's office after the budget was virtually settled. The leaders were told there was some discretionary money in the budget for small legislator projects. The leadership was expected to take the budget back to the members and pass it as it stood. They usually did so."[21]

In 1983 Mario Cuomo was the new Democratic governor. He presided over a budget negotiated among himself, the president of the Republican-held senate, and Speaker of the Democratic-held assembly. Afterwards he claimed most of the credit for passing the budget. The legislative leaders, angered by his credit claiming, negotiated the next budget between the two houses, and then presented it to the governor with instructions to sign it.[22] The process had changed.

The combination of a more professional legislature and divided control of the legislature has reshaped the decision process. There are now ongoing institutional battles between the houses and between the legislature and the governor. Each house of the legislature first establishes its own positions internally and then begins negotiations with the other house and the governor. There is less willingness to make quick accommodations.

The combination of political parties with clearly different constituencies and policy concerns, divided house control, strong leadership, and professional legislators makes decision processes more difficult and lengthier. In recent years no budgets have passed by the April 1 deadline. The last decade has seen some significant delays past the April 1 deadline. While much has been made of these delays, they are really part of a long-term trend of institutional development and longer decision processes in Albany. Figure 8.4 indicates how many budgets have been passed before and after the April 1 deadline since that deadline date was adopted in 1944. The present divided control of the legislature has surely accentuated the problems of delay, but the primary change has been in the ability of the legislature to formulate its own proposals, pursue them, and hold out until they get some of what they want. Delays are likely to persist, and they reflect serious substantive disagreements which take time to resolve.

PUBLIC FRUSTRATIONS

The delays in the budget process are enormously frustrating to the public and the press.[23] There is a widespread expectation that a deadline should be

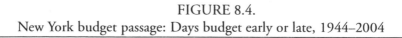

FIGURE 8.4.
New York budget passage: Days budget early or late, 1944–2004

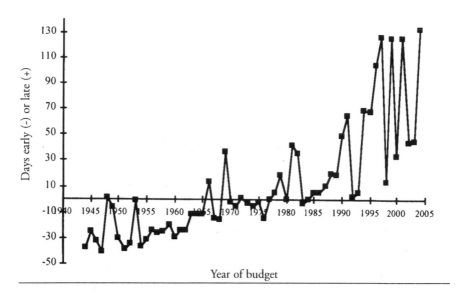

met, and delays cause enormous problems for organizations dependent on state funds, such as school districts. In recent years these delays have prompted numerous assessments that the legislature is in serious trouble and should be reformed.[24] There are periodic proposals to change the budget deadline date, impose a continuation of the prior year's budget, or severely penalize legislators for late budgets.

While these reactions are understandable, they neglect two crucial matters. The primary reason for these delays is that the state contains remarkable diversity (see chapters 3 and part 3, on policy issues) and there are significant policy differences between the parties. These conflicts between the parties are difficult to reconcile. Further, even before the parties can negotiate with each other, they must reconcile the differences within their diverse party conferences. New York City members do not constitute a majority of the Assembly, so to create a majority Democrats must also allocate benefits to upstate and suburban members. In the senate, the leader must create a consensus among members from rural upstate, New York City, and the suburbs around New York City. Negotiating within the conference and then with the other house is a laborious process, and one in which it is important not to look too eager to reach an agreement.

The crucial matter is that there are serious underlying conflicts and it takes time to negotiate a compromise. Delays are not because of incompetence or because members are not representing their districts. Indeed, they occur because members are holding out for their views, and cajoling them into a compromise is not an easy task. It is easy to create a simple portrait that three stubborn leaders in Albany are holding up budgets, but leaders are in reality struggling to build a consensus that members will accept. While this process frustrates the public, the argument that the legislature is failing denies the extent of conflict in the state and the impact of the relentless representation and advocacy that individual members are engaged in. Building support and legitimacy for compromises within a democracy is difficult, and the process in New York reflects how protracted that process can become in a legislature filled with veterans from diverse districts who take issues seriously.

In 2004 the legislature set a record for lateness in passing a budget. The primary reason for the delay was the conflict over how to respond to a court decision that New York City schools were underfunded and the state should provide more funds to the city. The conflicts involved in this issue are enormous. Conservatives are not convinced that the solution is more money and they do not want to permanently increase funding and taxes, but they do not want to look antischools or anti-New York City, since they have members in the city, so stalling becomes an important strategy. Liberals and Democrats in the Assembly saw this as a once-in-a-lifetime chance to increase funding to education and lower-income districts, so they were unwilling to yield quickly. The result was further delay.

CASE STUDIES: CONSTITUENCIES, MEMBERS, LEADERS, AND PUBLIC POLICY

Legislative leaders in New York clearly lead, but to do so effectively, they must listen to members of their caucus. When leaders advocate policy positions and the majority conferences are lined up behind their leaders, the leaders enjoy considerable influence in negotiations with the other house or the governor. When leaders fall out of sync with their legislative constituencies by advocating policies that do not benefit members, they lose support and bargaining power. The following policy negotiations provide examples of the dynamics of decision making and power of legislative leaders when they have strong conference support, and what happens when that backing does not exist. The policy areas are welfare reform, rent control, and the linked issues of local property tax relief and school aid.

Leaders and Members in Agreement: Welfare Reform

In the wake of the national welfare reform of 1996, Governor George Pataki proposed a series of reforms designed to change the way New York's 1.2 million welfare recipients were treated. Two-thirds of welfare recipients live in New York City and are overwhelmingly represented by Democratic senators and assembly members. In an effort to "replace welfare checks with paychecks," Pataki's recommendations included an immediate across the board 25 percent cut in benefits from existing levels and a further gradual reduction in benefits over two years, a five-year lifetime limit on eligibility for benefits, and measures requiring retraining, drug testing of recipients, and denial of benefits to immigrants and people convicted of crimes. Instead of cash grants to recipients, Pataki's plan called for a voucher program which would provide specific assistance for housing and basic necessities.[25]

Pataki's plan came under immediate fire from Democrats in the assembly and county-level Republicans. Democrats were opposed on several grounds. Because many of their members represent urban poor areas, the planned cuts were liable to disproportionately affect people in their districts. This was particularly unacceptable because the new federal welfare legislation gave states more funds than necessary to support the existing welfare case loads of 1997. Democrats saw no need to cut support. Democrats were also resistant to the vouchers approach because Pataki did not specify how the program would be implemented. Finally, the combination of the proposed elimination of rent control coupled with welfare-benefit reductions would create an intolerable and untenable political situation. In response, assembly Democrats proposed changes that would move the state into compliance with national regulations, but without the substantial cuts proposed by the governor. Republican county executives across the state resisted the idea of drug testing as expensive and unnecessary for most welfare clients. Because individual senators represent small portions of the state, Senate President Joseph Bruno of Rensselaer County suggested that the county positions would likely effect how the senate considered any reform legislation.

With organized opposition from the Democrats, led by Assembly Speaker Sheldon Silver of Manahttan, and no particular clamor of support for Pataki's plan from rural and suburban voters, Pataki's plan was repeatedly defeated throughout 1996 and 1997. In the end, faced with a federal deadline to comply with new regulations and little interest in Pataki's proposed changes among the public or among members of the Republican senate conference, Bruno and the governor agreed to the assembly Democrats' two main points of reform regarding the continuation of cash benefits and an upward adjustment of the level of earnings welfare recipients could receive while maintaining eligibility. The provisions the legislature passed included a small shift toward vouchers while maintaining overall benefit levels.[26] Assembly Democrats, adamant in their opposition and more unified than the Republican governor and senate, won the day. A leader with a unified party conference and little public attention to the issue prevailed.

Rent Control: A Leader Who Outran His Conference

Originally established as temporary measures in 1947, laws governing the costs of rental housing were politically popular and staunchly defended by the citizens who enjoyed the benefits of fixed rental costs in some of the most expensive real estate markets in the state. More than 1.1 million units of rental housing are covered under these regulations in New York City and downstate counties of Nassau, Rockland, and Westchester. Rent control laws were up for renewal in June, 1997, and elected officials in these areas were loathe to go against the tide of local opinion.

In December 1996, Senator Joseph Bruno, president leader of the senate, launched a major initiative to dismantle rent control laws. Bruno, who represents an upstate district, proposed eliminating all rent controls by 1999 or letting existing laws expire if a new plan could not be developed. While extremely popular in and around New York City, Republicans generally disliked rent regulation because they favor less government intrusion and reliance on market forces to govern private transactions such as housing. On its face, it would seem that Bruno's proposal would have no problem sailing through the Republican-controlled senate. The proposal, however, was highly controversial in downstate districts held by Republican senators and was met with a firestorm, not just from angry tenants and the Democratic opposition seeing a Republican attack in areas it overwhelmingly represented, but from within Bruno's own party.

Bruno's proposal had the most significant implications for Republican senators from areas where rent control laws existed. The proposal offered them the choice between fulfilling the obligation of party loyalty in Albany or the obligation of supporting a program that was overwhelmingly popular in their home districts. As a fierce political and public relations battle raged among renters, landlords, the assembly and senate, it became apparent that the costs of successfully getting a bill through the senate would likely irreparably damage several downstate Republicans, which could endanger the Republican five-seat majority in the senate. Confronted by the needs of New York City conference members who found Bruno's proposals dangerous to their reelection, Bruno had to agree to a Pataki-backed compromise that made incremental changes to rent control, but left the program essentially intact through 2003.[27] For a review of the dynamics of these negotiations, see the accompanying "summary box" on rent control.

Rent Control: A Leader Simply Can't Ask
Members to Vote against Their Districts

The process of negotiating compromise on legislative initiatives can involve many actors within the legislature and beyond and can be quite time consuming. Among the more dramatic episodes of public negotiation, Senate President Joseph Bruno's attempt to eliminate rent control played out over several months. In the end each of the participants in this process had some piece of what they wanted, but no one got everything they wished.

December 1996: With little advance warning, Senator Bruno reveals intentions to radically reform rent control laws or allow existing laws to expire in June 1997.

April 1997: Rent control supporters in New York city pressure six Republican Senators from areas affected by rent control laws. Two senators, Guy Velella and Nicholas Spano, announce support for extension of existing laws instead of Bruno's proposed reforms. Four other senators, including a deputy majority leader picked by Bruno, remain undecided. Party discipline narrowly holds in a procedural vote after the first debate regarding the Bruno Plan on the senate floor. Bruno, who controls participation of his party members is the only Republican to speak. Following the close vote, Bruno signals a willingness to compromise on the timetable for rent decontrol.

May 1997: After a long silence on the matter, Governor George Pataki proposes eliminating rent control subsidies for high-income tenants and a system of "vacancy decontrol"—ending rent subsidies when the current tenant moves out. Assembly Speaker Sheldon Silver announces strenuous opposition to vacancy decontrol.

June 1997: With days to go before existing rent control laws expire, a series of meetings between Bruno and downstate senators is held. Polls show over 70 percent of New York City residents wanting to retain some form of rent control and 80 percent opposed to the simple expiration of existing protections. Downstate Republican senators argue that even a vote of opposition to rent control would be politically damaging. Opposition within the Republican party would likely lead to a one-vote majority for Bruno, with several important Republican defections. This would be seen as a sign of weakness in the leadership.

With several Republican senators in open revolt, Governor Pataki offers public cover to Bruno to allow him to back away from his plan. Acknowledging Bruno's philosophical opposition to rent control, Pataki suggests that rent control "is a very important practical question for millions of people in New York City and other areas . . . that rely on rent control and . . . you simply can't insist on a philosophical position."

July 1997: Although opposed to such governmental interventions, Bruno is left with little choice but to back the plan his majority conference supports. A few days after existing laws expire, Bruno and Assembly Speaker Silver reach a compromise which eliminates rent subsidies for high-income tenants, limits the ability to pass apartments to relatives, and allows limited rent increases when vacancies occur, but leaves most of the existing program of rent control subsidies in place through June 2003. The legislation makes no provision for further decontrol.[28]

While the welfare reform process demonstrated the power of a party conference united behind its leader, the rent control controversy demonstrates what happens when a leader makes decisions without consulting the party conference. Without close communication and attention to the preferences and political imperatives of followers, a legislative leader can chart a path that is potentially destructive to maintaining the majority which allows the leader a role in the policy process.

Different Houses, Different Agendas: Property-Tax Relief and Urban School Aid

Sometimes party leaders are caught having to cope with how to counter a very popular gubernatorial proposal that does not do much for their party's constituencies. Their challenge is to bargain for something for their party while accepting the popular program. Property-tax relief was a major issue in Governor Pataki's election campaign and played well among the suburban and rural constituents of Republican senators. The primary source of revenue for local government and school districts, New York's property taxes are among the highest in the nation. The basic complaints were that property taxes were too high and that reliance on them created inequality across districts. In urban areas, property taxes do not generate as large a percentage of school operating revenues as in suburban and rural areas. Some of the shortfall is made up by the state, but it was a source of perennial resentment that little effort was made to equalize educational spending levels among the cities and suburbs. (Matters of local education and its funding are more fully discussed in chapter 12.)

Governor George Pataki ignored the inequality issue and chose to focus on cutting local property taxes. Under the State Tax Reduction (STAR) plan, property taxes would be reduced by 40 percent by 2002. A certain amount of the property value of each home would be exempt from local property taxes, and the lost local revenue would be made up from state funds. Pataki's program put the Democrats in a dilemma. Opposing a plan sold as general tax relief for everyone and providing the first relief to low-income senior-citizen property owners was political poison. As a practical matter, no political party can be opposed to a proposal which looks like a tax cut. Some have argued that STAR provides larger dollar cuts to Republican constituencies in the relatively more affluent suburban areas (downstate suburbs receive exemptions of $70,000 while others receive $30,000) than the Democrats' primarily urban constituency.[29] This awkward political position did not exclude Democrats from taking political advantage of the situation. While the Democrats were boxed into supporting Pataki's property-tax initiative,

Pataki was faced with moving the plan through the assembly. Any property-tax reform benefiting the constituencies of the governor and the Republican senate majority would have to be coupled with some sort of stable and plentiful funding formula for city schools.

A compromise was reached that resulted in the creation of two programs tailored to the two different constituencies represented by the majorities of both houses. While STAR would primarily benefit property owners in the Republicans' suburban and rural constituency, the Learning Achieving Developing by Directing Education Resources (LADDER) program would transfer greater state resources to primarily Democrat-represented urban districts. Property-tax reform easily passed through the assembly with the assurance that the LADDER program, featuring dedicated, annual state funding to urban school districts to assist with building maintenance and transportation costs, as well as funding to increase computer-based educational activities and to reduce class sizes, would soon follow.[30] With both programs in place, urban legislators got additional funding that was intended to provide some relief to urban districts, and Governor Pataki and the senate Republican conference got funds for lower taxes for their electoral constituency.

LEGISLATIVE LEADERSHIP: SOME OBSERVATIONS

Welfare reform was characterized by low public interest and uneven partisan interest in the legislature. Because of this, Republican agreement with the Democratic plan suggested no obvious political costs to members of the Republican-controlled senate. This left the leadership of both houses able to forge an agreement that was acceptable to both houses, leaving the governor with little choice but to accept. In the case of rent control, Majority Leader Bruno got out in front of an issue that was political dynamite for members of his conference. Rent-control reform represented a significant threat to the district interests of several Republican senators and had profound implications for the continuance of the Republicans as the senate majority party. Faced with a tremendous gap between the preferences of leadership and the practical needs of the conference, Bruno had little choice but to accept the compromise plan negotiated by Pataki and the assembly. Finally, the STAR and LADDER example demonstrates how chamber leadership and its members can negotiate programs appealing to their different constituencies.

In each case, the policy process is carried out through a process of bargaining over time between the house leadership and its conferees, between the houses, and between the legislature and the governor. Legislative leaders can bargain better to the extent that they know the preferences of their members and have their support for positions. As long as that relationship is effective, party discipline is maintained and policy is routed through a relatively simple process of negotiation and execution.

CONCLUSION

The legislature now is an equal partner with the governor in policy debates. The party conferences within the legislature serve as vehicles to form policy positions. The legislative staff generates information and studies to support party positions. At the same time the legislators have sufficient staff to explore policy issues in new areas to try to anticipate future situations. All this has allowed the legislative parties to participate in and structure policy debates within the state. There is now an ongoing dialogue between the houses and the political parties about what positions should be taken. The tradition of strong leadership allows them to create collective positions which allow a more focused debate. The legislature has developed both as a professional political institution and as a body fully capable of playing a major role in affecting policy choices.

NOTES

1. See also Gerald Benjamin, "The Political Relationship," in *The Two New Yorks*, ed. Gerald Benjamin and Charles Brecher (New York: Russell Sage Foundation, 1989).

2. For a discussion of the limits of the impact of the Black and Puerto Rican Caucus, see Ester R. Fuchs and J. Phillip Thompson, "Racial Politics in New York State," in *Governing New York State*, ed. Jeffrey M. Stonecash, John K. White, and Peter W. Colby (Albany: State University of New York Press, 1994), pp. 34–41.

3. Robert P. Weber, "The Speaker of the Assembly: Party Leadership in New York," Ph.D. dissertation, University of Rochester, 1975; Alan G.

Hevesi, *Legislative Politics in New York* (New York: Praeger, 1975); and John J. Pitney Jr., "Leaders and Rules in the New York State Senate," *Legislative Studies Quarterly* 7, no. 4 (November 1982): 491–506.

4. David W. Rhode, *Parties and Leaders in the Postreform House* (Chicago: University of Chicago Press, 1991), pp. 35–37.

5. Kwang S. Shin and John S. Jackson III, "Membership Turnover in U.S. State Legislatures: 1931–1976," *Legislative Studies Quarterly* 4, no. 1 (February 1979): 95–104.

6. Jeffrey M. Stonecash, "The Pursuit and Retention of Legislative Office in New York, 1870–1990: Reconsidering Sources of Change," *Polity* 27, no. 1 (Fall 1994): 25–47. The data were updated in January 2004.

7. An indicator of this is the proportion of legislators listing their occupation as "legislator" in the *Legislative Manual.* This proportion has increased dramatically in the last two decades. Informal discussions with legislators also suggest that relatively few of them have full-time occupations outside the legislature.

8. Interviews with Warren Anderson, temporary president of the senate, 1972–1988, and with Stanley Fink, speaker of the assembly, 1979–1986, in *The Modern New York Legislature: Redressing the Balance*, ed. Gerald Benjamin and Robert T. Nakamura (Albany: Nelson A. Rockefeller Institute, 1991), pp. 69 and 119.

9. Jeffrey M. Stonecash, *The Proposal and Disposal of Legislation in the New York Legislature* (Albany, NY: Assembly Intern Program, 2003).

10. *New York Times*, July 1, 1985, B2.

11. Jeffrey M. Stonecash, "Working at the Margins: Campaign Finance and Party Strategy in New York Assembly Elections," *Legislative Studies Quarterly* 13, no. 4 (November 1988): 477–93; Jeffrey M. Stonecash, "Campaign Finance in New York Senate Elections," *Legislative Studies Quarterly* 15, no. 2 (May 1990): 247–62; and Jeffrey M. Stonecash, "Where's the Party: Changing State Party Organizations," *American Politics Quarterly* 20, no. 3 (July 1992): 326–44.

12. Jeffrey M. Stonecash and Sara E. Keith, "Maintaining a Political Party: Providing and Withdrawing Campaign Funds," *Party Politics* 2, no. 3, (1996): 313–328.

13. Abby Goodnough, "Albany Legislative Leaders Quickly Agree on Most of Budget," *New York Times*, April 3, 1998, B1. Members reported being excited by the involvement, but they pointed out that it required much more work on their part. Whether they desire an increase in their workload remains to be seen.

14. Not all members, to be sure, are equally happy with the tradition of strong leadership. But enough have been placated that the tradition of strong leadership continues.

15. Those interested in press views of leadership and the process should see the articles or newspaper stories at sites such as *http://www.city-journal.org/html/5_2_new_yorks.html.* The Brennan Center has collected many of these at *http://www.brennancenter.org/programs/dem_vr_albanyreform_editorials.html* and *http://www.brennancenter.org/programs/dem_vr_albanyreform_newsstories.html.* A typical portrayal of the legislature is contained in a series run by the *New York Times* in 2002. See their series "The Albany Syndrome," October 2002. A particularly relevant story is James C. McKinley Jr., "Before Bills Move in Albany, 3 Leaders Cut Deals in Secret," October 20, 2002, A1. Another example is the *Syracuse Herald-American* series "Secrets of the Chamber," which ran in September 1994.

16. Interviews with Warren Anderson, temporary president of the senate, 1972–1988, Perry Duryea, speaker of the assembly, 1969–1974, and Stanley Fink, speaker of the assembly, 1979–1986, in Gerald Benjamin and Nakamura, *The Modern New York Legislature,* pp. 60, 115–18..

17. Perry Duryea, "Toward a More Effective Legislature," message to members of the New York State Assembly December 14, 1973; and New York State Bar Association, *Toward a More Effective Legislature* (Albany, NY: New York State Bar Association, 1975).

18. For studies of the development of the legislature and its conflicts with the governor, see Alan P. Balutis, "Legislative Staffing: A View from the States," in *Legislative Staffing,* ed. James J. Heaphy and Alan P. Balutis (New York: Wiley, 1975), pp. 106–37; Alan P. Balutis, "The Budgetary Process in New York State: The Role of the Legislative Staff," in *The Political Pursestrings: The Role of the Legislature in the Budgetary Process* (Beverly Hills, CA: Sage, 1975), pp. 139–72; Arthur J. Kremer, "The Resurgent Legislature in New York," *National Civic Review,* April 1978; and Alan G. Hevesi, "The Renewed Legislature," in *New York State Today,* ed. John K. White and Peter Colby, 2nd ed. (Albany: State University of New York Press, 1989), p. 168; interview with Warren Anderson, member of the Senate, 1952–1988, and temporary president of the senate, 1972–1988, in Benjamin and Nakamura, *Modern New York Legislature,* p. 60; Gerald Benjamin, "Budget Battles Between the Governor and Legislature: A Perennial New York Conflict," *Comparative State Politics Newsletter* 7, no. 4 (August 1986): 13–16; Diana Dwyre, Mark O'Gorman, Jeffrey M. Stonecash, and Rosalie Young, "Disorganized Politics and The Have-Nots: Politics and Taxes in New York and

California," *Polity* 27, no. 1 (Fall 1994): 25-47; Roman Hedges, "Legislative Staff as Institutional Partisans: The Case of Tax Reform in New York," *Journal of Management Science and Policy Analysis* 7, no. 1 (Fall 1989): 34–52; and Jeffrey M. Stonecash, "The Rise of the Legislature," in *New York Politics and Government*, ed. Sarah F. Liebschutz (Lincoln: University of Nebraska Press, 1998), pp. 80–92.

19. "On the Home Front," *New York Post*, March 31, 2003, p. 30; Kenneth Lovett and Frederic Dicker, "N.Y. Budget Late for 19th Straight Year," *New York Post*, April 1, 2003, p. 24.

20. Joe Stashenko, "Pataki Calls New York Budget Illegal," *Associated Press Online*, May 16, 2003 http://customwire.ap.org/dynamic/fronts/ARCHIVE?SITE:NYGLE&SECTION:HOME; Al Baker, "As Time Expires in Albany, the Budget Impasse Persists," *New York Times*, April 1, 2003, p. 5; Joe Mahoney with David Saltonstall, "It's a Deal: Soak Rich, Up Sales Tax," *Daily News*, April 30, 2003, p. 6.

21. Interview with Robert Herman, in Benjamin and Nakamura, *Modern New York Legislature*, pp. 239–44.

22. Based on discussion with legislators at the time, and stories in *New York Times*.

23. Again, the newspaper stories and editorials collected by the Brennan Center provide good examples: http://www.brennancenter.org/programs/dem_vr_albanyreform_editorials.html, or http://www.brennancenter.org/programs/dem_vr_albanyreform_newsstories.html.

24. http://www.brennancenter.org/programs/downloads/albany reform_finalreport.pdf.

25. James Dao, "Pataki's Welfare Plan In Brief: Amid Austerity, A Tax Break, Welfare," *New York Times*, January 6, 1996, p. B6; George Pataki, Governor of New York, "Welfare Reform: Memorandum and Proposed Legislation," 1996.

26. James Dao, "Pataki's Budget Plan Takes Another Blow," *New York Times*, March 12, 1996, p. B4; Raymond Hernandez, "Allies of Pataki Express Concerns on Welfare Plan," *New York Times*, March 11, 1997, p. 1; New York State Assembly, "A Democratic Consensus on Welfare Reform," 1997; Richard Perez-Pena, "Assembly Adopts Own Version of Budget," *New York Times*, April 1, 1997, p. 1; Raymond Hernandez, "Pataki Is Willing to Give Up Parts of Welfare Plan," *New York Times*, July 3, 1997, p. 1.

27. James Dao, "GOP Wins First Test in Albany in an Effort to End Rent Controls," *New York Times*, April 8, 1997, p.1; James Dao, "Pataki Urges End of Rent Cap When Apartment Is Vacated," *New York Times*, May

13, 1997, p. 1; James Dao, "GOP Waging Internal Battles on Rent Policy," *New York Times*, June 4, 1997, p. 1; David Firestone, "Rent Regulations Firmly Supported in New York City," *New York Times*, June 11, 1997, p. 1;. Raymond Hernandez, "In Rent-Law Battle, Focus is on Pivotal GOP Legislator's District," *New York Times*, April 7, 1997, p. B1; Raymond Hernandez, "Entering Debate, Governor Offers Rent Compromise," *New York Times*, May 12, 1997, p. 1; Raymond Hernandez, "Spano's Quandary: Bruno or Tenants," *New York Times*, June 14, 1997, 24; Randy Kennedy, "Easing Stand, Bruno Sees Rent Decontrol Over 4 Years," *New York Times*, April 18, 1997, B1; Richard Perez-Pena, "As Rent-Law Expiration Approaches, It Is Supporters Who Appear to Dig In," *New York Times*, June 11, 1997, 1; James Dao, "Deal Is Achieved as Rent Laws Expire," *New York Times*, June 16, 1997 (http://query.nytimes.com/search/advanced); Richard Perez-Pena, "N.Y. Lawmakers Approve Bill to Keep Rent Rules for 6 Years," *The New York Times*, June 20, 1997 (http://query.nytimes.com/search/advanced).

28. See stories cited in note 27.

29. William Duncombe and John Yinger, "The Star Program," Maxwell School, Syracuse University, 1997, and subsequent revisions of analysis in 1998. The Republicans, however, note that the percentage cuts are the same across the state. They argue (see exchange between Duncombe and Yinger and Senator Cook in the *Syracuse Herald-American*, "Opinion," Section, Sunday, March 28, 1998, p. 1) that downstate suburban homes are worth more and a $70,000 exemption results in the same percentage cut in affluent areas as a $30,000 cut does in less affluent areas. Duncombe and Yinger respond that, while this may be true, the amount of dollars of tax relief are much more to affluent downstate suburbs.

30. New York State Assembly. *Learning Achieving Developing by Directing Education Resources: A Report from the New York State Assembly*, 1997.

CHAPTER 9

New York's Courts

BRIAN J. NICKERSON AND THOMAS W. CHURCH

INTRODUCTION

New York's state trial courts accept more than four million new case filings every year.[1] This substantial caseload makes it one of the busiest court systems in the nation. Cases range in importance from petty misdemeanors and small claims actions in village justice courts to appellate cases having vast implications for economic and social life in the state. Despite the political significance of many of these judicial decisions, courts and judges are frequently omitted from discussions of the state's political system; indeed, courts are often seen as apolitical, with judges' decisions considered to flow from legal standards that are nondiscretionary and somehow above politics. Yet courts are incontrovertibly an essential component of any political system.

Furthermore, American courts are undeniably political in at least three additional senses. First, courts make decisions that can have dramatic impact on the allocation of power and resources in society—the essence of politics. For example, New York courts regularly resolve election disputes and, in so doing, have a substantial impact on who governs;[2] they have assessed everything from the winner of the America's Cup yachting race in 1990, to the legality of hospitals' plans to destroy frozen human embryos, the constitutionality of the "Son of Sam" law that prevents convicted criminals from profiting from their illegal acts through book and movie contracts, and the legal adequacy of the state's elementary and secondary public school funding system. Even when courts resolve private disputes over personal injuries or contractual obligations, they set down legal standards that guide the vast system of individual and business behavior, with enormous social, economic, and political implications.

Second, judges have considerable discretion in reaching many of their most important decisions. Judicial rulings might be of limited interest to students of politics if the decisions themselves were dictated by an autonomous, value-free entity called "The Law." Political scientists and legal scholars have long regarded this characterization of legal decision making, at least in American courts, as inadequate. Decisions of judges must be justified in legal terms, to be sure. And some provisions of statutes or constitutions are very clear and specific, leaving little room for judicial interpretation. But many legal enactments, from city ordinances to state constitutions, are deliberately vague, inviting judges to inject their own political values into the process of legal interpretation. For example, state courts have had to determine whether the constitutional protection of freedom of speech in the New York State Constitution is violated by a ban on political solicitation in privately owned shopping malls and to what extent do public employees have free speech protections in the workplace; whether a long-term same-sex relationship constitutes a "family" within the meaning of New York City rent-control regulations; and whether the constitutional prohibition of unreasonable searches and seizures is violated by police seizure of a gun in plain view during a routine stop of a vehicle for a traffic infraction, or by a school official's search of a student bookbag or locker. The words of ordinances, statutes, or constitutions may seem clear enough in the abstract, but when judges must apply those general words to the ambiguities of real-life situations such as those described above, they have considerable leeway in interpretation. In such circumstances, judges are necessarily exercising discretion and making policy.[3]

Finally, American courts at all levels are intimately connected to the political system through the ways in which judges and other court officials are selected. As will be discussed in more detail later in this chapter, most New York State judges are popularly elected; those that are not elected are appointed by the governor or by city mayors. Virtually all New York's elected judges are nominated by local political parties, through a highly political process that frequently rewards the party faithful with judicial nominations. Similarly, politics is seldom very far in the background when judges are selected by governors and mayors, even when, as is the case with the state's highest judges, they must be first nominated by a nonpartisan[4] selection committee. Political considerations also pervade appointment of other court-system officials, from selection of judges to serve on the appellate division of the supreme court,[5] to the administrative judges who supervise the state's judicial districts, administrative officials in the court system and the law clerks, assistants, and the legally trained "secretaries" who serve with trial court and appellate judges throughout the state.

This chapter first summarizes the organization of New York's state court system. This is not a simple task, for the court system has an arcane, highly complicated structure. The next section sets out how the court system is governed and administered. We then discuss three perennial political and reform issues regarding court reform in New York: proposals for simplification of the state's court structure and staffing, creation of a new geographical department to handle growing caseloads, and altering the system of judicial selection.

STRUCTURE OF THE COURTS

Historical Development

The present structure of the state's judicial branch is the result of a succession of patchwork responses to the dramatic social, political, and economic changes that have occurred in New York from its colonial origins to the present.[6] New York State has been governed under four different constitutions. The state constitution of 1846 (the state's third) laid the foundation for the current court system. Key judicial provisions of that document included popular election of judges, establishment of the court of appeals as the state's highest appellate court, a statewide trial court of unlimited jurisdiction named, peculiarly, the supreme court, and eight subdivisions (or "terms") of the supreme court to serve as intermediate courts of appeal. The organizational structure of the courts closely paralleled the political boundaries of local governments. County, city, town, and village courts were important parts of the judicial system, but they operated largely independently of the statewide court system. A new judicial article in 1869 redivided the state into the current four geographical departments, each with one general term of the supreme court to hear appeals.

The current state constitution (adopted in 1894) ratified the existing structure of the courts, although twentieth-century reforms have altered the system at the margins. Since the mid-1960s, the office of court administration has operated as the statewide administrative office for the courts, with the chief judge of the court of appeals as titular head of the court system. A change from popular election to gubernatorial selection was initiated for court of appeals judges, a commission on judicial conduct was established, and the state government assumed responsibility for funding most courts in the state.

The Current "Unified" Court System

Article VI of the New York State Constitution, as amended in 1962, defines the powers and structure of the judiciary and provides that all courts located in the geographical jurisdiction of the state (except the federal courts) are part of a "unified court system." This term, however, is something of a misnomer as applied to the courts of New York State. The 1962 amendment unified the financing of state courts, taking responsibility for support of most aspects of most courts from local government and vesting it in the state treasury. But "unified court system" is a term of art in judicial administration circles: it implies that all state courts are consolidated—not only financially, but operationally and organizationally—into one hierarchical, streamlined system without functional overlap. The National Center for the Study of State Courts defines a "unified" court as "more accurately a collection of characteristics or processes: centralization of administrative authority, centralization of rulemaking powers, unitary budgeting, state (vs. local) funding of trial courts, and trial court consolidation."[7] States that have adopted a unified structural reform (examples are Minnesota and Kansas) have also eliminated special-purpose courts (such as New York's present court of claims and family and surrogate courts), consolidated the organization and financing of the courts at the state level, and established a powerful administrative organization to manage all the courts in the state.

New York's unified court system, despite its name, still evidences its seventeenth- and eighteenth-century origins. It bears scant resemblance to the standard three-tiered model promoted by the American Bar Association or to the unified court systems in other states.[8] Indeed, no less a figure than the chief administrative judge of New York, testifying before a joint legislative hearing, called the structure, "the most antiquated, cumbersome, complex court structure in the country."[9] Moreover, even the current chief judge of the New York Court of Appeals has advocated, "We need to simplify our Byzantine court structure—a maze of eleven separate trial courts, each its own jurisdictional universe."[10] Figures 9.1 and 9.2 graphically illustrate this complexity, showing a schematic overview of the structure and the routes of criminal and civil appeals within the system.

Courts can be divided into trial and appellate courts. Trial courts hear disputes, take evidence from witnesses, determine facts, and apply the law to those facts. They conduct the proceedings embodying the popular image of courts: determinations of guilt or innocence in criminal cases, for example, or imposition of damages and compensation in personal injury actions. Decisions in trial courts can be made by either judges or juries. Appellate courts generally do not decide questions of fact (and thus do not hear witnesses, take evidence, or utilize juries), but rather correct errors of law made by lower courts that heard cases previously. Appellate courts usually employ several judges sitting as a panel, and make decisions after reading written briefs and oral argument by lawyers for the parties in a case.

FIGURE 9.1.
New York State court system: Criminal appeals structure

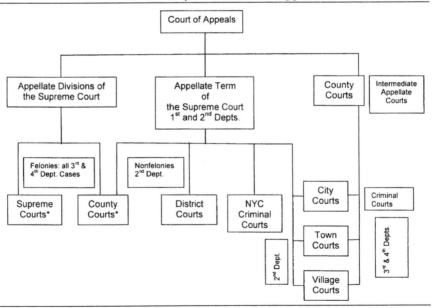

*Appeals involving death sentences must be taken directly to the Court of Appeals.

FIGURE 9.2.
New York State court system: Civil appeals structure

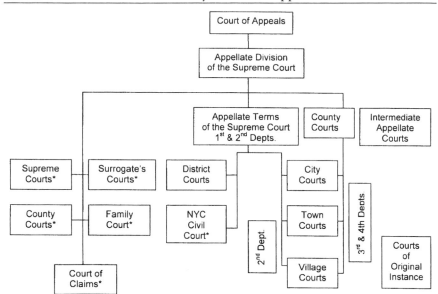

Source: 24th Annual Report of the Chief Administrator of the Courts for Calendar Year 2001
(New York: Office of Court Administration, 2002), p.2.

*Appeals from judgments of courts of records of original instance that finally determine
actions where the only question involved is the validity of a statutory provision under the New
York State Constitution may be taken directly to the Court of Appeals.

New York's state trial courts are made up of courts of superior and lesser
jurisdiction. The courts of superior jurisdiction are the workhorses of the
system; they include the supreme court and county courts, the multipurpose
courts that hear most of the serious civil and criminal matters. But in New
York they also include specialized courts—family court, surrogate's court,
and the court of claims.[11] Courts of lesser jurisdiction hear less serious civil
and criminal matters. They include the criminal court and civil courts in
New York City, and a seemingly endless variety of city courts, district courts,
and town and village justice courts outside New York City.

When a party is unhappy with the result in a trial court and believes a
legal mistake was made in some aspect of the proceedings, an appeal can be
lodged in an intermediate appellate court. The structure of the intermediate

appellate courts is especially confusing in New York since appeals can progress from the trial court to a variety of appellate courts, with different names and composition, depending on geographic location and type of case. Appeals from trial courts can be heard by the appellate divisions of the supreme court, the appellate terms of the supreme court, and the county courts acting as appellate courts. In another deviation in typical court nomenclature, the court of last resort (analogous to the United States Supreme Court in the federal system) is the New York State Court of Appeals.

Geographically, the New York courts are divided into four judicial departments, and each department is further subdivided into judicial districts consisting of one or more counties. Supreme court judges are elected by the voters in these judicial districts.

The courts of New York State are a patchwork quilt in which courts performing virtually identical functions across the state have different names, legal jurisdictions, judicial selection methods, and avenues for appeal. This confusing situation can be attributed to historical accident, but its continuation is directly related to political imperatives. As will be discussed later in this chapter, the major roadblock to reorganization and rationalization of the structure of the courts has been the issue of how the various judicial officials are selected. While many of the relevant actors profess an interest in simplifying the organization of the system, none seem willing to give up their role in choosing the various judicial officers who populate the current system.

A brief description of the distinguishing features of each court in the New York System is provided in table 9.1; the courts are described briefly in the sections that follow.

TABLE 9.1.
Characteristics of New York State judiciary

Court	No. of authorized judges*	How selected	Term
Court of Appeals	7	Gubernatorial appointment with advice and consent of senate	14 years
Appellate Division	55: 20 permanent plus 35 temporary	Gubernatorial designation from among duly elected supreme court justices.	Presiding justice: 14 years, or balance of term as supreme court justice. Associate justice: 5 years, or balance of term as supreme court justice.

TABLE 9.1 (*continued*)

Court	No. of authorized judges*	How selected	Term
Appellate Term	Varies	Designation by chief administrator of courts, with approval of presiding justice of the department, from among duly elected supreme court justices	Varies.
Supreme Court; Trial Parts	279	Elected	14 years.
Court of Claims	72	Gubernatorial appointment with advice and consent	9 years, or shorter if appointed to fill vacated term.
Surrogate's Court	30	Elected	14 years in New York City. 10 years outside the City.
County Court	128**	Elected	10 years.
Family Court	126	Mayoral appointment in New York City	10 years or if appointed to fill a vacancy, the period remaining in that term.
Civil Court of New York City	120	Elected	10 years
Criminal Court of New York City	107	Mayoral appointment	10 years, or, if appointed to fill a vacancy, the period remaining in that term.
District Courts outside New York City (Nassau and Suffolk Counties)	50	Elected	6 years
City Court	158	Most elected; some acting judges appointed by mayor or Common Council	Varies.
Town Court and Village Court	Over 2,300	Elected	4 years for towns; villages varied terms

Source: 24th Annual Report of the Chief Administrator of the Courts for the Calendar Year 2001 (New York: Office of Court Administration, 2002), p. 3.
Note: Mandatory retirement age of 70 for all judges except town and village courts.
*Numbers accurate as of December 31, 2001
**Includes one-, two- and three-hatted judges, that is, judges who function as county and/or family and/or surrogate court judges.

TRIAL COURTS OF LESSER JURISDICTION

Trial Courts of lesser jurisdiction process misdemeanors, violations, and minor civil matters. These courts also preside over arraignments and other preliminary proceedings in felony cases. The lesser jurisdiction courts in New York City are called the civil court and the criminal court. The former handles civil cases involving up to twenty-five thousand dollars and land-lord-tenant disputes.[12] Civil court judges are elected for ten-year terms. The criminal court handles misdemeanors and the early stages of even the most serious criminal cases. Criminal court judges are appointed by New York City's mayor for ten-year terms.

Outside of New York City, city courts have limited jurisdiction in both civil and criminal cases. City court judges are either elected or appointed by mayors or city councils; they serve ten-year terms and have jurisdiction in misdemeanors and in civil cases up to fifteen thousand dollars. In two down-state jurisdictions the lower courts are called district courts; judges in these courts are elected for six-year terms. Finally, most towns and villages in the state have justice courts, usually staffed by a part-time judicial officer referred to as the town or village justice (or justice of the peace). Justices in these courts are elected to four-year terms and need not be attorneys.[13] These courts have criminal jurisdiction over minor criminal cases and civil jurisdiction up to three thousand dollars; unlike courts in the rest of the court system, they are funded by local government.

TRIAL COURTS OF SUPERIOR JURISDICTION

Supreme Court. Unlike the federal court system and that of most states, where "supreme court" is the name given to the highest court in the system, New York's supreme court is the general jurisdiction trial court, the court that hears (or could hear)[14] nearly all civil and criminal cases. In practice, however, the supreme court hears serious civil and criminal matters, and all cases involving divorce, annulment, and separation. It rarely hears cases that could be handled by specialized courts, the county courts, or the other courts of lesser jurisdiction. Justices of this court are elected to fourteen-year terms by the voters of the judicial district within which the court is located.

County Courts. There is a county court in each of the state's counties except those making up New York City. The court has criminal jurisdiction over offenses committed within the county, including felonies, although minor offenses are usually handled in the lower courts. It also has civil jurisdiction for claims up to twenty-five thousand dollars. Judges are elected on a county-wide basis to serve ten-year terms.[15] Most appeals from the county court go to the appellate division of the supreme court.[16]

Family Courts. The family courts were established in the 1962 constitutional reorganization to deal with families and children in distress. There is a family court in each county of the state and in New York City. The family court decides matters relating to adoption, guardianship, foster care, juvenile delinquency, paternity and child support, custody, visitation, termination of parental rights, family offenses, and child protective services. Ironically, the issues most commonly associated with family cases—divorce, annulment, and separation—are not part of the family court's jurisdiction, but are rather in the exclusive domain of the supreme court. Jurisdiction over adoption proceedings is shared with the surrogate's courts.

The term of office for family court judges is ten years. Outside New York City family court judges are elected; as indicated previously, New York City family court judges are appointed by the mayor.

Surrogate's Court. The surrogate's court has colonial origins and today exists in every county in New York. The court's jurisdiction generally involves the affairs of decedents, including the probate of wills and administration of estates and trusts. The court shares jurisdiction over adoption of minors with family court. Surrogates are elected to ten-year terms except—in another example of the patchwork quality of New York courts—in New York City, where they serve fourteen-year terms.[17]

Court of Claims. The court of claims is a special trial court that hears cases, usually involving property or asset forfeiture, against the State of New York. The governor, with the advice and consent of the state senate, appoints court of claims judges for terms of nine years.

INTERMEDIATE APPELLATE COURTS
Litigants are generally entitled to at least one appeal from a trial court decision. Depending on which department a case originated in, this appeal may go to either the appellate division of the supreme court, or the appellate term of the supreme court.

Appellate Division of the Supreme Court. The first appeal in a case is most often heard by one of the appellate divisions of the supreme court. Each of the state's four judicial departments has an appellate division. Justices of the appellate division are designated by the governor from sitting members of the supreme court. The governor also designates presiding and associate justices in each division. These appointments do not require legislative confirmation.

Appellate Term of the Supreme Court. The New York State Constitution authorizes the appellate division in each department to establish an appellate term to ease the division's caseload. Currently, only two downstate departments have established appellate terms. These courts sit in panels of three supreme court justices, designated by the chief administrator of the courts. The appellate terms hear appeals from certain lower courts including the New York City civil and criminal courts and, in the second department, the district, city, town, and village courts in all civil cases and from the county courts in all civil and nonfelony criminal cases.[18]

THE COURT OF APPEALS

The New York Court of Appeals is the state's court of last resort. It consists of a chief judge and six associate judges. The current chief judge is Judith S. Kaye. All judges of this court are appointed by the governor for fourteen-year terms.[19] The governor's appointments must come from a list of persons found "well-qualified" by a bipartisan state commission on judicial nomination and must be confirmed by the state senate. Cases coming before the court of appeals have almost always been reviewed and acted upon by an intermediate appellate court—in most cases the appellate division of the supreme court—and the court has considerable discretion in the cases it decides to review.[20]

The New York Court of Appeals has traditionally been considered one of the most prestigious courts in the United States, with such justices as Benjamin Cardozo, Rufus Peckman Jr., and Ward Hunt going on to serve on the U.S. Supreme Court. The court's decisions have been especially influential in the development of American common law, particularly in the areas of tort and contract law.

The reputation of the New York Court of Appeals was founded on craftsmanship and originality in areas of the law that have traditionally been the creation of judges: the area of private law that governs contracts, the allocation of responsibility for accidental injuries, and the like. While the court continues to enjoy a high position among analogous courts in other states, most observers would agree that the court in recent years does not have the prominence that it had in the Cardozo era. Scholars attribute this situation to several factors: a decline in the relative importance of private law decisions in such areas as torts and contracts—traditionally the forte of the court of appeals—in favor of public law litigation involving constitutional and statutory interpretation, an emphasis in the court of appeals on correcting errors rather than developing new law, and strong norms on the court that encourage collegial decision making and consensual opinions rather than grand exposition of legal principles frequently seen in more activist courts. Unlike the state supreme courts (such as those of New Jersey and California) that have been generally regarded as the most influential in the recent past, the court of appeals has ostensibly tended to adopt a nonideological, pragmatic approach to legal issues.

However, the court of appeals has maintained an activist stance in several key constitutional areas, particularly in freedom of expression and privacy cases, and criminal cases involving search and seizure and right to counsel. But, in the words of one legal observer, "This is not a court with an agenda. It doesn't see itself as the avatar of a proper society, while the [U.S.] Supreme Court seems to be willing to remake the social structure."[21] There are suggestions by some legal scholars that under the chief judgeship of Judith Kaye, the court of appeals may be emerging from a period of relative obscurity to take a more prominent role in American jurisprudence.

COURT ADMINISTRATION, FINANCES, AND REGULATION OF JUDICIAL CONDUCT

Administration

New York's courts have a lengthy history of administrative fragmentation and inefficiency. Prior to 1962, most of the state trial courts operated as independent entities, with almost no central management or direction. Constitutional reforms in 1962 and 1978 moved toward a less fragmented system but, as indicated above, the state court system fails to achieve the hallmarks of a truly unified system. Since 1978 the chief judge of the court of appeals has been the designated chief judge of the state and its chief judicial officer. The chief judge appoints a chief administrator of the courts[22] with

FIGURE 9.3.

Administrative oversight of the New York courts

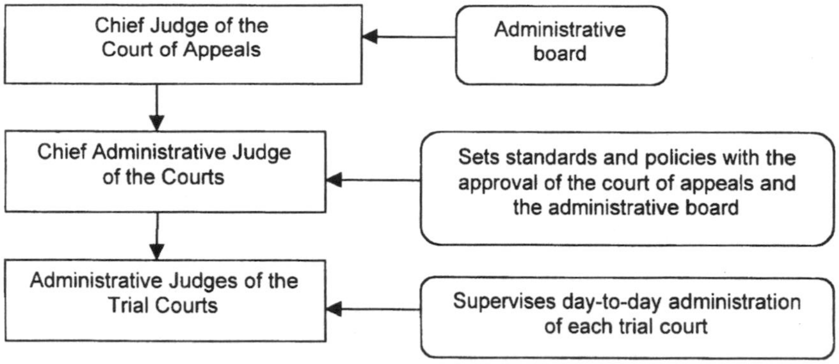

Source: *The Judicial Maze.* League of Women Voters, 1998.

the advice and consent of the administrative board of the courts—a body consisting of the presiding justices of the four appellate divisions of the supreme court and the chief judge of the state, who serves as chair. Interestingly, because the governor appoints the presiding justices of the appellate divisions, the governor has primary appointment power over this governing body of the judiciary. Figure 9.3 provides a schematic overview of the various entities responsible for court administration.

The chief judge is responsible for establishing statewide administrative standards in consultation with the chief administrator and the administrative board; important administrative policies must be approved by the court of appeals. The chief administrator, on behalf of the chief judge, is responsible for supervision, administration, and operation of the state's trial courts. The court of appeals and the appellate divisions are responsible for their own administration. Figure 9.4 illustrates the overall structure of court administration in the state.

The chief administrator also directs the Office of Court Administration (OCA), the administrative office responsible for management functions for the courts. Through the OCA, the chief administrator has several key functions, including preparing the judiciary budget, assigning of judges, conducting labor negotiations, and recommending legal changes to improve administration of justice and court operations. The OCA is also responsible for overall financial management in the courts, as well as legislative liaison, human resource management, public and external relations, data collection

FIGURE 9.4.

Administrative structure of the New York unified court system

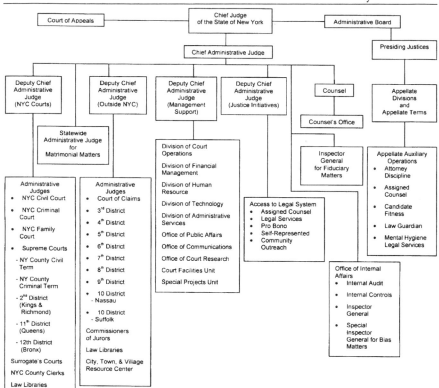

Source: 24th Annual Report of the Chief Administrator of the Courts for Calendar Year 2001 (New York: Office of Court Administration, 2002), p. 28.

and processing, maintenance of court libraries, judicial and nonjudicial education (such as staff development), and general technical assistance to the courts. In short, the OCA is responsible for most of the day-to-day management functions for the New York courts.

Finances

Historically, funding the courts in New York has been as chaotic as their administration. In 1976, however, the Unified Court Budget Act merged 120 separate court budgets into a single state judicial budget. By 1980, the

TABLE 9.2.

2004–2005 budget request for the New York court system

Category/fund/major purpose	2003–2004 Available	2004–2005 Requested	Change
Court & Agency Operations:			
Courts of Original Jurisdiction	1,164,438,029	1,175,237,583	10,799,554
Court of Appeals	13,251,535	13,256,293	4,758
Appellate Court Operations	59,121,171	60,437,947	1,316,776
Appellate Auxiliary Operations	76,947,019	81,490,784	4,543,765
Administration & General Support	18,563,864	18,860,299	296,435
Judiciary-Wide Maintenance Undistributed	8,895,227	8,837,678	(57,549)
Court & Agency Operations—General Fund	1,341,216,845	1,358,120,584	16,903,739
Special Revenue Fund—Federal	6,500,000	10,500,000	4,000,000
Special Revenue Fund—Other			
NYS County Clerks Operations Offset Fund	18,476,447	18,389,928	(86,519)
Judiciary Data Processing Offset Fund	12,933,484	12,015,501	(917,983)
Miscellaneous Special Revenue	3,000,000	2,500,000	(500,000)
Attorney Licensing Fund	19,785,734	19,849,980	64,246
Indigent Legal Services Fund	6,250,000	25,000,000	18,750,000
Court Facilities Incentive Aid Fund	2,183,275	2,083,451	(99,824)
Court & Agency Operations—All Funds Total	1,410,345,785	1,448,459,444	38,113,659

Source: Judiciary 2004–2005 Budget Request, www.courts.state.ny.us/admin/financialops/bst04-05/budgetwhole.pdf

state had assumed the noncapital costs of all state courts except those involving the town and village courts (which are funded by the municipal governments) and the repair and maintenance of court houses (which is funded primarily by the municipalities in which they are located).

In New York State's fiscal year 2003–2004, the appropriation to the unified court system reached $1.41 billion for general and special operations programs. Table 9.2 provides the judiciary budget request for fiscal year 2004–2005, representing a marginal increase from prior year expenditures.

While the amount of state funds appropriated to operate the court system is small in comparison to governmental expenditures from the general fund on big ticket items such as education ($14.1 billion disbursed in 2002–2003) and Medicaid ($8.4 billion disbursed), the size and content of the judiciary budget is a perennial source of conflict between the courts and the executive and legislative branches of government.[23]

The courts are, of course, an independent branch of government, and there is always a judicially expressed fear that the independence of the judiciary is compromised when governors and legislators have ultimate authority over court funding. But the legislature and governor are just as zealous in maintaining their established role in controlling governmental expenditures. The size and overall content of the courts' budget is usually established through informal negotiation between court officials, staff at the governor's Office of Management and Budget, and legislative staff. However, this system of informal accommodation does not always function effectively. The most recent example of this tension occurred in 1991, when former chief judge Sol Wachtler sued then-governor Mario Cuomo and the legislature for improper cuts to the judiciary's budget.[24]

The recurring debate concerning the appropriate size of the courts' budget in New York is grounded in different views regarding the necessary number of judges in the system, and the efficiency and productivity of those judges. Chief judges and chief administrative judges routinely make dire predictions at budget time concerning the impact of legislative failure to authorize new judgeships to deal with the state's allegedly "crushing" caseload. Budget officials in the governor's office and the legislature question whether the existing complement of judges is as hard working and productive as it might be, and whether the addition of more judges would dramatically affect the problems of delay and overcrowding that have bedeviled many of the state's courts for decades. Unfortunately, there is little reliable data that would allow officials to resolve these conflicting views. National studies conducted in the 1970s and 1980s examined the operation of the supreme court in two boroughs of New York City—Brooklyn and Bronx County—comparing them to big-city courts elsewhere in the United States in terms of delay and judicial workload. The studies portrayed these courts as among the country's most congested and delayed, but the data did not suggest that the judges on those courts were necessarily overworked, at least not in terms of their judicial brethren in other major cities.[25]

Judicial Conduct

After questions of funding, perhaps the most potentially contentious issue between the courts and the more explicitly political branches of government involves judicial conduct and how to address legitimate complaints of improper behavior of judges without compromising judicial independence. New York's constitution authorizes removal of judges by legislative impeachment or by a concurrent resolution of the senate and assembly. These are cumbersome devices, however, that are rarely used. The Commission on Judicial Conduct was established through constitutional amendment as part of the 1978 reforms to court organization and financing. Its functions include receiving and reviewing written complaints against judges, initiating complaints, obtaining witnesses and documents, and conducting formal hearings. Ultimately, the commission can dismiss, admonish, censure, or retire any state judge.

In the federal courts, and in many state court systems, judicial conduct commissions or committees are primarily judicial bodies, with most or all members appointed from within the courts. New York's commission, as another indication of the close linkage between politics and the operation of the judiciary, consists of eleven members, only three of whom are appointed from within the judiciary (by the chief judge); four members are appointed by the governor, and one each by the Democratic and Republican leaders in each house of the legislature. Members serve four-year staggered terms. As a further nod toward independence from the judiciary, the commission is funded directly by the legislature, without gubernatorial or court control over budgetary requests or allocations.

POLITICS, REFORM, AND THE COURTS

Politics and Staffing the Courts

American politics in the nineteenth and early twentieth Centuries was grounded on what was termed the "spoils system," a reference to the old political adage, "To the victor belong the spoils."[26] The spoils of electoral victory included a variety of forms of largesse to political friends and supporters: lucrative governmental contracts, selective law enforcement, and influence over land acquisition and public works projects. Perhaps the most important element of the spoils system, however, was government jobs for political friends and party workers. Starting in the early days of the nineteenth century, it was more or less expected that the party which controlled the executive branch of a city or state (or even the nation) would use government jobs to reward the party faithful. Changes in party control in state capitals (as well as the nation's cities) were inevitably accompanied by almost complete turnover in government employees—from high level policymakers to janitors and clerks.

This system of political selection of government employees ultimately brought about a chorus of complaints charging inefficiency, incompetence, and corruption. The system was cut back substantially at all levels of government with civil service reforms initiated in most states beginning around 1900. So-called merit systems were put into effect and a growing proportion of government jobs were awarded on the basis of scores on competitive examinations and objective indicators of experience and competence, rather than political affiliations and connections. The judiciary is the last vestige of the patronage system in many states—including New York. Indeed, as late as the mid-1970s, prior to the creation of the office of court administration in 1978, patronage was reportedly "a way of life" in New York courts at all levels.[27] While diminished, political patronage in one form or another continues to play a significant role in staffing New York's courts. Indeed, as recently as 2004 the *New York Times* described the courts of one New York City borough—the Bronx—as "a world suffused with politics" and "awash in patronage."[28]

The most common and direct route to a New York judgeship remains activity in either the Democratic or Republican Party. (For further analysis of the role of political parties in New York, see chapters 3 and 4). With few exceptions, judicial officers at all levels have been active in party politics and have "done their time" in party clubhouses; frequently judges have previously served as elected officials at some level of state or local government. For appointive judicial positions, such as judgeships in the criminal court and family court in New York City, the court of claims, or the appellate division, political connections to the appointing authority (whether the mayor or governor) are critical to the appointment; success in gaining one of the elected judgeships (as in the supreme and county courts, and family court outside of New York City) almost always requires nomination by one of the two major political parties, a nomination that is tightly controlled by party leaders. As A. Thomas Levin, president of the New York State Bar Association has observed, the system "pretty much excludes from the judiciary anyone who's not involved in politics—they're out of the game altogether."[29]

Since elections in most New York counties are dominated by either the Democratic or Republican Party, party nomination is usually tantamount to electoral victory. Judicial nominations at the county level are controlled by each party's county leader, whose influence over court jobs—from the judges' secretaries and law clerks to the judicial positions themselves—is a major political resource. Party nominations for most of the elected judicial officers are made formally through primary elections, but the choice of the regular party leadership is almost always confirmed in these low-visibility elections. Nomination of supreme court justices is even more directly controlled by party leadership, since they are made by nominating conventions in which the delegates are hand picked by party officials who exercise virtually complete control over the results.[30] When supreme court electoral districts span more than one county, nominations for judgeships are often negotiated between the Democratic and Republican Party leaders of the relevant counties. Specific judicial positions are designated to be the sole province of one party or the other, and through the system of "cross-endorsement," party leaders of one party agree not to field candidates for judgeships held or vacated by incumbents of the other party.[31] These arrangements are informal and break down on occasion, to the inevitable accompaniment of heated political recriminations.

The conservative *Albany Times-Union*, surveying several such cross-endorsement clashes in 1990, urged the end of the practice of electing judges in an editorial entitled "Judges, Thick Smoke and Pork."[32] Four years later, after another interparty dispute over cross-endorsements, the editorial staff came to the same indignant conclusion: "Supposedly, justices of New York's trial level court are selected by the voters. But that is a myth, and everyone knows it. In reality, judicial candidates are frequently handpicked by political leaders and cross-endorsed as part of a multiyear package deal that usually precludes even the possibility of a competitive election. Often, the only time voters have any say in the matter is when backstabbing politicos renege on a deal—as occurred this year . . . and the cross-endorsement pact is temporarily abandoned."[33]

Reappointment or reelection decisions are similarly subject to political control. While it is generally assumed that sitting judges will receive renomination from their party and (in light of the power of incumbency) reelection, parties have sometimes denied nomination to sitting judges, almost always for reasons unrelated to their competence or performance on the bench.[34]

Once on the court, judges are in a position (and are frequently expected) to reward party insiders with judicial largesse. Supreme Court justices appoint "fiduciaries" who serve as guardians to children and to the elderly or infirm; they also appoint "receivers" to protect the property of individuals and firms involved in litigation. The fees for these services are usually paid out of the assets of the parties and can frequently amount to very substantial sums.[35] The surrogate's court, a low-visibility court that deals primarily with wills and estates, is another major source of political patronage.[36]

There are other sources of patronage within the courts. Supreme court justices and most county judges are provided with a small staff including a court clerk, a legally trained "secretary" (or law clerk), and an administrative assistant. These positions, which can command an annual salary as high as one hundred thousand dollars or more, are not subject to civil service restrictions. In many courts occupants of these jobs are chosen more by local party officials than the judges.[37] Indeed, a frequent route to a judgeship is through the position of law clerk or legal secretary. There have also been allegations that the Office of Court Administration has its share of political appointees. A 1988 investigative article in an Albany area newspaper that called the OCA a "patronage haven" revealed that 65 percent of central staff personnel were listed as "indefinites," an unusual job classification that is exempt from civil service requirements for competitive recruitment.[38]

In light of the limited number of patronage positions available in executive agencies in state and local government, courts remain important repositories of jobs to reward the party faithful. The courts also provide a ready source of funds for party activities. Judges running election campaigns, even though they are seldom contested, frequently amass substantial funds for campaign expenses, much of which is donated by lawyers appearing before them in court. Some of these funds may not be needed for the judge's campaign in an election where the result is often preordained, but means exist for transfer of funds to the general party coffers or to insure that judicial candidates use funds during the campaign to reward politically favored campaign consultants and businesses.[39] Judicial candidates, judges, and court employees themselves are also frequently called upon to make direct or indirect contributions to support various party activities, and donations to the party by court personnel frequently constitute a significant proportion of the party's monetary resources.[40] In light of the foregoing, it is unsurprising that virtually all efforts at court reorganization and reform in New York are carefully assessed in terms of their impact on the number of political appointments lost or gained, by which party, and which appointing official, and their implications for party fund-raising activities. More than one court reform proposal has foundered on these shoals.[41]

Both elective and appointive systems have produced some excellent judges, in New York State and elsewhere. But reformers argue that the close relationship of the judicial selection process to state and local party organizations discourages qualified individuals from seeking judicial office, and sometimes results in selection of unqualified, or at least underqualified, judges. The so-called merit plan for judicial selection is often put forward as a response to this criticism. Under the typical merit selection plan, a nonpartisan committee of judges, attorneys, and other luminaries sifts through applications for judicial office and presents the governor with a short list of applicants deemed to be most meritorious. The governor then appoints one of the individuals on the list. The appointee usually serves a first term without election, and then stands for a "retention" election, where there is no opposing candidate, and the electorate is asked simply whether the judge should be reelected to another term.

A variant of the merit selection plan operates for court of appeals judges in New York. This selection process differs from the typical merit plan in the requirement of senate confirmation of gubernatorial selections and elimination of the retention election. Gubernatorial appointments must be approved by the Republican-dominated senate, a fact that may in part explain why former governor Mario Cuomo, a Democrat, appointed several Republicans to the court of appeals. An additional difference lies in the composition of the nominating commission. In New York, this body is explicitly bipartisan rather than nonpartisan, since its configuration virtually guarantees an equal number of Democratic and Republican members.[42]

The governor also appoints judges to the appellate division of the supreme court and to the court of claims. Recent governors have made these appointments from lists of candidates proposed by judicial screening committees. Governor George Pataki established a committee within each of the four departments for appellate division appointments, and a statewide committee for court of claims appointments. These committees, however, exist through executive order and have no constitutional standing. A dispute arose in 1997 when Governor Pataki announced that he would not be restricted by a department's judicial screening committee's list of acceptable candidates in making his appointment, but would look to the lists of other departments as well. It was widely assumed that this change would enable the Republican governor to fill vacancies on appellate divisions in strongly Democratic constituencies with Republican appointments, which the organized bar criticized as "of questionable merit" and "interference" with the evaluation process.[43] Whatever the merits of this particular change, it is reasonably clear the governors have had, and will continue to have, substantial flexibility in appointing judges at all levels on the basis of their political as well as legal qualifications. It is also reasonably clear that fundamental alteration in the methods of selecting judges in the trial and intermediate appellate courts of New York State will be resisted by the party officials who benefit so substantially by the patronage and fund-raising opportunities provided by the present system.

Organizational Reform

The perennial targets for court reformers in New York have been the Byzantine structure and organization of New York's court system and the state's system of judicial selection. These issues will be discussed in turn.[44]

TRIAL-COURT MERGER

Trial-court merger is a key element in the national movement for unified court systems. Merger of the trial courts in New York State would mean a substantial reduction in the number of superior jurisdiction courts, since most proposals involve merging county courts, family court, surrogate's court, and the court of claims into the supreme court. A plan proposed by Chief Judge Judith Kaye would also merge the limited jurisdiction courts throughout the state into one district court. Proponents of court merger argue that despite the constitutional declaration of a unified court system, the New York's courts are in fact highly fragmented, with unnecessarily complex and overlapping jurisdictions that cause public confusion and increased costs for both litigants and the court system.

Opponents of court merger typically argue that the current system allows for local administrative autonomy and responsiveness to local conditions and values, but merger plans also threaten political power relationships and the perquisites of existing supreme court justices. In the past, opposition to court merger has come from supreme court justices, who are often displeased with the prospect of having their ranks swollen by a large number of new judges from less prestigious courts, and who fear that they may find themselves sitting on less interesting and important cases (such as family court matters or less significant civil and criminal cases) that are currently relegated to county court or the specialized courts.

The major stumbling block to reform, however, concerns how the judges on the new court would be selected. As indicated above, the courts to be merged into the supreme court have a variety of selection methods—from countywide election to mayoral gubernatorial appointment. Most previous plans for court merger provided that after the existing terms of the merged judges expire, seats on the supreme court would be filled through the traditional districtwide election. But changes in judicial selection methods necessarily result in political winners and losers. Potential losers fought hard to maintain the status quo.

Chief Judge Judith Kaye proposed a court merger plan in 1997 and again in 2001 that seemingly finessed this difficulty. The proposal, while unifying all the superior jurisdiction trial courts into one supreme court, retains the selection system, including the terms of office, for all judgeships that existed when the merger took place. This nominally merged and unified court would thus be populated by judges who earn the same salary and have the same formal status and jurisdiction. But while existing supreme court judges and their successors would continue to be elected by judicial district for fourten-year terms, the successors to former court of claims judges on this new court would be appointed by the governor for nine-year terms; those succeeding former New York City family court judges would be appointed by the mayor for ten-year terms; successors of former surrogate court judges would be elected to ten-year terms (except those from New York City, where the term would be fourteen years), and so on. While these concessions to politics may have made the reform more likely to be enacted, one wonders whether this bizarre court will be unified in more than name, or whether this reform will simply add yet another patch to the complex quilt of New York's court system. In any event, there has yet to be significant legislative action on the proposal.

JUDICIAL SELECTION
The intensely political system of interparty deals, patronage, and clubhouse politics is a favorite target of governmental and legal reform groups. The most frequently proposed reform is to take judicial selection out of politics by establishing a nonpartisan merit selection process in which competence rather than political connections will presumably be paramount. Another is

to replace the system of solicitation of contributions for judicial campaigns with a system of publicly financed elections. Such moves would necessarily reduce the resources available to reward party stalwarts. It is unsurprising that in an era of limited patronage positions, a major reduction in the already diminished supply of such jobs would be met with strong resistance from party leaders. It was undoubtedly no accident that reform proposals of Chief Judge Kaye have included only minor changes in existing judicial selection methods.

Calls for reform of the system of judicial selection in New York State reached a peak in 2003, after a series of scandals involving bribe-taking and other forms of judicial misconduct in the Brooklyn Supreme Court resulted in indictments of judges, and even a prison sentence. In response to the furor, Chief Judge Kaye appointed a blue-ribbon commission to investigate reform in the way New York selects its judges. The commission recommended several modest reforms in the system designed to remove some of the more blatant forms of political interference with the courts, such as establishment of judicial screening panels that would produce lists of qualified candidates from which party officials would presumably choose judicial nominees. Despite widespread support among reform groups for more fundamental changes in judicial selection practices across the state, including a move to merit appointment procedures rather than partisan elections, the panel—at least as of this writing in February 2004—has not embraced them.[45]

As the foregoing suggests, even the most innocuous court reform proposals carry political implications, particularly in a state like New York, where the judicial system is so closely tied to the political system. This explains why a dry, seemingly apolitical discussion of court merger or judicial selection can raise the anxiety levels of political actors. It also explains why superficially bland administrative reforms in the courts are so difficult to put into place.

Courts in the American system of government—at both the state and national levels—are inevitably tied to politics and to the political system. Courts are staffed through a process in which politics is ever present. Court systems must compete for resources in that most elemental of political battles, the budgetary process. And judges in all American courthouses are called upon to make decisions that vitally affect the political process and the allocation of values in society. Recognizing the central role of courts in the governmental and political system, the central challenge is to maintain at the same time the separation of law and politics necessary to insulate judicial decisions from the political pressures of the day.

NOTES

1. There were 4,014,962 New York trial court filings in 2001, excluding activity in locally funded town and village courts and pleadings for standard parking tickets. Of the over four million trial court filings, approximately 42 percent occurred in criminal courts, 35 percent in civil courts, 19 percent in family court, and 4 percent in surrogate's court. Additionally, there were 166 records on appeal filed with the court of appeals and 10,023 records on appeal filed with the four appellate divisions for the year 2001. *Twenty-Fourth Annual Report of the Chief Administrative Judge of the Courts for the Calendar year 2001* (Albany, NY: State of New York, 2002, pp. 4–8). This chapter will be concerned with New York's *state* courts, the courts operated by state government. A parallel system of federal courts, operated by the national government, exists in New York, as in every other part of the United States.

2. For example, New York courts ruled on a lawsuit challenging the validity of complex Democratic primary rules that have the effect of keeping nonmainstream candidates off presidential primary ballots, they have upheld the legality of term limits legislation, they have examined the legality of district boundaries for a variety of offices.

3. Ironically, one area of judicial activity in which discretion is most accepted, that of sentencing individuals convicted of criminal offenses, has been increasingly circumscribed in recent years. Mandatory minimum sentences for particular types of crimes and criminals have been enacted in both the federal system and in many states, including New York State. These enactments were intended to confine judicial sentencing discretion, and they have had their desired effect. However, they have not resulted in elimination of sentencing discretion altogether, only a shift from the judge (who has little or no choice as to sentence in a growing number of cases) to the district attorney (who, through plea bargains can still have a substantial effect on the sentence). For an excellent summary discussion of the impact of various sentencing reforms, see Alfred Blumstein, Jacqueline Cohen, Susan Martin, and Michael Tonry, eds., *Research on Sentencing: The Search for Reform* (Washington, D.C.: National Academy Press, 1983).

4. The commission might be more accurately termed "bipartisan." See discussion of the court of appeals and judicial selection, #42 below.

5. The appellate division is the state's intermediate appellate court. See #8 below.

6. For a comprehensive summary of the constitutional and legislative reform efforts concerning the New York courts since 1846, see Frederick Miller, "New York State's Judicial Article: A Work in Progress," in *Decision 1997: Constitutional Change in New York*, ed. Gerald Benjamin and Henrik N. Dullea (Albany, NY: Rockefeller Institute Press, 1997), pp. 127–146. See also Henrik Dullea, *Charter Revision in the Empire State: The Politics of New York's Constitutional Convention* Ph.D. dissertation, Maxwell School, Syracuse University, 1982). For constitutional reform history in New York prior to the twentieth century, see Charles Lincoln, *The Constitutional History of New York* (New York: Lawyers Cooperative, 1906).

7. Statement available at http://www.ncsconline.org/WCDS/Topics/topic1.asp?searchvalue=Court%20Unification.

8. The American Bar Association advocates a simplified and functional system consisting of trial courts in the lower tier, followed by intermediate appellate courts in the next tier, and the courts of last resort in the top tier. This model does not make the multiple jurisdictional distinctions evident in the New York Courts. See *Law & The Courts* (Chicago, IL: American Bar Association, 1998).

9. John Caher, "Court System Needs Reform, Proponents Say," *Albany Times-Union*, January 22, 1998, p. B2.

10. Judith S. Kaye, *The State of the Judiciary 2003* (Albany, NY: New York State Unified Court System, 2003), p. 6.

11. There is some confusion in terminology regarding whether county and specialized courts fall into the category of courts of superior jurisdiction. Some would suggest that all trial courts but the supreme court are limited jurisdiction courts.

12. A separate division of the civil court, the housing court, handles these cases.

13. The existence of nonlawyer judicial officers has been a recurrent target of judicial reformers. Since the justice courts are located almost exclusively in Republican areas in upstate New York, even this seemingly nonpartisan effort to professionalize the courts takes on the political coloration of a Democratic attack on Republican strongholds.

14. The supreme court lacks jurisdiction where exclusive power has been given to the federal courts for certain types of cases, to the court of

claims for actions against the state, and to those cases where the appellate division exercises original jurisdiction. The family, surrogate's, and other specialized courts were established primarily to lessen the caseload of the supreme court, which still retains primary jurisdiction over cases in those courts.

15. The county court also possesses limited appellate jurisdiction in several parts of the state through which it hears civil and criminal appeals from city, town, and village courts.

16. An exception is in the first and second departments, where all non-felony and civil appeals go to the appellate terms.

17. Appeals from the surrogate's courts go to the appellate division.

18. Appeals in civil cases from the appellate term are taken to the appellate division, while criminal appeals go directly to the court of appeals.

19. Judges on the court of appeals were elected until reforms in the 1960s.

20. The court of appeals hears appeals of death penalty sentences directly from the trial court and appeals from determinations made by the commission on judicial conduct. The court also appoints and oversees the board of law examiners and promulgates rules for attorney admissions to practice.

21. David Lewis (president of the New York Association of Criminal Defense Lawyers), quoted in John Caher, "Taking a Conservative Swing?" *Albany Times-Union*, February 17, 1992, p. A1.

22. This official is called the chief administrative judge of the courts if the appointee is a judge; occupants of the position have, with few exceptions, been judges.

23. 2003–2004 Enacted Budget Report (Albany, NY: New York State Division of the Budget, 2003), pp. 19–21.

24. Chief Judge Wachtler requested a court order mandating the governor and legislature to provide the court system with an additional seventy-seven million dollars beyond the amount allocated in the budget passed by the legislature and signed by the governor. This figure represented the difference between the amount requested by the courts and the amount allocated in the final state budget. The issue was eventually resolved in the legislature.

25. A national study of trial court delay conducted by the National Center for State Courts in 1978 assessed the supreme court in Bronx County as one of the slowest, but also one of the least overworked, felony trial courts among the twenty-one urban courts examined. See Thomas Church et al., *Justice Delayed* (Williamsburg, VA: National Center for State Courts, 1978).

A follow-up study published in 1991 suggests that while disposition time in both Bronx County and Brooklyn had improved substantially by 1987, the supreme court operating in those jurisdictions still had one of the lightest workloads (in terms of felony filings per judge) of any of the thirty-nine courts surveyed. See John Goerdt, *Reexamining the Pace of Litigation in 39 Urban Trial Courts* (Williamsburg, VA: National Center for State Courts, 1991), table 2.5.

26.   This phrase, sometimes mistakenly attributed to President Andrew Jackson, was actually uttered by Senator William Marcy in remarks to the U.S. Senate in 1832. Suzy Platt, ed., *Respectfully Quoted* (Washington, D.C.: Congressional Quarterly, 1992), p. 249.

27.   New York City judges used to have "confidential attendants," which one court observer noted were usually "a district leader or district leader's nephew." The four appellate divisions all controlled their own hiring for all court jobs in the division, unconstrained by civil service regulations. Greg Smith and Dan Janison, "Disorder in the Courts: Agency Potential Patronage Haven," *Albany Times-Union*, October 9, 1988, p. A1.

28.   "A Bronx Judiciary Awash in Patronage" *New York Times*, January 3, 2004, pA1.

29.   "Albany Bobbled Court Restructuring," *Buffalo News*, August 15, 1998, p. C2.

30.   This system of nominating conventions for supreme court justices has come under substantial scrutiny after a series of judicial scandals in 2003 with its epicenter in Brooklyn. A *New York Times* editorial decried "New York's Fake Conventions." According to the *Times*, "The 'nominating conventions' are staked with employees and friends of the various bosses. Their job as 'delegates' is to pick up the resumes on the seat of the designated chairs and vote for candidates as swiftly as possible. Some conventions take less than the lunch hour." "New York's Fake Conventions," *New York Times*, July 28, 2003, p. A16.

31.   This system of cross-endorsement sometimes involves agreements with the minor political parties in the district and is frequently part of a much larger set of agreements covering a variety of political offices.

32.   *Albany Times-Union*, November 3, 1990, p. A10. Responding to criticism of the party control of judicial elections, Albany County Democratic Leader J. Leo O'Brien perhaps said more than he intended when he told the press, "I don't think I've ever put anybody in, mentioned anyone for a judgeship, that wasn't more than qualified. . . . Why should we change?"

John Caher, "Political Squabble Fuels Judge Selection Debate," *Albany Times-Union*, September 30, 1990, p. C1. Justice Gerald Esposito, administrative judge for the Bronx civil term and former Democratic district leader, defended the current system of judicial selection as "by and large, a terrific system." "A Bronx Judiciary Awash in Patronage," *New York Times*. A variety of reform commissions—most notably the 1988 Commission on Government Integrity—have advocated removal of judicial selection from partisan electoral politics.

33. "End Judicial Elections," *Albany Times-Union*, December 24, 1994, p. A8

34. A particularly noteworthy example occurred in 1983, when two sitting judges of the Bronx County Supreme Court (including William Kapelman, the presiding judge) were denied renomination by the Bronx County Democratic Party. The reason given by Stanley Friedman, Bronx County Democratic leader, was a desire to foster more ethnic diversity on the court, but it was widely assumed that the two judges had lost favor in the party. They attempted to run for reelection on the Liberal Party line, without the Democratic nomination, but failed to gain reelection. This affair raised the ire of the legal community, who argued that it was a direct assault on judicial independence.

35. The treasurer of the Bronx Democratic Party, a lawyer, was awarded more than $300,000 in legal work assigned by the court, and his daughter, not then admitted to the bar, received more than $50,000. Two other well-connected Bronx lawyers received, respectively, $175,000, and more than $235,00 in court work. *New York Times*, "A Bronx Judiciary Awash in Patronage," January 3, 2004, p. A1. Regulations put into effect by the Office of Court Administration in early 2003 were designed to "eliminate the cronyism affecting appointments of guardians, receivers and other referees." *New York Post*, "Court Gravy Train Derailed" December 3, 2002, p. 23. According to the *New York Times*, however, "It is unclear whether the rules will curb the cronyism in the system. Past efforts at reform have often failed." "A Bronx Judiciary Awash in Patronage," *New York Times*. As late as the end of 2003, several Brooklyn Supreme Court judges admitted that they were given a list of lawyers "approved" by the Democratic Party leaders for this kind of legal work. "Better Judges for New York," *New York Times*, December 24, 2003, p. A20. For an in-depth account of the close relationship between one politically connected lawyer and the court, see "Cozying Up to Judges, and Reaping Opportunity," *New York Times*, November 11, 2003, p. A1.

36. Surrogate judges are responsible for appointing lawyers to act as guardians or conservators of estates. According to a study by the Fund for Modern Courts, these lucrative assignments are frequently given to politically connected attorneys who are past or present party officials, or who have contributed to judges' election campaigns or to the party. Fund for Modern Courts, quoted in "Surrogate Politics," *Albany Times-Union*, December 20, 1986.

37. For example, in Bronx County, according to the *New York Times*, "Many [law clerks and judicial secretaries] were hired not through a process that featured the widespread recruiting of candidates, but through a system in which judges sort through a list of favored candidates sent by political leaders. Some have worked on judicial campaigns or carried petitions for the Democrats. Some are the spouses or relatives of political leaders, including district leaders, who serve as lieutenants for the party organization." While party officials argue that judges are not penalized for refusing these party referrals, the *Times* concluded that "there is ample evidence that judicial hiring discretion has often been constricted." "A Bronx Judiciary Awash in Patronage," *New York Times*.

38. Greg Smith and Dan Janison, "Disorder in the Courts Agency Potential Patronage Haven."

39. In late 2003, as part of the Brooklyn District Attorney's investigation into corruption in the courts of the borough, the borough's top two Democratic officials were indicted on extortion and grand larceny and charged that they tried to force judicial candidates into hiring consultants favored by the party. Two unsuccessful Democratic candidates for civil court told investigators that the indicted leaders "threatened to withdraw the party's support during the 2002 race unless they hired the party's choices to print brochures and work to get out the vote." Andy Newman and Kevin Flynn, "2 Brooklyn Democrats Indicted in Judicial Corruption Case," *New York Times*, November 18, 2003, p. A1.

40. The *New York Times* reported that in Queens, "roughly $200,000, or nearly 40 percent, of the $525,000 raised by the Queens Democratic Party last year [2002] came from courthouse donors." These figures include court staff from secretaries to judges. The *Times* reported that the law clerks to supreme court judges by themselves "donated close to 10 percent of the party's total." Clifford J. Levy, "Where Parties Select Judges, Donor List Is a Court Roll Call," *New York Times*, August 18, 2003, p. A1. The *Buffalo News* similarly suggested that judicial races in western New York are "cash cows"

for the political parties. They reported that cross-endorsed judicial nominees in Buffalo in 1992 were required to pay both the Republican and the Democratic Parties $7500 to offset the "costs" of the nominating conventions that officially selected them. Candidates are oftentimes asked to pay for administrative costs of running Democratic headquarters. While state election law and rules of the courts prohibit "direct or indirect contributions by a judge to any political campaign," it appears that such rules are not always followed and, in any event, the rules allow judges and judicial candidates to buy two tickets to each of the countless political fundraisers run by the party and its other candidates. According to the *News*, "some [judicial candidates] end up spending tens of thousands of dollars on the campaigns of others." Michael Beebe and Robert J. McCarthy, "Appeal for Reform as Spending on Judicial Races Escalates," *Buffalo News*, July 16, 2002, p. A1. Their conclusion: "Judicial candidates are pressured to take part in a political money-laundering system that skirts election law and turns supposedly nonpartisan judges into fund-raisers for powerful party leaders and their favorite candidates." Robert J. McCarthy and Michael Beebe, "Courting Big Money, Putting Politics First, Paying to Run, Buffalo News," July 14, 2002 p. A1.

41. See the discussion of court reform below.

42. The commission is made up of appointees of the governor, the party leaders in the legislature, and the chief judge of the court of appeals, each of whom selects four of the twelve members. The appointments by the governor and chief judge are constrained in that no more than two of their four appointments can be members of the same political party, and both are required to appoint two practicing lawyers and two nonlawyers. Assuming the legislative party leaders appoint members of their own political party, the commission is likely to have an equal number of members of the two major parties.

43. Gary Spencer, "Judicial Screening Panel Rule Changes 'Troubling' to City Bar," *New York Law Journal*, December 5, 1997.

44. The version of this chapter in the previous edition of this book included in the reform agenda an effort to add a fifth judicial department to the state's four existing departments, to handle to burgeoning caseload of Long Island. The addition of a new judicial department has frequently been proposed and Chief Judge Judith Kaye renewed the proposal in 1997. The plan was controversial, in large part because Democrats in the legislature were reluctant to give party leaders in largely Republican Long Island influence over judgeships and other patronage positions that they share with

Democrats under the existing geographical division of the departments. The plan failed to emerge from the legislature and it appears to have dropped from the court reform radar screen.

45. A typically pungent editorial in the *New York Daily News* predicted that the recommendations issued by the commission will "sit handsomely in a binder that will . . . be exhumed someday by researchers looking for museum-quality examples of good-government intentions that came to naught." The creation of independent judicial screening committees, called for in the report, will be by subverted "party bosses" who will see them as "a gaggle of fuddy-duddies who don't understand that the highest qualification for a judgeship is political fealty." The other "cosmetic reform proposals" fail to amount to the "bracing" solution that the panel was not allowed to consider: "blowing up the mess, scrapping judicial elections and appointing judges through merit selection." "Judith Kaye's Dust Collector," *New York Daily News*, December 4, 2003.

CHAPTER 10

Other Governments

The Public Authorities

KEITH M. HENDERSON

The Port Authority of New York and New Jersey, the New York State Thruway Authority, the Power Authority, the Dormitory Authority, and the Metropolitan Transportation Authority are among the most important public agencies in New York State, yet their structure and financing is little understood by the public. Only when a crisis occurs (such as the threatened bankruptcy of New York City in the 1970s, the purchase for one dollar of the 5.3 billion dollar Shoreham Nuclear Plant by an authority, or the destruction of the World Trade Center) does widespread attention befall this unusual form of government. Even then, the state authority may not be immediately visible in the crisis. For example, in the enormous media coverage of the September 11 terrorist attack on the World Trade Center—built and managed by the Port Authority—little attention was paid at first to the state level despite the fact that eighty-four Port Authority employees, including Executive Director Neil Levin, died in the attack. "Even 16 days after the attack—The New York Times carried a story headlined 'State Seeks To Play A Role in the Reconstruction Effort'—as though state government did not automatically have a major role."[1]

There are numerous major state-level public authorities (technically, public benefit corporations) in New York State with billions of dollars worth of assets and debt. In the fiscal year ending March 31, 2003, authorities had over $35 billion in state-supported debt outstanding. An additional $71.7 billion (as of December 31, 2002) was in non-state-supported debt such as revenue bonds.[2]

Throughout the United States these entities provide government or quasi-government functions which cannot easily be carried out by traditional government departments. Public authorities are sometimes used for those functions, particularly when long-term financing is required or businesslike activities conducted.

There are many tasks that government officials wish to do without going through general-purpose governments. They may wish to establish an entity that provides only one service (building a bridge) and collects fees for that service, and maintains a clear connection between benefits and costs. They may wish to establish an entity that provides a long-term benefit (the thruway) and can borrow money for a lengthy period of time and charge fees over time that repay the debt. They may also wish to establish an entity (the Port Authority) that will be more removed from political interference than a state agency would be. There may also be a desire to use an authority to resolve a complicated financial problem, such as how to decommission the Shoreham Nuclear Plant on Long Island. As discussed in more detail later, the need to pay off the debt from constructing, but not using, the plant led to a search for mechanisms to provide state assistance and finally, in 1998, to the largest municipal bond issue ever undertaken anywhere as of that time.

Public authorities play an important, though often hidden, role in reconciling political conflicts in New York State. Their generous streams of revenue make them attractive targets for elected officials and their ability to operate outside normal governmental restrictions places them under pressure to accommodate political demands, particularly those related to balancing the state budget.

The existence of these authorities is also a source of controversy. There are arguments that their accountability to the public and elected officials is too limited, and that they can pursue agendas not in keeping with the public interest. There are also arguments that they control huge resources that should be used for general purposes. The New York career of Robert Moses, as detailed in *The Power Broker,* best embodies the advantages and the problems with these authorities.[3]

THE CHARACTERISTICS OF PUBLIC AUTHORITIES

Each authority is created by a special act of the legislature. Generally, most share certain characteristics in their legal structure, their broad administrative autonomy, and their concern with financing, constructing, or operating revenue-producing facilities or providing public services outside the normal limitations of state government. Often, their activities span several local government jurisdictions, enabling them to deliver areawide services without recourse to the other jurisdictions. Since they have no authorization to levy taxes, they must finance themselves through user charges, fees, tolls, and revenue bonds. Additional funding may be provided by general-purpose governments. Revenue bonds—unlike general obligation bonds, which are legally enforceable obligations of the state—are repaid from project revenues. Like general obligation bonds and New York's unique 'moral obligation' bonds, they are tax-free securities sold to investors in the worldwide municipal bond market but of particular interest to those who otherwise pay New York State taxes on corporate bonds. The lower interest rates on "municipals" makes them competitive with other bonds and costs the issuing jurisdiction less.

Most authorities have the following features:

1. They are administered by boards or commissions, most of whose members are appointed by the governor with state senate confirmation.
2. They borrow outside governmental debt limits.
3. They are exempt from taxation for both bonds and property, although in the latter instance, payments may be made in lieu of taxes.
4. They have the power of eminent domain.
5. They have discretion in establishing charges.
6. Their employees are independent of the civil service system.
7. They can pay higher salaries to their employees than the state proper. (Some top executives make more than the governor.)
8. Their decision making is isolated from the normal political process.

Although New York may use (and some would say abuse) the authority form more than other states, the device is quite common. In the United

States, there are more than six thousand public authorities, equaling about 7 percent of all governmental units.

As in other jurisdictions, there are compelling political, financial, and administrative reasons in New York for creating and sustaining authorities. However, in New York there are additional constitutional factors: the state constitution limits the number of state departments to twenty; requires "full faith and credit" backing for state debt; and—very importantly—requires cumbersome statewide referenda for increases in state debt. The authorities escape these restrictions since they are separate, largely autonomous corporations and are not operating departments of the state.

To better understand authorities in New York, it is helpful to look at them as three functional groups. The transportation group includes the Thruway Authority and the Metropolitan Transportation Authority and its subsidiaries together with other authorities that provide transportation services including mass transit, highway, bridge, and port services. The commerce and development group includes Empire State Development, the Power Authority, and other organizations whose principal function is the development and promotion of New York's commercial environment. The finance group includes the Housing Finance Agency, Dormitory Authority, and other entities engaged in providing low-cost financing and other services to both public and private concerns. A variation of the finance group includes "financial control boards" that have been created to rescue the finances of several municipalities (including New York City) and one county (the Nassau County Interim Finance Authority). These boards have power to monitor, oversee, and restructure the jurisdiction's finances.

THE TRANSPORTATION GROUP

The Thruway Authority is well known to all motorists in New York State and the Metropolitan Transportation Authority to commuters in the New York City area.

Although created by an interstate compact as a bi-state agency and, hence, operating under different legal authorization, the Port Authority of New York and New Jersey (originally called the Port of New York Authority) is among the largest such agencies in the world. One author has called it the *Empire on the Hudson.*[4] It operates LaGuardia, Kennedy, and Newark Airports, as well as Teterboro Airport in New Jersey and the Manhattan heliport; the Port Authority Bus Terminal in New York City; six bridges and tunnels in the New York City area; the PATH Rail Transit System; AirTrain; ferry transportation; the World Trade Center site (privatized for ninety-nine years prior to its destruction), several other trade and industrial enterprises; and, as its name suggests, various marine terminals. By any standard—even the scale we are used to in New York State and New York City—it is a gargantuan operation. Prior to the terrorist attack at the World Trade Center, a $14 billion five-year capital budget plan—largest in the agency's eighty-year history—had been in effect (2001–2006) with projected spending on new PATH trains, airport modernization, harbor dredging, and bridge and tunnel upgrades.[5] The long-delayed AirTrain made its debut exactly one hundred years after the Wright brothers first flew, with a great deal of fanfare for this monorail which will take passengers to Kennedy Airport from Jamaica and Howard Beach with Long Island Railroad and subway connections to Manhattan. The World Trade Center PATH Station reopened in late 2003 after a $323 million, 16-month rebuilding effort. Interestingly, the architectural competition for the World Trade Center memorial was not overseen by the Port Authority but by another public-benefit corporation, the Lower Manhattan Development Corporation.

Generally, the Port Authority has gone its own way, occasionally using differences between New York and New Jersey, whose governors each appoint half of its Board of Commissioners, to its advantage. It has been criticized frequently for avoiding risky projects, subsidizing some commuters and not others, and failing to make enough of a contribution to the region's economy.

In recent years, the Port Authority's role as the foremost U.S. seaport has declined because of competition from other East Coast ports and trade with Asia through the ports of Los Angeles, Long Beach, and others on the West Coast.

Just as the Port Authority has branched out from its original mandate into a variety of economic development projects, so has the Thruway Authority in its assumption of responsibility for the Erie Canal. Part of the official explanation for this unusual arrangement was that since the Thruway Authority had almost forty years of toll-collecting experience, it would be the logical agency to implement a canal toll-collection plan. A more plausible explanation is that pressure from the legislature was applied to the authority to help balance the state budget by relieving the Department of Transportation of the costs of maintaining the canal. Aggressive efforts have since been underway to promote the canal as a recreational and tourist attraction.

Federal funds have been sought and attained for the previously neglected 524-mile canal with both the federal Department of Housing and Urban Development and U.S. Department of Agriculture, as well as other federal agencies, infusing significant funds. In 2003, the Canal Corporation was involved in conflict over the sale of exclusive development rights to a Buffalo developer. "Selling Off Miles of the Erie Canal" was the banner in a New York Times article which described the no-bid process by which only thirty thousand dollars was paid for the right to cut private channels into the canal for housing construction.[6] The state comptroller later rescinded the contract.

A third important transportation authority is the Metropolitan Transportation Authority (MTA), which operates the New York City subways (through the Transit Authority) and the Long Island Railroad, among other activities.

One interesting subsidiary of the MTA, with a long and colorful history, is the Triborough Bridge and Tunnel Authority. It operates the Triborough, Bronx-Whitestone, Throgs Neck, Henry Hudson, Marine Parkway, Cross Bay Veterans Memorial, and Verrazano-Narrows Bridges and the Queens Mid-town and Brooklyn-Battery Tunnels.

The spectacular Triborough Bridge, originally planned by New York City in 1929 with municipal bond financing, could not be built when the stock market collapse rendered municipal credit useless. Robert Moses, whose name recurs again and again when authorities are discussed, was able to arrange for the financing and construction of the bridge by establishing a public authority. The legendary Moses, whose career spans over forty years, had been effective in New York State government as an aid to Governor Al Smith and had already established a popular base of support by the time he began to spearhead the Triborough to completion. The obstacles he faced were considerable, including a personal grudge against him by the president of the United States, Franklin D. Roosevelt, who—through his secretary of the interior and administrator of the Public Works Administration (PWA), Harold Ickes—vowed to withhold federal PWA funding unless Moses was removed from the Triborough board. The measure of Moses's aggressive political skill was that he outmaneuvered the president with carefully timed press releases that made it appear FDR was "playing politics," ultimately forcing the president to relent.[7] When completed—FDR reluctantly participated in the opening ceremonies—the Triborough Bridge began almost immediately to generate more traffic and revenue than even Moses had anticipated and became a model PWA project.

In later years, the authority was expanded, also under Moses's vigorous manipulating, to include other bridges and tunnels. In a revealing statement Robert Moses described the significant governmental role which public authorities play: "The nearest thing to business in government is the public authority, which is business with private capital under public auspices, established only when both private enterprise and routine government have failed to meet an urgent need, and this device is often attacked because it is too independent of daily pressures, too unreachable by the boys and therefore essentially undemocratic."[8]

In virtually every corner of the state there are bridge authorities, port authorities, or other transportation authorities. A partial listing includes the Niagara Frontier Transportation Authority, Rochester-Genesee Regional Transportation Authority, Capital District Transportation Authority, Central New York Regional Transportation Authority, New York State Bridge Authority, Ogdensburg Bridge and Port Authority, Buffalo and Fort Erie Public Bridge Authority, and Port of Oswego Authority.

THE COMMERCE AND DEVELOPMENT GROUP

Some public authorities have been primarily concerned with commerce and development rather than transportation or finance, although they may be involved in project financing. For example, Empire State Development (technically, the Empire State Development Corporation) was established as New York's premier economic development agency under Governor Pataki, combining previous activities of the Job Development Authority, the Urban Development Corporation, and other entities. Officially, its "mission is to provide the highest level of assistance and service to businesses in order to encourage economic investment and prosperity in New York State."[9] It has a network of offices throughout the state and even around the world intended to promote new companies, relocate companies to New York, expand existing operations, and retain and enlarge company workforces. The controversial Urban Development Corporation (see below) remains as the 'parent agency' in the new Empire State Development Corporation which resulted from an effort by the governor—with the cooperation of the legislature—to integrate the state's economic development agencies and "allow one-stop shopping for businesses needing assistance."[10]

In a very different field of activity, the New York State Energy Research and Development Authority was created in 1975 as a response to the energy crisis. The former Atomic and Space Development Authority was transformed into the new agency and given a mandate to accelerate the development and use of energy technologies consistent with the state's economic growth and protection of its environmental values. "Energy research and development" now includes everything from implementation of energy efficiency measures in industries, schools, and hospitals to site management of the former nuclear fuel reprocessing plant at West Valley, Cattaragus County. One important activity undertaken by this authority is administration of the New York Energy $mart program, which is designed to facilitate the transition to a more competitive electricity market.[11]

By far the largest authority concerned with commerce and development is the New York Power Authority, which generates and transmits electric power at wholesale rates through its various facilities including, until recently, nuclear power plants. Under the leadership of Robert Moses, who served as Chairman from 1954 until 1962, the authority expanded its role, completing the St. Lawrence Power Project and the Niagara Power Project. The final generating unit of the latter was placed on line on November 11, 1962. It is now part of an impressive complex that tourists on the Niagara Frontier may visit. The Power Vista, a public observation building, crowns the south buttress, some 350 feet above the river, and provides a view of the 1,840–foot plant which houses thirteen hydro-generators. In the background are the twelve units of the Lewiston Pump Generating Plant. In order to meet power demands of the twenty-first century, upgrading of facilities is occurring and to adjust to the new competitive, deregulated environment for utilities, the authority has attempted to come to terms with private utilities. However, the state comptroller has criticized the Power Authority for using revenues from two hydroelectric plants to subsidize operating losses from nuclear and fossil fuel plants and transmission facilities. In addition, the comptroller faulted the authority's accounting practices. In a follow-up to its initial study, the comptroller's office noted that "NYPA officials generally had not implemented the recommendations contained in our prior report. However, NYPA had sold its two nuclear power plants, which were the target of several of our recommendations."[12]

The Power Authority has participated in the dismantling of another and more expensive ($5.3 billion) nuclear facility which was constructed by the privately owned Long Island Lighting Company (LILCO) but never allowed to operate. After much controversy and protracted negotiations, the Shoreham plant was "sold" to an authority created for this purpose—the Long Island Power Authority—for one dollar and decommissioned under contract with the Power Authority of the State of New York. Shoreham was built by LILCO in the 1960s, when nuclear power looked promising, but with threats of nuclear disaster appearing more real it was never allowed to operate. Several years of effort by the Long Island Power Authority (LIPA) to take over or break up LILCO and refinance Shoreham-related debt with tax-exempt state bonds led to the state legislature's requirement that LIPA assume some of LILCO's assets as well as debt. Meanwhile, campaigning for governor in 1994, George Pataki promised to shake up the unloved electrical and gas utility (LILCO) which supplied power to over one million customers on Long Island.

An opportunity developed several years later when the Brooklyn Union Gas Company agreed to merge with LILCO and acquire its operations in electricity generation and natural gas while LIPA bought its electric transmission and distribution business plus the debts that LILCO still owed for Shoreham. Clearances were required from the state Public Service Commission, the federal Nuclear Regulatory Agency, and the Internal Revenue Service, and all were eventually obtained. Not until 1998 was the deal completed with the floating of the largest authority bond issue ever to that time (dwarfing the second biggest, a New Jersey Turnpike Authority $2 billion issue.)

FINANCE GROUP

One of the most controversial of the finance authorities was the Urban Development Corporation (now incorporated into the Empire State Development Corporation, described above), which was allowed not only to raise its own funds but, also, to override local building and zoning codes. One expert has maintained that the UDC was created in order to build at top speed and "was rammed through the legislature (by Governor Rockefeller) on a 'message of necessity' following the assassination of Martin Luther King."[13]

Officially, the UDC was created to "provide or obtain the capital resources necessary to acquire, construct, rehabilitate or improve industrial, manufacturing, commercial, public, educational, recreational and cultural facilities, and housing accommodations for persons and families of low income, and to carry out the clearance, replanning, reconstruction, and rehabilitation of substandard and unsanitary areas."[14] Its original focus was to provide financial aid for construction of low-income housing, industrial parks, shopping malls, sports facilities, schools, hotels, and new communities (Audubon, near Buffalo; Radisson, near Syracuse; and Roosevelt Island, in New York City). The UDC had been involved in various ways, from partial funding to lending of technical help, in the Javits Convention Center (New York City), the 42nd Street redevelopment (New York City), the Carrier Dome Stadium in Syracuse, the Grand Hyatt Hotel (New York City), the Albee Square shopping mall in Brooklyn, the Sheraton Motor Inn in Utica, and other projects.

A growing fiscal crisis compounded by curtailment of federal housing subsidies caused an overextended UDC to default on $100 million of bond-anticipation notes in 1975. Although this was less dramatic than some media accounts suggested (the default only lasted two months), when combined with the larger fiscal problems of the City of New York it precipitated a frantic search for new financial guarantees from the state which would satisfy the bond market. The state legislature agreed to pay contractors and suppliers during the default period and then came up with a plan to bring UDC reserves up to an adequate level. As of 1977, a completed reorganization for the agency had its focus shifted from housing to economic development, a reduction in its staff, and a new state corporation, the Project Finance Agency, to purchase and refinance some UDC mortgages. Although no longer involved significantly in housing, the UDC funded numerous research, cultural, recreational, and other civic facilities and, following legislation enacted in 1983, issued special obligations to finance correctional facilities and has entered into a lease/purchase arrangement with the state for such facilities. In 1991, it "purchased" the Attica prison from the state in a paper transaction designed to ease the State's budget problems.

Interestingly, a controversial constitutional amendment to rein in such financing, supported by both the governor and the state comptroller, was defeated by the voters in 1995. Again, in 1997, voters rejected a constitutional convention, which might have addressed such issues. Apparently, suspicion of any Albany-controlled reform measures accounts for both defeats.

Another agency heavily involved in complex financing through lease/purchase and other financing arrangements is the Dormitory Authority. The Dormitory Authority, as its name suggests, provides financing and construction services for student dormitories (public and private) but it also provides for many other college and university buildings, court buildings, hospitals, nursing homes, and medical research centers. Projects range from low-cost renovations of single buildings to multi-million-dollar capital-expansion programs. The authority has quietly grown into one of the nation's largest public financing agencies; under Governor Pataki, it has absorbed the former Facilities Development Corporation and the Medical Care Facilities Finance Agency. One of the older of New York's Authorities—established in 1944—it now has outstanding bonds and notes of $31 billion, mainly in health-care facilities, state and city university projects, and other state agency and independent institution projects.[15]

Another important finance authority is the Environmental Facilities Corporation which until 1989/1990 was relatively inactive. Since then its role has been to run the Drinking Water Revolving Fund and the Water Pollution Control Revolving Fund, which in the first instance, makes loans to municipalities at low rates of interest for construction of water pollution control facilities and, in the second, provides both public and private community water suppliers with financial help for projects which improve public water supplies.[16] Other significant authorities include the New York State Housing Finance Agency and State of New York Mortgage Agency. The latter makes low-interest mortgages to lower-income, first-time homebuyers through the issuance of mortgage revenue bonds, and also provides insurance on mortgage loans.

In 1975, when New York City could not pay its debt obligations, the Municipal Assistance Corporation for the City of New York (quickly nick-named Big Mac) was created and, in conjunction with it the New York State Financial Control Board for the City of New York was designed to rescue the finances of the city. A public-benefit corporation was the instrument for aiding the nation's largest city and, although its financing mission on behalf of New York City has been completed, it continues to manage its existing debt. Similar arrangements were made for Yonkers and Troy ("Mini Macs"), terminating oversight in 1998 and 1999, respectively. More recently (2003) the City of Buffalo also fell under a "Fiscal Stability Authority" after its finances were judged to be at the crisis point. Buffalo was also the location for a restructuring of the Erie County Medical Center as a public-benefit corporation and for financing the Roswell Park Cancer Institute expansion by the Roswell Park Cancer Center Corporation.

Responding to the criticisms of finance authorities, the state legislature has taken steps to reassure the public as well as bondholders. "Capping legislation," for example, has been enacted which limits the amount of "moral obligation" bonds that certain corporations may issue. This affects the Municipal Assistance Corporation, Dormitory Authority, Housing Finance Agency, and UN Development Corporation. The latter has financed One, Two, and Three United Nations Plaza as well as other office space in the vicinity of the United Nations.

LOCAL AUTHORITIES AND OTHER PUBLIC CORPORATIONS

In addition to the three groups of state-level authorities discussed above, there are literally hundreds of housing authorities, urban renewal agencies, parking authorities, sewer authorities, water authorities, industrial development agencies, and other organizations associated with general-purpose local governments. In the larger cities, particularly New York City, a dizzying array of organizations with the legal status of public-benefit corporation can be found. New York City has its unique agencies such as the New York City Health and Hospitals Corporation, which took over operation of city hospitals in 1969, and the 1988 New York City School Construction Authority, which has built schools and repaired and renovated existing school buildings. The Hugh L. Carey Battery Park City Authority is another New York City organization intended, originally, to provide moderately-priced housing through private development contracts on land leased from the City but afterward involved in commercial real estate ventures (and—at one point—an elaborate topiary garden proposal) which yielded substantial income, some of which has been returned to the City government. The Battery Park City Authority emphasizes public-private partnerships for multiple-use (commercial, residential, retail, park) development within its designated ninety-two- acre site on the lower west side of Manhattan.

Local authorities are affiliated either with cities, counties, towns, or villages and generally are similar in their functioning to state-level authorities. The oldest are the housing authorities—some of them go back to the 1920s and early 1930s—which receive revenues from tax-exempt bonds and federal and state subsidies as well as income from rental of their housing units. Related, but less important in recent years due to reductions in federal funding, are the over one hundred Urban Renewal Agencies which were originally intended to qualify for financing under federal urban renewal programs. Another grouping with large membership is the industrial development agencies that finance commercial projects intended to be advantageous for development of their areas. They issue taxable as well as tax-exempt bonds, particularly since the 1986 Federal Tax Act severely limited use of tax-exempt financing.

PUBLIC AUTHORITIES: PROBLEMS AND PROSPECTS

From the foregoing description, the careful reader can deduce the two significant problems—distinct but related—of New York's public authorities: accountability and financial integrity. Each has received considerable attention but by rather different groups. Legislative investigations, state commissions, watchdog organizations, and academics have been very concerned with accountability of the authorities. Moody's, Standard and Poor's, and other bond-rating agencies have been closely monitoring the soundness of authority notes and bonds, as has the state comptroller.

In the first instance, it is clear that authorities are not held to the same standards as general-purpose governments. As in other states, the legislative and gubernatorial intent to establish business like agencies with the power to issue tax-free bonds has resulted in a profusion of authorities removed from direct accountability to the public. In Jerry Mitchell's view, "In the United States, as well as many other countries, policy-makers have sought to transform the structure of pressure on government administration by creating self-financing, quasi-independent authorities (referred to also as public enterprises or government corporations)."[17] Some refer to a "Fourth Branch of Government"[18] or "Underground Government."[19] A particularly critical view is expressed by Donald Axelrod, who describes the "shadow government" and shows the ploys used by public officials to make public debt appear lower than it really is.[20] Similarly, New York State's independently elected attorney general, Eliot Spitzer, has recently indicated that authorities are where things are hidden from the public and tough decisions are moved off the balance sheet.[21] In New York, clearly some authorities have taken advantage of their position and have directly thwarted the public will, often with the collusion of the governor. On several occasions in the 1960s, for example, voters turned down financing proposals for low-income housing and slum clearance only to find the newly created Urban Development Corporation engaged in just such activities. Similarly, in 1981, voters rejected a prison construction bond issue only to have the UDC subsequently float bonds to build prisons. The practice has not disappeared in recent years.

Even more disturbing, some have charged that authorities use law about debt to protect themselves and prolong their existence. Robert Moses was able to establish legislation that an authority could not be eliminated or interfered with as long as it had debt outstanding as a means to protect the integrity of obligations to bondholders. Authorities, aware of this provision, can continue to issue small amounts of long-term debt and prevent any intrusion into their existence, or any requests that their funds be used for other purposes.

Proposals for reform, at least as far back as the Temporary State Commission on the Powers of Local Government (1973) and the Moreland Commission (1976)[22] have stressed the need for greater accountability and access. In partial response, a "Public Authorities Control Board" was legislated, but it was more symbol than substance. The 1990 report of the State Commission on Governmental Integrity urged creation of another Moreland Commission and suggested a variety of reforms including a merit system (similar to civil service) for hiring, better internal control procedures, more stringent conflict-of-interest guidelines, greater openness of records and transactions, and, generally, conduct by officers and employees "with a full awareness of their obligations to the public."[23] Prospects for such reforms are not good; as Annemarie Hauck Walsh has pointed out, adding formal controls has not significantly changed the role of authorities in the past.[24] The ongoing controls over authorities include regular reports to the governor, the legislature, and the state comptroller. Annual independent financial audit and budgetary reports are made.

The related problem of credit-worthiness of bonds and notes issued by authorities and some of the more creative solutions to financial problems in New York State has been addressed frequently by state comptrollers, who have cautioned against fiscal gimmickry and even attempted lawsuits to redress the excesses of the state legislature and authority managements. State Comptroller Regan, in 1991, called a sale of Thruway Authority bonds to provide money to purchase the Cross-Westchester Expressway, "the worst fiscal gimmick ever in this state." Along with the selling of Attica prison, in effect, to itself (the UDC bought it from the state for $200 million) and similar transactions, serious questions were raised about New York State's approach to budgeting. While some of the gimmicks have lessened in recent years, State Comptroller McCall was concerned, as is his successor, Alan Hevesi, both of whom referred to "back-door" borrowing.[25]

Because of the severity of the overall state debt problems, the state's credit-worthiness—it is one of the lowest-rated states—has been in continuous peril. Throughout the last thirty or more years, however, general obligation, revenue bonds, and other forms of debt remained, with a few exceptions, of investment quality and could readily be sold in the marketplace.

Thus, in recent years, authorities have been able to accommodate the demands of the bond market and withstand criticisms of their lack of accountability. They have bargained and negotiated effectively with other actors in New York State politics and have developed useful alliances. They have acquiesced in efforts to improve the state's general budget, have simultaneously maintained their autonomy, and have emerged from most political struggles without suffering any of the often-suggested dismantling, privatization, or downsizing measures. Generally, they are well regarded by the interested public, who may see them as flexible, businesslike, and less immersed in politics than other parts of state government. Authorities will continue to play an important role in New York State.

NOTES

1. Robert B. Ward, *New York State Government: What It Does, How It Works* (Albany, N.Y.: Rockefeller Institute Press, 2002), p. 304.

2. Comptroller, State of New York, *Comprehensive Annual Financial Report for the Fiscal Year Ending March 31, 2003*; http://www.osc.state.ny.us.

3. Robert A. Caro, *The Power Broker: Robert Moses and the Fall of New York* (New York: Alfred A. Knopf, 1974) a 1,200 page study of Moses. Moses is also discussed in detail in Eugene Lewis, *Public Entrepreneurship: Toward a Theory of Bureaucratic Political Power* (Bloomington, IN: Indiana University Press, 1980) and Jeanne R. Lowe, *Cities in a Race with Time* (New York: Random House, 1967).

4. Jameson W. Doig, *Empire on the Hudson*, (New York: Columbia University Press, 2001).

5. "Port Authority Approves Budget, Putting Capital Plan in Motion," New York Times, February 23, 2001.

6. "Selling Off Miles of the Erie Canal," New York Times, September 29, 2003.

7. See Robert A. Caro, *The Power Broker*, pp. 426–442.

8. Editors of *Fortune, The Exploding Metropolis* (New York: Doubleday, 1958), p. 81.

9. http://www.nylovesbiz.com.

10. State of New York, Executive Budget 1997–98 (Albany: 1997), p. ix.

11. *New York Red Book*, 97th ed., 2003–04 (Albany, N.Y.: N.Y. Legal Publishing Co.), p. 929.

12. Comptroller, State of New York, Report 2001–F-37, 11/29/01, http://www.osc.state.ny.us/audits.

13. Charles R. Morris, *The Cost of Good Intentions: New York City and the Liberal Experiment, 1960–1975*, (New York: McGraw-Hill, 1980), p. 37.

14. *Manual for the Use of the Legislature of the State of New York*, 1990–91, (Albany: Department of State). (This is known as the "Blue Book.")

15. Comptroller, State of New York, *Comprehensive Annual Financial Report for the Fiscal Year Ending March 31, 2003*, (Albany, N.Y.: Office of the Comptroller, 2003), p. 77.

16. *New York Red Book*, 97th ed., 2003–04, p. 949.

17. Jerry Mitchell, "Accountability and the Management of Public Authorities in the United States," *International Review of Administrative Sciences* 59 (1993): 477.

18. See, for example, Jane Shapiro Zacek, "The Executive Branch," in *New York Politics and Government, Competition and Compassion*, ed. Sarah Liebschultz, et al. (Lincoln: University of Nebraska Press, 1998), p. 119.

19. Commission on Government Integrity, *Underground Government: Preliminary Report on Authorities and Other Public Corporations*, (New York: Fordham University School of Law, April, 1990).

20. Donald Axelrod, *Shadow Government: The Hidden World of Public Authorities and How They Control Over $1 Trillion of Your Money* (New York: John Wiley, 1992).

21. Quoted on *New York Week in Review*, WNED/PBS, November 30, 2003.

22. Temporary State Commission on the Powers of Local Government, *Strengthening Local Government in New York*, part 2, Albany, N.Y.: 1973, pp. 83–88; Moreland Commission, *Restoring Credit and Confidence: A Reform Program for New York State and its Public Authorities*, Albany: March 31, 1976).

23. Commission on Government Integrity, *Underground Government,* pp. 5–6.

24. Annmarie Hauck Walsh, "Public Authorities and the Shape of Decision Making," in *Urban Politics: New York Style,* ed. D. Netzer and J. Bellush (White Plains, NY: Sharpe, 1990), p. 217.

25. http://www.osc.state.ny.us/press.

PART III

Public Policy

Introduction to Part III

Public Policy in New York

JEFFREY M. STONECASH

Public policy discussions in New York are often contentious and protracted. Negotiations about what and how much the state should do are difficult, and are likely to remain so for several reasons. Costs are a central issue. New York, either directly or indirectly, provides extensive public services. As the subsequent chapters will indicate, very large sums of money are involved in public policy issues in the state. New York is among the highest in spending per capita for Medicaid and education. The state spends a great deal on a vast system of roads, bridges, and mass transit systems. In general, government spending per capita in New York is higher than almost all other states.

The sheer magnitude of many programs means that decisions to make further policy commitments in the area can have enormous impacts in subsequent years. There is also an inevitable interdependency of decisions among decisions. Increasing funding for local schools, health care, welfare generally prompts the question of what this will mean for current and future resources for other programs. While the governor and the legislature might like to proceed by considering just the need for more health care, or just a better metropolitan mass transit system, they must continually calculate how such a commitment will limit policy options in other areas in the future.

The extensiveness of state policy involvements also means that, directly or indirectly, a large proportion of the public may be affected by policy decisions. Efforts to change policies can affect many constituents. In some cases these policy impacts are clear and immediate. If the state provides more aid for local schools, it directly affects school programs and local tax rates. If the state seeks more power to approve and control Medicaid costs, it immediately and directly affects many recipients of services. When battles develop over how much Tuition Assistance Program (TAP) aid will be provided, or how much state support will be provided to the SUNY system, they affect students and their families all over the state. In many cases the impacts are largely confined to the less affluent, such as when decisions are made about welfare, aid to attend college, and Medicaid, which provides health-care support for the less affluent. But middle-income and more affluent residents are also affected by state government. When state government provides less aid to local schools and governments, it puts pressure on local governments to raise local property taxes. State decisions about how much to support mass transit in the New York City metropolitan area affect the performance of city subways and of commuter lines from the suburbs. If this system does not work well, it makes it difficult for more affluent commuters to get to work. It also makes it more difficult for employers to rely on employees.

The policy choices of the state affect not only individuals but local governments. State government "provides" many policies by requiring local governments to provide services, and then state government distributes local aid to support these programs. For example, the state requires that local governments provide welfare, Medicaid services, and elementary and secondary education, and then provides considerable state aid to support those services. Over 60 percent of the state budget is devoted to state aid to local governments, and this level of support creates a complicated ongoing relationship between state government and local constituencies and officials. This intergovernmental entanglement means that not only is there extensive lobbying by groups about policy decisions, but local officials are continually worried that the state will not provide enough aid to support the policy requirements imposed by the state.

Finally, all the policy decisions made in New York are constrained by the recent history of economic growth in the state. While many other states have experienced steady growth in jobs and population, growth in New York has been relatively limited in recent decades. That history has resulted in more concern that the conservative arguments that state and local taxes are too high, and that state and local governments spend too much money, may have some validity. There is now more concern about constraining the growth of government programs and restructuring them to try to save money and use existing funds more effectively.

All these conditions make the politics of public policy contentious. For every policy area there are strong advocates arguing that the state should make more of an effort in their area. These advocates are also aware of the need to establish the merits of their area relative to others. They realize they must anticipate the widespread argument of the need to lower taxes and ease state mandates. The result is difficult choices. To provide an indication of the variety and nature of state policies and the issues that are involved in each area, the following chapters cover some of the major policy concerns in New York: taxes and the economy, local and higher education, public welfare, transportation, health care, and the environment.

CHAPTER 11

The Economy, Taxes, and Policy Constraints in New York

STEPHANIE LUNDQUIST AND AMY WIDESTROM

Many public policies require fiscal resources. The policy areas reviewed in the following chapters—local and higher education, welfare, health, transportation, and the environment—all require some state expenditures. In some cases, the public dollars involved are enormous. To fund these programs, the state must acquire revenue. This prompts questions of what tax levels are acceptable, what kinds of taxes should be imposed, what tax burdens are fair to impose on individuals of different means, and whether charges for services should be relied upon instead of taxes.

The political debate about taxes has been intense and prolonged in New York State. The essential question of recent years has been whether taxes and regulation are too burdensome and hurt the state's economy. The tax issue has emerged at both the state and the local level because taxes are high for both levels of government. The economy of the state has not grown much in recent years, particularly upstate,[1] prompting even more criticism of state taxation and regulation policies. This tax debate is important because its outcome affects the resources raised by the state to support the policy areas discussed in later chapters. This chapter reviews the evolution of tax policy in the state and the steps taken in recent years to respond to this issue.

THE ECONOMY—TAX POLICY DEBATE IN NEW YORK

New York state and local tax levels increased steadily and significantly starting in the 1960s and by the 1970s New York had developed the highest combined state and local tax burden in the nation.[2] Figure 11.1, presented on page 254, illustrates the rise in state and local tax effort since the 1950s. "Tax effort" is defined as state or local taxes divided by total personal income, which represents the portion of income taken by government in taxes. The increase in both of these taxes was met with strong criticism. Critics argued that high taxes make the state less attractive to business.[3] They contended that state mandates and high Medicaid costs were increasing the state and local tax burdens.[4] Critics also argued that the progressive taxes enacted by the state— a higher percentage of income taken at higher levels of income—were driving out the well-educated and affluent younger population.[5]

By the mid-1970s this argument had more credibility. The state's population stopped growing and reports of a decline in jobs emerged. Later years showed significant losses in jobs. The situation became particularly serious by the mid-1970s, with New York City and the state facing a fiscal crisis. The practice of filling shortfalls in budgets by borrowing large sums had to be stopped as the short-term debt obligation became too large to pay back while sustaining regular operating budgets. The consequence was that the proponents of cutting taxes began to have more influence in the ongoing dialogue about tax levels throughout the 1980s.

Not everyone agrees that the solution to New York's problems is to cut taxes and public programs. There are those who have consistently argued that the key to enhancing the state's attractiveness to business is to have a well-educated labor force and a good infrastructure. A report by the Fiscal Policy Institute points out that New York State's income inequality is the highest in the nation, and continues to grow.[6] Some politicians favor more state-sponsored programs to alleviate the human capital gap between people from high- and low-income families.[7] Additionally, the advocates of "investing in New York" have continually pushed for allocating more money to highways, bridges, mass transit, and education on the premise that it will produce an environment more attractive to business and a better-trained workforce. These advocates have supported state retention of revenue so it can provide state aid for these activities. Peter Goldmark, former executive director of the New York Port Authority, and Stanley Fink, former speaker of the assembly, argued that the quality of infrastructure is very important for attracting business. They contended that the state should retain revenue to make sure that the state's bridges, roads, and mass transit systems are maintained. This argument has had an effect on the debate about taxes because numerous studies have suggested that the state's infrastructure is declining. Democrats, led by Assembly Speaker Sheldon Silver, have argued that the state is making significant progress in lowering business taxes, and want to focus on improving the state's education system and infrastructure.[8]

There are also those who argue that, if anything, the state should play a larger role and reduce the burdens on local governments and school districts by assuming responsibility for programs or providing more state aid. As discussed by Donald Boyd in chapter 2, the state provides large sums of aid to local governments. If the state reduces its revenue-raising activity and relatively more of this funding comes from local governments, there will be greater reliance on local tax bases with all the inequities that accompany such a situation. This may also mean that state funding for public transportation and education will decline.

Despite these counterarguments, the tax cut proponents became even louder and more influential as New York's economy struggled during the early 1990s. Many businesses left New York because of what they considered the state's antibusiness tax and regulation policies.[9] From 1989 to 1993, as a national recession unfolded, New York saw approximately six hundred thousand jobs leave the state.[10] Even as the nation's economy began to recover, the recession in New York continued to linger. Despite some small signs of an economic upturn, unemployment remained a serious concern and the economic recovery in New York lagged well behind that of the nation as a whole.[11] From November 1992 to March 2001, New York State's total job growth was 12.6 percent (967,600 jobs), while the national job growth rate was 21.4 percent (23,322,000 jobs).[12] Finally, New York State has suffered a higher percentage of job losses since the recession of March 2001 than the nation as a whole.[13] Many business leaders blamed the economy's continued poor performance on New York's policies of high taxes, burdensome regulations, and ever-rising fees toward business.[14] In 2003, the Public Policy Institute of New York State, published a report suggesting that taxes levied on New York State's businesses constituted one-third of the state's tax revenues in the projected 2003–2004 New York State Executive Budget.[15]

By 1993, Mario Cuomo, New York's liberal Democratic governor, began to admit there was at least some validity to the claims being made by business.[16] Cuomo proposed a package of tax cuts and regulatory reforms aimed at helping business. Business, however, argued that Cuomo's measures did not go far enough.[17] Senate Majority Leader Ralph Marino, a Republican, agreed and pushed for even greater tax cuts.[18] By 1994, the question was not whether the tax and regulatory burdens imposed on business in New York should be eased, but rather by how much.

During the 1994 gubernatorial campaign, Republican challenger George Pataki repeatedly attacked the incumbent Governor, Mario Cuomo, claiming the governor's tax and regulatory policies toward business were responsible for the severe job loss and poor economic performance that New York had suffered.[19] After Pataki won the election, he claimed a mandate to improve the economic climate in New York: "On Election Day, the citizens of New York looked to the future and chose a new direction for state government—a path of less spending, lower taxes, fewer regulations."[20] Pataki has acted on his perceived mandate, making the rejuvenation of the state's economy through lower taxes and fewer regulations on business one of the priorities of his administration.[21]

Pataki acted quickly on his commitment to lower taxes. In the 1995 session he proposed and was able to win significant tax cuts. From when he took office in January 1995 through September 1997, 225,000 new jobs were created in New York State.[22] However, the Fiscal Policy Institute published a report indicating that the jobs created in the 1990s were not sufficient to provide a "balanced economic future" for New York State.[23] This report finds that the jobs created were predominantly low-paying jobs, while those leaving New York State were higher-paying jobs.[24] Further, as previously mentioned, New York State lost jobs at a higher rate than the nation as a whole from March 2001 to December 2003. As a result, even assembly leaders often speak about attracting business to New York State by reforming regulations and lowering energy costs.[25] Current political rhetoric from both major parties is framed mostly in terms of helping business and improving New York's economy, and whether enough has been done to reduce taxes and regulations.

New York State's economy continues to lag well behind the rest of the nation as a whole. While the employment rate decreased 2 percent in the United States from March 2001 to July 2003, it decreased 3.1 percent (265,000 jobs) in New York State.[26] Additionally, while the national real hourly wage increased 7.8 percent between 1995 and 2000, it increased only 0.9 percent in New York State.[27] Finally, New York State has one of the highest state and local tax burdens in the nation, and is among the five largest economic slow-growth states.[28]

THE POLITICAL RESPONSE: TAX CHANGES

The pressure to cut taxes has been a central issue for the last thirty years. When Hugh Carey became governor in 1975 it was widely agreed that the state needed to bring down its spending and taxes. At the same time the state was experiencing these specific problems, the general political climate in the country regarding taxes shifted. Resistance to taxes, symbolized most clearly by Proposition 13 in California, increased dramatically in the late 1970s. The election of President Reagan in 1980 was regarded as another indication of the hostility to taxes in the nation.

Governor Carey and the legislature made the first of several tax cuts. The tax which received the most attention during this debate was the personal income tax. Politicians believe this tax is the most visible and critics of state tax policy tend to focus on this tax. Governor Pataki also made a reduction in the personal income tax one of the central components of his economic rejuvenation plan. As a consequence, the top rate for this tax has been reduced from about 16 percent to under 7 percent. As these changes have occurred, a persistent focus has been how much individuals with different incomes should pay.[29]

Despite the various cuts, state and local tax efforts have declined only modestly since they peaked during the early 1970s. Figure 11.1 indicates state and local tax effort over time.[30] During the 1950s state tax effort was consistently lower than local tax effort. Most services were paid for with local tax dollars, and state aid was relatively limited. During the 1960s state tax effort climbed significantly as the state provided more aid and assumed direct responsibility for some services. For a few years during the 1970s the state was raising more in taxes than local governments, but since then state taxes have declined somewhat, leaving local taxes higher than state taxes. Perhaps most important to the tax debate is that the state's high tax levels are due to the combination of state and local taxes. While much of the debate has focused on state taxes, local taxes in New York continue to be very high.[31] In most states, beginning in the 1960s state taxes surpassed local

FIGURE 11.1.
State and local tax effort, 1950–2000

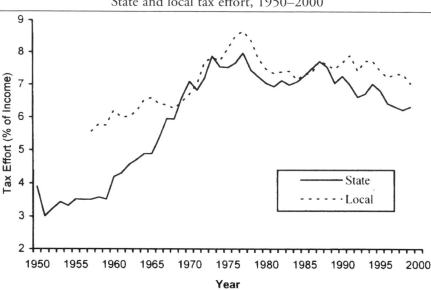

taxes, and as state aid increased local taxes declined.[32] That has not occurred in New York.

Because overall tax levels have not declined, critics continue their argument that taxes in New York are too high. A 2002 report by the Public Policy Institute of New York State stated that New York had the highest per capita tax burden in the nation.[33] Critics also argue that the state is too generous in its programs, and the commitments of the state are consistently beyond the revenues the state generates.[34] Local education is very expensive, with school personnel receiving some of the highest salaries in the nation (see chapter 12). Critics argue that there are too many mandates on local governments, such as for Medicaid (see chapter 14) and that mandates are costly.[35] This mandating has been a target of complaints from local officials for some time. All these arguments lead to the conclusion that the state must cut back. The senate, held by the Republicans, and the Business Council have consistently made these arguments.

There continue, however, to be strong supporters of the state playing a strong and even greater role. As discussed in the following chapters, there are enormous inequalities among local schools in the financial resources they have. Some of Medicaid costs continue to be paid by local property taxes. Large segments of the population are struggling to obtain jobs and become regular participants in the labor force with adequate health care. Advocates who work in these areas argue that the state should do more, rather than less, to alleviate these burdens.

A POLITICAL RESPONSE: CHARGES AND FEES

While tax levels have been restrained in recent years, more revenues are being raised through other means. State officials, including Governor Pataki, have kept their promise to not increase broad-based taxes by increasing the role of fees and charges as a means of raising revenue.[36] Faced with a strong resistance to general taxes, more fees have been imposed and those already in existence have been increased. Fees for car registration and driver's licenses continue to increase, as do tuition and fees at state universities.[37] Additionally, new fees have been imposed in a wide array of areas, such as paying for access to facilities at public campsites.[38]

The consequence has been a significant increase in the role of charges and fees in state and local revenue. In 1957 New York State and its local governments raised $599 million in revenue from charges and miscellaneous sources. Most of that total was raised at the local level. In 2000 the state and its local governments raised $27.8 billion in charges and miscellaneous revenue, with 62 percent of that raised at the local level. Charges and miscellaneous revenues have become a significant proportion of state and local revenues.[39] In 2000, charges and fees contributed 20.1 percent of the state's own general revenue, not including federal aid. Meanwhile, they contributed 27.7 percent to local governments' general revenue.

Charges represent a nontax approach to paying for government. Rather than pay for services out of general taxes, citizens who wish some service (a health test, use of a park, education at a community college or a state university) or a right of access (driver's license, hunting or fishing license, campground usage) pay for it directly. The growth of fees has drawn very mixed reactions. Advocates argue that citizens who use services should pay for them. This makes citizens who want services aware that it costs the state money to provide them. For example, campers must help pay for the state resources that accompany this past time. This also serves to constrain the growth of some services beyond what people "really" want. The essential argument is that government engages in many activities that provide direct benefits to individuals, and there should be some connection between benefits and costs in these areas.

Not everyone is happy with the growth of charges. Critics think that activities of general social benefit should be paid for through general taxes. Others argue that politicians have gradually increased the role of charges because there is so much attention to tax effort indicators—charges and fees receive much less attention. Fees in particular have drawn sharp criticism.[40] The Business Council has argued that they make doing business harder, and they are just another (but less obvious) way for politicians to find money to spend.[41] Additionally, many of the new and increased fees in the 2004–2005 budget would "hit the insurance and health care industries hard, and affect other businesses like tire sales and nuclear power," which increases the cost of doing business in New York and "perhaps [results] in job loss or even the flight of business from the state."[42] Further, many argue that fees place an unequal burden on the middle and working classes because, as the director of the Center on Budget and Policy Priorities in Washington says, "The fees have no relationship to ability to pay."[43] In other words, fee increases on transportation, marriage licenses, or birth certificates take a larger portion of middle-class and working-class disposable income.

It is unclear if increasing charges and fees is simply a hidden way to raise money. If this is the case, the real extraction from citizens is higher when all sources of revenue are considered. If all sources of state revenue are divided by total income, overall state effort has remained unchanged for over a decade. However, it has gone up at the local levels, where charges and fees have become more significant.[44]

THE ONGOING DEBATE AND POLICY LIMITS

The ability of the state to provide more funding for programs is limited by the amount of revenue the state can generate. As of now, the dominant view among state officials is that taxes should not go higher. Indeed, a substantial proportion believes that they must be cut. The crucial point is what this has done to public policy debates. The current climate makes it difficult to respond to problems just by raising more money through taxes. Additional revenues must come primarily from economic growth.[45] This also means that significant short-term responses to specific policy problems can come only from reallocating resources from other areas.

NOTES

1. Richard Deitz and Mike DeMott, "Is Upstate New York Showing Signs of a Turnaround?" *Current Issues in Economics and Finance, Second District Highlights* 5, no. 6 (May, 1999) (New York: Federal Reserve Bank of New York): 1–4; Fiscal Policy Institute, *The State of Working New York* (Albany, NY: Fiscal Policy Institute, 2003), p. 8.

2. Roy Bahl and William Duncombe, *Economic Growth and Fiscal Planning: New York in the 1990s* (New Brunswick, NJ: Center for Urban Policy Research, 1991), p. 118.

3. Peter D. McClelland and Alan L. Magdovitz, *Crisis in the Making: The Political Economy of New York State Since 1945* (Cambridge: Cambridge University Press, 1981); Michael Wasylenko, "Employment Growth and the Business Climate in New York and Neighboring States," Metropolitan Studies Program Occasional Paper No. 140 (Syracuse, NY: Maxwell School, Syracuse University, 1990).

4. Robert Ward, "The $163 Lightbulb: How Albany's Mandates Drive Up Your Local Taxes," The Public Policy Institute of New York State, (Albany, NY: November 1999), p. 3; Public Policy Institute of New York State, Inc., *Putting Stock in New York State* (Albany, March, 2000).

5. Richard Alba and Katherine Trent, "Population Loss and Change in the North: An Examination of New York's Migration to the Sunbelt," *Social Science Quarterly* 67 (December, 1986): 690–706.

6. Frank Mauro and James Parrott, The Fiscal Policy Institute, *New Study Finds Income Inequality in New York Worst of Any State . . . and Getting Worse Rather Than Better* (Albany, NY: Fiscal Policy Institute, April, 2002).

7. Ibid.

8. David McKay Wilson, "Corporate Cravings," *Empire State Report*, February 1997, pp. 23–27.

9. Alan Breznick, "Taking Care of Small Business," *Empire State Report*, March 1993, pp. 27–30.

10. Jon Gertner, "New York's Return On Investment," *Empire State Report*, December 1993, pp. 30–33.

11. Lawrence Van Gelder, "Unemployment Is Higher in New York City and State," *New York Times*, November 5, 1994, p. 54, Barry Meier, "New York Region Shows Big Gains in Job Market," *New York Times*, June 4, 1994, p. 47.

12. Public Policy Institute of New York State, *Facts and Figures About New York's Economy* (Albany, January, 2004) http://www.ppinys.og/nyecon/stats.pdf.

13. Ibid.

14. Public Policy Institute of New York State, *The Key to the Upstate Economy? Manufacturing—Still* (Albany, NY: Public Policy Institute, September, 2002), pp. 8–10.

15. Public Policy Institute of New York State, *A Fair Share—At Least!* (Albany, NY: Public Policy Institute, March, 2003).

16. Alex Storozynski, "How to Create a Business-Friendly Environment in New York," *Empire State Report*, September 1993, pp. 29–34.

17. Breznick, "Taking Care of Small Business"; Jeff Plungis, "The Governor's Budget: Reading the Tea Leaves," *Empire State Report*, February 1994, p. 54.

18. James Dao, "Silver Asks Giuliani's Aid in Pressuring Republicans," *The New York Times*, April 13, 1994, p. B5.

19. Kevin Sack, "Political Notes: Statistics Cast Doubts on Pataki's Job-Loss Ads," *The New York Times*, Sptember 4, 1994, p. 36.

20. Jeff Plungis, "The Pataki Blueprint," *Empire State Report*, March 1995, pp. 21–28.

21. Amy Terdiman, "Rebuilding New York's Business Image," *Empire State Report*, September 1995, pp. 27–32, 67; Andrew Danzo, "Beyond Tax Cuts and Deregulation," *Empire State Report*, December 1996, pp. 35–40; "The Governor's Chief 'Bureaucracy Buster,': An Interview with Robert L. King," *Rockefeller Institute Bulletin*, 1998, (Albany, NY: The Nelson A. Rockefeller Institute of Government), pp. 104–109.

22. Eileen A.J. Connelly, "The Road Back," *Empire State Report*, December 1997, pp. 41–44.

23. Fiscal Policy Institute, *The State of Working New York*, p. 40.

24. Ibid.

25. Erik Kriss, "The Legislature's Unfinished Business," *Empire State Report*, June 1995, pp. 19–28.

26. Fiscal Policy Institute, *The State of Working New York*, p. 5.

27. Ibid., p. 8.

28. Public Policy Institute of New York State, *Tax Watch '04* (Albany, NY: Public Policy Institute, November, 2003).

29. Diane F. Dwyre, Mark O'Gorman, Jeffrey M. Stonecash, and Rosalie Young, "Disorganized Politics and the Have-Nots: Politics and Taxes in New York and California," *Polity* 27, no. 1, (Fall 1994): 25–47; Citizens for Tax Justice, *A Far Cry From Fair* (Washington, D.C: 1991).

30. This approach is not without its limits. It does not measure the extent to which taxes are paid by residents of other states (as with the hotel occupancy and commuter taxes) and ultimately shifted (exported) to residents of other states by passing higher costs along when products are sold elsewhere. It does not capture the extent to which residents of New York actually pay the taxes collected. Nonetheless, it is a good indicator of the inclination of politicians to tax wealth and economic activity.

31. Jeffrey M. Stonecash, "Are We Really Reducing Taxes?" *Empire State Report*, June 1985, pp. 9–14

32. Jeffrey M. Stonecash, "The Politics of State-Local Relations," in *Governing Partners*, ed. Russell Hanson (Boulder, CO: Westview Press, 1998), p. 81.

33. Public Policy Institute of New York State, *Budget Watch '03* (Albany, NY: Public Policy Institute, December, 2002).

34. Public Policy Institute of New York State, *Putting Stock in New York State* (Albany, NY: Public Policy Institute, March, 2000); Public Policy Institute of New York State, *Budget Watch '03* (Albany, NY: Public Policy Institute, 2003).

35. For an analysis of the situation of local governments and the mandate issue, see Jeffrey M. Stonecash, "Home Rule in New York," in *Home Rule in America: A Fifty-State Handbook*, ed. Dale Krane, Platon N. Rigos, and Melvin Hill (Washington, DC: Congressional Quarterly, 1998); Ward, "The $163 Lightbulb," pp. 79–82.

36. Elizabeth Benjamin, "Taxes May Not Increase, but Fees Would," *Times Union*, January 21, 2004.

37. Michael Powell and Christine Haughney, "Wary of Higher Taxes, Officials Boost Fees," *Washington Post*, April 7, 2003, p. A3.

38. Public Policy Institute of New York State, *Fees That Ate New York*, (Albany, NY: February, 1992); Stacy Albin, "Camping Fees to Rise," *New York Times*, April 8, 2003, p. D5.

39. Jeffrey M. Stonecash, "Cash or Charge," *Empire State Report*, January 1990, pp. 23–25.

40. Alan Breznick, "Tax Policy," *Empire State Report*, January 1992, pp. 33–36.

41. Public Policy Institute of New York State, *The Fees That Ate New York*.

42. Al Baker, "Fees, as Surely as Taxes, Will Rob the State of Jobs, Critics of Pataki Budget Say," *New York Times*, February 16, 2003 p. 38.

43. Powell and Haughney, "Wary of Higher Taxes," p. A3.

44. Stonecash, "Cash or Charge," pp. 23–25.

45. Roy Bahl and William Duncombe found that is where additional revenue came from during the 1980s. See *Economic Growth and Fiscal Planning* (New Brunswick, NJ: Center for Urban Policy Research, 1991), pp. 136–141.

CHAPTER 12

The Politics of State Education Aid

Is "Demography Destiny"?

ROBERT F. PECORELLA

A merican culture is grounded in notions of individual political rights and personal economic achievement. In large part, governance in the United States is designed to safeguard the former and encourage the latter. In modern American society, the communities in which people live clearly reflect their personal levels of economic achievement. Few Americans object to the fact that residents of upper-income communities have bigger homes, newer and more expensive automobiles, and generally nicer private amenities than their less well-off counterparts. Indeed, such manifestations of private wealth are not only tolerated but celebrated in a competitive culture. On the other hand, however, concerns arise when the level of public services available in different communities reflects or even exacerbates private wealth differentials.

In no other policy area are such concerns more fundamental than in public education. After all, the legitimacy of a social system based on economic disparities rests on the shared belief in the concept of equal opportunity. If children in some communities, however, begin the competitive race for success with disadvantages based not only in the uncontrollable lottery of life's fortunes but in government policies that act to reaffirm the circumstances of these varied fortunes, that is, with "inequities of fate compounded by failures of public policy," then the very idea of equality of opportunity is called into question.[1] In short, government may not be able to redress many of the personal inequities that distinguish individuals from each other, but it can enact public education policies that seek to counterbalance the impact of private-sector inequities. With these twin notions in mind, this chapter examines educational funding in New York State.

Education is one of New York State's biggest "big-ticket" budget items. In fiscal year 2000, the state allocated nearly $13.7 billion in general education aid to local school districts, an amount equal to 44 percent of total education spending in New York and more than 15 percent of total state spending.[2] The local school districts, in turn, spent 15.98 billion of their own dollars on education. Factoring in federal monies, government spending on public education in New York State rose to over 31 billion dollars for fiscal year 2000, reflecting a 23 percent increase after inflation in total education spending since 1996. Two-thirds of these expenditures support the instructional work of the more than 260,000 teachers and other educational professionals who are charged with educating the 2.84 million students enrolled in the state's public schools. Although the student numbers reflect a decline in enrollment from the "baby boom" years of the early 1970s, they represent a more than 10 percent student increase since the early 1990s.

During most normal budget years, the politics surrounding overall education expenditures are fairly predictable. The governor's initial budget proposal usually includes smaller education expenditures than the final budget adopted by the legislature. In exchange for the annual opportunity to claim credit for increased education spending within their districts, legislators give due consideration to gubernatorial initiatives in other policy areas. Although this tactical aspect of the education budget process is relatively harmless, the intrastate inequities in spending included within the education budget are not. At best, state education aid only partially alleviates the existing inequities in per-pupil expenditures in school districts around the state. Depending on where one sits or, perhaps more to the point, where one's children sit, these funding inequities may well represent a major problem. In recent years, concerns about educational quality have become sufficiently widespread, information about educational spending inequities sufficiently well documented, and the legitimacy of education bureaucracies sufficiently questionable to require more than the usual rhetorical response from decision makers.

This chapter examines the politics surrounding the distribution of state education aid in New York in a three-part analysis. The first part reviews the constitutional and statutory context within which state school aid policy in New York is developed. The second part examines comparative data concerning educational expenditures, school environments, and student outcomes in an effort to distinguish between and among the state's school districts based on their relative economic capacity. The third part analyzes the politics of the major arenas within which state education funding is formulated, the legislature and the court system. The analysis suggests that although the legislature has repeatedly failed to correct the inequities in state school aid, recent state court decisions may well force significant change in the funding of New York's schools.

THE FORMAL EDUCATIONAL STRUCTURE
IN THE STATE OF NEW YORK

In 1784, New York became one of the first states in the nation to establish a free and universal public school system. Article XI of the New York State Constitution is the basis for the state government's role in New York's education system. Section 1 requires the legislature to "provide for the maintenance and support of a system of free common schools, wherein all the children of this state may be educated." This section has been interpreted by the courts to require "not simply schools, but a system; not merely that they shall be common, but free; and not only that they shall be numerous, but that they shall be sufficient in number so that the children of the state may, unless otherwise provided for, receive in them their education."[3] Section 2 of Article XI provides constitutional status to the regents of the University of the State of New York, created by statute in 1784, as the governing body of the state's system of common schools. Currently, there are sixteen regents, one from each of the state's twelve judicial districts and four from the state at-large, who are selected by majority vote of the entire state legislature for overlapping seven-year terms.

The regents are responsible for New York's comprehensive educational system, including "all public and nonpublic elementary and secondary schools; all postsecondary institutions including State University, City University of New York and all independent and proprietary schools; all museums, libraries and historical societies; vocational and rehabilitation agencies; and it also has jurisdiction of 31 major professions." The regents select the state's commissioner of education, who serves at their pleasure. "Comparative research has found no other state in which a single education authority has been assigned, either by constitution or by statute, the breadth of responsibilities assigned to the Board of Regents/Commissioner of Education."[4]

The state legislature's role in selecting the Board of Regents represents a significant limitation on the governor's appointment authority in general and a major impediment to the governor's ability to influence education policy in New York. Moreover, because the Regents are chosen by a majority vote of all state legislators, the large Democratic majorities in the 150-seat assembly coupled with relatively small Republican majorities in the smaller senate have allowed the Democrats in the legislature to control the process of selecting the regents in New York State. Although that selection process has always been a source of institutional tension between the two branches, it became a directly partisan matter with the election of George Pataki as the first Republican governor in twenty years in 1994.

Responsibility for the actual delivery of public education services in New York lies with the state's 741 local school districts, the overwhelming majority of which function as independent entities charged with hiring local superintendents and exercising budgetary authority, subject to voter approval, within their districts.[5] Although these local boards are independent, their day-to-day operations are subject to statewide mandates from the Board of Regents that tightly constrain their hiring and curriculum policies. The five school districts representing the cities of Buffalo, New York, Rochester, Syracuse, and Yonkers, however, are not independent of their city governments. Within these five districts, which include over 41 percent of students in the state, school budgets are part of the overall municipal budgets. Not surprisingly, the New York City school district is the state's largest with nearly 37 percent of total student enrollment.

FINANCING PUBLIC EDUCATION:
LOCAL CONTROL, STATE AID, AND EQUITY

The American emphasis on local control of education reflects a cultural distrust of central authority as well as doubts among cultural and religious traditionalists about the values inherent in modern public education. Local control, however, means that a large proportion of the funding necessary to run schools must be raised at the district level. While the five large-city districts are dependent on general municipal budgets for their funding, the independent school districts in the state are heavily dependent on property taxes to support their operations.[6] Significant inequities can result from such a system as evidenced by the fact that in some instances wealthier independent school districts are able to secure much larger per-pupil revenues than districts in poorer communities employing similar property tax rates.[7]

There are a number of possible reactions to this fiscal situation ranging from market-based acceptance—that is, that such inequities are natural in a society based on individual competitive effort—to more radical left perspectives that view education funding as simply another form of class reproduction. In New York State, however, the mainstream political perspective has long rejected the notion that school-funding inequities are either natural or systemic. Instead, state policy has sought to move toward increased spending equalization in school districts around the state by using state resources to counterbalance uneven local tax capacities. Since increased educational equity through state intervention has been the model in New York for decades, it is reasonable to evaluate education spending in the state from within this equity paradigm. Before analyzing state efforts at equalization, however, some mention of the federal role in education funding is useful.

The federal government became directly involved in allocating money for education with the passage of the Elementary and Secondary School Act (ESEA) of 1965.[8] The federal fiscal role in education, however, has been small relative to total expenditures. Since the passage of ESEA, federal expenditures have accounted for less than 5 percent of New York State's education spending. Moreover, because it was structured as a categorical grant-in-aid program, federal aid through ESEA has been focused on supporting specific educational initiatives rather than on providing general funding assistance. Although the reauthorization of ESEA in 2002, the No Child Left Behind Act, designed to "ensure that all children have a fair, equal, and significant opportunity to obtain a high quality education," increased the federal regulatory role at the state and local levels, particularly in large city school districts, the national government remains a junior partner in education funding.

State governments, on the other hand, are the primary entities charged with counterbalancing the inequities resulting from uneven local revenue capacity. On average, state resources account for more than 50 percent of total education spending nationwide.[9] In New York, however, the state share of the burden has historically been 6 to 10 percent lower than the national average, although it has increased somewhat since the later 1990s. Notwithstanding the fact that more than one-half of education funds are raised locally in New York, the state share of funding could still go a long way toward alleviating the inequities generated by differential local tax bases.

STATE AID AND EDUCATIONAL EQUITY:
THE OVERALL VIEW

Table 12.1 highlights the impact of state aid on total per-pupil expenditures. The data point to three general conclusions about school district funding capacity in New York State: (1) Although the data are skewed somewhat by the fact that New York City is considered as one school district, the majority of the state's primary and secondary students attend schools in districts with less than average locally generated district expenditures. (2) Schools in the "low need, high resource" districts of the state generate on average over 212 percent more local education revenues than schools in the state's rural areas. (3) New York City generates a larger percentage of local revenues for education than any other district except for those in the wealthiest areas of the state. In fact, excluding the wealthiest districts, New York City raises over 8 percent more local money for education than the average of the remaining districts.

The data in Table 12.1 also point to four general conclusions about the impact of state aid on educational equity in New York. (1) State education aid notably increases and to some extent equalizes educational expenditures across the board, largely in the large-city upstate school districts, the lower-income small cities and suburban areas, and the rural areas of the state. In fact, the large cities other than New York as well as the smaller upstate cities and suburbs emerge from the state aid process fiscally better off than the state average. (2) Although rural school districts remain below the state per-pupil spending average following the allocation of state aid, they receive the highest percentage increases in the state. (3) Despite the fact that their local per-pupil revenues are already 165 percent higher than the state average, upper-income school districts are provided with nearly $1.1 billion more ($2,826 per pupil) in state education aid. (4) After state aid is factored in, per-pupil expenditures in New York City are $571.00 below the state's average and represent only 80 percent of the amount spent in the wealthier districts.

Table 12.2 helps clarify New York City's relative situation concerning state aid. If the state education aid appropriated in 2000–2001 had been apportioned based on student numbers, New York City would have been allocated $460 million more than the amount of aid it received. This $436.73 per-pupil deficit reflects the fact that historically the city has received somewhere between 2 and 4 percent less than its pupil-based share of aid from the state legislature. Indeed, other than the wealthier school districts already spending above the state average, New York City is the only

TABLE 12.1
Per-pupil expenditures in New York State by district type, 2000–2002

District types*	Students		District revenues**		State aid		State-district expenditures		
	Numbers	% State total	Per pupil	% State average	Per pupil	% State aid average	Per pupil	% State average	% Increase
High N/RC Districts:									
New York City	1,048,692	36.9	$6,118	97.8	$4,351	90.9	$10,469	94.8	71.1
Large-city districts	126,650	4.5	4,262	68.1	7,657	160.1	11,919	108.0	179.7
Urban-suburban	216,400	7.6	5,094	81.4	6,347	132.7	11,441	103.6	124.6
Rural	179,578	6.3	3,309	52.9	6,888	144.0	10,197	92.4	208.2
Average N/RC districts	868,545	30.5	5,902	94.3	4,868	101.8	10,770	97.6	82.5
Low N/RC districts	383,737	13.5	10,347	165.4	2,826	59.1	13,173	119.3	27.3
BOCES	20,508	0.7	n/a		n/a		n/a		
Total New York State	2,844,110	100.0	$6,256	100.0	$4,784	100.0	$11,040	100.0	

* N/RC is the ratio of "need," i.e., poverty as measured by a weighted average of the kindergarten through grade 6 free- and reduced-price lunch percent, to "resource capacity," i.e., the ratio of per pupil district wealth to the statewide per pupil wealth average. *High N/RC Districts* have the greatest amount of poverty relative to resources on the need-resources ratio; *Low N/RC Districts* have the least amount of poverty relative to resources; and *average N/RC Districts* reflect the statewide mean on the need-resources ratio.

**BOCES is the Boards of Cooperative Educational Services.

***District revenues include federal funds.

Source of state aid data: New York State Education Department, *New York: The State of Learning* (Albany, NY: The University of the State of New York/State Education Department, June 2002), table 3-2, p. 74 and table 3-6, p. 82.

TABLE 12.2.

Race bases of parties among nonwhite voters:
percentage of seats won by district race, 2002

District types	Actual state aid		Proportional state aid		Differenes between actual and proportional	
	In millions	In percent	In millions	In percent	In millions	In percent
High N/RC districts:						
New York City	$4,562	33.5	$5,020	36.9	($458)	(3.4)
Large City districts	969	7.1	612	4.5	357	2.6
Urban-suburban	1,373	10.1	1,034	7.6	339	2.5
Rural	1,238	9.1	857	6.3	381	2.8
Average N/RC districts	4,228	31.1	4,149	30.5	79	0.6
Low N/RC districts	1,084	8.0	1,836	13.5	(752)	(5.5)
BOCES	n/a	n/a	95	0.7	—	—

Note: For definitions of district types, see table 12.1 notes.

Source of the data: Calculated from data found in New York State Education Department, *New York: The State of Learning* (Albany, NY: The University of the State of New York/State Education Department, June 2002), table 3-7, p. 83.

school district that does not receive an amount of education aid at least as high as its proportion of the state's student population would dictate.

Because there are differences in per-pupil spending within the district types presented in the first two tables, considering the data in decile format allows a more comprehensive look at the situation in New York. As Robert Berne wrote in a previous edition of this book, "To some degree the averages for the groups of districts conceal the substantial within group disparities."[10] The data in table 12.3 indicate that Berne's warning offered more than ten years ago is still quite valid. Although there has been some equalization in per-pupil expenditures since fiscal year 1996, the movement has been marginal at best. Indeed, among both rural high need and suburban low need school districts there were greater within-category differences in per-pupil spending in fiscal year 2000 than in fiscal year 1996. Moreover, from a statewide perspective, a number of school districts continue to spend less than 50 percent per pupil of the wealthiest school districts in the state; and New York City, which includes 37 percent of the state's students, spends just over 56 percent as much on those students as the wealthiest districts. The continued existence of such inequities among school districts in New York is particularly troubling given the fact that the state legislature appropriated record school-aid increases, totaling nearly 33 percent, in the four fiscal years beginning in 1996.[11]

TABLE 12.3.

Intra-district per-pupil expenditures in New York State 1999–2000

District types percentile	Expense per pupil 1995–1996	As percent of category high	As percent of state high	Expense per pupil 1999–2000	As percent of category high	As percent of state high
High N/RC districts						
New York City	$8,207	--	49.7	$10,469	--	56.1
Large-city districts	$9,749	--	59.1	$11,742	--	62.9
Urban-suburban						
10th	$7,799	61.6	47.3	$9,247	65.3	49.6
50th	9,598	75.8	58.2	11,095	78.3	59.5
90th	12,670	--	76.8	14,162	--	75.9
Rural						
10th	$7,235	73.0	43.8	$8,840	70.0	47.4
50th	8,212	81.9	49.2	10,155	80.5	54.4
90th	9,914	--	60.1	12,621	--	67.6
Average N/RC districts						
10th	$7,409	63.1	44.9	$8,703	63.0	46.6
50th	8,575	73.0	52.0	10,176	73.7	54.5
90th	11,748	--	71.2	13,809	--	74.0
Low N/RC districts						
10th	$8,952	54.3	54.3	$10,087	54.1	54.1
50th	12,229	74.1	74.1	13,760	73.7	73.7
90th	16,500	--	--	18,661	--	--
New York State						
10th	$7,512	57.2	45.5	$8,943	60.9	47.9
50th	8,931	68.0	54.1	10,604	71.9	56.8
90th	13,143	--	79.7	14,756	--	79.1

Note: For definitions of district types, see table 12.1 notes.

Source of the data: Based on data found in New York State Education Department, *New York: The State of Learning* (Albany, NY: The University of the State of New York/State Education Department, June 2002), table 3-7, p. 83.

STATE AID, EDUCATIONAL EQUITY, AND STUDENTS AND TEACHERS

The special needs of many of the students in the state's poorer districts, including particularly the five biggest urban centers, only exacerbate the existing inequities in the distribution of education funds. As the data in table 12.4 show, nearly three-quarters of the elementary school children in New

TABLE 12.4.
Student characteristics by district type and race Fall 2000

District types	K-6 Students in free-lunch program %	Nonwhite students	Student English language learners	Drop out rates	Annual absence rates	Students going to four-year colleges
High N/RC districts						
New York City	74.2	84.8	17.8	6.5	11.5	47.8
Large-city districts	69.4	73.6	8.4	4.0	9.5	45.2
Urban-suburban	51.3	49.5	6.9	3.9	6.9	40.9
Rural	34.2	7.2	0.7	3.6	5.4	36.2
Average N/RC districts	16.6	13.9	1.8	2.0	5.0	48.5
Low N/RC districts	3.2	12.7	2.2	0.6	4.4	72.2
Total New York State	43.5	55.1	8.4	3.8	7.7	54.2
Schools by race						
Low minority*	9.6	--	n/a	1.8	4.8	53.3
High minority*	65.6	--	n/a	10.0	12.1	

Note: Low-minority schools are defined as having 0–20 percent minority students; high-minority schools are defined as having 81–100 percent minority students.

Source of the data: Based on data found in New York State Education Department, *New York: The State of Learning* (Albany, NY: The University of the State of New York/State Education Department, June 2002), table 3-3, p. 75; table 3-4, p. 76; table 3-17, p. 101; and table 3-19, p. 104.

York City qualify for the free-lunch program, a figure more than 70 percent higher than the state average and including a substantial majority of nonwhite students. Educating children is not an easy job under the best of circumstances but it is particularly difficult when dealing with low-income students. As the New York State Department of Education (NYSED) asserts, "Children who have been placed at risk by poverty, homelessness, poor nutrition, or inadequate care, often require special educational and support services to master required competencies." The SED goes on to acknowledge, "These services incur an extra financial burden for the district and increase the cost of education."[12] Furthermore, students in the vast majority of below-average school districts are more likely to require English language training, exhibit higher drop-out and absence rates, and are less likely to attend four-year colleges following graduation than their counterparts in average or wealthier districts.

Although New York City teachers are responsible for more students with greater special needs in bigger classes than teachers in other parts of the

TABLE 12.5.
Teacher characteristics by district type and race Fall 2000

District types	Pupil-teacher ratio	Median teacher salary	Turnover rate 1999–2000 %	Median years teaching	Teaching outside certified area %	With master's plus 30 hours or doctorate %
High N/RC districts						
New York City	14.1	$51,020	18	12	26.9	42.9
Large-city districts	12.3	49,391	14	13	12.1	21.7
Urban-suburban	13.2	52,252	11	14	6.4	27.4
Rural	12.1	42,521	11	15	6.0	10.9
Average N/RC districts	13.2	49,605	11	14	4.4	21.3
Low N/RC districts	12.6	63,000	11	13	4.1	36.6
Total New York State	13.3	51,020	14	13	12.5	30.1
Schools by race						
Low minority schools		49,733	15*	14	6.0	22.8
High minority schools		48,650	22*	11	27.1	37.0

*Data based on 1998–1999 report.

Source of the data: Based on data found in New York State Education Department, *New York: The State of Learning* (Albany, NY: The University of the State of New York/State Education Department, June 2002), table 3-8, p. 84.

state, the data in table 12.5 indicate that they receive salaries that are more than 23 percent lower than those of their counterparts in upper-income districts. The fact that New York City teachers are 43 percent more likely than teachers in other parts of the state to be pursuing post-master's work or doctoral degrees only exacerbates these regional pay inequities. Indeed, such fiscal inequities may go a long way to explain the high teacher turnover rate in New York City. It is also noteworthy that New York City has the largest number of teachers—fully 115 percent of teachers above the state average—teaching outside of their certified areas of expertise, which also explains some, though certainly not all, of the salary differential.

To an unprecedented degree, teaching in the twenty-first century requires integrating up-to-date information and high technology into the classroom on a daily basis. A global economy requires people with technological literacy, and schools have a responsibility to provide students with the necessary skills to function in this economy. The five biggest cities in the state lag behind all other districts in terms of the numbers of computers and library books available to their students. In fact, with one-third fewer computers—although a relatively high proportion of them are classified as "new generation"—and 68 percent fewer books available per student than the state average, New York City lags behind other all other jurisdictions in the state on technology measures as well as general information sources available to students.

STATE AID, EDUCATIONAL EQUITY, AND STUDENT PERFORMANCE

Finally, it is useful to evaluate student performance data to ascertain whether there is a correlation—not to be confused with a causal relationship—between district spending and educational outputs. It is important to note in this regard that student performance is dependent on a host of variables, many of which are external to the school system itself, such as family situation and peer-group pressure. School district spending may be an important contributing factor to student performance, but it is far from the only factor. One generalization, however, would seem to be in order. From an educational-performance perspective, all things being equal, spending more on schools is preferable to spending less.

Several conclusions emerge from the student performance data in table 12.6. One, the relationship between spending and student performance on both the New York State Assessment and the Regents' tests is consistently and notably linear. In fact, when NYSAP test results are controlled for students' family income, the results across district types remain consistently linear for both advantaged and disadvantaged students: within each district type, lower-income students perform consistently less impressively than their more advantaged counterparts.[13] Moreover, on nearly every measure, there are greater problems with student performance in the large cities of the state than in any of the other jurisdictions, including the other two within the high-need districts. Indeed, it is staggering that in the large-city districts other than New York, fully 86 percent of middle-level students are not performing at grade level in mathematics. Second, students from low-need districts are awarded Regents' diplomas at a rate more than 160 percent higher than their counterparts in the four large-city districts of the state, and more than 146 percent higher than students from New York City. Conversely, students from the four large-city districts are 82 percent more likely and students from New York City are 70 percent more likely to receive IEP certificates than their counterparts in low-need districts.

TABLE 12.6.
Student performance by district type and race Fall 2000

District types*	NYSAP tests, elementary level		NYSAP tests, middle level		Regents Exams, high school level			High school diplomas	
	ELA* % at or above level 3	Math % at or above level 3	ELA % at or above level 3	Math % at or above level 3	English % passing scoring 65 or higher	Math % passing scoring 65 or higher	Global history % passing scoring 65 or higher	Regents % awarded	IEP % awarded
High N/RC districts:									
New York City	44	52	33	23	59	39	62	27.3	3.7
Large-city districts	41	50	25	14	65	32	64	25.7	6.0
Urban-suburban	57	67	35	29	71	45	73	40.6	5.3
Rural	60	74	41	39	85	63	84	50.0	4.7
Average N/RC districts	72	82	52	49	87	66	88	58.7	2.6
Low N/RC districts	86	93	69	68	94	84	95	67.2	1.1
New York State	n/a	n/a	n/a	n/a	77	54	79	48.5	3.1
Race									
White	73.7	73.7	55.3	52.6	n/a	n/a	n/a	58.3	2.1
African American	39.3	45.7	23.8	13.4	n/a	n/a	n/a	20.3	5.1
Hispanic	39.6	49.3	26.1	16.0	n/a	n/a	n/a	21.4	4.2

*ELA stands for English-Language Arts.

Level 3 is the baseline stratum for students to demonstrate proficiency in the standards of their grade level.

Source of state aid data: New York State Education Department, *New York: The State of Learning* (Albany, NY: The University of the State of New York/State Education Department, June 2002), figures 3-6, 3-7, and 3-8, p. 86; figure 3-13, p. 90; figure 3-14, p. 91; and table 3-16, p. 101.

The correlation between income and race is yet one more troubling component of education inequities in New York. Members of minority groups comprise nearly 45 percent of students attending public primary and secondary schools in New York State, representing almost three-quarters of the student population in the large cities upstate and nearly 85 percent of the students in New York City. An increasing percentage of minority students attend schools with high minority enrollments. The State Education Department considers a school as high minority if its student population is 80 percent or greater nonwhite; it considers low minority schools as those with student populations of 20 percent or lower nonwhite. The data in table 12.4 indicate that in comparison with low-minority schools, high-minority schools are nearly seven times more likely to have low-income students, have dropout rates more than five times higher, have absence rates more than two and one-half times greater, and graduate fewer students going on to four-year colleges. Table 12.5 clearly indicates that the distinctions between high- and low-minority schools also involve instructional staff. Teachers in high minority schools are less experienced, less well paid, and have turnover rates 47 percent greater than teachers in low-minority schools. Moreover, teachers in high-minority schools are more than four times as likely to be teaching outside of their certified areas as those in low-minority schools. As the New York State Education Department acknowledges, "The close association between minority status and poverty is cause for grave concern."[14]

THE POLITICS OF EDUCATION
IN THE NEW YORK STATE LEGISLATURE

The primary vehicle for transferring state money to the more than seven hundred school districts in New York is the state education formula. Over the years, the technical aspects of New York's convoluted education formula have become increasingly and intentionally complex. As one report notes, "Previously described as an 'elegant formula,' the distribution mechanics now involve a complex amalgamation of formula factors, many of which bear no rational relationship to any describable state aid goal."[15] In the early 1970s, the state's education aid formula had three separate categories; a decade later, it included ten distinct categories; and in 2004 it incorporated nearly fifty separate formulas and program grants. The policy goal of the state aid program is to promote increased equalization in educational spending around New York and, as table 12.1 indicated, to a certain extent it accomplishes that purpose. In its present incarnation, however, the formulas that allocate state education aid tend to protect, and according to some analyses, at times actually enhance existing inequities among some of the school districts in the state.[16]

There are four major components of state education aid in New York: unrestricted funds, reimbursement assistance, categorical aids, and the LADDER program.[17] First, as the name suggests, unrestricted aid can be used for any educational purposes that the local district considers necessary. As such, it is the most popular form of state aid among the districts. In 2000, more than one-half of state education money was allocated to the districts as unrestricted aid. Nearly 88 percent of unrestricted money was operating aid; another 9 percent was targeted to extraordinary needs, a category focused on districts with large numbers of "disadvantaged pupils"; and a small portion was awarded based on local tax effort. Second, roughly one-third of state aid was allocated as reimbursement funds or "spend-to-get" money designed to help defray local costs for services like transportation and building mainte-nance. Third, 9 percent of total state aid is dispersed through categorical aid programs that target money to state-mandated priorities, including formulas focused on gifted and talented or limited-English-proficiency students, text-book, software, and library services, and professional development initia-tives. Fourth, the Ladder program, representing less than 4 percent of total state aid, was added in 1997 to fund prekindergarten programs and smaller class sizes in early grades. Its funding has become an annual source of politi-cal tension between assembly Democrats and the governor.

Regardless of the specific formula, a substantial share of state school aid is allotted based on the ratio of student need to district resources. "Need" is defined as the percentage of a district's kindergarten through grade 6 stu-dents eligible for federally subsidized school lunch programs, and "resources" are represented by a school district's "combined wealth ratio," that is, the ratio of the district's per-pupil property and income wealth to the state aver-age. Generally, the program is designed to provide greater amounts of funds to districts with greater needs or fewer resources. There are, however, mech-anisms built into the formulas that keep them from being as equalizing in practice as they were intended to be in theory. One is the formula for deter-mining district wealth, which includes property values and income. The measures of district wealth based on income are expressed in per-pupil terms, which temper somewhat the greater income in suburban school districts with relatively large numbers of students in the public schools while augmenting the wealth measures of urban districts with less average income but proportionately fewer numbers of students in the public schools. Moreover, per-pupil counts are based on average daily attendance, which undercounts the number of students actually enrolled in urban schools and thereby exacerbates the skewing of the district wealth data even more.[18]

Other formula mechanisms also serve to lessen comprehensive equalization. A "transition adjustment," enacted in the early 1990s, includes both "save harmless" provisions, designed to protect all districts from any reductions in aid regardless of their current need or changes in their relative situation from year to year, as well as expenditure caps on the amount of funds allotted to any particular district or set of districts in a given year. Moreover, in an effort to secure "maintenance of effort" by local school districts, that is, to ensure that they will not employ state funds solely to diminish their own revenue efforts, the formulas contain a number of "spend-to-get" provisions—state aid conditioned on spending by local districts. Such provisions reward high local taxing and spending and thereby tend to assist better off or perhaps less efficient school districts with increased state aid. Because such leveling mechanisms have also been included within many of the categorical school aid formulas added in recent years, and because the funding for these categorical grants is growing faster than that for unrestricted categories, their regressive impact on the school aid program as a whole becomes ever more pronounced. In analyzing increases to education aid between fiscal years 1996 and 2000, for example, a state comptroller's report concludes that "nearly two-thirds of the $3.4 billion increase has been paid through various categorical and 'spend-to-get' aids."[19]

Perhaps the greatest impact on the equalization of spending, however, lies in the actual manner of allocating state education funds each year. As part of their annual negotiations, the governor and the legislative leaders eventually agree on an appropriation for the Department of Education to be included in the state budget. Budget specialists are then charged with manipulating the individual formulas and grants programs included within the education aid budget so that they conform to the overall figure agreed to by the leaders. The impact of this informal reconciliation process varies. During the fiscal stress period of the early 1990s, "deficit reduction assessments" reducing the amount of money available in the education aid budget and thereby forcing changes in the individual formulas actually "had the overall effect of making school aid payments more equalized."[20]

In summary, despite the numerous leveling mechanisms they include, the education aid formulas in New York do result in school districts around the state being in a more equitable spending situation than they would have been in if their funding were based solely on local revenues (see table 12.1). In other words, the overall impact of state education aid is to some degree redistributive. Yet, the data indicate clearly that even after a substantial amount of state aid, notable spending inequities between and among school districts remain. In fact, although New York spends more per pupil than most other states, it consistently ranks very poorly on measures of funding equity.[21] If these inequities were simply a function of the lack of state resources, they would represent another of the predictable fiscal limitations on government's ability to achieve any specified goal. The fact is, however, that the limitations are less financial than political in nature. Referring to "America's Geography of Inequality," Stephen Macedo concludes, "Well-off suburbanites are doing very well in our stratified system. They have little incentive to upset the status quo, and they are more apt to vote than inner-city residents."[22] It is to politics that this chapter now turns.

THE POLITICS OF EDUCATION AID IN THE NEW YORK LEGISLATURE

Analyzing the distribution of state education aid requires a brief review of the context surrounding legislative politics in New York. Since 1975, control of the state legislature has been divided, with the Democrats in charge of the assembly and the Republicans holding a smaller but stable majority in the senate. Under a partisan system, majority-party conferences charge their leadership with developing unified policy positions and representing them in negotiations with the other house and the governor. The majority conferences in each house reflect regional party politics in the state. While the Republican majority in the senate comprises largely rural and suburban members, there is a decidedly urban and downstate base to the Democratic conference in the assembly. (For a complete analysis of the regional basis of legislative politics in New York State, see chapter 8).

In terms of state education aid, two distributional outcomes lead to one fundamental question. Outcome number one is that low-need school districts in the senate's suburban base augment their already high local spending with more than a billion dollars of state aid, and high-need districts in the senate's rural base receive the highest percentage increases in aid in the state. Outcome number two is that New York City's high-need school district, the electoral heart of the assembly majority, receives less than its equitable share of state school aid even if equity is defined strictly in terms of percentage of students and not in relation to special educational needs. The fundamental political question that emerges from these two outcomes is obvious: why has the senate been so successful in tending to its educational backyard while the assembly has historically proved unable to produce a more favorable distribution of education aid for New York City schools?

Part of the answer lies in the nature of the school funding process itself and part in the makeup of the two majority conferences. Keeping three general political rules in mind helps focus the analysis. First, political intensity is a function of the saliency and visibility of a particular issue. Second, among the defining traits of successful legislators is the ability to recognize and then translate constituent intensity into public policy positions. And third, relative political strength in legislative politics depends in part on unity among members of policy coalitions.

Local school boards in the nearly seven hundred independent school districts in the state are responsible for raising and appropriating education monies in their districts. Their budgets, funded largely from property taxes, must be submitted to local voters for approval. To the residents of the independent districts, therefore, the specifics of school funding are immediate and the state role is highly visible. Conversely, the "Big Five" city school districts derive their local operating revenues from the overall municipal budgets in the cities in which they operate. Consequently, to the residents of these urban districts, although the issue of education may be important, particularly for those with school-age children, the funding mechanisms for schools are more opaque and the specific state role is less visible than in the independent school districts.

Because the overwhelming majority of their constituents live in independent school districts, state education aid is a visible, salient, and unifying issue to Republican members of the state senate. Indeed, state funding for the independent school districts becomes an annual test case, evaluated in biennial elections, of senators' ability to secure funds for their districts. Characterizing state aid for schools as "the single most important issue" on their political agendas, Berne writes, "The Republican senators bargain hard for their school district state aid because of the personal identification with specific districts and the importance of state aid for education for their con-

stituents."[23] Such issues are especially relevant to the nine Republican senators from Nassau and Suffolk Counties, where local property taxes are
among the highest in the nation and where citizen dissatisfaction with
county Republican governance has led to Democratic victories in recent
years. In the Assembly, however, the education aid issue is framed quite dif-
ferently. Nearly three-quarters of the Democratic majority in that body are
from big-city school districts where local education allocations are included
within overall municipal budgets. Without the mandated referenda held in
the independent districts, the numbers in the education budget are less visible and the connection between taxes and expenditures less direct. As a
result, the relative share of the state/local burden is less obvious to constituents and, in turn, less immediately politically pressing on members.

The less visible nature of school finance, however, only partly explains
the assembly's relative ineffectiveness in securing equitable state education
aid for New York City. The heterogeneous nature of the Democratic conference in the assembly is also a factor. Democrats from upstate suburban areas,
Long Island, and even upstate cities often share portions of their districts
with Republican senators who generate significant state education aid for
these areas. As a consequence, the distribution of education aid is not an
immediate political issue to this portion of the majority conference; indeed,
open support for increased aid to New York City among non–New York City
legislators might well be politically injurious to their reelection efforts and
ultimately threaten the party's control of the assembly. Moreover, New York
City's status as one school district muddies the political waters. In many
neighborhoods of the city, the schools are functioning quite well and
although the members representing these areas undoubtedly support
increased education funding for the city, the issue does not have the saliency
with their constituents that it has in lower-income communities.

Downstate assembly members also have a variety of difficult and
expensive social issues on their policy agendas. Unlike most other states,
New York mandates that its local governments, including New York City,
contribute to the state's social welfare and Medicaid programs. Because New
York City has a preponderance of the state's poor, such programs are much
more important to the city's voters than they are upstate or in the suburbs.
As a result, there are competing social issues on the plate of the Democratic
conference in the assembly which, depending on the political climate at any
time, might well put education issues on a political backburner. All of this
means that the assembly leadership, although it may be personally and

politically committed to increased equity in education funding, does not
have the same strong conference support base reinforcing its commitment
on this issue as does the senate leadership.

The political context within each legislative conference constrains the
leaders in their negotiations with each other and with the governor. On
some policy matters, conference members afford leaders relatively wide discretion in negotiating agreements; on other matters, however, a leader
brings more directive marching orders from the conference defining a more
restricted area of permissible compromise; on still other matters, one conference is more directive than the other. Education financing fits into that
third category with the senate Republican conference being significantly
more directive than its assembly counterpart. To the senate majority leader,
education aid is a bottom-line issue not to be traded away for other political concessions in negotiations with the speaker and the governor. The
intensity of this issue in the senate is evidenced by the fact that disagree-
ment over state education aid was the immediate catalyst for the 1997 conference rebellion that replaced Majority Leader Warren Anderson with
Long Island's Ralph Marino.

For the past two decades, governors of New York have weighed in on
the education aid formula. Given his political base in New York City, it is
not surprising that Governor Mario Cuomo spoke out in favor of increased
equity in education financing.[24] Considering the senate's unrelenting commitment on the issue, however, Cuomo had little chance of changing the
state's education aid policy without risking even later budgets or sacrificing
other policy initiatives. With Republican George Pataki's ascension to
office in 1995, New York City's overall electoral importance diminished.
With the exception of a brief and expensive flirtation with unions in the
city during the 2002 elections, Pataki's electoral base has never much
depended on support from the city, relying instead on Republican votes
from upstate and suburban Long Island. Nevertheless, under political pressure from a highly visible court case, in which his administration defended
the current funding process, Pataki has begun criticizing the school aid
process, terming the current set of formulas "'incomprehensible' and 'a
dinosaur'—worthy of extinction."[25]

In summary, while senate Republicans approach the issue of education
financing with single-focus intensity, assembly Democrats approach it as one
of a number of issues that must be dealt with by a sometimes fractious party
conference. Governor Cuomo provided rhetorical support for increased

equity in education financing with little effect, and Governor Pataki has only very recently indicated dissatisfaction with the current formulas. Under such political circumstances, it is not surprising that New York City as well as a number of other high-need districts around the state have fared so poorly under the state's school-funding formulas.

ENTER THE COURTS

To students of legislative politics, where the accommodation of competing interests almost always result in incremental adjustments to the status quo, the decisiveness of a court ruling may well appear as a political bolt out of the blue. To the participants in court cases, however, the legal process often seems nearly interminable. (For a complete description of the New York State court system, see chapter 9). Such contradictory assessments were both correct on January 10, 2001, when New York State Supreme Court Justice Leland DeGrasse issued his opinion in *Campaign for Fiscal Equity v. State of New York.*[26] The trial court judge ruled that, in relation to students from New York City, the state's method of distributing education aid violated the mandate for a "sound basic education" included in Article XI of the state constitution as well as the rights of minority students as defined in Title VI of the 1964 Federal Civil Rights Act. The trial court's decision was finally affirmed by a court of appeals ruling on June 26, 2003, after it had been overturned by an appellate division ruling in 2002.[27]

A brief history helps put the decision in context. In 1982, after more than eight years of litigation, the New York State Court of Appeals ruled in *Levittown v. Nyquist* that, despite "significant inequities" in the distribution of funds and "significant unevenness in educational opportunities," the state's education-funding mechanism afforded students educational services "above the minimum standard" and, therefore, met New York's constitutional mandate that the state provide a "sound basic education."[28] In 1992, following a series of state cutbacks in education aid, a coalition of education advocacy groups and community school boards formed the Campaign for Fiscal Equity (CFE) to fight for increased funding of New York City's schools. With Michael Rebell as its attorney, the CFE began what was to become an eleven-year court struggle to overturn the state's method of financing schools, contending, in light of the Levittown decision, that "minimally acceptable educational services and facilities are not being provided" in New York City's schools and that this was in violation of both the State Constitution and Federal Civil Rights Law.

In a 1995 decision, the Court of Appeals, "distinguishing" the Levittown ruling, found that, stipulating the truth of the assertions, "plaintiffs have alleged facts which fit within a cognizable legal theory."[29] The court also recognized that, again given the stipulation of truth, the plaintiffs' argument that such inequity, when visited upon a racial minority, violated the "disparate impact" standard of federal regulations.[30] Accordingly, the state's highest court remanded the case to a trial court with directions to focus on three questions: what a "sound basic education" was; whether students in New York City were provided with the opportunity to receive such an education; and, if they were not, whether the state funding mechanism was the reason.

Based on these directives and relying on testimony of experts, Justice DeGrasse in his 2001 ruling rejected the state's contention that a "sound basic education" required only that high school students be capable of reading at an eighth-grade level and of understanding sixth-grade math, skills measured by the Regents Competency Examinations and evidenced by receipt of local diplomas. Instead, DeGrasse defined a "sound basic education" as imparting the skills necessary for "civic engagement" and "productive employment," including the capability to "evaluate complex public issues" as voters and jurors as well as the technical and mathematical skills necessary to compete in a postindustrial economy, talents better measured by the traditional Regents Examinations and evidenced by qualifying for a Regents' Diploma.

In addressing the second question, Degrasse examined the personnel (quality of teacher preparation), the facilities (buildings and classroom facilities), and the instrumentalities of learning (textbooks, library resources, and instructional technology) available in New York City's schools. He deemed all three "inadequate," citing in each case the lack of funding to secure the required resources. The judge tied the inadequacy of school resources to comparatively lower graduation rates, higher dropout rates, and less impressive performance on standardized tests among city students. Finally, rejecting arguments of local blame, DeGrasse affirmed the state's constitutional responsibility for education, concluding that there was a causal relationship between state funding mechanisms and the lack of educational opportunity for students in New York City: "The State's school aid distribution system has for over a decade prevented the New York City public school system from receiving sufficient funds to provide its students with a sound basic education."

Once affirmed by the court of appeals in 2003, this thirty-years-in-the-making bolt out the blue puts the onus for fixing the problem on the legislature with the proviso that the courts would monitor the effort. The Legislature was given a July 30, 2004, deadline to establish the baseline cost of a sound basic education and to devise a funding system around that baseline.

STRATEGIES TO INCREASE FUNDING
EQUITY IN NEW YORK STATE

Whatever strategy the legislature and governor eventually choose to address the court mandate, it will be enacted within a larger context of continuing and dramatic change in education policy in New York State. Over the past ten years, the regents have implemented rigorous new standards complemented by testing instruments to assess movement toward those standards at all grade levels; the legislature has approved a process for certifying and evaluating charter schools; and, after years of lobbying by mayors in New York City, the legislature has placed the state's largest school district under direct mayoral control.[31] The climate of reform notwithstanding, officials in New York have thus far resisted calls for voucher programs that advocates claim promote educational improvements and funding efficiencies through school-based competition, though such programs have been enacted in a number of other states.[32]

New York's attempt to restructure its school aid formula will involve debate over the meaning and cost of a "sound basic education"; provoke tensions between often mutually exclusive notions of fiscal efficiency, social justice, and political feasibility; and possibly result in open conflict between the judicial and legislative branches of state government. Some states have used court rulings as an opportunity to enact basic reforms. Michigan, for example, eliminated the connection between local property taxes and school funding by approving a 2 percent increase in the state sales tax with all the additional revenues earmarked for education. Early reports note some degree of redistribution among school districts in that state with upper-income areas seeing their state-based "foundation allowances" decreased in favor of increased funds for lower-income districts.[33] Fears of diminishing local control as well as predictable and intense resistance in some suburban areas make this an unlikely outcome in New York State. Other states have seen open battles between branches of government. In Ohio, the state supreme court's 1997 mandate for a "complete systematic overhaul" of school financing was addressed only at the margins by the legislature and a more conservative court has retreated in recent years.[34] In Arkansas, on the other hand, the state supreme court named two "special masters" in 2004 to evaluate the efforts toward equalization of school funding taken thus far by a largely recalcitrant legislature and governor.

Most observers agree that reform in New York must begin with some consensus about a regionally adjusted baseline cost for a sound basic education in the state and then award state funds on an equalization basis, that is, in a fashion to bring per-pupil spending up to that baseline around the state. Moreover, given the political power that suburban communities wield in the state senate, most observers also appear to agree that whatever equalization system is developed, redistribution of resources will be deemphasized in favor of leveling up mechanisms that will save harmless current spending on education in all districts. In short, leveling up is less redistributive and therefore, both more politically feasible and more costly.

Several options are on the table. A state education department proposal, released in 2003, would implement a basic foundation cost for school districts throughout the state, develop regional and pupil needs indices to adjust the foundation cost upward, and require local districts to contribute local revenues based on average income per pupil. The proposal, incorporating a nearly $6 billion increase in current state aid, would not be implemented fully until fiscal year 2011.[35] A study commissioned by the Campaign for Fiscal Equity and released in 2004 also recommended that overall state education spending be increased by roughly $6 billion dollar per year. Establishing a per-pupil baseline of $12,520 for the 2001–2002 school year, which represents a 13 percent increase in actual per-pupil costs, the study recommended a 24 percent increase in per-pupil spending in New York City as well as a nearly 11 percent increase in per-pupil expenditures in the low-need suburbs.[36]

The controversies surrounding any of the options are intense. Establishing the baseline per-pupil cost will be quite difficult. In the first instance, there are significant disagreements over how much money is required to produce a sound basic education generally. Second, there is the matter of regional adjustments in need. Some are reasonably obvious. Transporting students is more expensive in rural areas than in other districts around the state and heating costs vary regionally. The most difficult adjustment issue, however, concerns the relative costs of providing a sound basic education for students from diverse socioeconomic backgrounds. The basic question is as simple to state as it is difficult to answer: how much additional money, if any, is needed to educate a disadvantaged student?

In the wake of the state legislature's failure to produce a school funding plan by the court-mandated July 30, 2004 deadline, Justice DeGrasse appointed a panel of three special masters to resolve the dispute. Having received legal briefs from both parties to the case, the panel scheduled oral arguments for September 2004. As of this writing, some observers predict that now that the matter is back in court it may well remain there for quite some time as appeals follow appeals. The stakes are extraordinarily high. The answer that eventually emerges will speak volumes not only about politics in the state but also about New York's basic values. In the short term, public policy choices are reflections of political influence, political process, and the temper of the times. In the long run, however, some policy choices define the type of people we are.

NOTES

1. Assembly Committee on Education, *Testimony: Education Finance Reform*, Robert Lowry (Albany, NY, October 3, 2003).

2. Unless otherwise indicated, the data on school district spending and performance in this chapter are taken from Nicholas W. Jenny, "Education in New York State: A Back-to-School Preview of the 2003 NYS Statistical Yearbook," *New York State Statistical Briefs: The Rockefeller Institute* 2, no. 5 (September 2003); and New York State Education Department (NYSED), *New York The State of Learning*, Report to the Governor and Legislature (Albany, NY: The University of the State of New York/State Education Department, June 2002).

3. New York State 1894 Convention Document, no. 62, quoted in Robert D. Stone, "Education," in *The New York State Constitution: A Briefing Book*, ed. Gerald Benjamin (Albany, NY: Nelson A Rockefeller Institute, 1994), p. 178.

4. Stone, "*Education*," pp. 179–180.

5. This number includes the thirty-eight BOCES districts around the state.

6. In addition to the property tax, which raises over 90 percent of local school district funds, some counties allot a portion of their share of the

sales tax to school districts; others allow the school districts to levy consumer utility taxes.

7. New York State Council of School Superintendents, "Campaign for Fiscal Equity v. New York: Carpe Diem," *NYSCOSS Policy Report* (Albany, NY: NYCOSS, September 2003), pp. 7–8.

8. For an insightful political analysis of the federal role in education, see Edward Schneier, "The Politics of Local Education," in *Governing New York State,* ed. Jeffrey Stonecash, 4th ed. (Albany, NY: State University of New York Press, 2001), pp. 217–220.

9. Elise St. John, "Revenues and Expenditures for Public Elementary and Secondary Education: School Year 2000–01" (Washington, D.C.: U.S. Department of Education, National Center for Education Statistics, May 2003).

10. Robert Berne, "Primary and Secondary Education," in *Governing New York State,* ed. Jeffrey Stonecash, John Kenneth White and Peter W. Colby, 3rd ed. (Albany, NY: State University of New York Press, 1994), p. 253.

11. Office of the State Comptroller, *A $3.4 Billion Opportunity Missed* (Albany, NY: Office of the State Comptroller, November 2000).

12. NYSED, *New York: The State of Learning,* p. 68.

13. Ibid., pp. 88–89.

14. Ibid., p. 123.

15. Office of the State Comptroller, *School Finance Reform: A Discussion Paper* (Albany, NY: Office of the State Comptroller, October 1995), p. 11. The description of the state aid formula included here is based in part on this and a later report from the state comptroller's office, *A $3.4 Billion Opportunity Missed,* November 2000.

16. Office of the State Comptroller, *A $3.4 Billion Opportunity Missed.*

17. This analysis includes both "computerized categories" and "other" aid.

18. In other words, the denominator in the per-pupil formula for the cities is smaller than it otherwise would be because of the use of attendance figures as a measure of student numbers and the large private-school enrollment in the cities. As the denominator decreases, per-pupil measures of wealth rise.

19. Office of State Comptroller, *A $3.4 Billion Opportunity Missed,* p. 6.

20. Office of State Comptroller, *School Finance Reform: A Discussion Paper,* p. 12.

21. Office of State Comptroller, *A $3.4 Billion Opportunity Missed*, p. 26.

22. Stephen Macedo, "School Reform and Equal Opportunity in America's Geography of Inequality," *Perspectives on Politics* 1, no. 4 (December 2003): 743–756.

23. Robert Berne, "Primary and Secondary Education," p. 260.

24. See Edward Schneier, "The Politics of Local Education," for an analysis of Governor Cuomo's annual education "budget trifecta," p. 231.

25. New York State Council of School Superintendents, "Campaign for Fiscal Equity," p. 2.

26. For the trial judge's opinion in the state supreme court, see *CFE v State of New York* 719 NYS ²D 130 [2001].

27. For the appellate court's decision, see *CFE v State of New York* 744 NYS 2D 130 [2002]; for the court of appeals decision, see *CFE v State of New York* 100 NY 2D 893 [2003].

28. *Levittown Union Free School District v Nyquist* 57 NY 2D 27 [1982].

29. *CFE v State of New York* 86 NY 2D 307 [1995].

30. Under a "disparate impact" standard, no proof of intent is required to affirm that discrimination has occurred. See 34 Code of Federal Regulations 100.3[b][2] for specific regulations.

31. Since 1996, the regents have replaced the Pupil Evaluation Program with the more rigorous New York State Assessment Program for elementary and middle schools; phased out the less demanding Regents Competency Exams and required high school students to demonstrate proficiency in the Regents Examinations; and increased the number of math, science and second-language units required for high school graduation.

32. For analyses of voucher programs elsewhere, see Paul E. Peterson, "A Choice Between Public and Private Schools: What Next for School Vouchers?" *Spectrum: The Journal of State Government* 76 (Fall 2003): 5–8; Terry Moe, *Schools, Vouchers, and the American Public* (Washington, D.C.: Brookings Institute Press, 2001).

33. Hank Prince, *Proposal A and Pupil Equity* A report of the House Fiscal Agency, Michigan State Government (Lansing, MI: December 1996).

34. Peter Schrag, "Adequacy in Education: Why Is Clear. But How?" *New York Times*, June 28, 2003, p. A29.

35. Subcommittee on State Aid and Full Board, "Regents Proposal on State Aid to School Districts for 2004–05" (Albany, NY: New York State Education Department, December 10, 2003).

36. American Institute for Research/Management Analysis Planning, Inc., *The New York Adequacy Study: "Adequate" Education Costs in New York State,* Preliminary Report (Washington, D.C.: AIR/MAP, February 2004).

CHAPTER 13

Contested Futures

Public Policy and the State University of New York

HENRY STECK

As it celebrated its fiftieth anniversary in 1998, the State University of New York (SUNY) appeared to have reason to feel good about itself.[1] Since 1948 SUNY had developed a solid record of achievement. But for many at SUNY the celebrations were clouded by persistent uncertainty about the university's future direction. Nearly twenty years of fiscal disinvestment had seen to that. But for almost fifty years nothing before had called into question SUNY's basic mission or institutional character. With the 1994 elections, however, a new governor, Republican George Pataki, strode into office with an apparent mandate to change the direction of public policy that New Yorkers had known for generations. As the new regime of conservative policymakers set about cutting spending and taxes, SUNY became an early target of opportunity. Within days of taking office, Governor Pataki proposed budget reductions that were the deepest in SUNY's history and within months he began to put the university's leadership in the hands of trustees who brought to the board an outlook antithetical to SUNY's traditions and even to its mission. The "Pataki Trustees," as they came to be called, quickly developed a strategic plan, *Rethinking SUNY,* that enunciated radically different values and goals for the university. Within two years, the Pataki Trustees became the model for what came nationally to be called "activist trustees"—aggressive trustees determined to put a conservative stamp on the universities they controlled. SUNY faced a new era.

289

During the demonstrations set off by Pataki's initial budget proposals, angry students sent up the chant, "Fight! Fight! Fight! Higher ed is our right." But this was precisely the claim that was now at issue. Is there a right to higher education? Who should go to college? Should public higher education be simply a safety net for the unfortunate? Is higher education a public good that cannot be priced by the marketplace, or a private good to be purchased by individuals for their individual well-being? How much should the state spend and how much should students spend on their college education? Such questions are recurring, but now, confronted with a quite different philosophy of government, they acquired a fresh urgency.

The Pataki election initiated a "paradigm shift," to use Peter Hall's term, that compelled New Yorkers to ask old questions in new ways. In the 1980s, the question on the table was how good and how large a state university did New York need and want? In the mid-1990s, that question was still relevant, but now another question was on the table: What kind of state university would SUNY be and what values would it embody as it approached the twenty-first century? Would it follow the path laid down in 1985 in its statutory mission statement or would it follow a different path, one shaped by the precepts of a conservative philosophy of education, of the public sector, and of society?

HIGHER EDUCATION IN NEW YORK:
A TALE OF TWO SECTORS

New York contains the largest and most diverse higher education system in the country. No other state encompasses public and private sectors of such distinction and variety. From red brick to Ivy, from urban streets to pastoral countryside, from plain classrooms to distance learning networks, all manner of institutions come together to educate over one million students, of whom 80 percent were undergraduates in 1996. Of all enrolled students (including community college students and graduate and professional) approximately 38 percent are enrolled in SUNY; 21 percent in the City University of New York (CUNY); and 41 percent in private schools. SUNY includes world-class research universities, liberal arts colleges, specialized colleges, health science centers, professional schools, and two-year community colleges. Few counties in the state lack a SUNY campus of one kind or another. The private or independent sector is equally diverse and is among the nation's most distinguished university communities.

The existence of two strong sectors is a post-1948 development. Until the twentieth century, higher education was firmly in the hands of the private sector. The rapid growth of state universities in the nineteenth and early twentieth centuries, driven by what Allan Nevins terms the "fundamental emotion" of a passionate belief in "the cause of greater democracy,"[2] left New York relatively untouched. Several normal schools for training teachers had been established in the nineteenth century and these became the foundation stones for SUNY in 1948. By the 1930s, New York City had established several municipal colleges to meet the needs of the city and these achieved notable distinction. But these scattered institutions do not constitute a system of higher education, much less a state system. Nor could they meet the massive demand for entry to universities that reached crisis proportions following World War II. Growing pressures for direct public responsibility for higher education were resisted well into the twentieth century. Despite their responsibility for all education in the state, the regents resisted pressure for direct public responsibility for higher education, believing that existing private institutions provided adequate opportunities. Until after World War II, higher public education was restricted, minuscule, and, with the exception of the City College of New York, undistinguished and unknown outside the boundaries of the state.

By contrast, the private sector was large and varied in terms of size, quality, financial strength, and prestige. Above all, it was powerful—a fact reflected in the historical partiality to private education by the state Board of Regents and by the extent to which its alumni dominated politics, the professions, and commerce. The religious and racial discrimination practiced by many, but certainly not all, private schools, especially in medical education, was as significant as the pressure of numbers for creating a political climate that pushed Governor Thomas Dewey to recommend the establishment of a state university to the legislature.

SUNY's birth pains were intensely political and bitter. All New York's traditional political divisions came into play: downstate Democrats and representatives of minority groups, concerned with equal opportunities, particularly in medicine, supported the idea of a state university. The regents, the State Education Department, private colleges, and upstate Republicans fought any but the most minimal expansion of public higher education. Private schools were interested in self-preservation; the American Medical Association opposed the establishment of state medical schools; the Board of Regents sought to preserve its power; and Governor Dewey's aides worried about costs—and about the upcoming presidential election.

The question of access and opportunity was central to the struggle to establish a scheme of state-provided higher education. Young people who sought entry to a college faced a series of barriers: there were not enough places, especially given the flood of returning veterans; there was racial and religious discrimination; the price of a college education was out of reach for many families. The pressure for expansion of medical education was particularly strong. The harsh fact of discrimination was so significant in the debates that as part of the legislative package establishing the state university, the legislature also enacted a Fair Educational Practices Act, a clear signal that the legislature meant what it said about fair access and opportunity.

But even after the stormy debates and hard-fought compromises that led to the establishment of SUNY, the regents sought to control (if not cripple) the fledgling university, restrict its mission, and stifle its growth. SUNY's role was to "supplement" and to serve "as a secondary alternative, suitable mainly for the would-be teacher or those seeking vocational training, or for students unable to afford private institutions."[3] Until the 1960s, its funding was sparse, its enrollment growth minimal: between 1948 and 1960 total undergraduate enrollment grew by only twelve thousand, while in the next ten years it would grow by nearly one hundred thousand. Despite evidence of popular support for expanding the university, SUNY was kept under wraps for its first dozen years; the ideals of its founders were not matched by the initial reality. As one analyst noted, there was "a vacuum, an abdication of responsibility for higher education which prevented any significant policy proposals or master plans. . . . There was no system at all; there was merely a weak and undistinguished group of public institutions lumped together in a State University on the one hand, and a diverse group of private institutions on the other. . . . Higher education in the spring of 1959 lacked focus and direction and was . . . hopelessly bogged down in the face of an impending crisis."[4]

SUNY's initial development was "fitful" and, as the baby boomers approached college age, "pitifully underdeveloped."[5] The best that could be said was that New York had a new state university—the last in the nation— but did not know what it wished to do with it.

It fell to Nelson Rockefeller in the 1960s to give the state university the direction that characterized it into the 1990s. Expanding higher education was a major priority of Rockefeller's leadership and developing SUNY into a major state university was at the heart of this effort. A series of special reports—the Heald Report, the Keppel Report, and the Bundy Report charted the way for SUNY and for all higher education in the state. A core feature of Rockefeller's vision for SUNY was seeking excellence at all levels rather than identifying excellence with a single flagship institution.[6] Rockefeller freed SUNY from the limits that had been imposed on it in 1948.

During Rockefeller's tenure, New York moved into the era of mass education. In addition to expanding and transforming SUNY, the state assumed 50 percent of CUNY's costs, the first step toward full state funding of CUNY. A program of student aid, the Scholar Incentive Program, followed in 1974 by the creation of the Tuition Assistance Program (TAP), was initiated, and as a result direct aid to students increased eightfold. The expansion was, as the Bundy Commission put it, "a veritable educational revolution." In 1948, 12 percent of New York's high school graduates went to college; in 1965, 60 percent; by 1995 the number had increased to 81 percent, including 36 percent to SUNY. By the late 1960s, SUNY's institutional profile was fixed: It was a statewide system, comprehensive in its offerings; it was administered by an autonomous board of trustees appointed by the governor; health-care education was enlarged; graduate and professional schools were expanded; four centers for graduate and professional education and research were created; former teachers colleges were converted to colleges of arts and sciences; a vast network of community colleges was expanded; a policy of free and then very low tuition sealed an egalitarian commitment to access. The trustees rejected a single campus for the university and they rejected the idea of a flagship campus. They believed strongly in the advantages of the geographic reach of SUNY—that "collegiate programs should be provided where students live."[7] They believed in systemwide institutional leadership so that SUNY did not become simply a scatter of obscure units.

In short, State University became SUNY—a uniquely configured state system with a distinct identity and enormous potential to become one of the truly great public universities of the nation.

SUNY's expansion into a major state university transformed postsecondary education in the state and created a new political dynamic within the higher education community and between higher education and state government. There remained one additional element in New York's policy framework. By the late 1960s, the once dominant private schools looked on the rapid growth of SUNY and CUNY uneasily as they found themselves forced to compete with growing public institutions in a shrinking education marketplace. As their situation worsened, they pushed aggressively for state assistance. From the start, Rockefeller's aspirations for the public sector were balanced by a commitment to aid private institutions. In 1968, Rockefeller made good on his assurances to the private sector by securing passage of a program of direct financial assistance to independent institutions, named "Bundy Aid" after the select committee that had recommended the policy. With Bundy Aid, the passage of the TAP, and the initiation of other programs of assistance to private colleges, the state sealed its commitment to support for private institutions. Today, New York remains the leading state in the nation in terms of its direct assistance to private colleges and universities. In 1996–1997 nearly $41 million of Bundy Aid was distributed to ninety-nine private institutions while another $36.5 million was distributed through other programs, not including TAP, which awarded $220 million to private school students in 1996–1997.

The enactment of Bundy Aid and TAP solidified the structure of higher education policy in New York State—what we can define as the "Rockefeller settlement." Balancing the demands of the two constituencies, New York's political leaders redefined the public/private relationship from one of private school dominance to one of relative parity, even if educational leaders themselves feuded over the allocation of resources implied by this formula. The settlement provided a political framework for managing higher education issues. Since the 1960s, responsibility for higher education policy has been a shared responsibility of legislative and executive branches. The Legislature in particular has carefully guarded its responsibility for oversight and for providing broad direction and accountability for higher education. The geography of the systems—CUNY in the city, SUNY on Long Island and upstate, and the privates throughout the state—gives politicians a vested interest in the well-being of public higher education, since a campus in one's district brings opportunity for constituents and economic development for communities surrounding the state and city systems. These are considerations that politicians, whatever their ideologies or partisan commitments, do not ignore. Periodic efforts by SUNY planners to remove SUNY from New York's volatile political process, with its swirl of regional, ethnic, ideological, and partisan forces, have invariably failed. SUNY, we will see below, is also linked to the executive through the budget, the governor's appointment of the trustees, and the executive's responsibility for key policies.

The Dilemma of the Independent Sector

As the fiscal noose tightened in the 1980s, the legislature's protector role, despite limits, became more important. The privates, no less than the publics, had their share of trouble, as private-school lobbyists were quick to point out.[8] The privates reacted uneasily as the shift in balance that began in the 1960s continued thereafter. Enrollments and financing were, of course, two central issues. Private-school costs nationally were rising rapidly, producing sticker shock for students and families: between 1990 and 1996 overall published tuition rose by about 46 percent while actual discounted tuition (that is, when aid was factored in) rose about 28 percent.[9] Their expenses were escalating, not least the expense of generating financial aid for less affluent students from those able to pay. While demand might be inelastic for the best private schools, the bulk of the private sector worried about enrollments as their prices outran both the consumer price index and personal income, especially for lower-income students. In the mid-1990s, these concerns were deepened by studies that showed that students from affluent families were heading for public colleges in increasing numbers. For these students, the SUNY tuition increases that hurt disadvantaged students were easily absorbed. For less talented students, a second-tier public institution was assuredly a better buy compared to less selective private institutions, and a first-rate SUNY institution was a best buy compared to all but the more selective, well-endowed private institutions. As public colleges became more gentrified there appeared to be a looming crisis for the privates.[10] In 1995, the Commission on Independent Colleges and Universities argued that thirty thousand places remained open, a gap created, the commission stated, by students who were selecting taxpayer-subsidized places in SUNY and CUNY. Reduced state spending on higher education impacted the private sector: TAP covered a declining proportion of tuition costs while Bundy Aid was cut by about two-thirds. These multiple trends raise troubling questions about access. Should taxpayers subsidize affluent college students in the public schools or should they pay their own way? The privates argued that policymakers should link tuition to the actual cost of educating each student and to family means. With competition becoming more ruthless, price competition from SUNY could not but be felt by private schools, although the increasing cost of SUNY after 1989 reduced the gap between SUNY and second-tier private schools.

Despite these pressures, legislators did not—would not—choose between the two sectors. "Broad coalition" and "protector" are the key terms that characterize legislative attitudes toward higher education. For most legislators, as for Rockefeller thirty years earlier, higher education was to be supported and there could be no uncoupling of the two sectors, whatever the political pressures and the real or imagined inequities. Legislators continued to support both sectors within the budget parameters available to them rather than favor one over the other. They could not do otherwise, for many legislators had both public and private institutions in their home district: SUNY Cortland and Cornell, Ithaca College and Tompkins-Cortland Community College, SUNY Environmental Science and Forestry and Syracuse University.

THE CHANGING FISCAL AND POLICY ENVIRONMENT: THE TRIALS OF THE 1980s.

New York has for long enjoyed—suffered with, some would say—a reputation as having one of the most generous public sectors in the nation. In the post-1945 era, liberal Democratic and moderate Republican governors believed that activist government could improve the quality of life of New Yorkers. By the end of Rockefeller's tenure in Albany, however, budgets were tightening up. With the New York City fiscal crisis of 1975, the zero-sum character of political choices became painfully clear as governor and legislature struggled to balance the expectations of New Yorkers with diminishing resources. The politics of scarcity became central to New York politics as first Hugh Carey, then Mario Cuomo, and finally George Pataki sought to bring New York's budget situation under control with conservative fiscal policies.

The pattern of disinvestment that began in 1975 was both deliberate policy and unplanned reactions to events, particularly downturns in the economy. Whether what was seen as the continuing fiscal crisis of the state was genuine or produced by state fiscal policy, most policymakers acted as if it were the real thing, an inclination encouraged by the state's low ratings from the wizards of Wall Street. Despite a recurring sense of crisis, the pattern of incremental budgeting was not broken. When recessions hit the state, as they did in the late 1980s and early 1990s, there were painful trade-offs and austerity, but the overall pattern of policy was not significantly changed. Confronted with both conservative pressure for less spending and lower taxes and liberal pressure for increased spending and progressive restructuring of the tax system, the legislature sought to split the difference. As times grew hard and pressures severe, legislators resorted to borrowing, raising fees and nuisance taxes, refinancing debt, and utilizing an array of financial gimmicks to balance the books—or to give the appearance that, consistent with the state constitution, the books were balanced. Changing social needs caused shifts in the way the fiscal pie was sliced: with its growth spurt over, higher education was bound to receive less while spending on prisons or Medicaid increased. The structure of New York politics—parties, interest groups, personal ambition, and local constituencies—promoted bipartisan activist government, but it also bred a contempt by the public for the political establishment and created an atmosphere hospitable to the message that George Pataki brought to the voters in 1994.

The genius of Albany policymakers for compromise and fiscal legerdemain permitted business to carry on almost as usual—but not quite. Despite popular impressions to the contrary, there was a new fiscal caution at work in the 1980s. From 1982, Governor Carey's last year, to 1992, the share of state spending available for state programs (as distinct from assistance to localities) declined from 25.4 percent to 19.6 percent. Despite his liberal rhetoric, Governor Cuomo pursued a policy of fiscal conservatism. In 1987, during the Reagan boom, Cuomo and the legislature agreed on a three-year program of deep tax cuts. But when the downturn in the economy left the state unable to pay for policies it was committed to, the downside result of this conservative tax cut brought budget deficits and severe cuts in state programs.

Pain was not new to higher education in New York or, for that matter, to the nation. Nationally, higher education was underfunded since the mid-1970s, a reflection of "fundamental changes in government priorities."[11] There was an unmistakable erosion of quality in terms of a shrinking faculty and staff, reduced course offerings, deferred equipment purchases, erosion of library holdings, and increased workload.[12] Despite its widespread image as a tax-and-spend state, New York did not do well comparatively. By the end of the 1980s, it ranked thirty-ninth among the states in per student expenditures and forty-third in per capita expenditure, and this against a trend line that saw state appropriations across the nation at a thirty-year low in 1990–1991.[13] SUNY's fiscal pain continued well into the 1990s and was then intensified by successive Pataki budgets. Between 1985–1986 and 1995–1996, the percentage of state funds allocated to public higher education fell from just over 5 percent to just under 3 percent, compared with national figures of under 8 percent to 6 percent. Nothing was more stark than figures showing a drop in support of tax dollars to SUNY's budget from 90 percent in 1988–1987 to 43.5 percent in 1995–1996, with tuition income rising from 10 percent to 54 percent From 1993–1994 to

1998–1999, New York's average annual percentage increase in appropriations for higher education was 1 percent, compared to a national average of 5 percent and as states began to restore spending, New York continued to lag behind the rest of the nation.[14]

For students the picture was quite bad. Between 1989 and 1995, the proportion of household income necessary to meet tuition costs had more than doubled (from 4.64 percent to 11.25 percent). Nationally, the cumulative percentage increase in tuition from 1980–1995 was nearly three times more than the increase in household incomes and consumer prices, with the sharpest part of the increase coming between 1990 and 1995. In three years, from 1992–1993 to 1995–1996, the percentage of students nationally borrowing money for a bachelor's degree jumped from 46 percent to 60 percent while—a sign of the decrease in public support for students—the greatest percentage increase in student borrowing occurred in public institutions, with the percentage of students borrowing money jumping from 42 percent to 60 percent. For many students and their parents, then, affordability was not an abstract or remote policy issue, but a close-to-home concern.[15]

Hard though the budgets of the 1980s were, the fiscal and political storms that struck in the early 1990s were far more severe. The election of 1990 saw a particularly strong expression of tax rebellion that appeared to end the liberal framework that had characterized New York politics since the 1930s. In retrospect, of course, the 1990 election was not the fundamental break it appeared at the time, but it did drive Governor Cuomo and the legislative leadership to an understanding, more conservative in temper than before, that resolution of the long-term budget mess could not be avoided and that any solution must satisfy an unhappy electorate, an aggressive business community, and, above all, Wall Street bond raters. For the state university, this shift in outlook brought harsh new realities. Already a fifteen-year record of cuts, from the mid-1970s through the early 1990s, produced the equivalent of the elimination of the university centers at Albany and Binghamton, four four-year colleges, and one statutory college. Faced with the prospect of still further reductions, Chancellor Bruce Johnstone prepared a set of grim options for a stunned university community. These included permanent downsizing, campus closings, and increased tuition. Ultimately, SUNY avoided implementing the Johnstone doomsday options because it did, with more fervor perhaps, what it had learned to do so well, namely, make do with less, watch quality suffer, increase tuition, lobby hard, and, finally, Micawber-like, hope that something would turn up. Like Chancellor

Wharton before him, Johnstone sought to force the issue on legislative decision-makers whose talent lay as much in nondecisions as in decisions. "Muddling through"—that excellent British stratagem—was the hallmark of the political system and, it seemed, SUNY's last best strategy for survival. It was left, to Governor Pataki, in 1994, to break the muddle.

INSIDE THE BELTWAY: SUNY'S POLITICAL ENVIRONMENT

With the expansion of SUNY, higher education became a matter of big politics as well as big budgets. With the disinvestment of the 1980s, the SUNY community grew accustomed to fighting for survival just like any other state agency. Over the years, this necessitated deploying lobbyists and advocates, bargaining with Division of Budget (DOB), mobilizing a grassroots base, making deals, facing new enemies (e.g., the ultraconservative group, Change-NY), and summoning new friends into existence (e.g., the SUNY Mayors' Coalition). Repeated firestorms of protest on campuses that spilled over into the legislature and the executive branch signaled that SUNY policy was high on the Albany agenda. We have seen in the previous section that the fiscal crunch of the 1980s and early 1990s produced a shift in public philosophy. Before exploring the changes associated with the Pataki election, it is worth surveying the political landscape so as to understand the political environment of higher education decision making.

Governors in a Changing Environment

The governor is the key policymaker for public higher education and particularly for SUNY. Unlike many state universities elsewhere, SUNY is not constitutionally autonomous but is part of the executive branch. The governor appoints the trustees, sets budget and policy priorities, defines the policy agenda for the legislature, directs negotiations with faculty and employee unions, and articulates values and charts the direction of the state. The governor is gatekeeper to the key circles of state policy-making and to the eyes and ears, perhaps even the hearts and minds, of the public. But not all governors are alike. In the SUNY community, Governors Carey and Cuomo were not seen as altogether sympathetic supporters.[16] Aside from rhetorical flourishes and occasional involvement in questions of policy, higher education was a secondary issue for Carey and Cuomo except for budgets. On the other hand, Pataki's administration, as we shall see below, has had more impact on SUNY than any governor since Rockefeller. As an element in his overall policy direction, Pataki engineered a paradigm shift in higher education policy, budgets, and personnel—a shift that found little acceptance on SUNY campuses. Unlike his predecessors, Pataki responded to criticism of SUNY's new directions by tightening his control over SUNY by appointing top officials from his administration to key SUNY positions, by encouraging counterattacks by SUNY officials on their critics, and by stepping up positive publicity about SUNY achievements.[17] Still, the public perception was that Pataki maintained a languid disinterest in SUNY policy.

While the three governors differed in their ideological outlook, they shared at least one core policy objective in common—reduced state spending. The state budget, as they saw it, was simply too big; the state's deficit, the obstacle to economic growth; and SUNY's sizeable budget, an attractive and, because spending on the university was discretionary, an easy target. Despite its anguished protests, SUNY demonstrated a capacity to make do and politicians wondered, sometimes justifiably so, whether SUNY managers were simply crying wolf. For the governor's budget experts, SUNY's enrollment levels were proof that student demand was relatively quality insensitive and therefore inelastic as long as the price was right. Over the long term, it was not clear that tuition increases really had a depressing effect on enrollment. That the university differed from other state agencies in that it could not contract and expand without grave damage to quality was not an argument that swayed Cuomo's DOB in the 1980s or Pataki's trustees in the 1990s. As higher-education budgets nationally took a dive, DOB officials could argue that SUNY would not suffer competitively with peer institutions and that New York paralleled national trends. There were competing policy needs and SUNY would simply have to make do. "Tell me where to take the money from" was Cuomo's mantra, while Pataki supporters simply asserted that SUNY was too fat, too inefficient, too unproductive—too many overpaid professors doing too little. The new trustees weighed in, moreover, on the governor's side in repeated budget battles. Unlike their Carey-Cuomo predecessors, they saw their task not as advocating for the university but as keeping SUNY's budget in line with the governor's priorities; they were loyal foot soldiers in the governor's fiscal army.

Budget makers were doubtlessly aware that a university had alternative sources of income (i.e., tuition) that other state agencies lacked. During the

1980s, tuition increases were the third rail of higher education politics, but once the recessions of the late 1980s hit, producing an increase in the state's deficit, policymakers turned to tuition as a source of ready cash. As long as SUNY tuition did not materially exceed that of peer or regional institutions, tuition increases could be imposed on SUNY. The Pataki administration was less sensitive than its predecessor to the political heat generated by proposed tuition increases or by cuts to TAP, and it sought consistently to ratchet up the price of SUNY to students, 73 percent of whom receive financial aid. Between fall 1990 and fall 1995, SUNY undergraduate tuition more than doubled as the shift away from traditional "redistributivist liberalism" toward a "neoliberal" approach to the public sector that began under Cuomo continued under Pataki.

Players at the Table: The Legislature and the Organized Interests

For more than twenty years the legislature has shown itself to be SUNY's ultimate board of trustees, although its capacity to shape SUNY policy is shared with a constitutionally strong governor. By the mid-1980s, SUNY enjoyed strong bipartisan support generally, while the higher education committees, and particularly their chairmen—Assemblyman Ed Sullivan and Senator Ken LaValle—assumed the roles of watchdogs and mentors of higher education. Both the membership and the leadership of the two houses were willing to extend a helping hand to SUNY and CUNY whenever the executive proposed deep cuts—although it was never quite clear whether executive proposals were meant seriously, were tactical moves in legislative/executive negotiations, or were calculated on the assumption that the legislature would boost higher education budgets no matter what. From the early 1980s onward, defending SUNY while bashing successive governors for cutting SUNY was a low-risk political position that both Republicans and Democrats did not hesitate to take, as the titles of successive legislative reports indicate: *SUNY: 1975–1982: A Budgetary Battles of Access Versus Quality* (1982); *Fragile Giant: SUNY in the Age of Disinvestment* (1993); *SUNY: Rethinking, Shrinking or Sinking?*; *Reaffirming Our Commitment: Maintaining Access, Quality and Accountability for the State University of New York* (1996); *Shifting Shares of State Support for Higher Education in New York State* (1996). Nor is the legislature's interest purely academic or disinterested. Legislators fully appreciate SUNY's home town ("pork barrel") connection, and they do not hesitate to take positions of support or to claim credit when the legislative smoke settles. Few if any legislators could be found echoing calls for a smaller, less accessible SUNY.

Inevitably, there are nuances and subtleties. More concerned about budgets and taxes, Republicans, particularly in the Senate, are inclined to acquiesce to tuition increases or to argue for increases tied to the CPI or the Higher Education Price Index. Loyal to their roots, Democrats were more likely to resist tuition increases, and call for tuition rollbacks. But reaction to the "T-word" is so sensitive that an observer might well believe that tuition and TAP was *the* higher education issue. When, for example, the governor proposed both deep cuts and a radical restructuring of TAP in his 1999–2000 budget, the reaction of many legislators appeared to be that that item was dead on arrival.[18] More than once advocates for SUNY, whether union or management, were put in the position of trying to point out, sotto voce, that resisting tuition increases is all well and good, but only as long as state dollars for the operating budget are forthcoming.

Organized interests play a key role in the politics of higher education. Legislative responsiveness to SUNY issues has been aided, if not created, by the lobbying efforts of faculty and students who can say and do things that administrators cannot. When SUNY's administration argued for variable tuition and for detaching the hospitals from the university, it was successfully opposed by SUNY's influential faculty union, the United University Professions (UUP). Over the years, UUP proved adroit in its advocacy and in developing a network of friends in the legislature. By the early 1990s it was a player to be taken into account, aided no doubt by its affiliation with the New York State United Teachers (NYSUT), one of the state's most powerful and well-financed unions. As unions do, UUP and NYSUT reward friendly legislators, devote substantial resources to lobbying, and play interest group politics with sophistication and success. As the gap between SUNY administrators and trustees and the faculty widened in the late 1980s, and particularly after 1995, the union developed both policy and lobbying goals independent of the SUNY establishment. Across the board SUNY's best advocates—students, faculty, campus administrators—tend to work with legislators in a common direction.

For its part, System Administration (the new name for SUNY Central in the Pataki era) is generally accorded the natural deference that agencies receive, but this is no guarantee that its spokespersons, including chancellors, will consistently find receptive interlocutors in the legislature. A SUNY official who, at key budget hearings, begins successive answers with "I don't know" or comes up with a sizeable "rainy-day fund" after pleading dire poverty is not the most persuasive or credible spokesman. Throughout the 1980s and into the 1990s, SUNY Central's relationship with the legislature was often problematic, as political clumsiness, weak leadership, a touch of arrogance, or poor policy choices undermined its authority. Whether Wharton's Independent Commission in the mid-1980s or Pataki's radical trustees in the 1990s, legislators resisted, when and where they could, efforts to change the SUNY that the legislature built, protected, and regarded as its own.

Still, if SUNY got by with a little help from its legislative friends, often the operative word was "little." The legislature did not seek to micromanage the university or intrude on academic matters. It rarely set internal SUNY priorities or meddled with issues of curriculum or academic freedom. It seemed to have a sophisticated and wise appreciation of the proper relationship between the university and the people's representatives. The Legislature pursued the classic strategy of splitting the difference between what governors habitually proposed cutting and SUNY advocates wanted restored. "We'll help," legislators would say. "times are tough—you'll have to take some hits." It was the best the university could expect. Under Pataki, however, the cuts were so severe across the board and Republicans under such severe pressure to toe the party line that legislators felt besieged, making the task of winning relief more difficult than ever before. When, in Albany as in Washington after 1994, the Democratic assembly leadership hewed to a more moderate and less liberal line, the help grew more "little." Once the trustees made defending Governor Pataki's fiscal policies their top priority, "Save SUNY" campaigns were carried on almost exclusively by faculty and students. Inevitably, higher education could not be divorced from the general political context and SUNY issues were swept up in the whirlpool of broader partisan and ideological warfare: in spring 1998, to take one example, hard-crafted bipartisan add-ons to SUNY's budget fell victim to Pataki's massive across-the-board veto ax.

Legislators had to weigh one set of claims against another. In New York, as across the country, welfare, Medicaid, crime, and corrections all competed for scarce dollars against a backdrop of federal reductions in state aid. The Pataki agenda further tightened the fiscal screws. Then too, the legislative process is ill-suited for deciding fundamental policy within the constitutional deadlines imposed on the budget process or through the hard-fought bitter politics that characterizes an annual budget that is universally regarded as "dysfunctional," in the words of the comptroller. Legislators need to solve today's problems today—and these are fiscal and political; on the truly big questions that require long-term, thoughtful goals, they look to others to provide answers they can work with. Thus, SUNY came under increasing pressure to address its own problems. But when the internal constituencies (e.g., UUP, SUNY Central) could not agree on, say, flexibility for the hospitals or budget priorities, the result was a prolonged stalemate or simply drift. Often policy seemed to be the by-product of default or the result of measures taken as a fiscal quick fix. Comptroller McCall noted, to take one example, that TAP grant schedules were bent not to meet a policy objective but to meet immediate budgetary needs. Cuts to SUNY sometimes seemed to be driven by no greater motive than "That's where the money is." "'Policy,'" the Comptroller said, "ends up being whatever the budget dynamics produces."[19]

There is another point to be made here. Not surprisingly, professors look on SUNY as an academic institution. If they worry about policy questions at all, they worry about teaching, staffing, money for research, libraries, and colleagues threatened by layoffs. This produces a degree of disconnect between professor and legislator. Legislators often view the state university as a social program that meets the needs of real people. With Americans increasingly regarding a college education as an entitlement—as necessary to a secure personal future—legislators are concerned chiefly about opportunity: Can the sons and daughters of constituents find a place in SUNY? is there enough TAP to go around? Is there child care for the student-mother or remedial education for those who trail behind? Can parents save for their kids' education? These are the concerns of legislators worried about a single mother or a student who works at a convenience store to get by. The concerns of intellectuals matter less than the Educational Opportunity Program (EOP) student who drops out of school due to TAP cuts, the homeowner whose taxes are squeezed because the state does not pick up its full share of community college funding, or the layoff of another ten tax-paying faculty members. For legislators, the university is not an ivory tower but a human presence in their communities.

New Kids on the Political Block: The Pataki Trustees

In the past, SUNY trustees were seen as not much more than the legally constituted body responsible for the direction of SUNY—a slightly dull but worthy body, remote and anonymous, civic leaders or political notables content to defer to SUNY Central while maintaining a relaxed hand on the reins. This picture changed radically under Governor Pataki. For starters, he appointed conservative trustees who took it upon themselves to take charge of SUNY in an aggressive activist manner and to bring it into line with Governor Pataki's program. Like their counterparts in other states, they did not hesitate to push their agenda in the area of program issues, academic issues, and even areas defined as academic-freedom issues. Despite the frictions that this initially created with the holdover Cuomo trustees, the Pataki trustees took to the Albany political stage with an activism hitherto unseen from a board of trustees.

Buoyed by their self-confidence, a clear agenda, and a sense of mission, the new trustees regarded themselves as part of a movement of conservative trustees nationally who, in one description, are "largely social and political conservatives . . . [who] believe that they must act aggressively to cure sclerotic, selfish American higher education."[20] In the manner of any exuberant group bent on a mission, the new trustees pursued a variety of not always compatible goals. They put into place a plan (*Rethinking SUNY*) for restructuring or deregulating the university along cost-efficient lines (see discussion below), for devolving and decentralizing fiscal and managerial authority, and for compelling campuses to compete in the market for revenues and students. A new resource-allocation methodology linked revenues to enrollment. At the same time that they decentralized managerial authority in the name of efficiency, the trustees pursued a centralizing strategy in the broad areas of governance, curriculum, personnel, and standards.

Some of the reforms were long overdue, for example, fiscal flexibility and independence for local administrators. But others raised red flags: differential tuition would stratify the university; devolution would fragment the coherence of the university; a market-based approach would set campuses against each other; "basic curriculum" was an avenue for ideological direction; a pervasive cost-effective calculus would displace academic judgment. A fresh strategy on management issues—a trend throughout the country—was one thing; using such a strategy as a ramp for remaking the university and subtly redefining its mission was another. Trustee Arnold Gardner, a Carey appointee, was blunt in his assessment: "We all want standards, but not as a barrier to access. . . . These are codes for a lessened university, lessened in size, lessened in quality, lessened in terms of their ability to maintain quality programs and services."[21] Criticisms notwithstanding, the Pataki appointees were in control of the board and its agenda by 1997. They created a new political dynamic as they increasingly took a direct and supercharged role in the university's internal affairs.

Nothing demonstrated better, perhaps, the underlying conservative impulse that guided the trustees than the controversy that raged over a 1997 women's studies conference at SUNY New Paltz, a controversy that extended from the columns of the *Wall Street Journal* to campuses throughout the nation. Offended by the apparent over-the-edge subject matter, Trustee Candace de Russy sought to have the campus president fired. This was an action that some regarded as a proper exercise of trustee oversight but that others saw as clearly threatening academic freedom. Given the more cultural wars raging in American intellectual and academic circles, a controversy over sadomachismo might be seen as just another flap over postmodernist or feminist redefinition of the canon. But from the perspective of Trustee de Russy and her defenders, the "New Paltz Affair" was no small campus dust-up: the stakes were very large, namely, halting "the continuing corrosion of American culture as a whole."[22]

If "meddle" and "micromanage" was the common description at the outset, the adjectives grew stronger by 1999 as the new trustees showed little inclination to change course: politicizing the university, ideological takeover, a litmus test for appointments of administrators, infringing academic freedom, arrogance. The new trustees and their spokespersons responded in kind, denouncing union leaders as using the faculty as "pawns" for "your purpose of self-promotion."[23] By early 1999 at the latest the university community was polarized within, and often against, itself in a quite complicated manner. On many issues the Pataki Trustees were on one side while significant constituencies within the university community—faculty union and faculty senate, staff, students, and even some campus administrators who were obliged to carry out the decisions made by the DOB and the trustees—were on the other. Driven by their local interests, some campus presidents supported the trustees' efforts to implement management flexibility, campus authority regarding tuition, shedding the hospitals, and the like. On other issues, campus administrators, apprehensive about an overbearing board, concluded that discretion, not valor, was the best strategy. Nor were the divisions caused by the new trustees confined to the SUNY community. Some of SUNY's most ardent legislative friends plunged into open warfare against the new trustees who, at times, seemed quite determined to storm the Winter Palace and overthrow the *ancien régime.* The board did not hesitate first to drive one chancellor (Tom Bartlett) out and then, without a full search, appoint a more cooperative and agreeable chancellor (John Ryan). In a brutally frank report, the Faculty Senate sharply criticized the "erosion of academic due process in the selection of System Administration personnel" and the tendency of the new regime to ignore "the standard practices of professional employment in higher education in the U.S.[24] Nor did the board hesitate to impose, or attempt to impose, its judgment on a range of areas that previous boards had left to administrators and faculty. As many of the trustees' reforms did not require statutory approval, and as the governor continued to support his appointees, the critics lacked effective leverage to change or moderate the new policies. Some policies could be blocked: differential tuition was simply something that the legislature refused to accept; the new Resource Allocation Method was modified in 1998–1999. But as many of the new directions—for example, devolution and decentralization, the dismantling of SUNY Central—were institutionalized, and given the resounding reelection of Governor Pataki in 1998, it was clear that there would no easy return to the Rockefeller model, absent a major shift in state politics.

SUNY AND THE CHALLENGE OF RETHINKING SUNY

On the eve of the 1994 Republican takeover of the governor's mansion, SUNY's basic framework was generally secure, despite the disinvestment of the 1980s and early 1990s. The university had ducked the bullet of Chancellor Johnstone's desperate options and, despite continued fiscal pressures, was breathing somewhat easier. Following the electorate's repudiation of the Cuomo administration, however, it became clear SUNY would not be permitted to muddle through with basic issues left unresolved. But few observers were fully prepared for the shift in the framework of public policy that was now executed with a take-no-prisoners ferocity and speed—a shift signaled by the scope and depth of the fiscal year 1995 budget proposals. Even fewer expected, moreover, the new direction for SUNY that was set out in *Rethinking SUNY.* As large institutions, like large oil tankers, cannot change directions swiftly, over the next four years, the trustees found it more difficult than they had anticipated to realize their full vision or to carry out the more extreme ideas of some of their members. Much was attempted and much was done that was different. By 1999, certain institutional changes, as

suggested above, seemed firmly in place. These included greater fiscal autonomy for individual campuses, a change that increased enrollment-based
competitive pressures while accelerating centrifugal forces within the university and diminishing the overall coherence and identity of SUNY as a system.
But the trustees found far more impediments in their way than they had
probably anticipated. Their inability to imposed differential tuition or to
spin off the hospitals, mentioned above, are two examples. As their ideological kinfolk elsewhere in the nation discovered, sweeping change, not to say
revolutionary change, does not come easily to American political life. The
conflicts and disputes that characterized SUNY policy from 1994 onward, it
should be emphasized, were less about particular policies than about the
overall vision and philosophy that shaped those policies. The trustees were
successful in much, but not all, that they have attempted. By mid-1999, as I
discuss below, the trustees actions resulted in a major (and still unresolved)
effort by the faculty to compel the removal of the Board of Trustees—or a
least force a change in the governance of the university. But politics aside,
there was no consensus on the key question: What kind of university was
SUNY to be as it faced its second fifty years? To better understand the contested values in this continuing debate, it will be useful to refer to two broad
visions or models of the university—two contesting paradigms, two embattled camps. For simplicity, call them the "Rockefeller" and the "Pataki"
models as a way of conceptualizing the two visions that underlay the politics
and the debate over SUNY's future.

"TO PROVIDE TO THE PEOPLE": THE INHERITED VISION OF SUNY

When the Pataki administration came to office in early 1995, it inherited a
state university whose policy framework had been securely in place—whatever the ups and downs of budgeting, whatever the debates over mission and
size—for about thirty years. That framework was expressed in the 1985
statutory mission statement and in an institutional configuration that had
been largely constructed in the 1960s. The mission had been defined into
law in 1985 in statutory language of striking specificity and even eloquence.
As with any university, its mission encompassed "education, research and
service." But the legislature took care to define its mission in very special
terms and to enunciate some very clear policy values: "The mission of the

state university system shall be to provide to the people of New York educational services of the highest quality, with the broadest possible access, fully representative of all segments of the population in a complete range of academic, professional and vocational post-secondary programs. . . . These services and activities shall be offered through a geographically distributed comprehensive system of diverse campuses designed to provide a comprehensive program of higher education. . . . and to address local, regional and state needs and goals."[25]

The legislature defined the mission in detailed terms that a brief summary cannot do justice to. Fulfilling the Mission requires a "balance of . . . resources" that: (1) with respect to educational services, "recognizes the fundamental role of its responsibilities in undergraduate education and provides a full range of graduate and professional education that reflects the opportunity for individual choice and the needs of society"; (2) recalling the political struggle over medical education in the 1940s, "strengthens its educational and research programs . . . through the provision of high quality health care"; (3) with respect to access and tuition levels, "establishes tuition which most effectively promotes the university's access goals"; (4) and with respect to service, "shares the expertise of the state university . . . through a program of public service for the purpose of enhancing the well-being of the people of the state of New York." SUNY is enjoined to achieve the "broadest possible" access, a phrase that implied both expanded places and opportunity for socially and economically defined populations. Tuition must promote access rather than other objectives such as supplying a fixed percentage of operating costs. Educational excellence—of "the highest quality"—is the first obligation of the university. Excellence, access, affordability: these were the core values. Comprehensive offerings were the core programmatic commitment.

SUNY's institutional configuration is as important as its mission statement in defining the university's overall character and values. This point requires far more extended discussion than is possible here, but briefly I would like to identify five key features of this institutional profile, noting that they are in part accidents of history and in part a product of deliberate design.

1. *A public and a state university.* SUNY is a "public" university created by public legislation, state operated, and part of the general organization of government. Its faculty and employees are state employees. Its mission is to serve the public. The

statute does not define SUNY as a "state assisted" or "state-sub-sidized" institution, as is the case elsewhere. It is—or rather was—an organic part of the entire ensemble of public institutions, in the same way that public schools are. But in an age of "reinventing government" the line between "public" and "private" is blurry and, as we shall see below, SUNY increasingly is a state institution that is subtly becoming privatized in a number of ways.

2. *A unitary and comprehensive system.* SUNY developed as a unitary and comprehensive system rather than as a scatter of autonomous campuses tied together by administrative strings. A crucial expression of this unitary and comprehensive character has been the policy of applying a single common tuition fee for each level of instruction (e.g., baccalaureate, doctoral) rather than a variable or differential campus-based tuition. (Indeed, until 1963 tuition was free in SUNY.)

3. *No flagship campus.* As SUNY developed, a decision was made to support several advanced professional, graduate, and research centers rather than a single dominant flagship campus, a pattern found elsewhere in the country. This was consistent, as noted above, with the virtue that the trustees found in the geographic breadth that characterized SUNY.

4. *The role of the legislature and public accountability.* As noted earlier, SUNY was not made a constitutionally autonomous institution. Although the trustees exercise authority in directing the university, SUNY has remained linked to the political process. Without putting too fine a point on it, the legislature is the democratic link between SUNY and the public.

5. *A finely tuned balance—a common identity.* Finally, SUNY developed and earlier trustees sought to maintain a delicate balance between (as noted earlier) the advantages of decentralization and "the unity of purpose achieved by its units and central administration." This balance also permitted SUNY, I believe, to develop a coherent and readily identifiable identity that

stood all its campuses in good stead throughout the country and state. It had the potential of making SUNY one of the elements that, as one finds elsewhere across the country, link the people of the state with their university.

BREAKING THE MUDDLE WITH RADICAL MEASURES: THE PATAKI ADMINISTRATION AND THE NEW PARADIGM

Governor Pataki's general program and the decidedly conservative outlook of his appointees to the Board of Trustees signaled that the administration would seek to remake SUNY along different lines. The new vision was drawn from the panoply of conservative political ideas: greater fiscal belt tightening and reduced funding, attention to productivity, emphasis on conservative intellectual values, a reduced public sector, and support for the private sector. For conservatives, SUNY was neither well managed nor cost effective, nor doing the academic job it should. As the new board took charge, it became evident that university life would be subject to far greater trustee direction than before and that for the first time this would be extended to academic matters. Nor could there be doubt that this effort would provoke an extended debate about SUNY. What was not anticipated was just how radical this effort would be or just how bitter and protracted the ensuing controversy would become. We turn now to a review of the strategies that defined the new regime.

Shock Treatment: The Impact of Fiscal Policy

It is not surprising that SUNY was a prime target of opportunity for Pataki's budget officials, especially given the large budget deficit they were seeking to close. It had long been conventional wisdom that SUNY was too big, too inefficient, too costly, and poorly managed. Thus, the first strike was at SUNY's budget, not its classrooms. In his initial budget proposals, Governor Pataki proposed—when the numbers were finally added up[26]—a cut of nearly one dollar in three. The proposed budget also included reductions in TAP, the elimination of SUNY's Equal Opportunity Program (for economically and educationally disadvantaged students), and a general tuition increase. This last package of proposals reflected a marked indifference, if not class bias, toward precisely those social constituencies that SUNY was meant to serve. Faculty, students, administrators, and even seasoned legislative supporters of SUNY were stunned by the depth of the proposed cuts. Not even in its worst moments had the California system, which until then had taken the deepest cuts nationally, been hit as hard. Was the administration serious, or was it simply laying its cards on the table for the bargaining that would follow? Whatever the answer to this question, the proposals were taken very seriously.

What these "radical" measures might be was suggested by reports that the chancellor and trustees were considering the closing of eight campuses. When, as so often in the past, the legislature rescued SUNY from the worst of the governor's proposed cuts, a threshold had been passed. There would be no return to a fiscal status quo ante. Over the next four years, the Governor proposed budgets that contained deep reductions or else held the existing budget steady, producing a de facto budget cut. There would be no growth. Given divided control of the legislature, negotiating budgets became protracted stalemates; SUNY lobbyists were compelled to take what they could get, namely, very partial restorations.

Even when both chambers restored some funding, there always existed a possibility that they would disagree on whether additional revenue should derive from increased tuition charges or from appropriated tax dollars. Nor, after 1994, could the SUNY community of students, faculty, and campus administrators look to the trustees or, after Chancellor Ryan assumed office, SUNY's senior administrators for help with the legislature. They were working to a different brief and were defiant in their focus on cost efficiency in the face of criticism. In the rough and tumble of budget politics, rational discourse was a rare commodity, and debates were noisy and nasty. For the new administration, radical measures were necessary. If campus closings were taboo, then other measures had to be found. The following four years saw turmoil sweep the university as a result of the proposed budget reductions. The impact of the instability was enormous: applications slumped; faculty flight set in as talented faculty found opportunities elsewhere or took early retirement; the faculty as a whole fell by nearly 1600 from 1994 to 1997; the proportion of part-time faculty rose across the system; course sections were canceled. What cannot be shown with numbers is the demoralization of staff, the uncertainty of students about their planned program, the erosion of the reputation of an institution that, in terms of the long sweep of university history in American, was still building a reputation.

When the state's surplus grew to $1 to $2 billion in mid-1997, the pressure eased somewhat, although New York continued to lag behind the recovery evident elsewhere in the nation.[27] Nor was austerity lessened in the proposed 1998–1999 budget which, despite the provision of funding for capital improvements and the upbeat election-year tone with which the governor delivered it, continued the downsizing which began twenty years earlier. And once the 1998 election was behind him and national ambitions apparently shaping his policy agenda, the governor returned to the hard-line fiscal and social strategies that were the hallmark of his administration. Despite a budget surplus of about $2 billion, he proposed cuts in SUNY's operating budget that some calculated at $52 million and others as high as $213 million and contained the most severe proposed cuts ever in TAP. Moreover, TAP was restructured to accomplish nonfiscal goals, for example, shortening time to graduation, that fell the hardest on low-income and working students. As it faced the new century, SUNY continued to exist on short rations in an environment marked by a budget surplus, and, in fact, it faced the prospect of a worsening situation in the early 2000s as tax cuts, the STAR program, and federal welfare cuts together threatened a new state budget deficit.

"SUNY Bashing": The Discourse of Denigration

The political storm that raged as a result of the Pataki budgets spread beyond budget politics. Conservative politicians and right-wing groups such as Change-NY initiated a campaign of denigration—"SUNY bashing"—whose political purpose seemed to be to undermine SUNY's credibility. A series of reports by Change-NY's Empire Foundation for Policy Research attacked SUNY for what it saw as a core curriculum that lacked intellectual coherence and standards. Others attacked SUNY faculty as overpaid and underproductive, despite external evidence to the contrary. Such attacks conveyed the notion that there was little reason for SUNY to be anything more than a safety net for those who were neither rich enough nor bright enough to afford private education. Inevitably, the campaign of disparagement and the polemics it occasioned could not but contribute to the erosion of SUNY's reputation in the academic community and of its appeal to potential students and their families. In time, as the Pataki administration itself appeared to be moving in a more pragmatic direction, what might be called the "trashing of SUNY" eased up, but did not totally vanish.

A New Blueprint: Rethinking SUNY

Confronted with intense opposition to the first Pataki budget and frustrated at SUNY's apparent inability to bring its budget problems to resolution or to chart a course for itself, the legislature directed the trustees to emphasize cost efficiency. If legislators expected a process that would at last create a consensus on SUNY's future, they were dealt a sharp surprise when *Rethinking SUNY* was published in late 1995. Although presented as a plan for utilizing state resources efficiently, raising academic standards, and ensuring accountability, *Rethinking SUNY* projected a quite different vision for SUNY. It was, in fact, the first shot in a policy dispute that five years later had still not been resolved.

What was the fuss about? On one level, *Rethinking SUNY* was not as novel as it appeared. Many, if not most, of the ideas in the report were common currency among administrators in national higher education circles as a reflection of a movement to reform university management. Restructuring with an eye to cost efficiency, enhanced learning productivity, eliminating tenure in order to create a more flexible labor market, performance funding, "selective excellence," decentralized fiscal responsibility, outsourcing, user fees (shifting the cost burden to students)—these were managerial precepts that since the early 1980s were seen as solutions for the problems of higher education.[28] Fundamental to this managerial philosophy were propositions that, in effect, assumed that the university should be run along corporate lines, employing modern management practices. The notion was that students should be regarded as consumers, colleges should respond to the needs of the market place, education was about advancing individual interests, and intercampus competition was a good thing. Higher education was a service industry, an all-important engine in the process of economic growth, individual advancement, and global competition—but a service industry, nonetheless. At a time when virtual universities and for-profit corporations were blurring the lines between traditional universities and what some now called "education management organizations" (EMOs), *Rethinking SUNY* was in step with the new zeitgeist of higher education.[29]

In addition to its general neocorporate perspective, *Rethinking SUNY* projected a new institutional architecture. Campus autonomy and self-sufficiency would replace systemwide leadership and policy direction; undergraduate education would become SUNY's highest priority, replacing the long-time balance of undergraduate, graduate, and professional education—the latter presumably would again be the work of private institutions. The hospitals would be spun off from the health-science centers and converted into public benefit corporations, thus severing their organic connection to SUNY—a prime motive for the founding of SUNY in the 1940s. Differential tuition—with all its implications of hierarchy, prestige (not to say snobbery), and brand competition—would replace the long-standing policy of uniform tuition and introduce a prestige-based dynamic into the university. In a decisive departure from the 1985 mission statement, quality and access were to be balanced against cost. To its critics, *Rethinking SUNY* reverberated with meanings that violated honored traditions of the university as an institution, and of SUNY itself. In the end this is what the fuss was about.

In time some of these ideas proved to be nonstarters and some were fairly reasonable approaches to tidy management. But *Rethinking SUNY* was more than a technician's manual or a handbook for SUNY managers. It sought to install the neoliberal view that a market approach to management would be more efficient than SUNY's somewhat clumsy state-agency model. A second premise, one that guided the general approach of the Pataki administration, held that the private sector was superior to the public and that a downsized and less public SUNY would be a better SUNY. SUNY could not be totally privatized, but SUNY campuses could be forced to compete—become more "entrepreneurial" was the way it was put—in a market environment. The new resource allocation method, which also set off a small political firestorm when it was introduced, was one example of this.[30] SUNY campus presidents felt a steady pressure to manage their campuses as if they were in the private sector. As for campuses that could not compete successfully—well, perhaps in time they would need to be closed and if so, it would be the market and not the political process that would administer the coup d'grâce. In short, such approaches tended to emphasize fiscal considerations or competitive outcomes in academic decision making. And while the trustees did not neglect quality, many in the university were led to wonder whether managerial concerns were taking precedence over academic considerations or over SUNY's broad social mission.

Rethinking SUNY and the ensemble of managerial and ideological objectives pursued by the Board of Trustees and the Pataki administration set SUNY on a new, if contentious, direction. *Rethinking SUNY* and its progeny forced professors, administrators, and staff to ask hard questions as they watched their institution change around them. If the student is redefined as a consumer, rather than as an apprentice learner, does that mean that the "the customer is always right" and that the university should simply respond to market demand in designing programs and setting standards? Is the faculty member now also defined as an entrepreneur in search of self-advancement through a market calculus rather than a member of a community of scholars? What traditionally distinguished SUNY from some of its sister state systems was the principle that the SUNY whole is greater than the sum of its campus parts—*Rethinking SUNY* would change that by encouraging the parts to the detriment of the whole. Would the more decentralized SUNY envisioned by *Rethinking SUNY* face a slide back to what it was at the outset of its life: "a secondary alternative, suitable mainly for . . . students unable to afford private institutions," just a scatter of disconnected campuses with all but a few drifting into obscurity and even mediocrity—almost a higher-education welfare safety net? By 1998, some of its more extreme ideas, for example, differential tuition, scrapping professional training, perhaps even cutting back on access, were abandoned or defeated and with the trustees' decision to require a systemwide core curriculum (see below), more serious issues were on the table. Did the trustees really understand the deeper problems facing higher education or were these cast in the sometimes simplistic terms produced by the raging culture wars? And what would become of the university's reputation for learning, teaching, and scholarship if the trustees succeeded in giving SUNY a neoconservative ideological image—was SUNY destined to become the poster child for the anti-PC project of some trustees? Were the trustees correct that the curriculum was shapeless and lacked rigor? And did those trustees most concerned to limit, say, feminist, deconstructionist, or multicultural studies understand that the origins of public education stressed greater access and opportunity but also, as Nevins put it, a "rejection of the tyranny of classical and theological studies," that is, to explore new avenues of knowledge?

Whatever the conversations in the winter of 1999, *Rethinking SUNY* still provides direction for SUNY's managers. Its tenets are being realized as "new facts on the ground." To see the shift in emphasis and direction, one need look no farther than the key values embedded in the text of *Rethinking SUNY*: the word "market" appears four times, the word "efficiency" seven times, and the word "democracy," not at all.[31] The SUNY of 1998 is a far cry from Rockefeller's SUNY of 1968.

FROM CONFLICT TO CONFRONTATION

Given the importance of SUNY—its budget, its structure, its mission—within the ensemble of state policies, the politicization of SUNY policy that occurred between 1995 and 1999 comes as little surprise. SUNY was born in bitter controversy and major moments in its development were also marked by intense and rancorous political dispute. For all participants—faculty and trustees, students and taxpayers, legislators and governors—the stakes were very high, whether in 1948 with the establishment of the university, in 1985 with the effort by the Independent Commission to restructure it, or in 1995 with *Rethinking SUNY*. But the depth of conflict and the degree of polarization triggered by the Pataki Trustees was unusual, even for SUNY and even for New York.

Disinterested observers and friends of public higher education might well have wondered whether university norms of shared governance, democratic discourse, empowerment of university constituencies, and even civility could be restored given the tensions between the activist trustees and the community of students, faculty, and administrators for whom they have responsibility. This last question was given special urgency as the spring semester of 1999 drew to a close. In a clear effort to transform SUNY intellectually as *Rethinking SUNY* had sought to do in other areas of university life, the Board of Trustees, at its December 1998 meeting, approved a uniform thirty-hour core curriculum for all SUNY campuses. Encouraged by their allies in the neoconservative National Association of Scholars and in Change-NY, the trustees, with a single vote, sought to redress what they regarded as the lack of standards, intellectual rigor, and proper curricular content. This effort to impose a single curriculum on thirty or so quite diverse campuses was astonishing in its ambition and audacity. But that was not the problem. Nor did the problem necessarily lay with the content of the curriculum itself—reasonable people could disagree on both the desirability of a university-wide core curriculum and on the content of that curriculum.

The difficulty lay with the nature and implications of the action itself. It was consistent with the top-down governance more common among governing boards around the country. Thus, the faculty (and campus presidents too, for that matter) had been denied any input on the curriculum that the trustees finally approved—a clear breach, it seemed, both of the traditions of shared university governance and of the trustees' own policies. Moreover, the new requirements were approved with little or no regard for the difficulties or expense involved in implementing them. The decision was an unfunded mandate imposed from above. It did not help that at the same meeting the trustees, at the direction of the governor's office, proposed a meager 2.8 percent budget increase for the forthcoming year.

The firestorm of opposition and protest that followed these events resulted, as winter turned to spring, in the collaboration of the University Faculty Senate and United University Professions—the two core voices of the faculty—in crafting a formal resolution of no confidence in the trustees, a resolution addressed to the governor, the legislature and the public. To the degree that college faculties are conservative and cautious, slow to anger and slower to act, the speed with which support grew for the resolution reflected a degree of collective determination that was as breathtaking as it was rare. As the resolution took shape, and as campus senate after campus senate and union chapter after union chapter voted overwhelmingly to approve the resolution, a bill of particulars was articulated, indicting the trustees for what the faculty regarded as a long train of abuses and usurpations. In April, the University Senate adopted the resolution by a vote of 37 to 2.

In university politics, votes of no confidence are generally followed by the resignation of the target of the vote, usually a college president. But with lines drawn deeply in the dirt, passage of this vote of no confidence appeared to have little immediate effect on an embattled Board of Trustees that looked upon both the senate and the union with undisguised disdain. Nonetheless, votes of no confidence are sufficiently rare and sufficiently grave as to to pose a major challenge to the legitimacy of the trustees.

As this is written, the end game has yet to be played out. Will a governor intent on building a national reputation, move quickly to quell the disturbance in his own backyard by removing the most abrasive of the trustees or will he, intent on building credibility among conservative Republicans nationally, simply ignore the vote and play up his steadfastness in what his administration has stood for? Will he be the skilled politician and quietly move to bring the parties together to build some bridges of trust, communication, and common purpose? Will the trustees themselves move to moderate their agenda or will they persist on the activist path they have been charting since 1995? Will the vote simply ignite a further extended period of ill will, with all sides carrying on business as more or less usual? Whatever the outcome, the confrontation signals more clearly than any event since 1948 the extent to which the future of SUNY continues to be a bitterly contested issue of public policy and politics.

POSTSCRIPT
POLITICS, BUDGETS, AND THE DEMOCRACY OF EXCELLENCE:
LOOKING BACK FROM 2004

Since the analysis above was written, the contentious politics surrounding the State University of New York following the 1994 election of Governor Pataki appeared to calm down. While deep policy issues continued to produce political disagreements, the noise subsided and some of the gloomy predictions that brought this chapter to a close in the earlier edition did not come to fruition.

Let us pick up the analysis roughly a year after the tragedy of September 11, 2001. As so often in the past, SUNY policy in this period was shaped by budget issues.[32] During the winter of 2002–2003, many believed that the SUNY budget would be cut again and everyone knew that after seven years tuition would go up.[33] SUNY was not alone in facing the fiscal storm: across the country, the policy environment was changing with respect to public higher education. For the first time in nearly a dozen years, state spending on higher education was down and the overall decline was the biggest ever. In the words of one study, "public higher education—once considered untouchable—became an easy target for both budget cutters and external critics" in the early 1990s.[34] Nationally, the share of state general funds going to higher education had dropped by more than one-third since 1977 and reductions in direct aid to higher-education institutions accelerated dramatically after 1990.[35]

Budgetary austerity was not the only problem facing SUNY. The years immediately following 1994, as described above, had been tumultuous. Initially, the "Pataki Trustees," as they were called, wanted a smaller university, perhaps even shutting down some campuses; they wanted a more efficient university with significant fiscal decentralization and the use of market strategies; and they sought to exert more centralized direction over elements of academic policy. Throughout the 1990s, there were incidents that set faculty against trustees. There had been, for example, a firestorm over a 1997 New Paltz conference on women's sexuality that led ultimately in 2001 to the forced resignation of Roger Bowen as New Paltz's President. For some, this led to the perception that academic freedom was problematic in SUNY. Then there had been the imposition of a trustee-defined general education program that led in 1999 to a vote of no confidence in the trustees by the faculty union and the university senate. In 1998, the comptroller deplored the "policy vacuum" that characterized the making of higher-education policy.

By 2002, however, things had eased. The 1999 appointment of a polit-ically adroit chancellor, Robert L. King, seemed to push some of the ideo-logical concerns to the margins while bringing stability to SUNY's central administration. While the disputes did not disappear, King brought a wel-come change of tone and policy. He seemed to want to take SUNY to the first rank of universities and his international initiatives recognized that in a globalizing world major universities must be truly international. Among his initiatives was an energetic promotion of fund raising and grant seeking—a $3 billion campaign was announced in spring 2004—and of corporate part-nerships. Also in the spring of 2004, King made common cause with others such as the faculty union in requesting an additional $50 million from the legislature for the SUNY system, over and above the amount the governor allocated in the executive budget proposal. In his public pronouncements, King spoke proudly and enthusiastically about SUNY, a marked change from the negativity of the 1995–1996 period.

But there were marks on the negative side of the ledger. Critics argued that King's close relationship with the governor might limit his continued ability to speak out for the university. Moreover, King was still seen by many as the chancellor who forced Bowen from the New Paltz presidency and this won him no fans among the faculty.

THE FISCAL CRISIS OF SUNY: CUTTING BUDGETS—RAISING TUITION

If tight budgets were not SUNY's only problem, they were the most serious. By 2003, New York's economy was in a profound slump. The economic and human devastation of September 11 took place against the backdrop of the collapse of the Wall Street, the bursting of the dot-com bubble, and a national recession. Policymakers faced severe pressures from competing policy areas—Medicaid, K–12 education, prisons, and the fiscal plight of local communities. Spending on higher education was discretionary rather than mandate driven and thus a tempting target for budget reductions. The impact of these forces was intensified by the program of tax cuts and fiscal discipline that were core to Governor Pataki's small-government, free-market agenda. The governor's formula was simple: less revenue = less spending = smaller government. One way to achieve this was to shift the cost of public services from general taxpayers to the users of particular services, such as public parks and beaches, the Thruway, auto licenses, and, of course, tuition for SUNY, CUNY, and community colleges.

The Governor's proposed fiscal year 2004 budget was austere. Legislators, including the Republican Senate, knew full well what the spending cuts would mean for local taxes, K–12 education, Medicaid, universities, and other programs. Throughout the spring, legislators were under intense pressure. In the end, a defiant legislature passed a budget containing sufficient new taxes to meet policy needs and then overrode Pataki's veto of its budget. It was a historic moment, not one likely to be repeated anytime soon.

SUNY: Budgets, Tuition Increases, and Policy Choices

For SUNY, the governor's budget proposal was severe: there was no midyear tuition increase but there was a proposed cut of 15 percent or $185 million in SUNY's operating budget and a tuition increase of $1200. There were other important issues as well, such as the long-running dispute over proposals to privatize SUNY's hospital centers, but tuition and operating funds defined the debate and took the headlines.

By national standards, New York's public institutions were not cheap: they were the fourteenth most expensive in the nation.[36] Tuition had last been raised in 1995 by $750 against a backdrop of a massive deficit and an extended debate over the role, size, and mission of SUNY. And now, a tuition increase of $1200? This was no small sum for many SUNY students, even with the additional relief that financial aid provided.

But crises trump all. For the governor, a massive deficit meant that everyone had to sacrifice, so why not students? But the legislators had to answer to their constituents. When a compromise was reached, the legislature authorized a $950 or 28 percent increase in undergraduate tuition.[37] It seemed to be a straight swap: tuition increase for more operating funds.[38] But within a year, a rueful Chancellor King noted that the continuing lack of adequate funding "caused a considerable disruption in our campus budgets; a disruption that still exits even now."[39]

Whatever the philosophical or ideological arguments for or against charging tuition, in the real world of New York's fiscal policy, tuition is about money. During the debate, one point was usually lost: *The proposed tuition increase was a symptom of SUNY's underlying and on-going fiscal shortfall and a reflection of a changing balance between private sector and public sector.* As elsewhere in the country, withdrawal of state support would inevitably be balanced by increased tuition at a time when higher education was facing cost pressures from technology, enhanced student services, and the like.[40] The real question then was the lack of adequate state funding for SUNY (a situation shared by CUNY and even by private schools that saw their own state subsidies cut). For SUNY advocates the dilemma was this: if legislators were persuaded by students and their families not to raise tuition and if spending cuts were not restored, then SUNY's budget situation would force program cuts and layoffs of staff and faculty. This complex dynamic pitted faculty and institutional needs against students. Administrators were forced to argue for a tuition increase in order to salvage their institutions.

To say that the real battle was a struggle over the budget is to highlight the long-term problem that SUNY faced. SUNY had learned to live with a "pattern of flat budgets" whether measured in terms of actual or inflation-adjusted dollars.[41]

There is no doubt that legislators faced a difficult question. What is the best way to fund a major university in a time of shrinking resources and do so in a way that allows long-term planning and growth? Many legislators on both sides of the aisle opposed ever heavier tuition burdens. This position, of course, created an almost insoluble dilemma. If they rejected regular tuition increases but failed to make up the funding gap, students might have a university to come to, but what would be there to greet them? And so, year after year, the Albany political class finessed the issue by keeping SUNY on short rations and muddling through.

NEW POLICY OPTIONS?

As this is written, however, the situation might be changing. In December 2003, SUNY Chancellor King, supported by the Board, took the bold step of proposing the "creation of a rational tuition policy, which would provide for modest, predictable annual increases in tuition at the state-operated campuses."[43] He also proposed a three- to five-year tuition increase from $4350 to $5100. Though his proposal put on the table what many thought was necessary, the reception was not friendly. The chair of the Assembly Higher Education Committee, Democrat Ronald Canestrari responded that "it was shocking," a comment that effectively killed the idea for the time being.[44]

While as of this writing there is no sign that anything will come of it, a trial balloon has been floated.

There is a curious political feature to all this. As the budget drama unfolded in 2003, students seemed less exercised over the proposed increase than in prior years. How could policymakers impose a hefty tuition increase without paying a political price? Several answers suggest themselves. The most cynical might be that New York's highly gerrymandered legislators are insulated from electoral repercussions for their decisions, especially those that lack widespread saliency across the population. Another answer is that 2003 was not an election year and by time of the next election, new issues would be on the table. It may be that demand for a SUNY degree is relatively price and quality inelastic and students will flock to SUNY even if tuition does go up. Even as tuition was being raised applications for admission were soaring and the quality of students was improving. Although enrollment dropped following the tuition increase in 1995, it picked up again within two years and increased by 21,000 from 1997 to 2003.

Perhaps SUNY is becoming a university with a more affluent student body for whom a $950 tuition increase is simply not all that much—just another price rise, along with food, dorms, and books. As SUNY's quality and reputation continue to grow, it will be a more attractive college choice with a much lower sticker price than most private colleges and universities, and tuition may well matter even less.

While the public clearly supports SUNY, higher education is not an issue that mobilizes voters and decides elections. According to a freshman survey reported in the *Chronicle of Higher Education*, students today are somewhat more conservative than first-year students in 1970.[45] Students and their families simply do not rally around the university at election time. Perhaps the overall dynamic of higher education politics is in a process of transformation.

CHOICES FOR CITIZENS AND POLICY MAKERS

As noted above, state support for higher education has declined sharply since the late 1970s. Depending on how one calculates the numbers, state support for SUNY has dropped from approximately 80 percent to around 40 percent since the mid-1980s. In 2003, nine of thirty-one state-operated campuses received less than 30 percent of their funding from tax dollars. Assessing the impact of continuing austerity is difficult but let us try to frame the key issues as policy questions for citizens and policymakers alike.

Uncertainty. Uncertain budgets and unpredictable tuition make it difficult for campuses to plan for instructional improvements or programmatic initiatives. Do state policymakers want New York's public universities to achieve international prominence, or are they toning down their ambitions for SUNY along with its budgets? The question that Chancellor Wharton asked in the 1980s is still pertinent: how big and good a university do the people of the state want and what are they willing pay for it?

Alternative Sources of Money. In an environment of scarce resources, it is inevitable that SUNY would turn toward external fund raising. That was one intended outcome of *Rethinking SUNY*, the strategic plan produced by the new trustees that looked to a model of a decentralized state system characterized by campus self-sufficiency. By permitting campuses to keep tuition dollars, the trustees encouraged campuses to behave like private schools, even though most lack the endowment base to do so. The university is now reaching out for large gifts and partnerships with the corporate sector—the Wang Center at Stony Brook is one leading example. In 2001 Governor Pataki unveiled a $1 billion high-technology and biotechnology plan that would create multi-million-dollar "Centers of Excellence" on SUNY campuses. With Bioinformatics at the University at Buffalo, Nanoelectronics at the University at Albany, and Wireless and Information Technology at Stony Brook, SUNY was moving into the world of corporate partnerships and advanced technology.[46]

For many observers, this is an important new direction. For some, however, it is an unwelcome degree of privatization. Will such trends toward what is termed "corporatization" bring in the money but compromise the academic mission of SUNY?[47] The question that policymakers and citizens must face is this: as SUNY is de facto privatized, can it continue to fill its mission of serving all segments of the population?

Access and Affordability. As SUNY costs rise and as financial aid decreases[48] will SUNY become less accessible to lower-income students? In a study of cost impacts, the New York Public Interest Research Group (NYPIRG) found that tuition as a percent of median family income grew from 4 percent to 6 percent from 1990 to 2000. At the same time, there has been a long-term shift in financial aid from grants to loans. Do these combined trends act as a disincentive to the American dream of a college education for every qualified child? If the social base is changing, can SUNY's social mission of providing "the broadest possible access, fully representative of all segments of the population" be realized if vast segments of the population are unable to afford the price?

Impact on Enrollment. As noted above, SUNY enrollments have increased by 21,000 since 1997 but without a commensurate increase in resources. As Chancellor King put it, "We are now seeing clear signs that our campus budgets, stretched so thin these past few years, are nearing the breaking point. Campus reserves have been exhausted."[49] Can SUNY continue to open its doors to an increasing number of students or will it be forced to limit access by the sheer pressure of dollars? And if access is not limited, will quality be compromised?

Faculty. Between 1993–1994 and 2002–2003, the percentage of full-time faculty fell from 73 percent to 62 percent while the percentage of part-time faculty rose from 27 percent to 38 percent.[50] True, the number of faculty went up over the ten years, but that was because the number of part-timers had gone up by 50 percent. While part-time and adjunct faculty members may be qualified, they cannot fill the role of full-time faculty. Moreover, SUNY's ability to attract and retain faculty is doubtless impaired by the inability of the university to support faculty in terms of salary, library resources, and support for scholarship and research. While being a college professor has never been a route to wealth, professors in public institutions suffer by comparison to their private-school colleagues and in this respect SUNY salaries have been particularly weak.[51] Can a public university maintain a critical mass of faculty and professional talent in a competitive academic job market?

Politicization. For much of SUNY's history, governors and legislators alike respected the autonomy of the university and many of the battles over academic freedom that one has seen elsewhere have been largely absent in New York. But as long as a public university is subject to the ultimate control of elected officials and receives its support from taxpayers, the prospect that the culture of politics will compromise the culture of academe remains a real one. Is there a need to look again at the ways in which SUNY's academic mission and culture can be protected from political intervention without foregoing democratic accountability?[52]

CONCLUSION

In his inaugural address in 1959, Thomas H. Hamilton, then SUNY president (later chancellor), spoke of the mission of SUNY as achieving the "democracy of excellence." He spoke of the Jeffersonian faith that education can help any person, regardless of socio-economic background. His words reflect both the optimism held for SUNY as the university entered upon what might be called the Rockefeller era and they reflect the aspiration of American public higher education—the aspiration of the Morrill Act. The issue facing the people of the state and Albany policymakers is whether this remains the mission they want the university to fulfill or whether, in a society that looks to private means to achieve social ends, the university shall be simply a utilitarian service provider.

NOTES

The author is a participant observer, as an active campus-based advocate for the state university. Many of the observations and conclusions herein reflect the author's experience. I am indebted to the editors for their patience and encouragement and assistance. I am indebted to Dr. Thomas Kriger of the Research Office of United University Professions for sharing materials, suggestions, and ideas with me.

1. The State University of New York consists of thirty-one state-operated campuses, five statutory colleges administered by private institutions, and thirty community colleges administered by local county authorities. The state-operated campuses consist of four university centers, thirteen four-year university colleges of arts and sciences, five colleges of technology, five specialized colleges, and four health science centers, two of which are associated with university centers. Unless otherwise indicated, this chapter will be concerned with the thirty-one state-operated campuses

administered from Albany by SUNY System Administration, previously termed SUNY Central.

2. Allan Nevins, *The State Universities and Democracy* (Urbana: University of Illinois Press, 1962), p. 16.

3. State University of New York, *SUNY 2000: A Vision for the New Century,* A Report from the Board of Trustees and the Chancellor of the State University of New York (Albany, NY: Office of he Chancellor, 1991), p. 19.

4. Scher quoted in Robert H. Connery and Gerald Benjamin, *Rockefeller of New York: Executive Power in the Statehouse* (Ithaca, NY: Cornell University Press, 1979), p. 298, p. 301.

5. SUNY, *SUNY 2000,* p. 21.

6. Gerald Benjamin and Normal T. Hurd, *Making Experience Count* (Albany, NY: Rockefeller Institure, 1985), p. 106.

7. *Annual Report of the Board of Trustees, 1961-1962,* (Albany, NY: Office of the Chancellor, 1961), p. 8.

8. Patti Magill Peterson, "Current Status and Future Prospects of Independent Higher Education in the State of New York," in *Higher Education in Crisis: New York in National Perspective,* ed. William C. Barba (New York: Garland Publishing, 1995), pp. 105–120.

9. Peter Passell, "The New Economics of Higher Education", *New York Times,* April 22, 1997.

10. See Peter Passell, "Affluent Turning to Public Colleges, Threatening a Squeeze for Others," *New York Times,* August 13, 1997.

11. Stephen Carroll and Eugene Bryton, *Higher Education's Fiscal Future,* report prepared for the Council for Aid to Education (Santa Monica, CA: Rand, 1997), p. 18.

12. See the discussion in *Sharing the Challenge,* report of the New York State Regents Commission on Higher Education (Albany, NY: Board of Regents, 1993).

13. William C. Barba, ed., *Higher Education in Crisis: New York in National Perspective* (New York: Garland, 1995), p. 6.

14. *Chronicle of Higher Education,* November 27, 1998, p. A-26; William Zumeta, "Fiscal Prospects for Higher Education: 1999," *The NEA 1999 Almanac of Higher Education* (Washington, D.C., 1999), 80.

15. M. O'Loughlin, B. Horner, and F. Abdalah, *Opportunity Costs* (Albany, NY: New York Public Interest Research Group, 1997); and U.S. General Accounting Office, *Higher Education Tuition Increasing Faster than*

Household Income and Public College Costs, (Washington, D.C.: U.S. Government Printing Office, 1996).

16.   Governor Carey's involvement in CUNY, however, was significant. He presided at a time of momentous changes in CUNY, including its fiscal stabilization, the imposition of tuition, and open admissions.

17.   See the article by AP reporter Joel Stashenko, "SUNY Works to Rebut Criticism," *Legislative Gazette*, September 28, 1998.

18.   It should be noted that politically higher education budgets are seen as covering both student aid (e.g., TAP) and SUNY-CUNY operating budgets. Proposals on student aid that are sure to be rejected do serve to strengthen the governor's leverage in negotiations on operating and other budgets.

19.   H. Carl McCall (state comptroller), *New York State's Higher Education Policy Vacuum* (Albany, NY: Office of the Comptroller, 1998).

20.   Catharine R. Stimpson, "Activist Trustees Wield Power Gone Awry," *Chronicle of Higher Education*, January 16, 1998, p. B4.

21.   Amy Terdiman, "Changing Courses," *Empire State Report*, August 26, 1996, p. 32.

22.   Candace de Russy, "'Revolting Behavior': The Irresponsible Exercise of Academic Freedom," *Chronicle of Higher Education*, March 6, 1998.

23.   Joel Stashenko, "SUNY Works to Rebut Criticism," *Legislative Gazette*, September 28, 1998.

24.   "The Appointment of System Administration Senior Staff," *Faculty Senate Bulletin*, #2, 1997–1998, p. 1.

25.   McKinney's Consolidated Laws of New York, *Education Law*, vol. 16, Art. 8, section 351 (St. Paul, MN: West, 2001).

26.   The Pataki Administration proved itself adroit at masking the full extent of its budget proposals. The published budget proposals gave far less information about the budgets than had been customary; complexity in the structure of the budget proposals had the effect of obfuscating what was proposed. Thus, for the fiscal year 1995–1996 budget, it appeared that the proposed cut was a modest 4.8 percent of SUNY's overall budget, or $73.5 million on a base budget of $918.7 million, and this is the figure that administration defenders used. But the budget contained a revenue requirement of $215 million, bringing the loss of state support to $289.5 million or 31 percent. To meet the requirement, either a tuition increase of $1000 to $1200 or else extremely deep spending cuts would be required. In its 1998–1999 proposal, the administration touted a budget of $3 billion in capital expen-

ditures, but, again, disentangling the budget numbers reveals that much of the "new" money would be bonded and that operating funds would be cut.

27. Over the two-year period of 1995–1996 to 1997–1998, New York's expenditures on higher education dropped by 4 percent (adjusted for inflation), compared with a 6 percent national increase; New York ranked forty-sixth in the nation. *Chronicle of Higher Education,* November 14, 1997, p. A30.

28. For an important early work, see George Keller, *Academic Strategy: The Management Revolution in American Higher Education* (Baltimore: Johns Hopkins University Press, in cooperation with the American Association for Higher Education, 1983). See also Commission on National Investment in Higher Education (established by the Council for Aid to Education), *Breaking the Social Contract: The Fiscal Crisis in Higher Education* (1997). For a sharply critical view, see Langdon Winner, "The Handwriting on the Wall: Resisting Technoglobalism's Assault on Education" in *Tech High: Globalization and the Future of Canadian Education,* ed Marita Moll (Ottawa: Fernwood, 1997). See also Michael Berube and Cary Nelson, *Higher Education Under Fire* (New York: Routledge, 1995).

29. "Towers of babble: Whatever happened to the university?" *Economist,* December 25, 1993–January 7, 1994, p. 72–74. See also Henry Steck, "'Let's Pretend We're a Corporation': Rise of the Walmart University" presented to Conference of Alliance of Universities for Democracy, Nitra, Slovakia. 1998.

30. Thomas J. Kriger, *White Paper on RAM* (Albany, NY: Research Department, United University Professions, 1999). "RAM" stands for "Resource Allocation Method." At this time, this essay is written, a new term—"Budget Allocation Process"—has apparently replaced "RAM."

31. I am indebted to T. J. Kriger for bringing this to my notice.

32. The discussion herein will refer to the state-operated campuses of the state university and will not include the statutory colleges at Cornell or Alfred or the community colleges, unless otherwise noted.

33. In the discussion that follows, "tuition" will refer to undergraduate tuition. Readers should be aware that (a) tuition differs for undergraduates, graduates, out-of-state students, students in professional programs, and so on; (b) fees are set by individual campuses so that the price of a SUNY education as measured by tuition and fees will differ somewhat between campuses.

34. Joseph Burke and Associates, *Funding Public Colleges and Universities for Performance* (Albany, NY: Rockefeller Institute Press, 2002), p. 7.

35. Ronald G. Ehrenberg and Michael J. Rizzo, "Financial Forces and the Future of American Higher Education," *Academe* (July-August 2004), p. 28–31.

36. U.S. Department of Education, National Center for Education Statistics, *Digest of Education Statistics 2002.* See also, Miriam Kramer et al., *Shifting the Burden: Shifting the Costs of higher Education from State Government to New York Families* (Albany, NY: New York Public Interest Research Group, Albany, n.d.).

37. SUNY doubled the national average in tuition increase of 14 percent. See Elizabeth F. Farrell, "Public-College Tuition Rise Is Largest in 3 Decades," *Chronicle of Higher Education,* October 21, 2003.

38. Things are not as simple as this makes it out to be. The $950 tuition increase was not enough to make up for the full $183.5 million cut in state money. So the legislature raised out-of-state tuition by $2000, without really considering whether an increase that large would drive international and out-of-state students away. A year later, the issue is still cloudy. An Albany insider told this to the author: "SUNY claims this state money for tuition swap left them $36 million short. The legislators believe otherwise."

39. Testimony of Robert L. King, Chancellor, State University of New York, submitted to Senate Finance and Assembly Ways and Means Committees, February 5, 2004.

40. See Ehrenberg and Rizzo, "Financial Forces."

41. Testimony of William E. Scheuerman on the 2004–2005 Executive Budget, presented to Senate Finance Committee and Assembly Ways and Means Committee, February 5, 2004. It should be emphasized that state support is only one of several sources of funding. Others include tuition, federal aid, grants, residence halls, hospitals, and the like. From 1993–1994 to 2002–2003, all sources of funding increased by 60 percent. Research revenue, for example, increased by 68 percent since 1995. State University of New York, Board of Trustees, Finance and Administration Committee, "Financial Overview and Program Highlights," (Albany, NY: Office of the Chancelor, October 23, 2003).

42. Kramer et al., *Shifting the Burden,* p.11. The NYPIRG group calculated the increase in actual dollars from 1989–1990 to 2001–2002 as 12 percent, compared to the national average of 62 percent. For other measures, see *Postsecondary Education Opportunity,* Policy Research. State Reports, "New York Appropriations of State Tax Funds for Higher Education," January 2004 (and on-line, http://www.postsecondary.org). This shows a relatively steady drop of appropriations per capita.

43. See *SUNY News*, "Chancellor Presents Budget Proposal for Upcoming Year," December 3, 2003. For a flavor of the reaction, see "SUNY Faces an Annual tuition Rise," *Pipe Dream on the Web* (SUNY Binghamton), December 5, 2003.

44. "SUNY: Tuition Could Rise $750 in Five Years," *Cortland Standard*, February 6, 2004.

45. Megan Rooney, "Freshman Show Raising Political Awareness and Changing Social Views," *Chronicle of Higher Education*, January 31, 2003.

46. See Albany NanoTech, "Governor Announces College of Nanotechnology," January 7, 2004, http://www.albanynanotech.org.

47. Henry Steck, "Corporatization of the University: Seeking Conceptual Clarity," *The Annals* 585 (January 2003): 66–84.

48. There has been a long-term shift from grants to loans in terms of federal financial aid and each year, it seems, TAP and other forms of New York State support are threatened with cuts. For the 2004–2005 budget, for example, the governor proposed withholding a third of the TAP award until after graduation. In the 2004–2005 executive budget, the Governor proposal 5 percent cuts in opportunity programs such as EOP and Higher Education Opportunity Program (HEOP). In general, Pataki's budgets have fairly regularly proposed cuts in student aid programs and the legislature has regularly restored the funds.

49. Testimony of Robert L. King to Senate Finance and Assembly Ways and Means Committees," February 5, 2004.

50. UUP Research Department,"Number and Percentage of SUNY Full-and Part-time Academic Faculty, State Operated Campuses, 2993–2003." The figures are from the SUNY Institutional Research, *Statistical Release: Employees of the Institutions of the State University of New York, 1993–2003*.

51. See Scott Smallwood, "The Price Professors Pay for Teaching at Public Universities," *Chronicle of Higher Education*, April 20, 2001; *Chronicle* report on salaries, April 18, 2003, AAUP, *Academe*, March-April 2003.

52. Roger W. Bowen, "The New Battle Between Political and Academic Cultures," *Chronicle of Higher Education*, June 21, 2001; and John Ryder, "The American University Today: A Tale of Three Cities," presentation at Annual Conference of Alliance of Universities for Democracy, Belgrade, Yugoslavia, 2001.

CHAPTER 14

Health Care in the Empire State

Expanding Access and Escalating Costs

JEFFREY KRAUS

In terms of dollars spent, health care is the number one priority of New York State's government. In fiscal year 2004, the budget for the Department of health was more than $40.5 billion. More than $30.7 billion went to fund the Medical Assistance Program (Medicaid), the largest single expense item in the state budget. The massive commitment of resources reflects a desire on the part of the state's leaders to provide access to health care, and is testimony to the influence that the groups in the field have on the state's political process.

Yet, at the same time, there are still millions of New Yorkers lacking access to basic health care, and there is considerable doubt as to whether the present rates of spending are sustainable in the long term.[1] In this chapter, I examine the history of New York's health care policy; outline the state's administrative structure; describe current services and how those services are financed, and ask the question, "Can the state's taxpayers continue to afford this?"

HEALTH CARE IN NEW YORK: A VERY BRIEF HISTORY

The Beginnings

New York has long been a leader in health care. In 1736, the hospital that would eventually become Bellevue opened its doors, becoming the first

333

hospital in the North American colonies. In 1791, a second facility, New York Hospital, opened. Three years later, the first facility for care of the poor opened in what was then the Public Workhouse and House of Correction, on the site of what is now New York's city hall. In that same year, a "pesthouse" was opened (on the grounds of what was to be dedicated as the Bellevue Institution in 1816) to treat patients during one of the city's periodic yellow fever epidemics. In 1795, Governor John Jay asked the Health Committee of New York to investigate the causes of a yellow fever epidemic in New York City. Their report recommended improvements in environmental sanitation, including eliminating filth in the streets, clearing obstructed water mains, draining low-lying areas, and reducing air pollution by slaughterhouses and soap factories. The health committee also concluded that these changes would not be possible until New York City created a permanent health organization.[2]

After another yellow fever epidemic killed 1,600, the state legislature, in 1798, granted New York City the authority to enact its own health laws. In 1804 the city appointed its first health inspector. By 1823, improved sanitation procedures would bring yellow fever epidemics to an end. In 1850 the state legislature enacted legislation requiring every city and incorporated village to appoint a board of health and a health officer.[3] In 1866, the state legislature created the Metropolitan Board of Health. The state-appointed board was to monitor public sanitation and write health regulations. The board is credited with minimizing the death toll during the city's cholera epidemic.[4]

In addition to advances in public health, the state would lead the way in treatment. During the first half of the nineteenth century a number of specialized facilities would be opened, including the New York Eye Infirmary (1820), Bloomingdale Insane Asylum (1821), New York Infirmary for the Treatment of Diseases of the Lung (1823), and the New York Asylum for Lying-In-Women (1823).

In 1843 the State Asylum for Lunatics opened in Utica, becoming the first state-funded hospital for the mentally ill. Over the next fifty years, the state would open sixteen additional asylums. An 1890 law abolished county-run asylums, establishing operating standards for the state facilities.

In the years after the Civil War, New York hospitals were at the forefront of change. The first hospital-based ambulance service in the world was established at Bellevue in 1869. Four years later, the first nursing school in the United States opened at Bellevue. In 1887 the nation's first cancer hospital opened in Manhattan. In 1898, the first cancer research, treatment, and education center was established by Dr. Roswell Park with a $7,500 grant from the state legislature.

The Twentieth Century

In 1901 the New York State Health Department was created. In a short time, the department would become a national leader in the field of public health. The department started a health education program (1914), employed nutritionists (1917), and aired the first radio show on health in the United States called *Keeping Well.*

In 1921 county governments were authorized to form health districts and the state offered matching grants for the construction of hospitals. In 1926 the Department of Mental Hygiene was created by the state legislature. With the onset of the Great Depression in 1929, the state required welfare districts to provide medical care to those receiving assistance and others unable to afford medical care, a group that would grow larger as the economic crisis deepened.

The Era of Reform

In 1965 the first stories appeared in the *Staten Island Advance* about abuse of patients at the Willowbrook State School, a state psychiatric hospital located on Staten Island. Follow-up stories in the paper in 1971 led to television coverage, notably Geraldo Rivera's undercover reports for WABC, the ABC-owned- and operated- television station in New York City.[5] Litigation by the families of Willowbrook residents against the state resulted in a consent decree in which the administration of Governor Hugh L. Carey agreed to changes in the operation of Willowbrook which led to additional reforms in the treatment of the mentally ill, notably the policy of deinstitutionalization, the movement of patients from the state's psychiatric hospitals to smaller, community-based group homes.

Administrative reforms included the establishment of a Commission on the Quality of Care for the Mentally Disabled (1977) to monitor the treatment of those in the state's care, and the reorganization of the Department of Mental Hygiene. In 1978, the department was reorganized into the Office of the Mentally Retarded and the Developmentally Disabled (OMRDD), the New York State Office of Mental Health (OMH), and the Office of Alcoholism and Substance Abuse Services (OASAS). OMRDD was given responsibility for developing and delivering, in conjunction with local governments and the not-for-profit sector, the community-based programs that were part of the state's new approach to treating the mentally retarded. OMH was given authority for the state's psychiatric centers and for overseeing the community-based programs run by local governments and not-for-profit agencies. OASAS was part of the Department of Health from the 1930s until 1962, when it was transferred to the Department of Mental Hygiene. It serves about 120,000 New Yorkers who receive treatment for alcoholism and substance abuse from 1,200 community-based providers and thirteen state-operated treatment centers.

MANAGING HEALTH POLICY TODAY

The Department of Health (DOH) is administered by a commissioner, who is appointed by the governor and confirmed by the state senate. The Commissioner must have been a doctor for at least ten years and have "skill and experience in public health duties and sanitary science."[6] The present commissioner (2004) is Dr. Antonia Novello, who was appointed by Governor George E. Pataki in 1999. Previously, Novello had been surgeon general of the United States for three years (1990–1993) during the administration of George H.W. Bush.

The department is organized into two major program units: the Office of Public Health (OPH) and the Office of Health Systems Management (OHSM). OPH's mission is preserving the health of New Yorkers through education, research, and accident and disease prevention. The office emphasizes encouraging child growth and development through prenatal care, newborn screening, providing food for pregnant women programs, and teen counseling. Other OPH programs focus on occupational health and children, immunization, school health safety hazards, and combating communicable diseases.

OHSM inspects the state's health-care facilities to insure that they comply with regulations governing patient care. Those facilities that fail inspection can be sanctioned. The department's functions include administering and enforcing the Public Health Law and State Sanitary Code; addressing outbreaks of diseases; regulating health-care facilities by setting standards for personnel, cleanliness, and patient nutrition which are enforced through inspections of hospitals and nursing homes; supervision of local health agencies; and administering federal health-care financial aid.

The department also operates a number of research facilities, including the Wadsworth Center for Laboratories and Research in Albany (affiliated with the School of Public Health at the State University of New York at Albany), the largest public health laboratory in the United States. The center conducts laboratory tests and public-health research.

Another DOH facility, the Helen Hayes Hospital, located in West Haverstraw, Rockland County, is the largest physical rehabilitation and surgical center in the state, and treats patients with chronic disease and physical disabilities. One of its more famous patients was Christopher Reeve, the actor, who was paralyzed in a horse-riding accident. The department operates four veterans' nursing homes. They are located in Batavia (Genesee County), Oxford (Chenango County), Jamaica (Queens County), and Montrose (Westchester County).

In 1983 the AIDS Institute was created within the department. Its mission is to focus on prevention and to provide services to HIV-infected people and their families. Working with the Johns Hopkins University School of Medicine Division of Infectious Diseases, the AIDS Institute has also created a set of clinical guidelines. The Roswell Park Cancer Institute, located in Buffalo, was managed by the Department of Health until 1997. At that time, it became a public benefit corporation. It is not only a research center, but a hospital that admitted 3,800 patients in fiscal year 2002 (April 1, 2001–March 31, 2002). It is affiliated with SUNY-Buffalo, and is the third largest cancer center in the United States.

There is a Public Health Council, which includes the commissioner of health and fourteen other members, appointed by the governor and confirmed by the state senate, for six-year terms. Their duties include advising the commissioner of health, and establishing the state sanitary code.[7]

THE HEALTH SECURITY CONTRADICTION:
EXPANDING ACCESS WHILE CONTAINING COSTS

As stated at the outset, the largest health initiative in New York is Medicaid. Prompted by federal legislation and Governor Nelson A. Rockefeller, the New York State Legislature adopted the Medicaid Program in 1966, providing access to health care for the medically indigent.[8] The program would be administered by the New York State Department of Social Services (DSS), as Governor Rockefeller believed that the agency providing the funding (in this case DSS) should not be the same agency setting the program's standards (Department of Health).

In 1998 this division of responsibility was ended when the Department of Health was given responsibility for Medicaid when DSS was eliminated as part of New York's welfare-reform program.[9] The program provides cash payment to those providing medical services and nursing-home care for the needy. Medicaid is actually two programs. One program serves the state's poor families. The second program pays for long-term care for the elderly, mentally ill, and developmentally disabled. About 70 percent of Medicaid expenditures annually pay for services for the elderly and disabled.[10]

The federal government reimburses the state for 50 percent of the cost of Medicaid, with the state paying 35 percent, and New York City and the fifty-seven counties picking up the remaining 15 percent. New York State is one of fifteen states that require local governments to contribute to the financing of Medicaid.[11] (See the analysis of intergovernmental grant programs in chapter 2). The state does pick up 80 percent of the nonfederal costs of nursing-home care, which is a larger component of the program in the counties outside of New York City.

From its inception, Medicaid has proven to be a costly endeavor. Initially, families of four with incomes up to $6,000 were eligible, meaning that almost half the state's residents were entitled to coverage.[12] During fiscal year 1966 (the program's first year), costs exceeded appropriations by 36 percent.[13] In 1967, New York State accounted for 35 percent of the nation's Medicaid expenditures. By 1968 Governor Rockefeller was calling for changes in the program because of its cost to the state and local governments. However, notwithstanding Rockefeller's concerns, the program continued to grow, even as Rockefeller's successors called on the legislature to rein in costs.

Part of this growth has been due to the demographics of the state. According to the Kaiser Family Foundation, New York has a greater percentage of residents living in poverty when compared to the national average.[14] New York has a greater proportion of elderly and disabled individuals than the national average, and has the largest number of residents living with AIDS.[15]

Another factor has been the escalating cost of health care in New York State. Health-care costs have been driven by a number of factors: hospital workforce shortages, which have increased labor costs (those account for about two-thirds of hospital costs); the escalating cost of prescription drugs; technology costs; increases in medical malpractice insurance premiums; utilization of emergency rooms by the medically uninsured, and most recently, the need for hospitals and other health-care providers to pay for disaster and bioterrorism preparation.

Another reason for the growth of Medicaid has been the willingness of state policymakers to offer optional coverage to medically needy individuals in order to obtain additional federal funding.[16] In 1993, about 44 percent of the state's spending on Medicaid was on optional services.[17] New York spends as much on Medicaid as Texas and California combined.[18] All of Rockefeller's successors have tried to cut costs while at the same time expanding access to the program.

While initially limited to welfare recipients, the program was extended so that a number of optional populations—that is, individuals who do not have to be covered under federal law—could be covered. Among the additional family recipients were pregnant women and infants with family incomes between 133 percent and 200 percent of the federal poverty level, children ages six to eighteen with family incomes between 100 percent and 133 percent of the federal poverty level, and parents with incomes up to 150 percent of the federal poverty level. Also included were single adults and childless couples with incomes up to 100 percent of the federal poverty level, the medically needy (those who have spent down their assets and, as a result, qualify for Medicaid), women diagnosed with breast or cervical cancer who were screened under the Centers for Disease Control and Prevention's Breast and Cervical Cancer Early Detection Program, and individuals with disabilities who earn up to 250 percent of the federal poverty level.

Some of these additions have not been costly. Child Health Plus was created in 1990 during the administration of Mario Cuomo.[19] The program provided subsidized coverage to children under the age of thirteen. Child Health Plus originally covered outpatient services, excluding hospitalization or mental health services (except for alcohol and drug abuse counseling). This was a relatively inexpensive expansion of the program since medical expenses for children tend to be low. Subsequently, inpatient care was added, and coverage was extended to children between the ages of fourteen and nineteen.[20]

By 1997, the number of children covered statewide was 140,000, making it the largest subsidized health insurance program in the country.[21]

The program grew further following the enactment by Congress in 1997 of the State Children's Health Insurance Program (SCHIP).[22] SCHIP would provide $40 billion in matching funds over ten years to help states insure the nation's uninsured children.[23]

The New York program's coverage was improved to include dental care, speech and hearing services, vision care, inpatient mental health and substance abuse services, and durable medical devices. Free coverage would be provided to children whose families had incomes of less than 160 percent of the federal poverty level. Children in families with incomes up to 250 percent of the federal poverty level would be eligible for the subsidized insurance. By February 2002 there were 552,280 children enrolled in the program.[24]

In contrast, financing long-term care for the elderly has been extremely expensive for the taxpayers of the State of New York. Medicare, the federal health insurance program for older Americans, does not cover nursing-home care. Nursing-home care can cost more than $100,000 a year in New York City.[25]

Today, 72 percent of Medicaid expenditures are for those over the age of sixty-five and the disabled, who account for 28 percent of all the recipients. The bulk of these expenditures are for payments to nursing homes. Many of the individuals receiving institutional Medicaid became eligible by making gifts and establishing trusts for family members, thereby making themselves medically indigent and eligible for the program. Indeed, one of the great ironies (and some would argue, the inequity) of this situation is that many of the taxpayers who are paying to underwrite these long-term care payments are not as wealthy as those receiving the benefits.

OTHER EFFORTS TO EXPAND ACCESS TO HEALTH CARE

New York State has attempted to improve access to health care for those not eligible for Medicaid. Family Health Plus was established in 1999 to provide health insurance coverage for families that are not poor enough to qualify for Medicaid. The program was funded by a fifty-five-cent increase in the cigarette tax and with a portion of the state's share of the Federal Tobacco Lawsuit Settlement.

Families are able to purchase insurance through Medicaid at low rates. Many of the people signing up for the coverage are individuals holding low-wage jobs with employers who do not offer health insurance coverage to their employees and their families. There are 280,000 New Yorkers enrolled in Family Health Plus at an annual cost of approximately $880 million, with local governments paying for 25 percent of the program. While providing health insurance to working people, the program serves as a disincentive for employers to provide health benefits to their employees. It is now the fastest growing part of the Medicaid program.[26]

Healthy New York was created as part of the Health Care Reform Act in 2000 to provide low-cost coverage for small businesses (defined by the statute as having fifty or fewer employees, one-third of whom must be earning less than $31,000 annually) and individuals (with an income of $23,275 or less; $47,125 for a family of four). This is health maintenance organization (HMO) coverage that is less expensive because the state offers it as a group.

Since its creation about thirty thousand individuals have obtained coverage through Healthy New York.[27] The relatively small number of individuals taking advantage of the program was foreseen by Swartz, who wrote that "the lower Healthy New York premiums are not likely to create great demand among eligible people."[28]

Disaster Relief Medicaid was established as a temporary program after the September 11, 2001, terrorist attack on the World Trade Center to provide coverage for individuals who lost jobs (and their health insurance benefits) due to the business dislocations caused by the attack. With New York City's Medicaid computer system disabled by the terrorist attack, streamlined application procedures were implemented to allow those affected by the attack to apply for Medicaid. More than 342,000 people were covered by the program.[29] Under this program, which operated from September 24, 2001, to January 30, 2002, individuals were covered for 120 days. After their covered ended, they could apply for regular Medicaid or Family Health Plus.

MEDICAID: THE COST

Despite the efforts of policy makers, the state's efforts to provide access to health care had serious shortcomings. Foremost has been the high cost of the program. In the last five years, the cost of the program has risen from $30 billion to $42 billion, an increase of about 40 percent.[30] It is the most expensive Medicaid program in the country, costing $9,047 for each beneficiary, compared with the national average of $4,301.[31] Because of the mandate that New York City and fifty-seven county governments contribute to the program, Medicaid has proven to be a major strain on local budgets. In some counties, Medicaid expenditures take as much as half of local tax revenues.

Another cost factor is the program's financing. The state's portion of Medicaid is partially financed by a tax on private health insurance, making health insurance rates higher in New York State than in other states. This impacts not only New Yorkers who do have private health insurance (through higher premiums), but also many New Yorkers who do not have health insurance because their employers won't pay for it; their family incomes exceed the eligibility criteria for Family Health Plus, and they can't afford the higher cost of individual policies.

Nursing-home care (which is reimbursed by Medicaid) is also more expensive in New York due to the reintroduction of a nursing home gross-receipts tax in 2002. The tax is another part of the funding stream that finances the state's Medicaid expense. The tax increased total Medicaid spending by $270 million in fiscal year 2003.[32]

Yet while the tax may have triggered $135 million in additional federal aid, it did drive up costs for localities which had to provide additional funding, as well as make nursing-home care more expensive for residents who are not Medicaid eligible. Even with the state's efforts, there are more uninsured New Yorkers (3.2 million) than New Yorkers on Medicaid.

THE REVERSE SIDE OF THE POLICY COIN: COST CONTAINMENT

As the costs of the program have escalated, a number of efforts have been made to cut or contain costs. Cost cutting measures have included the following:

Cuts in provider reimbursement rates. In an effort to limit cost increases, the Medicaid reimbursement rate has not kept up with the increasing cost of health care. One consequence of this has been that a number of providers have dropped out of the program, reducing access for Medicaid recipients to private physicians and forcing many to rely on clinics or hospital emergency rooms.[33]

Tightening eligibility. This has included administrative efforts to more accurately verify eligibility for Medicaid and legislative initiatives designed to limit entry into the program by senior citizens seeking to become eligible for institutional Medicaid. These measures included lengthening the look-back period for the transfer of assets, repealing the cap on the penalty period, and tightening loopholes regarding trusts and estate planning.[34]

Greater emphasis on combating fraud. In 1975 the Office of New York State Special Prosecutor for Nursing Homes, Health, and Social Services was created, the nation's first Medicaid fraud unit. In 1995 the Medicaid Fraud Control Unit became part of the Criminal Division of the state attorney general's office.

Managed care. The Department of Health has attempted to contain costs by encouraging Medicaid recipients to enroll in managed-care programs. Historically, medical care has been provided in the United States on a fee-for-service basis. In managed care, the provider is paid a monthly fee for each subscriber (a capitation fee).[35]

During the 1980s many employers started looking at HMOs as a way of limiting their health insurance costs. State governments, seeing their Medicaid costs escalate, also began looking at HMOs as a means of cost containment. In 1984 the state legislature authorized the Department of Social Services (DSS) to develop, with the Department of Health, managed-care demonstration projects that would enroll Medicaid recipients on a voluntary basis.[36] In 1991 the state legislature mandated that New York City and the counties develop plans for enrolling at least half of their Medicaid recipients in managed care programs over the next five years.

Following the election in 1994 of Governor George E. Pataki, a fiscal conservative, interest in managed care intensified. In 1995 the Department of Health's Office of Managed Care began developing a statewide program of mandatory enrollment in HMOs and prepaid health services plans (PHSPs). In 1997, the federal government's Health Care Financing Administration (HCFA) gave the state a waiver of Medicaid regulations to move forward with its managed care program. By the end of 2001, 26.7 percent of New York's Medicaid recipients had enrolled in managed-care programs.[37] By moving Medicaid recipients into managed care, the state expects to realize significant cost savings through the increased use of primary care, fewer emergency room visits, and fewer inpatient days.

Denial of benefits to undocumented aliens. After Congress enacted the Personal Responsibility and Work Opportunities Reconciliation Act, the state legislature in 1997 passed an amendment to the Social Services Law that denied Medicaid to "unqualified" resident aliens, except for those in nursing homes or who had been diagnosed with AIDS, and to lawful permanent residents who entered the United States after August 22, 1996. In

Aliessa v. Whalen, this law was struck down by the New York State Court of Appeals on equal-protection grounds.38

Copayments and service limits. One way of discouraging unnecessary utilization of Medicaid is to require, as do virtually all private insurance plans, a copayment. Medicaid patients are required to pay minimal copayments when visiting a clinic, taking a laboratory test, or obtaining prescription drugs. A twenty-five dollar copayment is required for hospital in-patient care. While not particularly onerous when compared to private insurance plan copays, any copay may deter a poor person from seeking medical care until they are very sick—and their care is even more expensive.

Coverage limits have also been introduced. Medicaid recipients are now limited to an annual number visits to clinics, dentals, and private doctors. Such limits were established to combat so-called "Medicaid mills," that is, clinics that proliferated in New York City's poor neighborhoods where health-care providers would encourage repeated visits to treat minor or non-existent illnesses.

THE POLITICS OF MEDICAID

The Medicaid-Industrial Complex

These cost-cutting measures have been half-hearted because of politics. New York City legislators, especially those in the Democratic-controlled state assembly, have historically supported the program. New York City is home to not only a majority of the program's beneficiaries, but also to a large and politically powerful industry that has come to depend financially on Medicaid. Republicans, who control the state senate, generally oppose higher taxes, but have been sympathetic to the interests of hospitals and nursing home operators.[39] Industry groups such as the Hospital Association of New York State (representing hospitals outside the New York City area), the Greater New York Hospital Association (representing hospitals in the New York metropolitan area), the Home Care Association of New York, and the New York State Association of Homes and Services for the Aging constitute a significant political force in defense of the program, one which has been labeled the "Medicaid-industrial complex."[40] This is a complex that has been willing to use its resources to protect its interests. According to the New York State Temporary Commission on Lobbying, five of the top ten spenders in 2001 were organizations that are part of this pro-Medicaid coalition.[41]

Support for the program comes not only from the industry, but from organized labor. Local 1199 of the Service Employees International Union represents 237,000 members in New York State. It is a politically active union which, at one time, almost exclusively supported the Democratic Party. (Longtime leader Dennis Rivera was once a member of the Democratic National Committee and a vice chairperson of the New York State Democratic Committee). In recent years, the union has developed a relationship with Governor George E. Pataki (endorsing the governor in his 2002 reelection campaign) and State Senate Majority Leader Joseph Bruno, both Republicans. The pair was impressed by the media campaign mounted by Rivera and his union to win public support for what ultimately became Family Health Plus. This relationship bore fruit with the lightning quick approval in 2002 of the Health Care Reform Act (HCRA).

HCRA, also known as the "Health Care First" reform package, provided worker recruitment and retention funds for hospital, nursing-home, and health-care workers as the basis for raises for members of Local 1199. The availability of these monies allowed Local 1199 and New York City's League of Voluntary Hospitals to reach a contract agreement. The source of funding for the program was the anticipated conversion of Empire Blue Cross-Blue Shield into a for-profit insurance company.

Challenging the Medicaid-Industrial Complex

As 2003 came to a close there were new challenges to the Medicaid status quo. While the county governments have long complained about the program's mandated costs, the leadership of the new challenge was led by Democratic county executives, notably Thomas Suozzi of Nassau County. Suozzi, who was elected in 2001 on a wave of dissatisfaction with rising taxes and budget deficits under Republican rule, criticized the state legislature for failing to act on Medicaid reform. He went so far as to threaten to target a Democratic assembly member and Republican state senator for defeat if no action were taken during the 2004 session.[42] Other county executives, while not as strident, have joined Suozzi in what is being called a "county rebellion."[43] Their immediate goal: a cap on increases in the local share of Medicaid expenditures.

A plan put forward by the state senate in December 2003 called for a state takeover of the counties' share of Family Health Plus, as well as other measures intended to slow the growth of the State's Health Care costs.[44] In

January 2004, the Governor's Working Group on Health Care released its report, which seemed to support an eventual state takeover of the county share of Medicaid, but concluded that "given the state's fiscal condition, it is unrealistic to expect a compete state takeover this year—or even next."[45]

The dilemma of Medicaid reform was articulated by State Senator James Wright, who observed, "There's not one area of Medicaid that is good. If you're going to reform it, [there's no reform] that doesn't have some political risk in terms of its impact on major employers, major service providers, major constituency groups. . . . That's just the reality of what we deal with. It's why you haven't seen major reform in 40 years."[46]

EPIC: THE GROWING OBLIGATION

The Elderly Pharmaceutical Insurance Coverage Program (EPIC) represents yet another expansion of the state's commitment to health care access in an age of limits. EPIC was established in 1986 and by 2002 had more than 260,000 participants.[47] The program provides subsidies for prescription drugs for the elderly. Coverage, on a fee basis, is available to single individuals over the age of sixty-five with incomes of less than $20,000 and to married seniors with incomes of $26,000 or less. The plan is available, on a deductible basis, to single seniors with incomes between $20,000 and $35,000 and married seniors with incomes between $26,000 and $50,000. In fiscal year 2004 the cost to the state was $900 million.

The future of the plan is in question because the Medicare reform legislation passed by Congress in 2003 requires senior citizens to enroll, beginning in 2006, in either the new Medicare drug benefit program or a comparable private plan.[48] The EPIC plan will be phased out or, if history is to be our guide, redesigned by the state's policymakers to serve as a wraparound plan that will pay the copayments and deductibles required under the new federal plan.

CONCLUSION

New York State has long been a leader in the field of public health. In the last four decades the state's policymakers have focused on expanding access to health care, primarily by leveraging federal dollars, while also attempting to rein in the cost. While bringing additional federal aid to New York, this strategy has also driven up costs for the state and its localities, which finance the local match for Medicaid.

The skyrocketing cost of these efforts has been financed by increasing taxes on health care, forcing the localities to assume some financial responsibility, or one-shot sources of revenue (the Federal Tobacco Settlement or the Empire Blue Cross-Blue Shield conversion). Today, New York City and the state's counties argue that they can no longer afford the burden of the unfunded health care mandate and the state's fiscal situation makes relief for the localities unlikely.

There certainly have been benefits to the people of New York as a result of these policies. The state is home to some of the finest health-care facilities in the world—nursing-home care is considered superior when compared to other states, and while many New Yorkers remain uninsured, others are able to obtain care. The question remains as to how much longer New York can continue to pursue this paradoxical policy goal of greater access while trying to restrain the cost.

NOTES

1. Thorpe and Florence estimated that there were 3.2 million uninsured New Yorkers in 1998, compared to 3.1 million enrolled in the Medicaid Program. Kenneth E. Thorpe, and Curtis Florence, *Medicaid Eligible But Uninsured: The New York State Experience* (New York: United Hospital Fund, 2000), p. 1.

2. Robert B. Ward, *New York State Government: What It Does, How It Works* (Albany, NY: The Rockefeller Institute Press, 2002), p. 218.

3. The 1880 Annual Report by the State Board of Health found that most localities had failed to comply. Ward, *New York State Government*, p. 219.

4. Paula Baker, "New York During the Civil War and Reconstruction," in *The Empire State: A History of New York*, ed. Milton M. Klein. (Ithaca, NY: Cornell University Press, 2001). p. 441.

5. For more on Willowbrook, see Geraldo Rivera, *Willowbrook: A Report on How It Is and Why It Doesn't Have to Be That Way* (New York: Vintage Books, 1972). A documentary film, *Unforgotten: 25 Years After Willowbrook*, was produced in 2002 by Danny Fisher and Jack Fisher (City Lights Home Video).

6. New York State Public Health Law, Section 203, *McKinney's Consolidated Laws of New York* (St. Paul, MN: West Group, 2001)

7. New York State Public Health Law, Sections 220, 221, and 225, *McKinney's Consolidated Laws,* 2001.

8. New York State Social Service Law, Section 363, *McKinney's Consolidated Laws,* 2001. The state law was enacted after Congress passed Title XIX of the Social Security Act, which required states to provide medical assistance to low-income individuals and families.

9. 1997 New York Laws 436.

10. Hospital Association of New York State (HANYS), *New York State's Medicaid Program: A Sound Approach to Care* (Rensselaer, NY: HANYS, 2003), p. 1.

11. Sarah F. Liebschutz, *New York Politics and Government: Competition and Compassion* (Lincoln, NE: University of Nebraska Press, 1998), p. 173.

12. HANYS, *New York State's Medicaid Program,* 1.

13. Liebschutz, *New York Politics and Government,* 175.

14. Henry J. Kaiser Family Foundation, *State Health Facts, 2001* (Menlo Park, CA: Henry J. Kaiser Family Foundation, 2001).

15. HANYS, *New York State's Medicaid Program,* 3.

16. Liebschutz, *New York Politics and Government,* 173.

17. Kent Gardner and Bethany St. Dennis, *Medicaid Cost Containment for New York* (Rochester, NY: Center for Government Research, 1995), p. 16.

18. New York's program is far more expensive than the California and Texas programs because of differences in the scope of services and the manner of delivery. For example, while New York's program covers virtually all in-hospital procedures at any hospital in the state, California will only pay for services that are provided, on a preauthorized basis, at hospitals that are contracted with by the state through a competitive bidding process. Texas imposes a $200,000 annual limit per adult beneficiary and hospital stays are limited to a thirty-day maximum.

19. Chapters 922 and 923 of the Laws of 1990 (New York Public Health Law Sections 2510 and 2511).

20. New York Health Care Reform Act of 1996.

21. Dennis P. Whalen, *State Child Health Plan Under Title XXI of the Social Security Act: State Children's Health Insurance Program* (Albany: New York State Department of Health, 1998), p. 2-1.

22. Title XXI of the Social Security Act.

23. New York's annual share is expected to be $256 million.

24. New York Academy of Medicine, *New York Forum for Child Health*, Update Number 7, 2002, p. 1.

25. Richard Perez-Pena, "Medicaid Plan Would Restrict Nursing Homes to Truly Poor," *New York Times*, December 23, 2003, p. 1.

26. Addressing the disincentive issue, the Greater New York Hospital Association (GNYHA) and Local 1199 of the Service Employees International Union proposed, in early 2004, a $3,000 tax per employee on businesses that do not provide health insurance to their employees. Governor Pataki, in his fiscal year 2005 Executive Budget plan, included a provision that would deny Family Health Plus coverage to employees of any firm with more than fifty employees. This is known as the "Wal-Mart Rule," based on reports that managers at the world's largest retail chain are encouraging their employees to sign up for the state-sponsored plan rather than the company's health insurance program. According to the Pataki administration, at least 2,500 of the 300,000 people enrolled in Family Health Plus work for large employers. William F. Hammond Jr., "Budget Contains 'Wal-Mart' Rule," *New York Sun*, January 22, 2004, p. 4. Both proposals seem unlikely to pass the State Legislature. The GNYHA/1199 proposal will be opposed by business interests and senate Republicans opposed to any tax increases. The Wal-Mart Rule will incur the wrath of Assembly Democrats. Assembly Health Committee Chair Richard Gottfried called the rule "cruel and insensitive" for denying health insurance to low-income families due to their employers' actions, Hammond, "Budget Contains 'Wal-Mart' Rule," p. 4.

27. Gregory V. Serio, *Statement of New York State Insurance Department Before New York State Senate Committee on Insurance; Testimony By Gregory V. Serio, Superintendent of Insurance, New York State Insurance Department*, April 15, 2003, p. 7.

28. Swartz, Katherine, *Healthy New York: Making Insurance More Affordable for Low Income Workers* (New York: Commonwealth Fund, 2001), p. 14.

29. Michael Perry, *New York's Disaster Relief Medicaid: Insights and Implications for Covering Low-Income People* (Washington, DC: Kaiser Commission on Medicaid and the Uninsured, 2002), p. 1.

30. James C. McKinley Jr., "Senate Republicans Eye Medicaid Cuts," *New York Times*, December 23, 2003, p. A1.

31. The Health Economics and Outcomes Research Institute at the Greater New York Hospitals Association, *Quantitative Analysis of New York*

State Medicaid Spending (New York: Greater New York Hospitals Association, 2003), p. 4.

32. HANYS, *New York State's Medicaid Program*, p. 14.

33. This shift to reliance on hospital emergency rooms has effected Medicaid spending and hospital finances. While the emergency room and clinic reimbursement is higher than for a private physician's office visit, it has not been increased since 1991. As a result, in 2003, hospitals were losing an average of $200 on every Medicaid patient they treated in an emergency room.

34. Chapter 170 of the Laws of 1994.

35. For a discussion of managed care, its financing, and the adoption of a Managed Care Bill of Rights in New York, see Alice Sardell, and Harvey Catchen, "Health Policy in New York State: Market Models and Access Issues," in *Governing New York State*, 4th ed., ed. Jeffrey M. Stonecash (Albany: State University of New York Press, 2001), pp. 275–290.

36. For more on this demonstration project see New York State Department of Health, Office of Health Systems Management and The New York State Department of Social Services, *Report to the Legislature on the Implementation of the Medicaid Reform Act of 1984* (Albany, NY: New York State Department of Health, January 1990).

37. Nicholas W. Jenny and Haidy Brown, "State Expansion of Medicaid Managed Care Slows," *Rockefeller Institute State Fiscal News* 3 (February 2003): 4.

38. Aliessa *ex rel.* Fayad v. Novello, 754 N.E. 2nd 1085, 1094–1099 (N.Y. 2001).

39. Bruce Bryant-Friedland, "Medicaid Makeover," *Empire State Report* 21 (March 1995), p. 47.

40. James E. Fossett, "The Complex Puzzle That Is Medicaid," (Albany) *Times Union* December 18, 1994, p. E6.

41. New York State Temporary Commission on Lobbying, *2002 Annual Report* (Albany, NY: State Commission on Lobbying, 2002).

42. Jordan Rau, "Albany's Odd Man Out," *Newsday*, November 20, 2003, p. A8. A similar implied pledge was made by Erie County Executive Joel A. Giambra, a Republican. Sandra Tan, "WNY County Leaders Rage Against Costs of Medicaid to Press State for Relief," *Buffalo News*, January 7, 2004, p. B3.

43. Al Baker, "Counties Aiming at Fixed Targets," *New York Times*, January 12, 2004, p. B1.

44. The plan intends to save $2.5 billion over a five-year period, mainly by limiting the kinds of drugs that Medicaid recipients can obtain and by making it more difficult for those entering nursing homes to shelter their assets. New York State Senate *Report of the Senate Medicaid Reform Task Force*, December 2003.

45. Jordan Rau, "Taking Aim at Medicaid Costs: Panel Looks to Save Billions," *Newsday*, January 15, 2004, p. A18.

46. Acebedo, Edwin, "Albany Seeks RX to Cure Medicaid: State Leaders Feel the Heat From Counties Crippled by the Program's Spiraling Costs," (Syracuse) *Post-Standard*, January 11, 2004, p. B1.

47. Margaret H. Davis, *Strengthening New York's EPIC Program: Options for Improving Drug Coverage for Medicare Beneficiaries; Field Report* (New York: Commonwealth Fund, 2003), p. vii.

48. Public Law 108–173.

CHAPTER 15

Social Services

SARAH F. LIEBSCHUTZ

New York's generosity toward persons in need has long been recognized. Such generosity flows from the state constitution's stipulation, adopted in 1938, that the "aid, care and support of the needy are public concerns, and shall be provided by the state and by such of its subdivisions, and in such manner and by such means, as the legislature may from time to time determine (Article XVII)." The affirmative language of this provision—among the strongest in the nation—came about in the aftermath of the Great Depression, when localities and private agencies were unable to meet the needs of the people. More than two-thirds of a century later, public policies for the "aid, care and support of the needy" account for a large share of spending by the state and its local governments.

Social services to assist low-income New Yorkers range widely across population groups and policy areas. The affected populations span children, families, and the elderly as well as individuals with substance abuse and mental health problems. Policy areas include temporary (income) assistance, child care, child support enforcement, child protection, domestic violence, health and mental health, foster care, food assistance, housing, employment education and training, and transportation.

This chapter focuses on social services intended to meet the immediate needs of low-income New Yorkers for assistance and, at the same time, foster self-sufficiency and thereby avoid future dependency. Four federal grants to the states are key in advancing these goals. Those are Temporary Assistance to Needy Families (TANF), the Child Care and Development Block Grant

(CCDBG), and two welfare employment programs—Welfare-to-Work (WtW) and Workforce Investment Act (WIA). All four programs are intergovernmental. The federal and New York state governments are involved in policymaking through legislation and regulations as well as funding. The state's fifty-seven county governments and New York City are involved in administration, funding, and limited policymaking (see chapter 2). Although the programs are administered by different agencies at the state level, they have much in common. They are directed toward families with young children, and they strongly promote self-reliance through work. Each program will be separately presented in terms of federal, state, and local dimensions. The last section of the chapter considers the interactive effects of these programs on low-income New York families and children.

THE INTERGOVERNMENTAL SETTING

Two contextual factors are important for understanding how social service policies are made and implemented in New York: the state constitution and the intergovernmental administrative structure. The social welfare article (Article XVII) of the New York State Constitution cannot be overemphasized for its influence on the shape of social services in New York. Article XVII is frequently cited as a symbol of New York's liberal political culture and its tradition of big government.[1] Until its adoption by the state's voters in 1938, "care for the needy was a local responsibility and services were delivered by local governments and by private institutions and charities."[2] The court of appeals, the state's highest court, has consistently taken the position that aid per se is not a legislative option; its opinions, however, have varied with respect to the extent to which the state must provide assistance to the needy.[3]

The other important contextual factor is that social services in New York are state directed and locally administered. Both the financing and the administration of many social services, most prominently welfare and Medicaid, are intergovernmental. New York's Social Services Districts (fifty-seven counties and New York City) are required by state law to administer welfare programs and to share their costs with the state government.[4] New York, in fact, is one of only eleven states in the nation that requires such cost sharing, and that local share is the highest among the states.[5] The Social Services Districts share equally with the state government the nonfederal share of cash benefits paid to local TANF recipients: the federal government pays 50 percent, and the state government and localities, each 25 percent. In the case of the state, that is, nonfederal, Article XVII Safety Net (formerly Home Relief) program, the state government and social services districts each contribute 50 percent of total expenditures for these recipients. Counties and New York City have very little discretion over eligibility for cash programs and amount of benefits, but considerable flexibility in designing and enforcing work requirements and other rules affecting individual behavior. This last point, plus the fact that they are equal funding partners with the state, gives New York's fifty-seven counties and New York City a huge stake in both TANF and Safety Net welfare programs.

PUBLIC ASSISTANCE AND WELFARE REFORM

The national context for public assistance for needy Americans was radically changed in 1996 with enactment by Congress of the Personal Responsibility and Work Opportunity Reconciliation Act.[6] Touted as producing a "devolution revolution," the act terminated the 1935 federal entitlement program for needy families with children—Aid to Families with Dependent Children (AFDC)—and replaced it with a fixed block-grant program—Temporary Assistance for Needy Families (TANF)—to the states.[7]

AFDC, created during the Great Depression for the purpose of providing income support to widows and their children, turned out to be far more controversial than anticipated. The controversy involved changes in recipients of assistance and in public attitudes toward welfare. By 1980, most adult AFDC recipients were not widows, but rather divorced, separated, or never married nonwhite women. A sizeable proportion of them had numerous children, many born while the mothers were receiving welfare. As of 1996, nearly two-thirds of adult AFDC recipients had been on the dole for eight or more years.[8] Some fifty years after its adoption, AFDC was viewed as a program that discouraged marriage and work, encouraged out-of-wedlock childbearing and dependency, and primarily served people of color.[9]

Public opinion, historically supportive of assistance for Americans in need, shifted strongly against the welfare system and toward doing something about it. Republicans—from President Richard M. Nixon in the 1970s—and Democrats—to President Bill Clinton, who campaigned two decades later on the promise "to end welfare as we know it"—railed against the politically unpopular program. After Republicans took control of the Congress in 1995, they pressured Clinton to end AFDC and create TANF in its place.[10]

TANF differs from AFDC in important ways. TANF set time limits on eligibility for assistance (a lifetime maximum of sixty months) and work requirements (for adults within two years of TANF eligibility, and for 50 percent of the caseload by 2002). In addition, the Personal Responsibility Act created a new block grant for child care, the Child Care and Development Block Grant (CCDBG), which increased funding by almost 50 percent above levels spent under AFDC child-care programs. The act required each state to adopt its own welfare reform legislation by October 1, 1997, when the law took effect, in order to receive the federal block-grant funds.[11] The Personal Responsibility Act was authorized for five years, until September 30, 2002. Annual TANF appropriations to New York in federal fiscal years 1998 through 2004 were $2.4 billion.

The New York State Welfare Reform Act of 1997

"We have an historic opportunity to change the failed welfare system," Governor George E. Pataki asserted after enactment of the Personal Responsibility Act. "We must return welfare to its original intent: a temporary benefit to help those in need move back into the workplace." The governor proposed a state welfare reform program, New York Works, that had the potential, he asserted, to "restructure the entire public assistance system in New York State in a rational and efficient manner."[12]

Welfare reform negotiations in New York were entangled with those of the state's 1997–1998 budget, a budget that set a record for late adoption 126 days after the start of the state's fiscal year. After protracted negotiations involving well-organized interest groups with their own varying agendas for both continuity and departure, the New York State Welfare Reform Act was adopted in August 1997. The Act was a compromise between the governor's original proposal and key concerns of the senate and assembly majorities.

The governor's 1996 proposal was intended to appeal to conservative Republicans and antitax groups. He recommended that AFDC and Home Relief (the state/local general assistance program for persons ineligible for AFDC) be replaced by two time-limited programs—Family Assistance, a five-year program for families with children, financed by TANF, and Article XVII Safety Net, the successor to Home Relief, the state/local general assistance program. To encourage work, both programs were more generous in disregarding earnings in the calculation of welfare benefits than their predecessors. Both, however, were less liberal in benefits provided. Family Assistance/TANF benefits were scheduled in the governor's proposal to decrease over five years; Safety Net assistance was in the form of in-kind benefits and vouchers, not cash. Governor Pataki also proposed limiting exemption from work requirements to parents with a child younger than three months, defining work narrowly, and establishing a Child Care Block Grant to supplement funding from the federal Child Care and Development Block Grant. He also would have replaced the current system of state reimbursement for welfare spending with a block grant to social services districts. These and other changes to New York's welfare practices were predicted by Governor Pataki to save the state nearly $500 million in the first full year of implementation.

The assembly and senate reflected their different constituency bases in responding to the governor's proposal. Assembly majority Democrats, receptive to organized labor and to advocates for the poor, children, and families, favored a broader definition of work to include vocational and educational training, stable benefit levels up to the five-year cutoff point, and minimum or, if applicable, prevailing union wages for working recipients (see chapter 8). Senate majority Republicans reflected the concerns of county officials that block grants as well as benefit cuts would shift greater costs of public assistance to county governments; and that vouchers and in-kind benefits only for Safety Net recipients would increase the costs of local operations.

In the end, the New York State Welfare Reform Act incorporated many basic features of Governor Pataki's NY Works proposal, but with important concessions to the senate Republican and assembly Democratic majorities. For example, the legislature approved the proposed Family Assistance program but rejected the governor's proposals for block grants to local services districts and New York City (thus continuing state reimbursement for local welfare expenditures), and decreasing benefit levels over the five-year Family Assistance limit. In addition, the legislature modified the governor's Safety Net proposal to stipulate cash assistance for two years followed by vouchers and in-kind aid.

Overall, in content, welfare reform represented continuity of the New York welfare program. The New York State Welfare Reform Act—in its provisions for assistance to the needy through the Safety Net, expansion of the income disregard, and liberal definition of work—reaffirmed the state's historic liberalism. However, the act's limited exemption from work require-ments, a residency requirement for full benefits, and reductions in benefits for substance abusers who fail to get treatment when medically indicated reflected changed public expectations about individual behavior.

Administrative Restructuring

In addition to these programmatic changes, the New York Welfare Reform Act of 1997 authorized major administrative restructuring at the state level. The Department of Social Services (with long-term responsibility for admin-istration of public assistance, social services, Medicaid, child support, and welfare-to-work programs) was eliminated and replaced with the Depart-ment of Family Services. The new department, basically a shell superstruc-ture, contains two new units: the Office of Temporary and Disability Assistance (OTDA) and the Office of Children and Family Services (OCFS). Medicaid administration was shifted to the Department of Health, welfare employment programs to the Department of Labor, and child support enforcement to the Department of Taxation and Finance.[13] In addition, the Office of Alcoholism and Substance Abuse and the Office of Prevention of Domestic Violence were assigned responsibilities for specific programs for welfare clients.

If administrative restructuring had not occurred, the former Depart-ment of Social Services would have directed the welfare, workforce, and child care programs that are the focus of this chapter. Instead, they are administered by the OTDA (TANF), the Department of Labor (WtW and WIA), and the OCFS(CCDBG).[14]

Despite—or perhaps because of—its difficult birth, New York's 123–page welfare reform law was characterized in 1997 as a mixed bag.[15] Consistent with the premise that welfare reform in New York was not a rad-ical departure was skepticism that little had changed. "Critics on both the left and the right," a *New York Times* reporter observed, "agree that this approach does not represent a significant financial carrot or stick for getting recipients off the welfare rolls."[16] That skepticism was not borne out by New York's TANF experiences through 2002, as will be discussed in later sections of this chapter.

WORKFORCE POLICY

Work among welfare recipients, most of whom are single mothers, is "widely regarded as part of the social contract—a quid pro quo for the provision of income support—as well as a source of self esteem and self-reliance."[17] A primary goal of the Personal Responsibility Act is that persons receiving welfare assistance either work in the private economy or engage in activities such as education and skills training that lead to employment. Not only were TANF funds made available to the states to move persons from welfare to work, two other federal grants were also enacted for this purpose.

The Welfare-to-Work (WtW) Block Grant Program

Part of the Personal Responsibility Act separate from TANF, WtW was authorized only for federal fiscal years 1998 and 1999. It provides additional resources to states and localities to help meet TANF work participation requirements. WtW grants were intended to supplement TANF funds for assisting the most disadvantaged recipients move into the work force, including noncustodial parents, mainly poor fathers. Unlike TANF, where states either directly administer the grants or, in the case of New York, direct their administration by social services districts, the lion's share, 85 percent, of WtW funds are stipulated in the federal legislation to be passed down from the state to private industry councils (PICs). PICs, the governing boards of local service areas,[18] were mandated to coordinate WtW funds with TANF expenditures.[19] A total of $3 billion over two years was authorized for WtW funds for allocation by formula to the states, of which about 9 percent—nearly $200 million—went to New York.[20]

The New York State Department of Labor emphasized two objectives in its implementation of the WtW program. One was substantive: helping TANF recipients with multiple barriers—for example, school dropouts, substance abusers, and persons with poor work histories—get and keep unsubsidized jobs. The other was procedural: coordinating local services providers and potential employers. Coordination of local agencies (public, nonprofit, for-profit, faith, and community based) who deliver such services as job assessment, education, training, and placement, case management, transitional health, transportation, and child care was a key component. So, too, was connection with local employers. Each PIC submitted a local plan to the state Labor Department detailing how hard-to-employ TANF clients would be identified, assessed, provided services, and tracked, how the roles of local service providers would be coordinated, and how potential local employers and required skills would be identified.

The Workforce Investment Act (WIA)

The other intergovernmental program, WIA, was enacted by Congress in 1998 and authorized to September 30, 2003. This act replaced the Job Training Partnership Act of with three new programs for adults, dislocated workers, and youth into a single grant with "somewhat enhanced flexibility [for states]. WIA features separate funding streams for adults, dislocated workers and youth—with different eligibility, targeting, services, and service delivery requirements—and also maintains distinct funding streams for adult education and family literacy" and other workforce programs.[21] WIA maintains local administrative arrangements, redesignating the PICs as "Workforce Investment Boards" (WIBs). Unlike the PICs, WIBs are proscribed from providing services directly to participants. "The major hallmark of WIA is the consolidation of services through the one-stop center system. About 17 categories of programs, totaling over $15 billion [in federal fiscal year 2003] from four separate federal agencies, are required to provide services through the system."[22] One-stop centers are stipulated as the delivery systems for core services and the access point for intensive and training services.[23]

Governor Pataki welcomed WIA, asserting:

> Long before the WIA was signed, we made it clear that New York's workforce development system must be keyed to the actual needs of the marketplace to ensure that workers receive the skills and knowledge required in the workplace. New York realized that the core issues of workforce development included access to the new system, accountability standards, programming and skill standards, common data base and definitions, and structure and governance. We are creating a system that will be customer-driven, performance-driven, and flexible enough to continuously improve. The fact remains, we must work together to establish and maintain an employment and training system that will continue New York State's leadership.[24]

New York responded to the infusion of WIA funds—more than $300 million in 2000—by passing through $223 million to the state's thirty-three local workforce investment areas with the "expectation that each local area would create their own service structure based on their local needs."[25] The initial local plans proposed diverse approaches to employers and economic development. They ranged from a "sectoral approach for entry level, technical and professional level jobs" of the Rochester Resource Alliance, under the guidance of the Monroe County/Rochester Workforce Investment Board, in which six key industry clusters were identified as high-growth areas, to a health-care, employer-led consortium in Chautauqua County with "representatives from hospitals, long-term care facilities and home health care agencies," and a Business Response Team in Tompkins County whose "goal is to provide a comprehensive package of services to eliminate redundancies and insulate companies from bureaucracy."[26] After one year of WIA experience, these three workforce investment areas all reported "strong emphasis on striving to meet the needs of local businesses" through services provided at the nationally mandated one-stop centers. The Monroe County/ Rochester Workforce Investment Board explicitly linked WIA and child care, approving use of $1 million of WIA funds to offset a reduction in the Monroe County Child Care subsidy program, thereby enabling 257 low-income adults to continue their employment and avoid receiving welfare.[27]

CHILD CARE

The importance of child care for families, particularly those headed by single women, has long been recognized. It is generally agreed that "two of the biggest impediments to employment that welfare recipients face are a lack of relevant job skills and access to quality, affordable child care."[28] The Child Care and Development Block Grant of 1990, itself an aggregation of existing categorical grants, was incorporated into the Personal Responsibility Act of 1996. Two groups are targeted for child care assistance: families on or transitioning off TANF, and low-income working families.[29] The objectives of the CCDBG are several, including maximum flexibility for states to develop child care programs and policies that best suit the needs of children and parents, and promotion of informed choice about child care by working parents.

Nearly $5 billion was appropriated nationally for the CCDB for distribution to the states in 2002. CCDB funds are typically supplemented by other federal grants; states may transfer up to 30 percent of TANF funds, and also use federal Social Services Block Grant (SSBG, also known as Title XX) to provide child care assistance. New York utilized all three grants to total nearly $625 million in federal aid alone for child care in 2002.

Child care for public assistance and low-income families is a high priority of the state government. A State Child Care Block Grant (SCCBG) was established in the New York Welfare Reform Act of 1997 to reimburse social services districts (counties and New York City) for child care assistance. Four categories of families are eligible for child care:

- TANF recipients "to enable a parent . . . to engage in work, participate in work activities or perform a community service; to enable a teenage parent to attend high school or other equivalent training program; because the parent or caretaker relative is physically or mentally incapacitated; or because family duties away from home necessitate the parent or caretaker relative's absence."
- Families "with incomes up to 200% of the state [TANF] income standard who are attempting through work activities to transition off a family assistance."
- Families that have left welfare—they can receive child care transition assistance for twelve months.
- Families that are deemed to be at risk of becoming dependent on TANF.[30]

Table 15.1.
AFDC/TANF caseload changes

	Families			Recipients		
	AFDC	TANF		AFDC	TANF	
	Aug. 1996	June 2003	% change	Aug. 1996	June 2003	%change
U.S.	4,408,508	2,032,157	-53%	12,242,125	4,955,479	-59%
N.Y.	418,338	146,941	-64%	1,143,962	333,522	-70%

Source: U. S. Department of Health and Human Services, Administration for Children and Families, www.acf.hhs.gov.

In 2002, New York expended more than $875 million through the SCCBG funds (largely federal, supplemented by the state general fund), and local matching funds[31] for child-care subsidies, child-care quality initiatives, and child-care provider reimbursements totaled more than $875 million. According to Governor Pataki, whose executive budget proposed more than $864 million for localities from the SCCBG alone in the 2005 state fiscal year, "New York continues to be a national leader in providing child care to low income families, ranking among the highest in both total spending and the number of children receiving subsidies."[32]

SOCIAL SERVICE PROGRAMS:
WHAT DIFFERENCE DO THEY MAKE?

When the Personal Responsibility Act was adopted in 1996, TANF was "hailed by some as a watershed in the way that the United States would design and deliver social assistance to its most vulnerable families. Other observers assailed the enabling legislation as a disaster for the poor and a betrayal of solemn pledges made sixty years earlier when AFDC was established."[33]

From 1996 to 1999, the United States experienced economic expansion, better employment opportunities, and high wages. During this period, the number of families receiving TANF in the United States decreased by 43 percent, from 4.4 million to 2.5 million. Supporters of the "work, not welfare" message of the Personal Responsibility Act argued that the message was working. Detractors contended that the strong national economy made otherwise unemployable welfare recipients attractive to employers in a tight job market.

Over the next three years, the nation slipped into recession. Business investment and output declined, employment slowed, and unemployment increased.[34] Yet "welfare caseloads for much of the county . . . stayed essentially flat or declined" during the recession.[35] Over the seven-year period, 1996–2003, as shown in table 15.1, the total number of TANF families decreased by 53 percent. If the downward trend in TANF caseloads was caused by a strong national economy, why did the trend continue when the economy was in recession? What happened to families made poor by the stagnant economy, who, before the Personal Responsibility Act, would have qualified for income assistance? These questions make for a continuing quandary.

While the welfare caseload story during the recession of 2000–2003 is puzzling, it appears that "the vision of apocalypse for poor families feared by many critics . . . has not materialized."[36] In the case of New York:

- Caseloads have plunged. The decrease in New York families receiving welfare (AFDC or TANF) between 1994—the highest year for welfare caseloads—and 2003 was 73 percent. Table 15.1 shows the effects on caseloads from 1996 (when the Personal Responsibility Act was adopted) to 2003. It is clear that the number of families in the nation receiving welfare has fallen dramatically in New York and the entire nation.

- More low-income mothers are working. The majority of persons (mostly single mothers) leaving welfare in New York, according to a Rockefeller Institute of Government study released in June 2002, found and maintained employment.[37] Nearly two-thirds of respondents in a 2000–2001 survey of families who left TANF from eighteen to twenty-four months earlier were currently working, and most were working at least thirty-five hours per week. About half were above the poverty level for their household size. More than 70 percent of the respondents considered themselves to be somewhat or much better off than at the time they left TANF; they attributed this greater sense of well-being to increased income, self-reliance, and self-esteem. These findings are consistent with other studies of women leaving welfare.[38]

- Poverty is down. Between 1996 and 2000, the proportion of New York children in poverty decreased from 25 percent to 19 percent.[39] Nationally, children in poverty decreased from over 20 percent in 1996 to less than 17 percent in 2002, and the proportion of female-headed households living in poverty fell from 36.5 percent in 1996 to 28.8 percent in 2002.[40]

- The teen pregnancy rate, another indicator of family well-being, also declined. Among New York teens between fifteen and nineteen years of age, the rate declined from 90 per 1,000 in 1995 to 71 per 1,000 in 2000. Although the rates were much higher in New York City (135 and 102) than in the rest of the state (61 to 50), they trended downward in both regions.[41]

Are social services programs that provide cash assistance, workforce preparation and placement, and child care unqualified successes? Policymakers in state agencies, as well as program administrators in New York's local social services districts and nonprofit agencies with whom they contract to deliver services readily acknowledge the successes of the Personal Responsibility Act. At the same time, they express concern about the people who are left behind. "What will happen," they ask," about those who have exited the rolls [because of employment], or those pushed off assistance by sanctions or time limits as different economic cycles play themselves out?"[42] Other questions focus on "the poor who no longer apply for help because the new signals discourage them," and whether "adequate federal and state fiscal support [will] be maintained into the future."[43]

These issues were considered in 2001 in four regional forums and a roundtable convened by the Office of Temporary and Disability Assistance and the SCAA-Schuyler Center for Analysis and Advocacy. The result was a series of recommendations regarding the reauthorization of TANF. Overall, the signatories stressed the need for "significant investments . . . to help those who have obtained employment retain their jobs and advance, as well as to help those remaining on TANF who have multiple obstacles to achieving self-sufficiency."[44] Adequate and ongoing funding as well as continued flexibility for TANF and child care were singled out in this regard. The recommendations were endorsed by New York State and 37 human services advocacy organizations representing religious, child care, youth, and other interests.

In sum, the "aid, care and support for the needy" continue to be concerns of New York State, its local governments, and its residents.

NOTES

1. Sarah F. Liebschutz, *New York Politics and Government* (Lincoln, NE: University of Nebraska Press, 1998), chapter 1.

2. Gerald Benjamin and Melissa Cusa, "Social Policy," in *Decision 1997: Constitutional Change in New York*, ed. Benjamin and Henrick N. Dullea (Albany, NY: Rockefeller Institute, 1997), p. 304.

3. See Sarah F. Liebschutz, *Bargaining Under Federalism: Contemporary New York* (Albany: State University of New York Press, 1991), pp. 31–32.

4. See Sarah F. Liebschutz, "Political Conflict and Intergovernmental Relations: The Federal-State Dimensions," in *Governing New York State*, ed. Jeffrey Stonecash (Albany: State University of New York Press, 1994), pp. 49–62.

5. Under the AFDC program that preceded TANF, New York local governments financed a much greater share of public welfare than the national average. As of October 1994, New York required its localities to fund 50 percent of AFDC benefit payments. Only ten other states required localities to fund a share of AFDC benefit costs, and of these states, only North Carolina required this share to be as high as New York's 50 percent.

6. The title of the act is itself important in conveying its purpose—behavior modification: "It seeks to modify two kinds of behavior, the *personal* labor force and reproductive behavior of poor family heads and the *bureaucratic* behavior of the agencies that administer programs to aid the most controversial welfare population—non-disabled, working-aged, poor family heads and their children." Richard P. Nathan and Thomas L. Gais, *Implementing the Personal Responsibility Act of 1996: A First Look* (Albany: Rockefeller Institute of Government, 1999), p. 1.

7. For a description of TANF, see Irene Lurie, "Temporary Assistance for Needy Families: A Green Light for the States," *Publius* 27 (Spring 1997): 73–87. The reauthorization of TANF coincided with that of other programs affecting low-income families, including the Child Care and Development Block Grant and the Workforce Investment Act. In November 2002, Congress passed a continuing resolution (P.L. 107-294) that extended the Personal Responsibility Act to March 31, 2003. In September 2003, Congress passed legislation to further extend TANF and child care programs through March 31, 2004. For a comprehensive analysis of the issues involved in reauthorizing TANF, see *Focus*, a publication of the University of Wisconsin-Madison Institute for Research on Poverty, vol. 22, no. 1 (special issue 2002).

8. U.S. House of Representatives, Committee on Ways and Means, *The Green Book* (Washington, D.C.: U.S. Government Printing Office, 1996).

9. See Martin Gilens, *Why Americans Hate Welfare: Race, Media, and the Politics of Antipoverty* (Chicago: University of Chicago Press, 1999).

10. 1R. Kent Weaver, *Ending Welfare as We Know It* (Washington, D.C.: Brookings Institution, 2000).

11. The federal fiscal year (FFY) runs from October 1 to September 30, and is named by its ending date. Thus, FFY 1998 ended on September 30, 1998.

12. George E. Pataki, *State of New York Executive Budget 1996–1997*, p. 63.

13. The New York State Constitution limits the number of departments in the executive branch to twenty. Governors since Nelson Rockefeller have circumvented this limit by creating executive agencies and authorities. See Liebschutz, *New York Politics and Government*, chapter 8.

14. Separate divisions of the Department of Labor are responsible for administration of these federal grants—the Welfare To Work Division for WtW, and the Employment and Training Division, for WIA.

15. Raymond Hernandez, "New York's No Model Welfare State," *New York Times*, September 22, 1997.

16. Ibid.

17. Robert A. Moffitt, "From Welfare to Work: What the Evidence Shows," *WRB Policy Brief*, January 2002, http:// WRBinfo@brookings.edu.

18. New York City and Onondaga County were exceptions; there the Human Resources Administration and Department of Social Services, respectively, serve as the local entities for the WtW funds.

19. Service delivery areas (SDAs) and their administrative entities, private industry councils (PICs), were established under the Job Training Partnership Act (JTPA) of 1982. JTPA was terminated with enactment of the Workforce Investment Act in 1998, and the PICs became local Workforce Investment Boards.

20. Under the federal authorizing legislation unexpended WtW grant funds could be carried over for expenditure up to three years from the date of the grant.

21. Christopher T. King, "Federalism and Workforce Policy Reform," *Publius* 29 (Spring 1999): 68. A good overview of the Workforce Investment Act of 1998 (Public Law 105-220) can be found at www.doleta.gov/usworkforce.

22. General Accounting Office, *Workforce Investment Act: One Stop Centers Implemented Strategies to Strengthen Services and Partnerships, but More Research and Information Sharing is Needed* (GAO-03-725): 8.

23. "Under the WIA, "core" services are "Intensive services [such as] individual employment plans, career counseling, case management, and

short-term pre-vocational services provided by one-stop centers or individual providers. "Training" services are occupational skills, customized and on-the-job (OJT) training, workplace training and academic instruction, and adult education. See Christopher T. King, "Federalism and Workforce Policy Reform," *Publius* 29 (Spring 1999): 53–71.

24. New York State Department of Labor, *New York's Workforce Investment Act Annual Report, Program Year 2000,* http://www.workforce-newyork.com

25. Ibid.

26. Ibid.

27. Ibid.

28. George E. Pataki, *New York State 2004–2005 Executive Budget: Overview,* p. 81.

29. States must spend 70 percent of their CCDBG monies to provide child-care services for families on or transitioning off TANF or at-risk of welfare dependency. http://www.acf.dhhs.gov/programs/ccb.

30. New York State Welfare Reform Act of 1997, Title 5-c, Section 410.

31. Local social services districts are mandated under state law to share equally with the state child-care expenditures for TANF recipients.

32. Pataki, *New York State Executive Budget 2004–2005: Overview,* p. 89. The New York State fiscal year (SFY) runs from April 1 to March 31, and is named by the ending date. Thus SFY 2005 ends on March 31, 2005.

33. Thomas Corbett, "The New Face of Welfare: From Income Transfers to Social Assistance? *Focus* 22 (special issue 2002): 4.

34. See U.S. Council of Economic Advisors, *2004 Economic Report of the President* (Washington, D.C.: Government Printing Office, 2004), chapter 1.

35. Center for Law and Social Policy, *CLASP Update* (Washington, D.C.: CLASP, March 2004).

36. Corbett, "New Face of Welfare," p. 4.

37. Rockefeller Institute of Government, "Leaving Welfare: Post-TANF Experiences of New York State Families," June 2002, http://www.rockinst.org.

38. "From studies of women leaving welfare we know that about two-thirds work at any given time after they leave, and 80 percent give evidence of some attachment to the labor force." Corbett, "New Face of Welfare": 4.

39. New York State Kids' Well-being Indicators Clearinghouse, http://www. nyskwic.org.

40. U.S. Census Bureau, *Poverty in the United States* (Washington, D.C.: Government Printing Office, 1997 and 2003).

41. New York State Kids' Well-being Indicators Clearinghouse.

42. Corbett, "New Face of Welfare": 4.

43. Ibid.

44. SCAA-Schuyler Center for Analysis and Advocacy and the New York State Office of Temporary and Disability Assistance, "Recommendations on the Reauthorization of the Temporary Assistance for Needy Families (TANF) Program," February 2002.

CHAPTER 16

The Politics of Transportation

JEFFREY M. STONECASH
with
Mitchell H. Pally

INTRODUCTION

Financing New York State's transportation systems has involved persistent political controversy. Regular battles have pitted the Metropolitan Transportation Authority (MTA), which operates the bus, subway, and commuter rails in the metropolitan New York City region, against advocates of highways. Conflict has revolved around how resources are raised, who should pay, and how and where funding is spent. Should revenue come from user fees (those who use roads or mass transit) or the general treasury? How much of the burden of paying for transportation should be placed on current users and how much should be spread out over time via borrowing and debt? How can regional balance in taxing and funding support be maintained? Amidst all this conflict, the state must make sure its infrastructure is maintained for safety, the health of the economy, and the convenience of residents. This chapter reviews the sources of conflicts about transportation, histories of specific decisions made, how legislators behaved during these decisions, and why they acted as they did.

SOURCES OF CONFLICT

Conflicts in transportation policy exist because regions of the state differ in their transportation needs (see chapter 1). Politicians are concerned with

securing the best deal for their area in order to get reelected. That creates per-
petual regional conflicts. Upstaters and those in the suburbs, usually represented by Republicans, want state funds appropriated to highways and
bridges. New York City suburban legislators are concerned about their highway needs and rail service since many of their constituents commute into
New York City. Both of these sets of legislators have little interest in pouring
funds into New York City. New York City residents, usually represented by
Democrats in the state assembly and the state senate, want large sums of
state money to improve subway and bus systems within the city and to hold
down the fares on these systems. Fares only cover 50 percent of the cost of
the ride on the system. Government subsidies are necessary to hold down
fares for the people who rely on the New York City mass transit system.

Differences in mass transit usage by region are shown in table 16.1. In
New York City 56 percent of people use mass transit to go to work, while
Upstate the percentage of residents utilizing mass transit to reach work is
considerably lower: 17 percent in Buffalo, 15 percent in Rochester, 24 percent in Yonkers, 14 percent in Syracuse, and 20 percent in Albany. On Long
Island, these figures are even lower. The majority of Long Island residents
travel by roads either alone or in a car pool. Their legislators want transportation funds spent primarily on roads.

There are also significant discrepancies among regions in miles of road
that need to be maintained. New York City has 40 percent of the state's population, but only 6 percent of road mileage. Upstate has 34 percent of the
state's population, but 73 percent of the state's roads. Table 16.2 presents

TABLE 16.1.
Public transit service by region in New York State, 2000–2002

Year	Passengers in each area (in millions)		
	Upstate	Downstate	Total
2000	68	2,324	2,392
2001	67	2,452	2,519
2002	67	2,493	2,560

Note: Upstate consists of all public and private operators in New York State outside the New
York City metropolitan area. Downstate includes all public and private operators of bus,
subway, commuter rail, or ferry services in New York City and Nassau, Suffolk, Westchester,
Putnam, Dutchess, Rockland, and Orange Counties.

Source: 2003 New York State Statistical Yearbook (Albany, N.Y.: The Rockefeller Institute,
2004), p. 505.

TABLE 16.2.

Distribution of population, highway miles, and driver
and vehicle registrations, by area, 2001

| | Percentage of: | | | |
Area	State Population	Highway miles	Vehicle registrations	Driver's licenses
New York City	41	5	18	22
Long Island	15	10	19	14
Hudson Valley	11	12	15	10
Upstate	33	73	48	54

Note: Long Island consists of Nassau and Suffolk counties. Hudson Valley consists of Westchester, Rockland, Putnam, Dutchess, Columbia, Orange, and Ulster counties. Upstate consists of all remaining counties.

Source: 2003 New York State Statistical Yearbook, (Albany, N.Y.: The Rockefeller Institute, 2004), pp. 487, 490, and 500.

some important regional transportation differences in New York State. The contrasts among regions are clear. New York City residents rely heavily on mass transit and want fare increases restrained. Upstate relies heavily on roads and they want more money put into maintaining that system. The suburban area relies heavily on highways but also must use a commuter rail system to get into and out of New York City.

Conflicts also emerge from how the regions differ in the revenues they generate to support transportation expenses. State revenues for transportation come primarily from motor vehicle registrations, driver's license fees, and gasoline and petroleum taxes. New York City comprises approximately 40 percent of the state's population, but its vehicle registrations make up only 18 percent of the state total. Driver's licenses on file in New York City amount to only 22 percent of the state total.

New York City does not produce motor vehicle related revenues comparable to its percentage of the state's population. Given this, upstate and suburban legislators oppose allocating large amounts of aid to the New York City bus and subway systems. They believe that motor-vehicle-related revenues should go back into transportation improvements and revenues should return to those areas of the state which produce the most funds, namely their own areas of the state. New York City legislators in the assembly want the state to play a much larger role in helping to finance the operating and capital needs of the New York City bus and subway system, no matter where the funds come from. Otherwise mass transit fares could become too expensive for their constituents. This situation has established a continuing conflict between the Democrat-controlled state assembly, with its powerful New York City delegation, and the Republican-controlled state senate, with its power base resting in upstate and suburban areas. These persisting conflicts have affected five major transportation funding battles during the last ten years. Their resolution indicates how the legislature deals with conflicts over transportation funding.

MASS TRANSIT CONFLICTS AND THE
1981 CAPITAL IMPROVEMENT PLAN DEBATE

The Metropolitan Transportation Authority, which controls the bus, subway, and commuter rail systems within the metropolitan New York City region, was in serious financial trouble by the late 1970s. The system had experienced significant deterioration. Cars were aging and not being replaced. Tunnels and tracks were old. Fewer and fewer trains arrived on time. Funds received in fares, which had been kept artificially low, were inadequate to purchase new equipment to improve the system. New York City was unable to provide sufficient resources to save the system. The serious decline in the system was widely recognized. There was concern that a declining mass transit system would harm the economy of New York City and the metropolitan area. Since two-thirds of the state's population and much of job growth was in that area (see chapter 11), politicians recognized that something needed to be done about the MTA. The difficulty was that upstate and New York City suburban areas were hostile to any proposal that appeared to use state resources to bail out just New York City.

By 1980 there was a consensus to try to resolve the difficulties of the MTA, but no agreement on how to do so among the Democratic governor and assembly and the Republican-controlled senate. There was not even a consensus within the Democratic party. In March 1981 Governor Hugh Carey called for a $5 billion, five-year capital program to try to save the MTA. The plan was criticized by fellow Democrat and New York City mayor Ed Koch because the proposal was concerned only with capital improvements for the system and contained no operating assistance.[1] Koch knew that he would have to either contribute more money from the city treasury or face a fare increase for his constituents, which would clearly hurt him politically.

Koch responded with a proposal for a statewide tax to fund mass transit, with most of the funds coming from the upstate and suburban constituents of the senate Republicans.[2] Senate Republicans were firmly opposed to this idea since it was predicated on motor-vehicle-related revenue that is paid primarily by non–New York City residents. In an attempt to prevent a fare increase, Koch placed pressure on Carey for additional state aid by threatening to press for a federal trade-in of the funds for the Westway project. This was a major highway project that was to run along the West Side of Manhattan, and was strongly supported by construction unions that supported Carey. Since under federal law either the governor or the mayor could call for the trade-in of the funds from the highway to the mass-transit system, Carey was placed in a situation where he had to come up with additional funds for the New York mass-transit system or face the hostility of New York City unions.

Carey responded with a plan with the MTA involving only a ten- to fifteen-cent fare increase, with further fare increases tied to the Consumer Price Index.[3] Surprisingly, the Democratic minority in the state senate, consisting primarily of New York City legislators, rejected the proposal, saying that without any new state subsidies another fare increase could be expected.[4] None of these Democrats wanted to be tied to legislation that might result in large and frequent future fare increases. Without the support of senate Democratic legislators, the plan would not pass the Republican-controlled senate. The senate Republicans would not pass any proposal for increased state taxes without a majority of the senate Democrats voting for the proposal. Democrat opposition would leave the Republicans in the senate to vote for a fare increase by themselves, allowing the Democrats in the Senate to say they voted against the fare increase when it came. Since the Republicans hold the senate only by retaining some seats in New York City, the Republicans would not allow their New York City members to vote for a fare increase while allowing the Democrats to vote against the fare increase and then use that vote in their reelection campaigns the next November. The senate Democrats had to be part of any agreement so that none of the New York City legislators in the senate could campaign against the others on the fare-increase vote. Partisan divisions within the senate were central to the negotiations.

Meanwhile, Koch was still facing a massive fare increase without the availability of additional state funds to stop it from happening. To lessen this possibility, he proposed regional taxes, consisting of an increase in the sales tax, payroll tax, and gasoline tax, and a rise in automobile registration fees.[5] Koch was aware that these taxes would not greatly affect a majority of his constituents since the motor-vehicle-related taxes would primarily be collected in the suburbs.

Everyone could say they were protecting the interests of their constituents. The mayor and the governor, both Democrats, were arguing over the amount of state funds which would go to the city under any agreement. The senate Democrats declared that they would only vote for a plan which would hold any fare increase to an absolute minimum by increasing local and state taxes, the majority to be paid for by non–New York City residents. The senate Republicans, who waited for the Democrats to fashion a position, let everyone knew they would not pass any plan unless a majority of senate Democrats from New York City supported the proposal.

Finally, both Carey and Koch realized that without compromise, senate Republicans would just sit back and let Democrats squabble and then blame them for any fare increase. Carey finally agreed that the only way to finance the entire MTA problem, including the suburban commuter rails, was to use a regional tax. The only people paying for the state subsidy would be those constituents within the region of the state in which the MTA operated. Upstate legislators would accept the tax since their constituents were not being asked to subsidize transportation operations within New York City. An advisory panel was formed to determine which regional taxes would be proposed.[6]

The panel proposed two new taxes: an increase of 0.25 percent in the state sales tax within the MTA region and an increase from 2 percent to 3 percent on the statewide tax on the gross receipts of oil companies. The Democratic controlled assembly rejected increasing the statewide sales tax.[7] Upstate Republicans in the assembly were opposed to the statewide tax on oil companies, which was really a gas tax increase in disguise. They saw the burden of the tax as being imposed primarily on their constituents. The revenues would only support mass transit and would be spent primarily in New York City. Given this opposition, the taxes were not passed.

The legislature chose another route. Democrats wanted a solution quickly and they knew they would have to compromise with the Republicans. On June 23, the assembly passed an MTA capital improvement plan which involved borrowing $5.6 billion over the next five years. Funds would be repaid almost exclusively by the riders of the system. This would produce immediate results and allow paying back funds over thirty years. The assembly also drew $100 million from the state general treasury. This allowed the fare increase to be held to fifteen cents. In order to make the plan attractive to senate Republicans, substantial aid was contributed to highways and bridges across the state.[8] All three regions of the state received a benefit from the package without any region believing it was paying for any other region.

THE 1981 OPERATING AID AND DEFICIT DEBATE

The issues of the MTA operating deficit and fare levels were still unresolved. Governor Carey proposed three taxes to close a two-year $954 million deficit. The taxes were a 1 percent statewide tax increase on oil company gross receipts which would be passed on to consumers, a 0.50 percent sales tax increase in the MTA area, and a thirty-five cent tax increase to $9.30 per $100 of assessed value on all property in the area. New York City would also have to increase its funding of the MTA by $104 million.[9] Mayor Koch opposed the plan because New York City residents would pay for it. He did support the statewide tax since non–New York City residents would pay most of it.[10] The governor's hope was that the heavy emphasis on the regional metropolitan area would allow upstate Republicans to support the proposal. Nevertheless, the Republicans rejected the proposal. They saw the statewide gross receipts tax as a gas tax on their constituents in both the upstate and suburban regions. They also saw no benefits.

After much negotiating, a compromise was reached. It involved a statewide tax increase of 0.75 percent on the gross receipts of oil companies which would be passed on to consumers, an increase of a quarter of a cent on the sales tax in the MTA area, a 10 percent tax on the sale and transfer of industrial and commercial property exceeding one million dollars, and a "long lines" tax that would bring the New York State portion of interstate commerce under the state corporate franchise tax.[11] The package was a mixture of regional and statewide taxes to try to overcome the objections of upstate Republican senators that their constituents could be paying for a New York City problem. The suburban Republican senators accepted the package because their commuter rail facilities would receive sizable benefits. Again, in a further effort to appease upstate Republicans, 45 percent of the total raised from the gross receipts tax would be appropriated to upstate highways and bridges.[12] The tax package was approved by one vote in the Assembly and three votes in the Senate.[13] Again, regional politics dominated.

The plan provided benefits to all regions of the state, even though the only major problem was the New York City transit system.

THE 1983 NEW YORK BOND ISSUE

Amidst all this, it was also recognized that more needed to be done about roads and bridges across the state. That concern ultimately resulted in the 1983 Rebuild New York Bond issue, which provided funding for transportation infrastructure improvements. When Governor Cuomo first proposed the bond issue, he wanted to leave the specifics of allocating funds to individual projects to the Department of Transportation (DOT) and future legislatures. However, both houses of the legislature felt that to obtain the approval of the voters at the next general election, it was necessary for them to have specific projects in their areas to sell to their constituents. The suburban and upstate Republicans in particular were worried about all the money going for the old bridges in New York City and would not consider the bond issue until regional allocations were specified.

Upstate and New York City suburban areas wanted funds distributed based on highway mileage and vehicle registrations. New York City legislators wanted funds distributed on the basis of population. Each region had reasons why it should get more funds than other regions. Legislators and interest groups from those regions sought their fair share based on criteria which favored their region.

A Memorandum of Understanding was created to accompany the authorization to ensure that all regions of the state were satisfied. The memorandum listed every project costing over $2 million from the bond issue funds. Projects were chosen by combining proposals made by individual legislators and a complex formula used by the DOT that involved lane miles and population per capita in each region. Need and politics were combined to make sure individual legislators could go home to their constituents with projects for their areas. All regions of the state got some funds allocated to them.[14] The allocation of funds from the bond issue, listed in table 16.3, was specified by site and region. A compromise between the parties based on political need became the basis of the allocation rather than using any transportation need formula.

Despite the heavy allocation of funds outside New York City, the bond issue met with resistance upstate mainly because of concerns about state debt

TABLE 16.3.
Distribution of population and Rebuild New York bond funds, 1983

Area	% 1980 Population	% of bond funds	Total bond funds (in millions)
		Distributions of:	
New York City	40	24	303
Long Island	15	14	172
Hudson Valley	11	9	122
Upstate	34	52	652

Source: Memorandum of Understanding, Rebuild New York Bond Act, 1983.

levels. In upstate counties, however, only 48 percent supported the bond issue. Elsewhere in the state, which is traditionally more supportive of public expenditures, the issue received greater support. It received strong support in New York City (72 percent for) and in the suburban areas around New York City (63 percent in Westchester County, 54 percent in Rockland County). On Long Island, which received a large allocation of funds, 56 percent of voters supported the bond issue.

THE 1986–1987 CAPITAL IMPROVEMENT PLAN AND OPERATING AID DEBATE

Despite all this funding, the MTA system still needed additional funds to repair its infrastructure. In 1986, the MTA proposed an $8.6 billion, five-year capital improvement program.[15] To finance this program, a panel organized by Governor Cuomo proposed an increase in gasoline taxes for the area served by the MTA and a rise in tolls for the East River Bridge and tunnels.[16] Mayor Koch endorsed these proposals because a large part of his constituency did not own cars and would not be heavily affected by the increased taxes and tolls. The Republican-controlled senate, however, ruled out a gasoline tax. Upstate and suburban regions opposed it because Cuomo wanted to spend all the funds raised outside the region on the MTA.[17]

Suburban legislators wanted large sums put into the commuter rails and highways to better serve their constituents. In contrast, the New York City legislators, mostly Democrats, supported the gas tax because, again, it did not heavily affect their electorate. Cuomo responded by criticizing senate

Republicans. He warned that their failure to pass the gasoline tax would result in an increased fare for New York City residents.[18] Democratic assembly speaker Stanley Fink, with New York City and suburban legislators to protect, proposed converting registration fees and the state sales tax on newly purchased motor vehicles into a new property tax which could be deducted from the federal income tax.[19] This was again rejected by the Republicans because suburban residents would constitute the majority of that tax base but would receive little in return. Republicans argued, "Two-thirds of it is going to be collected in the suburbs, but it will go to meet the mass transit operating deficit."[20]

Governor Cuomo then proposed drawing $75 million from the state treasury in the first year and $150 million in following years. Upstate Republicans opposed this.[21] They did not want the mass transit "sinkhole" drawing on state funds, especially when their constituents received nothing. The next proposal in the long line of defeated plans involved for the most part a six-month extension of an existing 17 percent downstate corporate surtax which already helped to pay the MTA operating deficit, as well as doubling the amount that New York City pays on capital interest. The decision on how to pay for parts of the program was put off until early 1987.[22] With New York City subway and bus systems receiving almost all of the funds, the Senate Republicans delayed passage of the bill to argue for more money for commuter rails, which many of their constituents use. Senate Republicans wanted 35 percent for suburban commuter rail lines while Cuomo and Democratic assembly members wanted the entire package targeted at the bus and subway systems in New York City.[23]

Facing a large fare increase and the wrath of voters everywhere, the legislature finally approved a financing plan for the MTA on December 31, the last day of the MTA fiscal year. Assembly Democrats were forced to give concessions to senate Republicans in the form of increased spending for the rebuilding of highways and state aid directed toward commuter rail lines.[24]

Then a new dispute arose. Republicans blocked the MTA capital funding program, arguing that too much of federal funds was going to pay for city bus and subway lines. They argued that the Long Island Railroad and the Metro North Commuter Railroad were receiving less than their usual 21 percent of federal aid.[25] There was also a squabble over how much each part of the MTA system (New York City and the suburbs) was generating in revenue.[26]

In an attempt to settle the dispute, Governor Cuomo reintroduced Speaker Fink's plan which would involve converting registration fees and state sales tax on newly purchased motor vehicles into a property tax deductible from federal income tax, a proposal which had been opposed by Republican senators in the past. A surcharge of six-tenths of one percent would be placed on this property tax for those living in the MTA area, excluding suburban Orange, Rockland, and Dutchess counties. It would also involve an increase of one-eighth of one percent on the mortgage-recording tax.[27] The governor hoped this package would please suburban Republicans as well as provide the funds for mass transit. Senate Republicans still rejected the proposal. They were concerned that if highway funding was done on a regional basis, their constituents would end up paying for New York City highways and bridges.[28]

Assembly Democrats finally broke away from the governor and proposed a new MTA financing plan that would drop the tax on newly purchased motor vehicles and would change the federal aid distribution from 79/21 percent split in favor of the city over the suburban commuter rail lines to a 69/31 percent urban/suburban split.[29] The plan would deal with MTA budget deficits by increasing the estimates of expected revenues from various sources and by drawing from state treasury bond issues and commuter rail line surpluses. The Republicans had bargained for and obtained more suburban-rural aid from the urban-minded Democrats. Suburban Republicans had prevented the imposition of a new regional tax on their constituents and had received substantial aid for their highways and commuter rails in return for passing a measure to solve the New York City fare issue. Once again regional needs had been dominant in fashioning a transportation solution.

1988 ACTION BOND ISSUE

The 1983 bond issue did not solve the problem of repairing New York's roads and bridges. More funding was still needed. Senate Republicans wanted a new plan to help the state's highway and bridge infrastructure. They still felt that the highway and bridge needs of the upstate and suburban regions were not being addressed. They proposed their plan in March of 1988. At the same time both the governor and the assembly submitted plans to deal with the obvious road crisis facing New York, but with a much different emphasis on how and where funds would be spent.

The assembly proposal would have covered repairs only for the next two years and would have left the issue of what to do in the 1990s for a new committee to study. The senate Republican plan, dubbed ACTION, was intended to provide long-term financing for upstate and suburban areas without raising taxes. Their $3 billion-dollar plan would utilize debt financing and earmark revenues from existing gasoline taxes. ACTION would borrow funds for fifteen years and earmark two cents from gasoline tax receipts to pay off the debt. The amount of the gasoline tax dedicated to transportation funding would later be raised to five cents. The goal was to devote a large portion of the gas tax solely to highway purposes specified by ACTION. Suburban and upstate legislators deemed this fair because the people who use the roads the most would pay for their upkeep. Also, ACTION would draw at least $500 million from the existing Infrastructure Trust Fund (ITF). The ITF was set up in the spring of 1987 when New York experienced a surplus in its revenues.

ACTION's proposed allocation of aid again reveals the enduring conflicts over transportation. The senate plan would allocate aid proportionate to that area's vehicle registration. Long Island would have received the highest percent of the aid, which was strongly supported by the area's nine Republican senators. New York City's Democrats were not happy with the plan because the city would receive only 21 percent of the aid. The rest of the state would divide up the remaining 55.5 percent of the aid.

The final bill contained a distribution of aid which was very similar to the original senate plan. As in the Rebuild New York plan, the state is divided into four regions, with the aid distribution shown in table 16.4. Senate Republicans were successful because upstate Democrats wanted a major public works program for the 1990 elections. The senate knew that sooner or later New York City Democrats would have to pass some major financing plan and thus could not afford to hold out for a major redistribution of the funds. Thus, the suburban and upstate legislators were able to bring home 77 percent of all of the funds while having only 60 percent of the population. The bond issue passed with 55 percent supporting it. Downstate again provided greater levels of support. In New York City, 67 percent supported the proposition, on Long Island 64 percent supported it, and in Westchester County 57 percent supported it. Elsewhere in the state the proposal was supported by only 46 percent of those voting.[30]

TABLE 16.4.
Distribution of population and Rebuild New York bond funds, 1988

	Distributions of:		
Area	% 1980 Population	% of bond funds	Total bond funds
New York City	40	23	690,000,000
Long Island	15	23	690,100,000
Hudson Valley	11	14	420,600,000
Upstate	34	40	1,199,000,000

Source: A 11980 / S 9207, 1988.

THE DEDICATED TRANSPORTATION FUND

The battles over how to fund transportation eventually resulted in an effort to permanently set aside revenues to fund transportation needs. The battle became how to create a dedicated highway fund to finance ongoing highways and bridge repairs. Supporters of such a fund argued that the only fair way to finance transportation needs is from revenues raised from motor-vehicle-related sales. They argued that highway and bridges should be guaranteed all funds from these sources each year. Supporters argued that New York State has not spent enough on highway and bridges because motor-vehicle-related revenues went into the state general fund, which encompasses all state revenues. Highway and bridge needs then had to compete with more prominent needs in the state, such as education. Highway and bridge needs suffered in this competition.

To opponents of a dedicated highway fund, a primary issue was whether this dedication of funds to highways and bridges would mean the neglect of mass transit. Given the importance of mass transit within the state, they argue it would be unfair for highway and bridge needs to be met automatically each year by the revenues in the fund, while mass transit needs would have to continue to compete with the other needs of the state.

Politically, the supporters and opponents of the dedicated highway fund were a part of the enduring regional conflicts which have affected transportation policy in the legislature. Support for the dedicated highway fund tended to come from upstate and suburban areas, since their constituents paid the greater majority of the motor-vehicle-related funds in the state—

funds which according to them should have been spent only for highways and bridges all the time. Republican senators from these regions were prime movers behind the creation of the fund, even if some of them, especially those from the suburban areas around New York City, knew that their commuter rail riders would have to be protected in some way from the onslaught of the highway and bridge needs of the state.

Opponents of the fund tended to be legislators from New York City, especially Democratic senators and assemblymen. They felt New York City would lose if highways and bridges had their own fund ensuring them a set amount each year, and mass transit needs were left to compete in the regular budget process. They thought that any dedicated fund would have to include mass transit needs, especially those of New York City.[31]

Both houses of the legislature had talked about creating a transportation fund for years, but nothing had happened. Both houses would have liked to pass such a fund to claim credit for its creation, but they knew the state could not afford to take all of these motor-vehicle-related funds out of the regular state budget process without harming other needs within the state.

Finally in 1991 the political need to create a dedicated fund of some find became too strong for even the legislative leaders and governor to ignore. Many of the major highway and bridge interest groups made the creation of a dedicated fund their number one priority for the year and brought increasing pressure on individual legislators, especially those from the upstate areas. The pressure became very intense during the lengthy discussions on the 1991–1992 state budget, which lasted well beyond the April 1 deadline. Enormous political pressure was exerted on upstate Republican senators and upstate Democratic assemblymembers during budget negotiations, even though everyone realized that no money could flow to a dedicated fund for at least two years because of the state's dire financial condition.

Upstate senate Republicans and upstate assembly Democrats then made it clear to their leaders that a dedicated fund of some type was an absolute imperative in the state budget negotiations. With the support of the suburban Republicans in the senate, who also believed that the creation of such a fund would give their regions additional highway dollars, the senate made a fund a quid pro quo of the settlement of the budget negotiations. However, they also realized they could not just create a fund for highways and bridges and leave mass transit out in the cold—New York City Democratic assemblymembers would absolutely have to have a dedicated fund of some type for mass transit.

The senate then proposed a dedicated transportation fund which would consist of motor-vehicle-related revenues, but could be used for both highway and bridge and mass transit purposes. Because they knew that negotiating such a distribution would be difficult and would delay the state budget settlement, both houses quickly agreed to put off the distribution formula from the fund and pay-out of the fund for two years, until the 1993–1994 state fiscal year.[32]

Legislators in both houses could indicate they had created a fund, but postpone establishing a formula for the distribution of such monies. Since the revenues in the fund would consist primarily of motor-vehicle-related funds, upstate and New York City suburban legislators would continue to argue for the greatest share of the funds to go to highways and bridges in their areas, since their constituents were not dependent on mass transit facilities. On the other hand, legislators from New York City and some suburban areas realized that it was absolutely necessary for their mass transit facilities to be given ample opportunity to compete for the funds by need, regardless of the funding source. In this case, location of the legislative district became the main criteria for the distribution analysis, rather than the actual party of the legislator. Both Democrats and Republicans from upstate knew that their areas would have to be taken care of, and those from New York City and surrounding areas knew that their mass transit needs would have to be a focal point of the discussions.

The Dedicated Highway and Bridge Trust Fund receives revenues from highway use taxes (taxes levied on truck mileage, fuel usage taxes, and highway use permit fees), four cents of the eight-cent per gallon motor fuel tax, a portion of motor vehicle registration fees, and a portion of the petroleum business tax.[33] During the 2004–2005 budget cycle the fund generated about $1.5 billion in revenues.[34] The distribution of funds to support roads and bridges has tended to follow a stable pattern, with New York receiving 24 percent, Long Island 20 percent, Hudson Valley 14 percent, and the rest of the state 42 percent.[35]

New York City receives less from this fund because it gets most of the money in the Dedicated Mass Transportation Trust Fund, which is funded with receipts from a 1/4 percent sales tax and a business tax surcharge levied in the New York City metropolitan region, as well as a portion of statewide taxes on transmission and transportation companies and petroleum-related companies.[36] During the 2004–2005 budget cycle approximately $50 million would be distributed from this fund.[37] The creation of these dedicated funds represented considerable progress in addressing transportation needs. Designating specific revenues guaranteed a consistent flow of funds to support transportation needs.

The funds have not solved the state's problems, however, for three reasons. First, the needs of the state are enormous. The state has the highest percent (70 percent) of deficient bridges in the nation.[38] Repair of existing roads was deferred over recent decades, resulting in the need for spending large sums of money.[39] The mass transit system in the New York City metropolitan area also needs extensive repairs and new equipment. In 2000, for example, the MTA proposed a $17.5 billion capital plan for the years 2000–2004. The magnitude of needs and the challenge of responding to these needs are widely recognized as serious problems facing the state.[40]

Second, the revenues dedicated to the trust funds are not sufficient to meet these needs. There are consistent attempts to increase transportation funds and periodic efforts to get voters to approve bond issues which allow the state to borrow more. In 2000 voters were presented with a bond issue in which the state was seeking to borrow $3.8 billion for highways and the mass transit system in New York City.[41] The bond issue was supported by only 47.9 percent of voters, with regionalism again playing a significant role. In New York City 72.9 percent of voters supported the bond issue, while in the remainder of the state only 39.7 percent voted for it.

Third, responding to transportation needs has been affected by efforts to divert funds to other purposes. The initial plan for these funds was that they would be "locked boxes," or funds that could not be used for other purposes. The recession of the early 1990s, however, resulted in declines in revenue and created significant budget gaps for the state. Desperate for funds, state officials agreed to raid the funds to provide additional revenues for several years after the creation of the trust.[42] Finally, with the state's economy growing, Governor Pataki agreed beginning in 1996 to stop raiding the fund, and even proposed spending beyond the level of the revenues generated by the trust funds. In addition, the federal government, also experiencing growing revenues, enacted significant increases in federal aid for highways and mass transit in the late 1990s. The revenue needs of New York, however, are enormous, and the problems of the state are by no means resolved.

CONCLUSION

Regional politics and the concern of the parties for regional interests are never far from the surface. The events of May 1999 illustrate how quickly these regional conflicts can emerge. A special election was being held for a seat in the state senate. Both the Republican and Democratic candidates, in an attempt to present themselves as concerned about suburban residents, proposed that the tax of .45 percent of the income of those commuting to work in New York City be repealed. The tax, in effect for thirty-three years, had been enacted to balance the needs of New York City (needing revenue for service demands—fire and police—created by commuters, and to help maintain the transportation system) and suburban residents' needs (a reliable transit system). The senate Republicans, in the majority and wanting to win the seat to retain their margin of seats, quickly embraced and passed the proposal to repeal the tax. Governor Pataki, seeing the political value of supporting suburban interests, said he would sign the legislation. No studies were made of the impact of the repeal, and the mayor of New York City vehemently opposed the repeal. The politics were clear to all involved, however. The senate was trying to look responsive to suburban residents, and argued that the city had a $2 billion surplus and could afford the estimated loss of revenue of several hundred million dollars.

The assembly, not wanting it to appear that Democrats were not sensitive to suburban concerns, quickly joined in repealing the tax. As noted in chapter 3, Democrats hold the majority in the assembly only because they win seats in the suburbs. They recognized the importance of regional politics in forming transportation policy, and the importance of not letting Republicans look more responsive. As this incident illustrates, the process is not one in which the concern is always with some best policy, but with policies that accommodate different political interests.

Regional conflicts are fundamental in transportation politics. New York suburban legislators propose solutions favorable to their constituents. New York City legislators propose solutions favorable to their constituents. Upstate legislators worry about upstate roads. The challenge within the political process is to find a way to accommodate the divergent needs of regions while still providing the revenue to support transportation. This produces intense bargaining and a continual focus on the fairness of proposals. Legislators hold out for proposals that help their constituents. The outcome is inevitably a compromise, with no initial proposal surviving intact. The process is erratic, filled with brinkmanship, and attempts to outlast opponents. The process is a struggle, but policies do get adopted.

NOTES

Thanks are due to two students who provided very valuable research assistance for earlier versions of this chapter. Heather Sanderson was an assembly summer intern in 1988, and Jon Fielder wrote a paper for PSC 122, a political science class, at Syracuse University in the summer of 1988. Both did very helpful research.

1. Richard J. Meislin, "MTA Improvements Totaling $5 Billion Proposed by Carey," *New York Times,* March 3, 1981, p. A1.

2. Edward A. Gargan, "Koch Seeks Statewide Tax for MTA," *New York Times*, March 5, 1981, p. B3.

3. Richard J. Meislin, "Accord on MTA Plan Set by Carey, Koch, and Others," *New York Times*, March 6, 1981, p. B3.

4. Richard J. Meislin, "Senate Democrats Reject Carey Plan to Aid MTA," *New York Times*, March 11, 1981, p. B3.

5. Richard J. Meislin, "Koch proposed New Taxes as Alternative to Fare Rise," *New York Times*, March 17, 1981, p. B1.

6. Richard J. Meislin, "Carey and Koch Support a Regional Transit Tax," *New York Times*, March 19, 1981, p. B1.

7. Richard J. Meislin, "Carey Panel Urges 2 Tax Rises to Help MTA With Deficits," *New York Times*, June 5, 1981, p. A1.

8. Robin Herman, "Assembly Passes $5.6 Billion Plan for MTA Aid," *New York Times*, June 23, 1981, p. B2.

9. Richard J. Meislin, "Governor Proposes 3-Part Tax Program to Close MTA Gap," *New York Times*, June 27, 1981, p. A1.

10. Robin Herman, "Koch and Albany Leader Far Apart on Transit Tax," *New York Times*, June 29, 1981, p. B3.

11. Richard J. Meislin, "Fare 75 Cents; Transit Tax Plan Drawn in Albany," *New York Times*, July 3, 1981, p. A1.

12. Ibid.

13. Robin Herman, "Five Taxes Voted in Albany to Give Mass Transit Aid," *New York Times*, July 10, 1981, p. A1.

14. Erik Rhodes, "The Past, Present, and Future of the 1983 Rebuilding New York Bond Act: Where Do We Go From Here?" (Albany, NY: The New York State Assembly Intern Committee, 1988), p. 69.

15. James Brooke, "Bid for Money Begins in Plan to Keep Rebuilding Subways," *New York Times*, September 25, 1986, p. D27.

16. Jeffrey Schmalz, "Cuomo Panel Urges Increase in Gas Taxes and Bridge Tolls," *New York Times*, November 25, 1986, p. A1.

17. Jeffrey Schmalz, "G.O.P. Opposes Albany Gas Tax Rise," *New York Times*, December 13, 1986, p. A30.

18. Jeffrey Schmalz, "Cuomo Warns of MTA Fare Increase," *New York Times*, December 16, 1986, p. B10.

19. Bruce Lambert, "Fink Proposes a Vehicle Tax to Aid Transit," *New York Times*, December 17, 1986, p. B1.

20. Bruce Lambert, "GOP Blocks Tax Rise For Mass Transit," *New York Times*, December 19, 1986, p. B3.

21. Jeffrey Schmalz, "Temporary Plan Urged in Battle on Mass Transit," *New York Times*, December 22, 1986, p. B3.

22. Jeffrey Schmalz, "Pact Reached on Rebuilding Transit System," *New York Times*, December 23, 1986, p. B1.

23. Bruce Lambert, "Republican Objections Stall Adoption of Pact on Transit," *New York Times*, December 24, 1986, p. B3.

24. Jeffrey Schmalz, "Financing Plan for Transit Aid Voted in Albany," *New York Times*, December, 31, 1986, p. A1.

25. "State Senate Republicans Assail Transit Aid Plan," *New York Times*, January 22, 1987, p. B8.

26. Jeffrey Schmalz, "Transit Plan Deadlock: Politics Fuel City-Suburb Clash on Tax Increase," *New York Times*, February 9, 1987, p. B2.

27. Mark A. Uhlig, "Cuomo Plans Tax Shift to Raise Transit Funds," *New York Times*, February 12, 1987, p. B2.

28. Ibid.

29. Elizabeth Kolbert, "Automobile Tax Dropped from New MTA Proposal," *New York Times*, March 11, 1987, p. B2.

30. George A. Mitchell, ed., *The New York Red Book*, 19th ed., 1989–90, (Albany, NY: Williams Press, 1989), p. 997.

31. Sarah Lyall, "$16 Billion Prompts Fight in Albany," *New York Times*, May 25, 1992, p. 21.

32. Sam Howe Verhovek, "Albany Chiefs Agree in Full on Budget," *New York Times*, June 3, 1991, p. B1.

33. "Revitalizing Transportation," *New York State 1997–1998 Executive Budget*, p. 124.

34. *New York State 2004-05 Executive Budget*, (Albany: Office of the Governor), p. 403.

35. Tom Murnane, "Construction's Call for Help," *Empire State Report*, January 1996, p. 47.

36. *New York State 1997-1998 Executive Budget*, (Albany: Office of the Governor), appendix I, p. 321.

37. *New York State 2004-05 Executive Budget*, p. 403.

38. *Highway Bridge Replacement and Rehabilitation Program*, 1991, Tenth Report of the Secretary of Transportation, to the United States Congress, September, 1991; Iver Peterson, "New York Region Concludes: Don't Expand Transit; Fix It," *New York Times*, March 13, 1992, p. A1.

39. Bruce Bryant-Friedland, "Construction Conundrum," *Empire State Report*, July, 1995, p. 32.

40. Richard Perez-Pena, "Assembly Speaker Links Subway to Budget Vote," *The New York Times*, March 15, 2000, p. B1; Richard Perez-Pena, "M.T.A.'s Plan Spawns Warnings of Debt Crisis and Higher Fees," *New York Times*, April 2, 2000, p. A1.

41. Richard Perez-Pena, "M.T.A.'s Plan." Despite the failure of the bond issue, which was to provide partial funds for the M.T.A.'s $17.5 billion capital plan, the authority can still draw on tolls and fares, New York City and state funds, federal funds, its own bonds, debt restructuring, and other revenues. See http://www.mta.info/mta/budget/feb2004-finplan/feb2004-3.pdf.

42. Bryant-Friedland, "Construction conundrum," p. 32; Murnane, "Construction's Call for Help," p. 48.

CHAPTER 17

Environmental Policy in New York State

THOMAS A. BIRKLAND
with
Sean Madden
Jeffrey Mapes
Katheryn A. Roe
Amanda Stein

INTRODUCTION

Many people, when they think about the environment or environmental policy, think of wilderness areas in the American West, in Alaska, or perhaps in tropical rainforests and African savannahs. They may think of the animals that make the wilderness wild, such as moose, bears, and the many species of birds, reptiles, and fish that are not commonly seen in our cities and suburbs. And others may think about clean air, clean water, and the role that a healthy environment plays in promoting public health.

All of these components are important in the history of environmental policy in New York State. Nearly all the past and current environmental conflicts that have occurred in other states—ranging from the protection of wild areas to the need for clean (and cleaner) air and water—have also been important in New York environmental policy. New York has adopted many of the same policies to deal with these issues as have other states and the federal government, and, in fact, is an innovator in many areas of environmental policy.

This chapter is an introduction to environmental policy in New York, including illustrations of current issues and controversies in the state, with

391

several examples drawn from the environmental policy history of the Hudson River and Valley and the Adirondacks. We selected these regions because they are central to the history of the development of the state and of the United States, and because they remain important to the state's identity and quality of life today.

Environmental policy in New York is often controversial and contentious, for at least three reasons. First, environmental conflicts often involve clashes between different people with differing beliefs and values. The sanctity of private property often clashes with the importance of land as part of an interconnected and beneficial ecosystem. Second, interest groups have a great deal of influence in New York by reflecting and amplifying the deeply held beliefs of group members and sympathetic members of the public. People, groups, and governments often argue and sometimes compromise to create environmental policy that balances, at least in a political sense, various commercial, recreational, and environmental interests. Third, New York is characterized by a strong home-rule tradition that makes regional approaches to environmental problems difficult to achieve.

ENVIRONMENTALISM IN THE NATION AND IN NEW YORK

The environmental movements in the United States and in New York have influenced each other considerably. Costain and Lester divide the history of American environmental policy into four eras.[1] The first phase, from 1890 to 1920, is called the "Conservation-Efficiency Movement," which was led by early conservationists who sought to replace wasteful uses of natural resources with more rational and efficient management of natural resources for current and future generations. This utilitarian view of natural resources is most commonly associated with forester Gifford Pinchot, and was the basis of the multiple-use concept adopted by the U.S. Forest Service and the Bureau of Land Management. Well before Pinchot, however, George Perkins Marsh wrote, in his book *Man and Nature,* that human influences on the environment could ruin the natural order unless human action was taken to preserve and protect those environmental products and services on which humans depend. Marsh's work was very influential on New Yorkers such as Theodore Roosevelt, who was an early proponent of conservationism.

The second era (1920 to 1960) is the "Conservation-Preservation Movement" because this movement shifted environmental policy's focus from the use of natural resources for human needs toward preserving nature as a valuable resource for plant and animal habitat and for recreational and aesthetic uses. During this period, the Sierra Club, the National Wildlife Federation, and the Wilderness Society opposed private mining and logging interests that were oriented toward conservation and use of resources, rather than the preservation of nature for its own sake.

New York State was one of the states in which the conflicts between utilitarianism and preservation became clearest. The "forever kept wild" (more often called "forever wild") provision of the New York constitution (Article 14, section 1), enacted in 1892, requires that the state Forest Preserve, as defined in law, be kept as free as possible from development or human exploitation. This early preservationist policy was promoted by Verplanck Colvin, an Albany native who explored and mapped in great detail the high peaks of the Adirondacks. The "forever wild" clause is the only state constitutional protection of wild land in the United States, and led directly to the creation of the Adirondack Park in 1892 and the Adirondack Park Agency (APA) in 1971, encompassing over six million acres in public and private ownership. While the "forever wild" provision was intended to protect the wilderness from commercial exploitation, it was not until the early twentieth century that environmentally injurious logging practices forced the active enforcement of the "forever wild" clause. Greater enforcement was driven by environmental groups such as the Adirondack Mountain Club (ADK), founded in 1922, as well as greater public interest in the recreational value of the park and preserve.

Even with the "forever wild" clause, from the late 1800s to about 1960, New York's environmental policy was primarily characterized by Pinchot's "efficient use" ethic. Conservationism in this period was generally concerned with the wise use of natural resources for human purposes, such as recreation, drinking and irrigation water, water power, minerals, timber, and the like.[2] In New York, Robert Moses's efforts to expand parks and parkways and to exploit hydroelectric resources on the Niagara Frontier are examples of conservationist thinking, which, in the end, had numerous unintended environmental consequences.[3]

The third era, from 1960 to 1980, contains what we generally consider to be the height of the modern environmental movement, based on what Costain and Lester call "Pluralism in Policy Making." The seeds for this new era were sown by emerging state and national conflicts between preservationists and conservationists.

The modern environmental movement treats humans as part of an ecosystem: humans are both influenced by and influence the environment, which is a different understanding from the traditional notion of humans as stewards of resources that would be used in the future. Aldo Leopold's *Sand County Almanac* is an early expression of the values of the modern environmental movement.[4] Although Leopold's conservation philosophies were not largely embraced during his lifetime, he sought to instill the importance of a land ethic. The land ethic recognized the importance of understanding and maintaining natural ecological processes through wise ecological stewardship of the land, not just stewardship for the sake of human uses.

The environmental movement was further catapulted into mainstream consciousness by the publication of Rachel Carson's very influential book, *Silent Spring,*[5] which portrayed a natural world decimated by the overuse of pesticides and other chemicals. Interest groups also mobilized over environmental disasters including most notably the Santa Barbara Oil Spill in 1969, and by the near total degradation of Lake Erie, which became a national symbol of what one author has called "the criminal folly of humankind."[6] These events awakened the public to the various forms of damage that could be done to the earth through existing agricultural and industrial practices.

Soon after the first Earth Day on April 22, 1970, environmental issues became solidly mainstream political concerns. In the late 1960s and early 1970s, groups such as the Sierra Club and the Natural Resources Defense Council (NRDC) were remarkably successful in gaining the enactment of the 1969 National Environmental Policy Act (NEPA), which requires any major development project in which the federal government is somehow involved to prepare and issue an Environmental Impact Statement, or EIS. In 1970, President Nixon created the United States Environmental Protection Agency (EPA), and other milestones included the Endangered Species Act, the Clean Air Act, the Clean Water Act, and the Alaska National Interest Lands Conservation Act (ANILCA).

In New York during this era, important groups such as Environmental Advocates, Scenic Hudson, Hudson River Sloop Clearwater, and Hudson Riverkeeper were formed and became very visible and active. Many of these groups were founded to block the construction of the Storm King power plant in the Hudson Valley. This power plant, proposed by Consolidated Edison and approved in 1964 by the Federal Power Commission, would have pumped water from the Hudson River to an artificial lake on the top of Storm King Mountain during low-demand periods, and then the water would be released through turbines to generate power during the day, when power demands are higher.

Opponents to this project said that the power plant would scar the landscape, and later it was found that the water intakes and outflows could seriously injure fish stocks. A coalition called the Scenic Hudson Preservation Conference led the opposition to both the scenic and environmental impacts of the Storm King project. This group sought to block Storm King and at least six other plants along the river, both for aesthetic and ecological reasons. In December 1980, after a seventeen-year impasse, the utilities that owned the plants, the regulators, and environmental groups reached a historic settlement outlining steps to reduce environmental impacts of these power plants.[7] The Scenic Hudson Preservation Conference, now Scenic Hudson, Inc., remains an active opponent to major industrial development projects along the river and is a key proponent of the controversial cleanup of chemicals known as PCBs (chlorinated biphenyls) from the river.

Finally, the fourth era of environmentalism—called "Strong Democracy" or "Grassroots Environmentalism"—began around 1980. In particular, mainstream groups have been accused of failing to address environmental issues such as the environmental equity problem, in which facilities that create environmental hazards are located in poor or minority areas. Grassroots environmentalism, by contrast, is more a community-based, self-help form of activism that is often motivated by and oriented toward particular issues, such as the location of an industrial facility in a particular area, or on the basis of actual or perceived unfairness in terms of environmental costs and benefits.

Grassroots environmentalism may be less a reaction to mainstream environmentalism than it is a parallel strain of environmentalism that pursues similar goals while addressing those goals at a different scale using different organizations and tactics. But we do know that grassroots environmental groups are important because they raise local environmental concerns that are sometimes ignored by larger regional or national organizations, which are often more interested in broader policy areas. Grassroots environmentalism is not new in New York, for both large and grassroots organizations have roles to play in environmental policymaking.

ENVIRONMENTAL POLICY IN NEW YORK—SEQRA AND THE ENTRENCHMENT OF ENVIRONMENTAL CONSCIOUSNESS

The successful opposition to the Storm King power plant has often been cited as the key event in New York's recent environmental history, but as Paul

Bray argues, "the environmental era in New York State truly began in 1975 with the enactment of the State Environmental Quality Review Act (SEQRA)."[8] This law was the culmination of a decade of environmental group activity that began with the initial opposition to Storm King. SEQRA was one of a number of "little NEPAs"[9] enacted at the state level to provide state-level equivalents to the NEPA. Much like NEPA, SEQRA requires the development of an EIS that would disclose the nature and extent of expected environmental impacts.

SEQRA's impact and importance remain controversial. Even supporters of SEQRA argue that SEQRA is subject to legitimate criticism on both environmental and economic grounds.[10] But one can also argue that SEQRA has been a more important and useful tool for environmental policy than has been NEPA, because it provides a tool for local and grassroots groups to intervene in large development programs and requires the airing of environmental issues in a more public process than does NEPA.[11] However, while SEQRA outlines a set of criteria for project review, it does not spell out the conditions under which projects must be approved or rejected. Rather, these criteria are often site or project specific.

The primary value of SEQRA is the mandate requiring the use of a consistent project review process, and, in particular, a system of public participation. SEQRA has caused some projects to be scaled back; it has led to improvements in projects that would enhance various environmental values while inviting greater public participation (perhaps its most important legacy).

The efforts of environmental groups and the passage of SEQRA have been influential statewide. For example, with the expiration of the law governing the review of electric power plant siting and construction, known as "Article X," and the continued demand for electrical power in the state, power plant permitting must now go through the more lengthy SEQRA process. Indeed, Article X was intended to streamline power plant permitting, but now that it has expired, SEQRA has become a key tool for opponents of industrial development, and in particular, power plant development

The legacy of environmental activism, culminating in SEQRA, suggests that for nearly forty years, a large number of people have realized that the Great Lakes, the Adirondacks, the Catskills, and the Hudson River and its valley, among many places in New York, are important places worthy of protecting. This increased environmental activism has led to greater environmental consciousness, which is shown in relatively high levels of public support for measures to improve environmental quality.[12]

The success stories reflect the enduring network of people mobilized to address environmental issues in regions of New York. Simply put, this is not a "not in my back yard" (NIMBY) movement, and broader environmental concerns do influence public policy.

WHO MAKES ENVIRONMENTAL POLICY IN NEW YORK STATE?

Environmental policymaking is very complex, involving many actors. With this in mind, it is important to note two key features of policymaking. First, no one level or even branch of government is monolithic—one cannot say, for example, that the executive branches of the governments of the United States or of the State of New York speak with one voice on environmental policy matters. Second, the organizations and functions described here are similar at the state and federal levels. But this parallelism should not be construed to mean that the federal government controls the actions of the state, or that the state and federal governments share each other's goals. There is often considerable conflict in environmental policy and in what public administrators call intergovernmental relations relating to this policy.[13] (See chapter 2 for an analysis of political conflict and intergovernmental relations).

Executive Branch Agencies

The New York State Department of Environmental Conservation (DEC) was created in 1970 to assume the responsibilities and functions of previously existing bodies, including pesticide control, air pollution, and water pollution regulation. The DEC brought together many dispersed environmental agencies, much like the United States Environmental Protection Agency (EPA) did at the national level. However, neither the EPA nor the DEC assumes all the roles that one might presume would be in one environmental agency. In New York, the Office of Parks (now the Office of Parks, Recreation, and Historic Preservation) became an executive agency outside of DEC. Similarly, one might assume that the National Parks would fall under EPA, but they are actually part of the National Park Service, a unit of the United States Department of the Interior, which also includes the Bureau of Land Management.

Legislative Bodies

In the American system of government, the executive branch can issue regulations and orders, but these are grounded in legislation. Many legislators in both parties have developed a reputation for supporting proenvironment policies, but it is sometimes hard to determine how "proenvironment" a particular legislator may be. Some have become known as key advocates for more stringent environmental regulation. But other members will seek to balance environmental and developmental goals. But particularly in Northeastern states like New York, which have had dramatic examples of actual environmental degradation, few members of the legislature can afford to be staunchly prodevelopment and antienvironment, in marked contrast with some Western states, where these cleavages between environmentalism and development are much more pronounced.

Media

The news media can be influential in environmental policy in New York, but political scientists and students debate exactly how influential the news media are in ultimately affecting policy. We do know that the news media have an important agenda setting role, in which the news highlights environmental problems and controversies. (See chapter 6 for a discussion of media coverage of New York State politics.) Extensive media coverage of the Storm King controversy in the *New York Times* and local papers, the Love Canal contamination crisis by the *Buffalo News* and by national and regional media, and, in more recent years, the pollution of the Hudson River with PCBs, covered extensively by the *Albany Times-Union*, has raised public consciousness of these issues and has created a sense of urgency that might not have existed had these problems been not revealed in the first place. The mere attention to these issues is often enough to create dissatisfaction with these policies, and this dissatisfaction can often—but not always—yield policy change.

Environmental groups have long sought media attention to their cause, a tactic also adopted in more recent years by the interests that sometimes oppose some environmental actions. A recent example of this was the heated debate between General Electric (GE), which opposed dredging the upper Hudson

River to remove PCBs from the river, and the various environmental and downriver interests that support dredging. GE spent millions on an advertising campaign to block, or at least modify, any dredging plan that would require GE's extensive financial participation; these ads were generally ineffective in preventing the EPA from ordering a clean-up. The media was where most people learned of this debate, so the goal of the two sides was to gain media attention to their preferred interpretation of the PCB problem and its potential solutions. In this case, at least, news reporting may have overcome what monetary advantage GE had in running antidredging advertisements.

Private Sector

The private sector has long been concerned with environmental policy, because many of the activities of the private sector rely on natural resources either as factors of production or as means to achieve other ends, such as rivers as transportation routes. The early history of New York involved many extractive industries, such as mining, fishing, and logging. Indeed, the pace of logging and the damage it did was a reason for creating the Adirondack forest preserve.

The industrial sector has historically had an advantage in environmental debates because of the importance of business and industry to the state's economy. But since the 1970s, at least, the playing field has become more level under SEQRA, and the mainstreaming of environmentalism has induced industry to be attentive at some level to environmental concerns, particularly by considering citizens' and consumers' expressed concerns with environmental issues. However, one should not assume that the private sector is solely interested in resource extraction or that it intentionally causes environmental damage. In other words, the private sector is no more monolithic than government in its attitude toward environmental protection. Some industries, such as tourism, and more especially nature guiding, camping, bird watching, hiking, skiing, hunting, sport fishing, and white water rafting, rely on healthy ecosystems, and these industries will often oppose activities that purposefully or inadvertently damage ecosystems. Indeed, many companies in New York are models of national responsibility and are creating innovative solutions to the most pressing environmental problems of our day, such as the emerging fuel-cell industry in the capital district.

Interest Groups

Interest groups are fundamental to politics and society in the United States. During the explosion of interest-group growth in the 1960s, the number of national environmental groups also grew. At the same time, established groups, like the National Audubon Society and the Sierra Club, became more active, and many groups formed to deal with local or regional environmental issues rather than national issues.

New York plays a key role in this interest-group history. (For an analysis of interest-group politics in New York, see chapter 5). The Adirondack Mountain Club dates to 1922 and the major national environmental groups have activities in the state. In 1966, the Hudson River Fisherman's Association was formed in response to continued loss of fish and fishing areas due to industrial pollution.[14] Also in 1966, famed folk singer Pete Seeger began the process that culminated in the building of the sloop *Clearwater,* a wooden sailing ship used to highlight environmental problems on the river and educate the public about solutions to those problems. In 1983, the Hudson River Fisherman's Association changed its name to the Hudson Riverkeeper, recognizing that the riverkeeper was hired to lead efforts in investigating environmental damage, violations of state and federal law, and other threats to the river's environmental health. This group is now among the most vocal advocates for environmental causes on the river.

WHERE WE ARE TODAY:
WHAT IS ENVIRONMENTAL POLICY ABOUT?

As the preceding history suggests, environmental policy in New York involves a broad range of sometimes compatible and sometimes conflicting interests, needs, and preferences. Indeed, two or more people can call themselves "environmentalists" and find themselves adamantly opposed to the ideas and beliefs of other environmentalists. This may be because the term "environmentalist" indicates to many people a positive image of concern for the natural world, so that the term can mean many things to different people. This is because environmentalists of various backgrounds have assorted interests in preserving different types of environmental qualities. For example, those who wish to hike and camp (or use all-terrain vehicles or snowmobiles) in the Adirondacks may have a different vision of the environment than that held by those who wish to preserve delicate alpine ecosystems. The three major environmental groups on the Hudson River—Scenic Hudson, Riverkeeper, and Clearwater—provide another example of different approaches to environmental advocacy. While the groups have often coalesced over issues affecting the whole river, they have carved out their own distinct niches reflecting the environmental issues that initially spawned the groups. Scenic Hudson focuses on land acquisition and scenic preservation, Riverkeeper on fisheries issues and litigation, and Clearwater on education and public awareness.

The breadth of the range of issues and the conflict these issues suggest are apparent when we consider current important trends and issues in New York's environmental politics.

Urban Sprawl and "Smart Growth"

Urban sprawl in New York State and across the nation has emerged as a major threat to the environment. Urban sprawl poses problems because it encourages infrastructure, industry, retailing, and housing to spread over a wide area, resulting in greater reliance on automobiles for transportation. Increased development beyond the urban fringe often overruns forests and destroys wetlands, which in turn decreases biodiversity and destroys the beneficial functions of these ecosystems. Sprawl is also is associated with large parking areas and road surfaces that are impermeable to water, resulting in polluted stormwater.[15]

One way to minimize the impacts of urban sprawl is through "smart-growth" planning that promotes economic and environmental efficiency while improving local quality of life. Although attempts were made in the early and mid-1990s by the State of New York to reform comprehensive planning, no smart-growth proposals succeeded.[16] In 1999 diverse state, local, nonprofit, and private interests met at the First Annual New York State Smart Growth Conference in Albany to address urban sprawl and smart-growth issues. The following year Governor George Pataki issued a Quality Communities Executive Order (Executive Order 102, signed January 21, 2000), under which a State Task Force and Advisory Group would work to develop an agenda for addressing urban sprawl. The Task Force and the Advisory Group have been charged with making recommendations encouraging coordination of local and state agency planning, encouraging community revitalization and redevelopment, and creating community development strategies.

Meanwhile, the New York State DEC is a leader in implementing the Open Space Conservation Plan, under which over 394,000 acres in the state have been conserved within the past decade.[17] Many environmental groups view open-space conservation as an important tool for curbing urban sprawl. Funding from the Environmental Protection Fund and the Clean Water/Clean Air Bond Act funds ($378 million) have been used to establish and prioritize conservation priorities set forth by regional advisory committees and the Governor's Quality Communities Task Force to conserve open space, protect vital natural resources and habitats, create recreational opportunities, and enhance historic, cultural, and scenic resources throughout the state.

Brownfields

One of the most important environmental events in New York and U.S. history was the discovery of the heavily polluted area of Love Canal, near Buffalo. This and similar problems led to the enactment of the Comprehensive Environmental Response, Compensation, and Liability Act (CERCLA), also known as the federal Superfund program, which uses industry money to clean up such sites in exchange for avoiding expensive and time-consuming litigation over who is responsible for cleaning up contaminated sites. Many such sites are so badly polluted that they may never be able to be used again.

But, particularly in urban areas, some moderately polluted areas, known as "brownfields," could be put back to use by cleaning up the site and making it available for redevelopment. Brownfields are "real property, the expansion, redevelopment, or reuse of which may be complicated by the presence, or potential presence of a hazardous substance, pollutant, or contaminant." Such sites are found throughout New York State. Policies that seek to address the brownfields problem may help to improve environmental quality while at the same time encouraging the reuse of urban lands in areas already well served by existing infrastructure, thereby removing the existing taxpayer subsidy of sprawling development.

Most states have instituted Voluntary Brownfield Cleanup Programs to provide incentives to businesses to remedy smaller contaminated properties and to avoid a legal tangle that would stall cleanup and redevelopment efforts. New York State's program was enacted in 2003. Brownfield development is now being explored as an alternative to sprawling development in infrastructure-poor areas, while bringing economic growth to areas where industry moved to the suburbs.[18]

Energy and Clean Air

Clean air concerns have been an important issue in New York for many years. Before national air pollution legislation and regulation, many cities in New York had poor air quality. Since the 1970s, air quality has improved, but some cities are struggling with pollution as a result of growth. For example, the New York City metropolitan area has been prone to high levels of ozone in summer months. New York State has been making efforts to improve air quality by adopting California vehicle-emission standards for light vehicles in 1994, the toughest in the country. New York is also working to set the toughest emissions regulations in the country for power generation in-state and is encouraging the federal government to do the same.

In 1996 New York State passed Governor Pataki's Clean Water/Clean Air Bond Act, which provides "$230 million for state investment in clean technologies including clean fuel buses and cars, helping schools switch from coal-fired furnaces to cleaner fuel, and helping retain jobs at businesses that need to reduce air emissions."[19] The New York State Energy Research and Development Authority (NYSERDA) disburses some of these funds to municipalities and school districts to purchase clean-fuel buses. This and other programs have made NYSERDA one of the leading organizations for promoting less polluting forms of energy. Other energy programs related to the Clean Water/Clean Air Bond Act involve developing electric mail vehicles and installing systems at truck stops to provide heating, cooling, and electricity to truckers, thereby eliminating diesel engine idling, which reduces emissions and fuel consumption. NYSERDA has long encouraged using renewable energy sources such as solar power and wind energy.

In June of 2002 Governor Pataki released his energy plan for the state, which includes increasing renewable energy use from 10 percent currently to 15 percent by 2020, reducing greenhouse gas emissions 5 percent below 1990 levels by 2010, and 10 percent below 1990 levels by 2020; and, perhaps most controversially, encouraging the federal government to set higher Corporate Average Fuel Economy (CAFE) standards for motor vehicles.[20]

Among the most important air pollution problems in the state is acid rain, which has been particularly harmful to the Adirondacks. Acid rain generally results from the emissions from coal-burning power plants in the Midwest. To improve local air quality, these plants' smokestacks are very tall, and send sulfur dioxide and oxides of nitrogen (NOx) into the air. These pollutants travel to the northeastern United States, where they mix with moisture in the air to create acid rain. Acid rain can deteriorate the facades of stone buildings and statues, form sulfates (acidic particles) that can cause respiratory problems in humans, kill or stress trees and other vegetation, and kill aquatic organisms such as fish and plants in acidified lakes.[21] The New York State DEC has, with some success, put lime into some acidified Adirondack lakes to mitigate the effects of acid rain. Treated lakes are then stocked with brook trout and acidity levels are monitored.

New York State is currently seeking to reduce acid rain at its source by suing the federal government to enforce emissions standards on Midwestern and western New York power plants. Governor Pataki has also supported legislation to decrease allowable emissions and to allow the Long Island Power Authority to purchase and retire emission credits from the former Long Island Lighting Company (LILCO).

Clean Water

Remarkable strides have been made in water quality in New York over the past thirty years, thanks in large part to better sewage treatment, stricter permitting of pollution discharges, and increased public awareness. The Federal Water Pollution Control Act Amendments of 1972—later amended in 1977 and renamed the Clean Water Act (CWA)—called for the nation's waters to be "drinkable, fishable, and swimmable" by 1985. While many of the state's waters are in much better condition today, this goal has not been fully achieved. For example, while the Hudson River's overall water quality has improved considerably, and while one can enjoy swimming, boating, and some fishing in the river, some lingering effects from the river's toxic heritage can still be felt. PCBs remain in the sediment in certain stretches of the river and work their way up the food web. A particularly important commercial and recreational fish species, the striped bass, is not suitable for human consumption as it tends to contain high levels of PCBs, which, if eaten in sufficient quantities, may harm public health.[22] Yet some people, particularly in communities where fishing is an important part of their culture, continue to catch and eat the bass despite the health dangers.

An ongoing success story in the preservation of water quality in New York State is the agreement that protected New York City's drinking water supply in the Catskills. New York City water is considered among the best in the nation, a point of considerable civic pride.[23] However in the 1980s and 1990s, the EPA enacted stricter safe drinking water regulations mandating that large municipalities that draw drinking water from surface water sources, like the city's Catskill/Delaware Reservoir system, must provide filtration. The city faced the prospect of building a filtration plant that would cost at least $9 billion dollars, plus $300 million dollars annually to operate. Instead, New York City embarked on an ambitious plan to avoid filtration and work with communities in the Catskills to help protect the water at its source. This plan culminated in a January 1997 agreement that focused on watershed management rather than treatment as a tool to protect the city's drinking water supply and convinced the EPA to grant the city a waiver from the filtration requirement.

Rather than spend $9 billion dollars on filtration, the city invested over $1 billion dollars in upstate communities. The money went toward purchasing land around the reservoirs and source streams, as well as incentive programs for farmers and residents to deal with the threats to the watershed: agricultural runoff, failing septic systems, and encroaching development.[24] The plan sought to strike a balance between downstate needs for clean water and upstate desires for economic growth. Many praised the agreement as a landmark in joining upstate and downstate interests and as a model for the compatibility between watershed management and sustainable growth, but some citizens of the Catskill towns that were most affected by the watershed regulations still question whether the agreement was the win/win situation New York City claims it to be. They argue that the city gets its clean water at the cost of limited upstate economic development.[25] In addition, New York City's filtration avoidance is tenuous at best and could be revoked if EPA review deems that watershed management measures have failed. But so far, the agreement between New York City and the Catskills is a precedent in watershed management and has been a success. Whether management alone will be able to curb the negative effects of continued growth on drinking water, or if filtration is inevitable, remains to be seen.

Species Diversity and Ecosystem Function

From molds to moose, thousands of species, as catalogued by the New York State Museum's Biodiversity Research Institute and the New York Natural Heritage Program, coexist and evolve, enriching the landscapes in which we live. Biodiversity is defined as the variety of species living together within an ecosystem. Healthy and biologically diverse ecosystems are needed to provide vital ecological functions and natural products upon which humans depend. Invaluable and irreplaceable services such as flood control and water purification, and nutrient recycling and food and fuel, and even the air we breathe, are produced in natural ecosystems. Ecosystems in New York face threats including habitat destruction, invasive species, pollution, land use change, overconsumption, and climate change.

New York State has recently organized a collaborative effort to protect its more than two hundred different ecosystems. In December 1999, the New York State Biodiversity Project was established by several environmental groups and state agencies to maintain and preserve the state's species and ecosystems.[26] The goals of the project are to assess the current biodiversity of the state, identify information gaps and needs, interpret and disseminate biodiversity information, prioritize future conservation actions, and emphasize collaborations with other relevant agencies and parties.

Local and state land managers, educators, business representatives, planners, and policymakers have been called upon to develop a statewide needs assessment to determine how best to provide accessible biodiversity information. Future goals of the project are to create a web-accessible biodiversity database clearinghouse, summarize the current status of particular species within the state, create a publication addressing species status and research needs, and provide outreach and education about the biodiversity of the state's ecosystems.[27]

CONCLUSION

While environmental policy has demonstrated considerable success since the 1960s, New York continues to face very real environmental challenges. These challenges affect those who seek stringent protection of key natural resources, as well as those who perceive such strictures as barriers to economic growth and development. Much of the human development of places like Long Island, the Hudson Valley, the Adirondacks, and western New York exists due to the unique nature, location, scenery, and environment of these places, coupled with outstanding human capital. Over seventeen million people live in New York State, and they often cluster in the most desirable areas to live, such as along the Long Island Shore, the Hudson Valley, or in the Finger Lakes region; many of these residents treasure the very things that make these areas desirable places to live. Paradoxically, their desire for the jobs, conveniences, and amenities that make modern life attractive may threaten the very amenities that that people value in these areas. The challenge will be in balancing these interests to allow people to enjoy the fruits of economic activity, while at the same time preserving the important social, cultural, and environmental features of the world-famous areas of our state. This is a challenge that will not easily be met, but the history of people working together in New York to address these issues continues to suggest that New Yorkers can successfully address these challenges.

NOTES

1. W. Douglas Costain and James P. Lester, "The Evolution of Environmentalism," in *Environmental Politics and Policy: Theories and Evidence*, ed. James P. Lester (Durham, NC: Duke University Press, 1995).

2. Zachary A. Smith, *The Environmental Policy Paradox*, 3rd ed. (Englewood Cliffs, NJ: Prentice-Hall, 1999).

3. Robert Caro, *The Power Broker: Robert Moses and the Fall of New York* (New York: Vintage Books, 1974).

4. Aldo Leopold, *A Sand County Almanac, and Sketches Here and There* (New York: Oxford University Press, 1949).

5. Rachel Carson, *Silent Spring* (Greenwich, CT: Fawcett, 1962).

6. Walter Stewart, "A Late Great Lake?" *Canadian Geographic* 123, no. 5 (2003): 36–42; Peter Annin and Sharon Begley, "Great Lake Effect," *Newsweek*, July 5 1999, pp. 52–54.

7. Ross Sandler, "Law: Settlement of Storm King," *Environment* 23, no. 1 (1981): 5–6.

8. Paul M. Bray, Twenty Fifth Anniversary of SEQRA, *Eye from Albany*, http://www.braypapers.com/52000EOA.html; Albany Law Review, "Discussion: The Historical Development of SEQRA," *Albany Law Review* 65 (2001): 323–350.

9. Chester L. Mirsky and David Porter, "Ambushing the Public: The Sociopolitical and Legal Consequences of SEQRA Decision-Making," *Albany Law Environmental Outlook* 6 (2002): 1–25.

10. Bray, "Twenty Fifth Anniversary of SEQRA"; Arthur Ientilucci, "SEQRA: Down the Garden Path or Detour for Development?" *Albany Law Environmental Outlook* 6 (2002): 102–124; Mirsky and Porter, "Ambushing the Public."

11. Ibid., p. 43.

12. Nancy A. Connelly and Barbara A. Knuth, "Using the Coorientation Model to Compare Community Leaders' and Local Residents' Views About Hudson River Ecosystem Restoration, " *Society and Natural Resources* 15, no. 10 (2002): 933–948.

13. Because our expertise is not in environmental law, we do not consider the judicial branch in this chapter, but by our omission we do not mean to suggest that this branch has no role in environmental policy. The federal courts, in particular, have been very active in enforcing and interpreting environmental policy.

14. Roger Rosenblatt, "Let Rivers Run Deep: A Forceful Band of Activists Fights to Protect the World's Waterways from Being Polluted and Exploited," *Time*, August 21, 1999, p. 74. See also Riverkeeper, *The Riverkeeper Story* (2002), http://riverkeeper.org/ourstory_history.php.

15. Gary S. Kleppel, "Urbanization and Environmental Quality: Implications of Alternative Development Scenarios," *Albany Law Environmental Outlook* 8 (2002): 37–51.

16. American Planning Association. Research/Growing Smart/New York, http://www.planning.org/growingsmart/States/newyork.htm.

17. New York State Department of Environmental Conservation, "New York State Open Space Conservation Plan," (Albany, NY: Department of Environmental Protection), http://www.dec.state.ny.us/website/opensp/.

18. For more information on the brownfields issue see Michael Greenburg, "Should Housing Be Built on Former Brownfield Sites?" *American Journal of Public Health* 92, no. 5 (2002): 703–705; L. Cheryl Runyon and Larry Morandi, "Liability Protections to Promote Brownfields Redevelopment," *NCSL State Legislative Report* 28, no. 14 (2003); United States General Accounting Office, *Superfund Program: Current Status and Future Fiscal Challenges*, (Washington, D.C.: General Accounting Office, 2003).

19. See New York Department of Environmental Conservation, "About the Bond Act," http://www.dec.state.ny.us/website/bondact/index.html.

20. Various sections of the energy plan are available as separate documents from http://www.nyserda.org/sep.html (accessed February 6, 2004).

21 United States Environmental Protection Agency, "Effects of Acid Rain," http://www.epa.gov/acidrain/effects/index.html.

22. United States Environmental Protection Agency, "Polychlorinated Biphenyls (Pcbs)," http://www.epa.gov/opptintr/pcb/effects.html.

23. Diane Galusha, *Liquid Assets: A History of New York City's Water System* (Fleischmanns, NY: Purple Mountain Press, 1999).

24. Catskill Watershed Corporation (CWC). Catskill Watershed Corporation homepage, http://www.cwconline.org.

25. Galusha, *Liquid Assets.*

26. The Biodiversity Partnership, New York State Biodiversity Project. http://www.biodiversitypartners.org/US/NY.html.

27. Environmental Law Institute, *Sustainability and Resource Protection Programs: State Biodiversity Program,* http://www.eli.org/research/statebiodiversity/NYSbiodiversityeffort.htm.

CHAPTER 18

Guide to Research on New York Politics

SARAH F. LIEBSCHUTZ

There are many sources of information available for the study of New York state politics and government. This chapter lists a number of them, including bibliographies, themselves useful in discovering additional sources. Both published and electronic resources are contained in the following listings.

GENERAL RESOURCES

Libraries provide the best starting point for research. New York State has a large number of both public and university libraries that can be easily accessed. The New York State Library, founded in 1818 in Albany, holds the largest collection of official state documents and many other sources of information on state government and politics. The state library also distributes copies of documents to approximately two hundred other libraries throughout the state and beyond.

An additional source of original documents is the New York State Archives, also in Albany. The Archives has copies of many records and has published the *Guide to the New York State Archives* (1981) to assist those who wish to search for specific records.

411

Internet Resources

The state library's document retrieval system on the Internet at
http://www.gopher://unix2.nysed.gov/ is an extremely useful resource. The
gopher provides access to:

- the Full Texts of State Library publications, including bibliographies and education law excerpts;
- the Checklist of New York State Documents—sorted by year
  from 1992 to the present;
- the New York State Information Locator, with lists of state
  agencies and services and connections to other governmental
  Internet resources; and
- the Full Texts of state government publications, including
  reports of the comptroller, public service commission, and the
  department of housing and community renewal.

Through its link to other governmental Internet resources, the Information
Locator provides access to current census information and materials about
state and local government projects.

New York State also has a home page on the Internet at
http://www.state.ny.us/ny. It is designed to provide the public with information about the Empire State. Topics include the governor, tourism, economic
development, citizens' access to state government, associations, and a search
index. The search index provides the opportunity to search a large database
of information using a basic keyword query system. While the Home Page
has some general use, the state library's gopher system is more useful for doc-
umentation, transcripts, and archived records.

Newspapers and Journals

Newspapers can provide excellent information for research. The *New York
Times* features regular coverage of state politics and is indexed by subject
matter to make finding references easier. Many libraries will have this news-
paper on microfilm. Several other large city newspapers such as the *Times
Union* in Albany, the *Buffalo News, Long Island Newsday,* the *Daily News* in
New York City, the *Democrat and Chronicle* in Rochester, and the Syracuse

Post-Standard provide information on state politics. These can be found at libraries as well, but usually on a more regional basis.

The principal journal dealing with New York politics and government is *Empire State Report*. Published monthly, it deals with current state policy issues, changes to laws, important figures in the state and other related topics. Magazines such as the *New Yorker*, and *New York* are useful sources of information on cultural aspects of life, particularly in New York City.

Other Sources of Information

Basic data on the state can be found in the *New York Statistical Yearbook* (Albany, NY: Rockefeller Institute of Government). It is published annually and contains current economic, population, election, and financial data for the state. *The New York Red Book* (Albany, NY: New York Legal Publishing), published and updated biennially, is a guide to the organization of state government: its departments, personnel, and the basic duties carried out by each unit of the government. It includes biographies of state office holders. The state university system and various state authorities and commissions are discussed as well. *The New York Gazetteer* (Wilmington, DE: American Historical Publications, 1983) is a directory of basic reference data as well as a listing of places of historical interest in the state. It also includes a biographical index of important people in state history.

Research centers that deal with New York state politics and government include the Nelson A. Rockefeller Institute of Government at the State University of New York at Albany. Established in 1982, the Rockefeller Institute publishes newsletters, reports, and papers dealing with a variety of public policy issues and conducts conferences on topics related to state and local government. Further information can be obtained at the institute's website (http://rockinst.org) or by contacting the Institute at 411 State St., Albany, NY, 12203, (518) 443–5522. The Edwin F. Jaeckle Center for State and Local Government Law at the State University of New York at Buffalo focuses on the legal structure of state and local government, problems encountered in the administration of municipal laws, and efforts to reform state and local laws. The Jaeckle Center publishes papers and sponsors conferences for local government officials and lawyers. The Center can be contacted at O'Brian Hall, Amherst Campus, Buffalo, NY, 14260, (716) 636–2052. The Center for Governmental Research is a nonpartisan

corporation based in Rochester that compiles and analyzes statistics to evaluate state and local government programs. The center has published studies
of various programs and their impact on local governments. Information
can be obtained at the center's website (http://www.cgr.org) or at 37 South
Washington St., Rochester, NY, 14608, (716) 325–6360. The Center for
the Study of Business and Government at the Bernard Baruch College of
City University of New York, 17 Lexington Ave., P.O. Box 348A, New
York, NY, 10010, (212) 505– 5902, was established in 1978 to analyze the
relationship between business and government and the effects that government policies have on the business world. The center's studies focus on the
effect of programs and policies on New York State or New York City business concerns.

Public opinion surveys are conducted about New York State by two
organizations. The Marist Institute for Public Opinion at Marist College in
Poughkeepsie regularly conducts polls about state issues. The institute is an
independent, nonprofit survey and research center focusing on studies of
voting behavior and electoral research. Their polls can be accessed at
http://www.maristpoll.marist.edu/. Quinnipiac College also conducts
statewide polls. Their website is http://www.quinnipiac.edu/x11358.xml.

Election data are made available by the State Board of Elections. Their
website can be found at http://www.elections.state.ny.us/. Established in
1974, the Elections Board is responsible for the administration and enforcement of election laws. It monitors campaign finances and practices, provides
assistance to local election boards, and investigates complaints concerning
election procedures. The Elections Board can be contacted at P.O. Box 4,
One Commerce Plaza, Albany, NY, 12260. The *New York Red Book* contains
a listing of current members of the Board of Elections as well as election
results. Each county in the state has its own board of elections. Addresses and
names of current chairpersons are listed in the *New York Red Book*.

STATE GOVERNMENT DOCUMENTS

The New York State Library has developed several excellent publications that
can be used to locate documents issued by and concerning state politics and
government. *New York State Documents: An Introductory Manual* (Albany,
NY: University of the State of New York, State Education Department, New
York State Library, Cultural Education Center, 1987) and *Official Publica-*

tions of New York State: A Bibliographic Guide to Their Use (Albany, NY: University of the State of New York, State Education Department, New York State Library, Cultural Education Center, 1981) provide extensive listings of available documents as well as suggestions to assist in locating them. The *Checklist of Official Publications of the State of New York* (Albany, NY: New York State Library, 1947–, vol. 1–) is issued monthly by the state library and lists all publications by state agencies.

Several sources provide information on the legislative process. The *Journal of the Assembly of the State of New York* and the *Journal of the Senate of the State of New York* are compiled annually and provide daily records of activity for each body, including floor proceedings, amendments, confirmation hearings, and voting records. The *Manual for the Use of the Legislature of the State of New York* (Albany, NY: Division of Information Services, Department of State, 1840–) is published biennially and contains information pertaining to the members of the legislature and their staffs such as committee assignments, voting statistics, and party strength and leadership. The *Legislative Digest* (Albany, NY: New York Legislative Bill Drafting Commission) is an account of all bills introduced and action taken on previous bills. An annual summary of the progress of all bills is also available. The *Majority Leader's Report* (Albany, NY: New York State Assembly, Office of the Majority Leader) is an annual account of the activities of the legislature from the perspective of the majority leader.

The executive branch produces numerous documents as well. The governor's office issues *Messages to the Legislature* (Albany, NY: Office of the Governor, 1777–) and *The Executive Budget* (Albany, NY: Office of the Governor, 1928–). Reports issued by executive departments include those of the Office of the State Comptroller (for example, the annual *Comptroller's Special Report on Municipal Affairs*, and the *Comptroller's Report on the Financial Condition of New York State*, 1996), the *Annual Report of the Attorney General* (Albany, NY: Department of Law, 1890–), and the *Annual Report of the Secretary of State* (1919–).

The Local Government Handbook (Albany, NY: State of New York, Department of State, 1975–) is the best single source for information on the structural and functional features of local governments in the state and their relations to the state government. The Department of State has produced various newsletters such as *State and Local* (Albany, NY: New York State Department of State, Division of Information Services, 1983–1988) dealing with general topics concerning state government, and *Excelsior* (Albany, NY:

New York State Department of State, Division of Information Services, 1988–), presenting various viewpoints on specific state issues.

The body of New York state laws and judicial proceedings can be found in publications such as *McKinney's Laws of New York Annotated* (St. Paul, MN: West Publishing, 1943–) and *West's New York Digest* (St. Paul, MN: West Publishing), which are updated and supplemented as changes occur. Selected opinions of the court of appeals, appellate divisions and lower courts of the first and second judicial departments are published in the *New York Law Journal* (1888–).

One of the best sources of information on the New York State government is an internship in the legislature or an executive branch agency. Semester-long assembly and senate internship programs provide superior firsthand experiences for undergraduate and graduate students. Contact points for assembly and senate internships, respectively, are: (518) 455-4704 and (518) 432-5470. Comparable experiences in a wide variety of executive branch agencies are available through the Albany Semester Program (518) 485-5964.

TOPICAL BIBLIOGRAPHY

Numerous sources, useful for future study of New York state government and politics, are cited in each chapter. Rather than repeat each listing, the following is a group of selected sources, arranged by topic area, beginning with general works.

General Works

Bahl, Roy, and William Duncombe. *Economic Growth and Fiscal Planning: New York in the 1990s.* New Brunswick, NJ: Center for Urban Policy Research, 1991.

Caldwell, Lynton K. *The Government and Administration of New York.* New York: Thomas Y. Crowell, 1954.

League of Women Voters of New York State. *New York State, A Citizen's Handbook.* New York: League of Women Voters of New York State, 1979.

Liebschutz, Sarah F., with Robert W. Bailey, Jeffrey M. Stonecash, Jane Shapiro Zacek, and Joseph F. Zimmerman. *New York Politics and*

Government: Competition and Compassion. Lincoln, NE: University of Nebraska Press, 1998.

Moscow, Warren. *Politics in the Empire State.* New York: A. A. Knopf, 1948.

Munger, Frank J., and Ralph A. Straitz. *New York Politics.* New York: New York University Press, 1960.

State of New York Management Resources Projects. *Governing the Empire State: An Insider's Guide.* Albany, NY: State of New York Management Resources Project, 1988.

Stonecash, Jeffrey, John K. White, and Peter W. Colby. *Governing New York State,* 3rd. ed. Albany, NY: State University of New York Press, third edition, 1994.

Stonecash, Jeffrey. *Governing New York State,* 4th ed. Albany, NY: State University of New York Press, 2001.

Zimmerman, Joseph. *The Government and Politics of New York State.* New York: New York University Press, 1981.

The State Constitution

Benjamin, Gerald, and Henrik N. Dullea. *Decision 1997: Constitutional Change in New York.* Albany, NY: Rockefeller Institute Press, 1997.

Dullea, Henrick N. *Charter Revision in the Empire State: The Politics of New York's 1967 Constitutional Convention.* Albany, NY: Rockefeller Institute Press, 1997.

Gallie, Peter J. *Ordered Liberty: A Constitutional History of New York.* New York: Fordham University Press, 1996.

Schick, Thomas. *The New York State Constitutional Convention of 1915 and the Modern State Government.* New York: National Municipal League, 1979.

Federal Government Relations

Elazar, Daniel J. *American Federalism: A View from the States.* 3rd ed. New York: Harper & Row, 1984.

Liebschutz, Sarah F. *Bargaining Under Federalism: Contemporary New York* Albany, NY: State University of New York Press, 1991.

———. *Federal Aid to Rochester.* Washington, D.C.: Brookings Institution, 1984.

Liebschutz, Sarah F., and Irene Lurie. "New York." In *Reagan and the States*, ed. Richard P. Nathan. Princeton, NJ: Princeton University Press, 1987.

Moynihan, Daniel P. *Came the Revolution: Arguments in the Reagan Era.* New York: Harcourt, Brace, Jovanovich, 1988.

Peirce, Neal R. *The Megastates of America.* New York: W.W. Norton, 1972.

Schechter, Stephen L., ed. *The Reluctant Pillar: New York and the Adoption of the Federal Constitution.* Troy, NY: Russell Sage College, 1985.

Schechter, Stephen L., and Richard B. Bernstein, eds. *New York and the Union.* Albany: New York State Commission on the Bicentennial of the United States Constitution, 1990.

History

Alexander, DeAlva Stanwood. *A Political History of the State of New York.* Port Washington, NY: I. J. Friedman, 1969.

Caro, Robert. *The Power Broker.* New York: Knopf, 1974.

Ellis, David M. *New York State and City.* Ithaca, NY: Cornell University Press, 1979.

Ellis, David M., James A. Frost, Harold C. Syrett, and Harry J. Carman. *A Short History of New York State.* Ithaca, NY: Cornell University Press, 1967.

Flick, Alexander C., ed. *History of the State of New York.* New York: Columbia University Press, 1933–37.

Tripp, Wendell. *Coming and Becoming: Pluralism in New York State History.* Cooperstown, NY: New York State Historical Association, 1991.

Trover, Ellen Lloyd, ed. *New York: A Chronology and Documentary Handbook.* New York: Oceana Publications, 1978.

The Legislature

Berle, Peter A. *Does the Citizen Stand a Chance? The Politics of a State Legislature: New York.* Woodbury, NY: Barron's Educational Series, 1974.

Calicehia, Marcia, and Ellen Sadowski. *The Lobbying Handbook: A Guide to Effective Lobbying in New York State.* Albany, NY: New York State School of Industrial and Labor Relations, Cornell University, 1984.

Chamberlain, Lawrence H. *Loyalty and Legislative Action: A Survey of Activity by the New York State Legislature 1919–1949.* Ithaca, NY: Cornell University Press, 1951.

Hevesi, Alan G. *Legislative Politics in New York State: A Comparative Analysis* New York: Praeger, 1975.

Pecorella, Robert F. *Guide to the New York State Legislature.* Rev. ed. Albany, NY: Assembly Intern Committee, New York State Assembly, 1998.

Ruchelman, Leonard I. *Political Careers: Recruitment Through the Legislature.* Rutherford, NJ: Fairleigh Dickinson University Press, 1970.

The Judicial System

Gibson, Ellen M. *New York Legal Research Guide.* Buffalo, NY: W. S. Hein, 1988.

Klein, Fannie J. *Federal and State Court Systems: A Guide.* Cambridge, MA: Ballinger, 1977.

MacCrate, Robert, James D. Hopkins, and Maurice Rosenberg. *Appellate Justice in New York.* Chicago: American Judicature Society, 1982.

The Executive

Bellush, Bernard. *Franklin D. Roosevelt as Governor of New York.* New York: AMS Press, 1968.

Chessman, G. Wallace. *Governor Theodore Roosevelt: The Albany Apprenticeship 1898–1900.* Cambridge, MA: Harvard University Press, 1965.

Cole, Donald B. *Martin Van Buren and the American Political System.* Princeton, NJ: Princeton University Press, 1984.

Connery, Robert H., and Gerald Benjamin. *Rockefeller of New York: Executive Power in the Statehouse.* Ithaca, NY: Cornell University Press, 1979.

Cuomo, Mario M. *Diaries of Mario Cuomo: The Campaign for Governor.* New York: Random House, 1984.

Davis, Kenneth S. *FDR: The New York Years 1928–1933.* New York: Random House, 1979.

Eldot, Paula. *Governor Alfred E. Smith: The Politician as Reformer.* New York: Garland, 1983.

Flick, Alexander C. *Samuel Jones Tilden: A Study in Political Sagacity.* Port Washington, NY: Kennikat Press, 1939.

Kramer, Daniel C. *The Days of Wine and Roses Are Over: Governor Hugh Carey and New York State.* Lanaham, MD: University Press of America, 1997.

McElroy, Robert. *Grover Cleveland: The Man and the Statesman.* New York: Harper and Brothers, 1923.

McElvaine, Robert S. *Mario Cuomo: A Biography.* New York: Scribners, 1988.

Mitchell, Stewart. *Horatio Seymour of New York.* New York: DaCapo Press, 1970.

Prescott, Frank W. and Joseph Zimmerman. *Politics of the Veto of Legislation in New York.* Washington, DC: University Press of America, 1980.

Rosen, Hy, and Peter Slocum. *From Rocky to Pataki: Character and Caricatures in New York Politics.* Syracuse, NY: Syracuse University Press, 1998.

Wesser, Robert F. *Charles Evans Hughes: Politics and Reform in New York 1905–1910.* Ithaca, NY: Cornell University Press, 1967.

Political Parties and Interest Groups

Benenson, Bob. "Wake Up Call: Politics Resurge Big and Bold Across the State." *Congressional Quarterly Weekly Report* 50 September 5 1992): 2638–46.

Kass, Alvin. *Politics in New York State 1800–1830.* Syracuse, NY: Syracuse University Press, 1965.

Scarrow, Howard A. *Parties, Elections, and Representation in the State of New York.* New York: New York University Press, 1983.

Zeller, Belle. *Pressure Politics in New York: A Study of Group Representation Before the Legislature.* New York: Prentice-Hall, 1937.

New York City

Arian, Asher. *Changing New York City Politics.* New York: Routledge, 1991.

Auletta, Ken. *The Streets Were Paved With Gold.* New York: Random House, 1979.

Bailey, Robert W. *The Crisis Regime: The M.A.C., the E.F.C.B., and the Political Impact of the New York City Financial Crisis.* Albany: State University of New York Press, 1984.

Benjamin, Gerald, and Charles Brecher, eds. *The Two New Yorks: State City Relations in the Changing Federal System.* New York: Russell Sage Foundation, 1988.

Brecher, Charles, and Raymond D. Horton. *Power Failure: New York City Politics and Policy since 1960.* New York: Oxford University Press, 1993.

Brecher, Charles, and Raymond D. Horton, eds. *Setting Municipal Priorities: American Cities and the New York Experience.* New York: New York University Press, 1984.

Fuchs, Ester. *Mayors and Money: Fiscal Policy in New York and Chicago.* Chicago: University of Chicago Press, 1993.

Mauro, Frank, and Gerald Benjamin. *Reconstructing the New York City Government: The Reemergence of Municipal Reform.* New York: Academy of Political Science, 1989.

Mollenkopf, John H., and Manuel Castells, eds. *Dual City: Restructuring New York.* New York: Russell Sage Foundation, 1991.

Riordan, William. *Plunkitt of Tammany Hall.* New York: Dutton, 1963.

Sassen, Saskia. *Global City: New York, London, Tokyo.* Princeton, NJ: Princeton University Press, 1991.

Sayre, Wallace S., and Herbert Kaufman. *Governing New York City.* New York: Russell Sage Foundation, 1960.

Local Government

Frederickson, H. George. *Power, Public Opinion, and Policy in a Metropolitan Community: A Case Study of Syracuse, New York.* New York: Praeger, 1973.

Kennedy, William. *O Albany!* New York: Viking Press, 1983.

Miller, Robert H. *Politics Is People.* New York: James H. Heineman, 1962.

New York State Department of State. *An Introduction to Local Government In New York State.* Albany, NY: New York State Department of State, Division of Information Services, 1985.

NOTE

This is a revised version of a chapter that originally appeared in Sarah Liebschutz, *New York Politics and Government* (Lincoln: University of Nebraska Press, 1998), pp. 179–187.

Contributors

Gerald Benjamin is dean of the College of Arts and Sciences and Distinguished professor of political science at the State University College at New Paltz. He was formerly director of the Center for the New York State and Local Government Studies at SUNY's Rockefeller Institute of Government in Albany, and between May of 1993 and March of 1995, he served as research director of New York's Temporary State Commission on Constitutional Revision. He holds a doctorate in political science from Columbia University and, alone or with others, has written or edited fourteen books and numerous government reports and articles, most of them on state and local government in New York.

Elizabeth Benjamin is the Albany *Times Union*'s political writer. She was the paper's lead reporter for the 2002 governors race, and is now gearing up for a perfect storm of races in 2006 when one of New York's U.S. Senate seats, the governor and lieutenant governor's offices, the state attorney general post and the state comptroller's office—not to mention all 212 legislative seats—will be up for election. Benjamin is one of three reporters covering the state Capitol for the *Times Union*. She has held that job for almost five years. Benjamin was hired by the *Times Union* in 1997 after graduating from Columbia University's School of Journalism. Since then, she has covered town, city and state government. Benjamin also holds a bachelor's degree from University of Rochester. She grew up in New Paltz, NY and is the daughter of Gerald Benjamin.

Thomas A. Birkland is an associate professor of Public Administration and Policy and Political Science in the Nelson A. Rockefeller College of Public Affairs at the University at Albany, State University of New York. He directs the Center for Policy Research. His research focuses on environmental and industrial disasters and crises, and he is the author of *After Disaster* (George-

423

town University Press, 1997), as well as a number of articles on environmental and natural hazards policies. He also codirects the University's graduate program in Biodiversity and Conservation Policy.

Donald J. Boyd is the director of the Fiscal Studies Program at the Rockefeller Institute of Government, the public policy research arm of the State University of New York. His past positions include director of the economic and revenue staff for New York State's budget office, and director of the tax staff for the New York State Assembly Ways and Means Committee. He is also deputy director of the Center for Policy Research at the University at Albany, where he focuses on research relating to education issues and teacher labor markets. Boyd holds a Ph.D. in Managerial Economics from Rensselaer Polytechnic Institute in Troy, NY.

Thomas W. Church is professor of political science and public policy at the University at Albany, State University of New York. He received his Ph.D. in Government from Cornell University and has worked in academic and research settings and as a court administrator in the federal courts of the Ninth Circuit. He has written extensively on issues of judicial administration, court processes and, more recently, on environmental policy.

Keith M. Henderson is professor of political science at the State University of New York College at Buffalo. He worked for the City of Los Angeles for five years, most recently as field deputy, Los Angeles City Council. He has published over forty books and articles in the field and has received two Fulbright Senior Lecturing awards (Iran, 1975–1976l Croatia, 1998–1999). He is president of the Fulbright Association of Western New York and Northwestern Pennsylvania and Secretary-Treasurer of the Western New York Chapter, American Society for Public Administration.

Rogan T. Kersh is associate professor of political science and public administration at the Maxwell School, Syracuse University. He has published on a variety of topics in American politics and political theory, including several studies on lobbying. He also has extensive practical experience, including working with a federal tax-lobbying firm in Washington.

Jeffrey Kraus is professor of political science at Wagner College. He received his Ph.D. in political science from the Graduate School of the City University of New York. He is a contributor to the *Encyclopedia of New York State* (2005), *Affirmative Action: An Encyclopedia of History, Politics, Culture and the Law* (2002), *The Encyclopedia of Third Parties in America* (2000), *We Get What We Vote For . . . Or Do We? The Impact of Elections on Governing* (1999), and *Contemporary Problems in Sociology* (1989). He has published articles in *The Forum, Politics and Policy, Commonwealth,* the *Journal of Urban Affairs,* and (with Bertram M. Gross) *Social Policy.* Since 2001 he has been chairperson of the New York City Voter Assistance Commission.

Sarah F. Liebschutz is distinguished service professor emeritus of the State University of New York, where she was a member of the political science faculty at SUNY College at Brockport from 1970 to 1997. She is currently adjunct professor of political science at the University of Rochester. She specializes in American intergovernmental relations. She is author or editor of four books: *Managing Welfare Reform* (2000); *New York Politics and Government: Competition and Compassion* (1992); *Bargaining Under Federalism* (1991); and *Federal Aid to Rochester* (1984), and numerous monographs for New York State and United States government agencies, articles, and book chapters.

Stephanie Lundquist is currently a Ph.D. candidate in the department of political science in the Maxwell School at Syracuse University. She received an M.A. in public administration from Syracuse University and a bachelor's degree from Michigan State University. Her research interests include partisan differences between urban and rural areas in the United States, the effects of public policy on citizenship and gender and American politics.

Sean Madden is a student in the master of science program in biodiversity and conservation policy at the University at Albany, State University of New York.

Jeffrey Mapes is a student in the master of arts in pubic policy program at Rockefeller College at the University at Albany, State University of New York.

Brian J. Nickerson is associate professor of public administration and director of the Edwin G. Michaelian Institute for Public Policy and Management of the Dyson College of Arts and Sciences at Pace University. He has worked extensively in the areas of applied policy research and public management and his research has appeared in numerous domestic and international publications and conferences. He teaches an array of graduate-level courses in public policy, law, and organizational management within Pace University's masters of public administration program.

Mitchell H. Pally is vice president for legislative and economic affairs for the Long Island Association. In that capacity he has conducted numerous studies about state and local issues in New York. He previously worked for the New York State Senate in Albany.

Robert F. Pecorella is an associate professor in the department of government and politics at St. John's University. He is the author of *Community Power in the Postreform City* and the coauthor of *The Politics of Structure*. He has published articles in *Polity*, *Public Administration Review*, and the *Journal of Urban Affairs*. He was a professor-in-residence for the New York State Assembly Intern Program between 1986 and 2005.

Katie Roe is a student in the master of arts in public policy program at Rockefeller College at the University at Albany, State University of New York.

Robert J. Spitzer (Ph.D. Cornell, 1980) is distinguished service professor of political science at the State University of New York, College at Cortland. His books include *The Presidency and Public Policy* (1983), *The Right to Life Movement and Third Party Politics* (1987), *The Presidential Veto* (1988), *The Bicentennial of the U.S. Constitution* (1990), *President and Congress* (1993), *Media and Public Policy* (1993), *The Politics of Gun Control* (Chatham House, 1995; 2nd ed. 1998), and *Politics and Constitutionalism* (2000). He is also a series editor for the book series "American Constitutionalism" for SUNY Press. He served as a member of the New York State Commission on the Bicentennial of the U.S. Constitution, and has been called for interviews in numerous media outlets.

Henry Steck is distinguished service professor of political science at SUNY Cortland. He has a BA from Kenyon College and Ph.D. from Cornell University. His current research deals chiefly with higher education. He is author of "Contested Paradigms of Higher Education Policy: Higher Education as a Social Entitlement" in Brecher, et al., *The University in a Liberal State*

(1996); and "Corporatization of the University: Seeking Conceptual Clarity" *Annals*, January 2003, and *Our Ecological Crisis* (1974). He is also director of the James M. Clark Center for International Education and of the project on Eastern and Central Europe at SUNY Cortland.

Amanda Stein is a student in the master of science program in biodiversity and conservation policy at the University at Albany, State University of New York.

Jeffrey M. Stonecash is professor and chair of the department of political science in the Maxwell School, Syracuse University, and has been the professor-in-residence in the New York Assembly Intern Program since 1984. His recent books are *Parties Matter* (2005), *Diverging Parties* (2003), *Political Polling* (2003), *Class and Party in American Politics* (2000), and he has published articles on parties and their political bases in *American Political Science Review, American Politics Quarterly, Legislative Studies Quarterly, Political Research Quarterly,* and *Political Science Quarterly.* He is currently working on a book about whether the incumbency effect increased during the last fifty years and how realignment affected incumbency trends.

Amy Widestrom is pursuing a Ph.D. in political science at the Maxwell School at Syracuse University, with concentrations in American politics and political theory. She received an M.A. in political science from Syracuse University and a bachelor of arts from Oberlin College. Her research interests include the effects of economic inequality and segregation on political participation, urban politics and redevelopment policy, and American political development. She is also currently working with Jeff Stonecash on a book reexamining the post–World War II incumbency effect.

Index